BRIAN BELLE-FORTUNE

oll crews

JOURNEYS THROUGH JUNGLE / DRUM & BASS CULTURE

vision publishing

Published by Vision Publishing Limited,
1 Trafalagar Mews, Eastway,
London, E9 5JG, UK

www.vision-publishing.co.uk / www.allcrew.co.uk

DESIGN
Nadine Gahr

COVER PHOTOGRAPH
Tristan O'Neill

PHOTOGRAPHY
Cleveland Aaron, Andy Cotterill, Steve Gullick, Courtney Hamilton,
Rob Hann, Tristan O'Neill, Brian Sweeney, Lu Vu, Des Willie

Printed and bound in Great Britain by Biddles Ltd, King's Lynn

Set in Notes / NotesMono by primetype, Germany (www.primetype.com)

ISBN: 0-9548897-0-3

Very special thanks to: Colin & Rachel Knowledge, Miss Pink and Nicky
Blackmarket, Laurence Electric PR, Tania UMC, Indy BBC and Nastya.

Dedicated to Mum & Dad and Kate – my best supporting producer

In memory of my friend Minako, who lived to be creative ...
... and John Peel – thank you for the music !

CONTENTS

PREFACE

Rows of people stand facing out from dark banks of speakers. Dancing with militancy, stepping on every tier of the Forum, Telepathy, AWOL, Desire, Exodus. The souls on the floor, individuals, all as one, are cuttin' animated human sculptures - poses frozen in strobes … facing Randall, Grooverider, the bass bins or nowhere in particular, they're 'avin' it.

Lasers reflected in sunglasses, whistles, horns and lighter flares burn the air. They dance with no room to dance … and scream for the rewind. The DJ drops the tune and it all goes off again. This is Roast, Stush, Innovation, VIP Champagne Bash.

The people love dressing up, enjoying an edge in the air. Above all, they love the crucible that is Jungle Fever. You're outside at dawn in a sand quarry in Luton with Exodus, or on that fairground ride at World Dance.

The rush of weed or E takes hold. With a breathless surge you move to another level. You're in it, it's in you, wrapped in the music, the air, the vibe. The mix is running and beats burst through the night with the visceral intensity of a tempest.

I'm floating in it, at the highest plane. The ravers weave multitudes of patterns. They look beautiful. They look wicked. There's nothing like this and I love it with all my soul …

To get the world of Jungle Drum & Bass (JDB) in context, imagine the opening of *Citizen Kane* that begins in space, focuses on the world and descends through the clouds to a country, eventually landing on a particular street. The same can be done with music. We live in a world of music. Go down from the broad range, Classical, Rock n Roll, Country & Western, Pop, Jazz to Dance music. JDB shares common land with Reggae, Hip Hop, Rare Groove, Soul, House, Techno and Hardcore. It's all good music. We respect other neighbourhoods with people just as passionate about Oasis or Garth Brooks as we are about Grooverider or Roni Size. People have their preferences. But this neighbourhood is Jungle.

'97 the scene rolls into another weekend.
MCs give out shouts to destinations
on the web of England's motorways.
The M1, M3, M4, M6, M20, M25,
not forgetting the M62 …
As you drift down the motorway,
lose the pirates, switch to CD,
sit back, enjoy a spliff, relax
and drift into the night.

"They used to call our music, 'Devil Music.' A lot of people don't understand the kind of struggle we've been through to make Dance Music predominant in the UK." GROOVERIDER, OCTOBER 2004

"They don't understand what we had to do. We'd drive way down to them far country places … drag record boxes over muddy fields and play for hours. The kids in this game don't appreciate what we had to do to get where we are today." DJ SS, OCTOBER 2004

MTV Europe – August 1998

Leisurely coffee in staff restaurant by Camden's canal. A group of TV researchers are putting together a series of pan European video diaries. I'm summoned to Executive Producer Stephen D Wright's office. MTV's open plan innards are covered by blue cushioned carpet. Beautiful Euro kids wearing Club Culture's clothes sit at PCs, others carry piles of videos or log rushes on TV screens. Robbie Williams is in reception. Davina McCall holds court with a group of interns.

The exec's cramped office has glass walls – feels like a goldfish bowl. "Have you found a DJ for the Jungle diary?" Yeah. That's all sorted. We're covering Wildchild." "Never heard of him." "Wildchild's on Kool FM, works at SRD, plays Carnival. And it's her not him." "Her?" "Yeah. Skibadee MCs for her. She's wicked." Wright's not happy: "Interesting but not exactly *Jungle* is it?" "Sorry. Don't get you." "Well *Jungle* is a black male thing. You need to get back out there – find someone else." "'A BLACK MALE THING!?'"

The other researchers clock the action through glass walls: "Oh mi god." "Look. It's all going off." "Shit." "What the hell that's about?" "Stop staring everyone. B's … coming out." Door opens "' … A BLACK MALE THING!' You haven't got a fucking clue!" People look up. Door slams. Glass reverberates. "He's coming back." "Alright B." "Not really. No." "Fancy a coffee?"

Back outside by the canal with Red Anna: "What is it with these media types? They're only interested in reinforcing stereotypes. Doesn't matter what the actual truth is. I mean, what is the point of hiring specialist researchers if they won't listen? I'm sick of them saying Jungle is x, y, z. It's multicultural that's why …" Mobile goes off. "It's a BBC producer – wants to meet soon as. "Where you going?" "To see a man who wants to make the definitive Jungle documentary." "You're goin' right now? Suppose they start asking for you?" "Tell 'em I'm off doing more 'research.' "

One hour later Wagamamas, Soho. Paul's from a program called *Modern Times*. He's full of questions. We chat for hours. "You've got your crews and massives, labels, there's pirates, and record shops, then there's your DJs and MCs, and producers making tunes in bedrooms, and there's Music House, and your promoters and your clubs, magazines, distributors, Rave History and people who design flyers, then there's drugs, fashions, carnival, Bristol, Leicester, the crowds, One in the Jungle, booking agents, multicultural music, has its own language. It's a uniquely British scene …" Walking along Wardour Street my head's buzzing with all the info I've downloaded. Slope back to MTV but can't focus. Try to sleep that night – can't sleep. Get up and start writing notes on scraps of paper.

Reach work early. Start typing an e-mail to Exec Producer. One hour later. Red Anna checks the screen: "Looks interesting. Church of Jungle, pirate stations, illegal raves … Is it a program proposal?" "No. It's an e-mail for Stephen D Wright but you know what? I don't think I'm going to send it." A couple of weeks later I say to my partner, "Kate … I think I'm writing a book."

Most of what was to be the first version of *All Crew Muss Big Up* was written in 18 months. I then wasted months trying to find a publisher. They weren't interested. I almost lost heart. Friends were saying that the book was good. I'm not sure how much I believed them until Sage, my MC on pirate station Ruud Awakening, asked to read the manuscript. At the time it was a bundle of paper held together with string. Sage calls me: "I was at some party last night and left your book on a sofa …" I think, 'He's gonna say he's lost it.' "… Left it on the sofa right. I've gone to get a drink, come back and there's four people trying to read the same page! Serious man. When's it being published?" "It isn't." *All Crew* was going nowhere. I went to retrieve a draft from a publisher in a shining tower on Euston Road and was directed to the post room in the basement. They thought I was a courier. It was depressing. I felt like chucking the manuscript into a skip. But I felt responsible for all those stories on the pages. *All Crew* belonged to the people.

With a Little Help From My Friends

Friends came to the rescue. I met designer Nadine Gahr at Berlin's Love Parade. She suggested that if we wanted *All Crew* out there so badly, we should put it out ourselves. Cameron, a friend from Melbourne, had written a poetry book, printed and distributed it himself. That started me thinking, "We'll print up 100 copies and see how they do." Nadine got busy with design. Tristan O'Neill (*DJ* magazine) arrived with photographs and we all went into the mix. We couldn't afford to print *All Crew* so we had it photocopied, spiral bound, then Nadine and I hawked them 'round record and book shops.

I gave Storm a copy. Goldie nicked Storm's, starts calling artists and reading bits to them. I crawl out my tent at the Eclipse festival in Plymouth and bump into Kenny Ken. Goldie had called him: "He's reading out stuff from that interview we did. So where's my copy?" Same day Resin at Excessive Sounds in Enfield bells me: "When can you drop off more copies? We've sold out."

Neither Nadine nor I had worked on a book before so *All Crew 1* was a little rough around the edges. We even missed out the word 'Culture' from the cover title. Both Nadine and Tristan stayed on board for the second version and took the book to another level. *All Crew* was re-released in Christmas 1999. There had been a mistake with the ISBN order number, which made it incredibly difficult to find but we sold all 2,000 copies. Then came stories of books being stolen from shops. Friends even nicked it from their friends. Four years later orders still came in — especially from clubbers and students from the UK / Europe, the US, Canada, Australia and New Zealand. I'm pleasantly surprised with the positive reaction the book has received. And it's humbling hearing people referring to *All Crew* as 'The Drum & Bass Bible.' I've had so many requests for a rewind that I've taken up my pen again.

All Crews — The Remix

Rachel and Colin of Vision Publishing, who produce *Knowledge* magazine, have made this third version possible. Their support, guidance and hard work have produced a dub plate special. It includes many new photographs, mostly courtesy of Tristan O'Neill, Cleveland Aaron, Courtney Hamilton and Andy Cotterill. Nadine Gahr has come up trumps again re-designing the whole book. She has broken up the text grid structure, making it flow and jump like Drum & Bass music with different typefaces reflecting different voices. Nevertheless — I'm dyslexic so it's been our mission to make the text easy to read aswell. Thanks to Rico our distribution is being handled by SRD — all proppa tings.

Think of this version as a remix. Part One includes the original *All Crew Muss Big Up* published in 1999. Many people featured in Part One have moved on and are now doing different things so some text will seem dated, but it represents a snapshot of the scene as it was. However, it features new interviews with characters missed out last time. Part Two covers the many changes and developments in Jungle Drum & Bass since 2000. *All Crews* is not a 'Who's Who' but a journey accompanied by music with the names of tunes woven throughout the text. I've rinsed out all the pages so additional information like 'Thanks', the popular 'Glossary' and colour pictures can be found www.allcrew.co.uk — Watch the ride.

Sending one out to all the heroes I met along the way.

SEPTEMBER '88

"Freedom is a road seldom travelled by the multitude."
SHOW 'EM WHAT YOU GOT, PUBLIC ENEMY, DEF JAM, '88

Don't know how I came to be buying a ticket for a rave at the back of a shoe shop in Islington. A guy on some pirate radio station went on about a party and gave out a telephone number. The girl on the phone sussed me out and gave me the address — the shoe shop in Islington. Bought the ticket without even knowing if I was going. I hadn't told any of my friends. I had an instinct that they'd think I was mad. Does seem crazy. I'm doing this alone. Chill in the flat till the 12am clubbing hour, then check the ticket for the address. No address — shit — only a mobile phone number. Engaged. Engaged. Engaged. Recorded message — M1, Junction what? Drive my rusty, red Spitfire across the East India Dock Road and head north for the M1, still wondering what the hell I'm doing. The North Circular's grey lines are softened by Roy Ayers in the speakers. Brent Cross, M1, alone in the capsule on a road to God knows where. I'm the funki-dreaded soul boy in a leather jacket chugging along in the slow lane, being passed by everyone: lorries, old-age pensioners and parents with kids asleep in the back. I turn down the stereo to see if the car's developed any new noises. Really shouldn't be out doing mystery tours in this motor. Remember the time the left wheel fell off outside the Astoria?

Flashback to a few weeks earlier when the new clubbing season began: there was a different kind of energy in Soho that evening. The queue outside The Wag bulged. Friday nights at The Wag with the good old faithful. Hip Hop downstairs, Rare Groove upstairs and the same trendy faces strutting their fashionable stuff. Pay the usual and realise I hadn't noticed the music booming beyond the doorway. Something odd happens in the four feet between the cash desk and the entrance. Captured by heat, smoke and the vibe, a brown-skinned Goddess with huge eyes and green face paint offers me a welcome and some water from a plastic bottle. Someone else is shaking my hand asking if I'm " 'Avin' a good one?" I pan round the room from the centre of a time warp. The place is one heaving mass of sweat-drenched flesh. A party in a steam bath. It's *Heaven's Gate* or *Dante's Inferno* and I've never seen anything like it.

A green laser cuts through the haze, striking a CD held aloft by a bald-headed, bare-chested black guy, rocking, perched atop a speaker. Below, the DJ dances from mix to mix, mouthing the words of Martin Luther King's speech *I Have a Dream* and applauding the audience. Beside him a bloke fiddles with projectors and slide machines shining colours on faces, laughing, dancing, shouting. A strobe throws the room into slow motion. It's packed from the front to the back to the sides – moisture runs down the mirrored walls. Even the staff are bouncing behind jugs of iced water on the bar. Everyone seems to know the music. Screaming together. All those hands in the air. And the music – unrelenting music. More smiling faces in my face. It's becoming claustrophobic. Difficult to breathe, I climb the spiral staircase at the rear of the club. Below, people at a table are hugging, stroking each other, looking up, waving. It's all too hypnotising, too much to take in. I withdraw from the scene like a zoom lens. Upstairs, it's dark and familiar. Rare Grooves play to a few of the 'faces' wearing Gaultier and Joseph. It's kind of mature, restrained, a bit empty. I clutch a can of trendy Pils beer and rest up by some windows overlooking the street. It's 2am and the queue is bigger. What the fuck is going on? I'm doing a retake: the lasers, smoke and hands in the air. So many people talking, touching. Those baggy trousers, t-shirts for towels. White people, black people, dancing so close together. Everyone so close together. The music pounds through the floor, upstairs to the dark and familiar, past the mature and restrained, trendy and too-cool-to-move brigade. The familiar had lost it. Downstairs … downstairs is frightening yet enthralling. I can't help but drift back down the spiral staircase and stare at the mayhem. My God could they party. I feel odd, out of place and decide to leave.

Back on the M1, a car packed with people glides by in the middle lane – it's bouncing, they're waving. I wonder where they've come from. More pensioners, more huge lorries with their over-sized unmellow wheels. Another car, a geezer's got the window down and is shouting at me above the music. A white Escort pulls level in the outside lane, horn honking, everyone screaming through open windows. They zoom off, leaving at the next junction. Which junction? Just follow the tail lights. In the rear-view mirror, I clock a stream of headlights leaving the motorway. I hope they're not following me. I haven't got a clue where I'm going. I'm caught up in something else here. We grind to a halt down some country lane. More shouts and calls. A guy in a white pork pie hat and fluorescent orange jacket walks back up the road, chatting briefly to each driver and giving up before he gets to me. I open the roof and stand. The sight is awesome. Too many cars to count at 2am down a country lane. Something connects us. It isn't a traffic jam, it's a convoy. Ahead there's movement. All the cars are doing three-point turns. Someone must know where we're going. After the last left, then right, a bloke with a walkie-talkie directs the traffic past a small sign in orange paint – *To Sunrise.*

Cars are abandoned as occupants head up the muddy road in baseball caps and Timberlands. Walking with a purpose. Distant music and flashing lights pour through the hedgerows. All those dungarees, baggy jumpers, big floppy hats and hooded tops. Three girls with shining faces sit on the back of the car until we wind the last few yards into a field / car park. Good friends for fifteen minutes. I stall, they leave with a 'see-you-inside' hug and dance off towards the music. Across the fields, a large black barn stretches back into the trees. To its left, there's a fairground in full swing. I'm surrounded by groups of people chatting 'round cars, shouting down the way, like everyone knows each other. I feel paranoid and wonder if I belong. I follow the music to its source and strangers chat to me in the queue. "Have some water, where you come from? Manchester? Yorkshire, London, where? What's yer name? See them cars? Did ya get lost? Gonna be a blinder, never been to this before either, lost me friends, what you on … ?" I'm confused again, trying to figure out what it is. Feeling what it isn't. Attitude, there's no attitude. If you don't belong, why are you here? The guys at the entrance, pony-tails, shaggy hair and broad grins, rip the tickets and open the way in. "If you're here, you belong."

It wasn't a barn. It was an aircraft hanger. The only time you see anything like this is in those 'Old Testament' films with a cast of thousands. All too much to be real. So many people dancing. They're doing that dance with their arms to that music – unrelenting, uplifting music. Others are bouncing up and down. A girl with a whistle runs around windmilling her arms and hugs someone. DJs I don't know play like Gods, rising from the masses on a huge scaffolding platforms along one wall. Above them, dark figures move between stage lights and barrages of lasers, releasing a shower of white balloons into the rising screams. I'm walking to the scaffolding, brain overloaded with images and faces, thousands of faces. Blag through the security, climb up past the speakers to the second storey and join others on the platform. We're taking in the whole thing, this vibe, from the best seat in the house. People are raving, well and truly raving. There's no other word for it. We're talking to each other above the music. The teacher, the burglar and the Saturday girl. Never met so many different people.

Sometime 'round six o'clock, I crash out with some others in a corner amongst plastic bottles, flyers and polystyrene cups. Lying down, there's a strange side-on view of bouncing legs and feet. Close my eyes and the music beats on. Open them to check that it's all still there. Everybody looking so good. Sleep till I'm woken, hearing people shouting for one more tune. The last record plays and I find the energy to stand and dance the night's maddest dance. Everyone claps everyone. A voice on the speakers is saying thank you to loads of names. The only one I recognise is Paul Anderson. When the system's turned off, I can still hear the music.

Outside, up the hill, there are faint sounds from a car stereo. In the sunlight, people are dancing on roofs and bonnets. England's never looked so pleasant. This is freedom. A group of policemen look on through binoculars. Have we been naughty boys and girls? Whose land is this anyway? Five miles on it feels like a dream. I stop the car and hunt for a cassette, knowing I've got none of that music. I need to see someone, tell a friend that ... So much to tell. My best friend from years back has become live-in House Master of our old boarding school. Reach the country village fifteen miles away and head for his cottage by the side of the Manor House. I walk into his living room. My friend looks old. I'm ten years younger chatting away, then realise that he doesn't seem at all interested. Perhaps it's all beyond his comprehension. Where the hell had I been? "I've been in this 'thing' man."

Wednesday 1pm, I'm day-dreaming in the coffee room at work. The Intensive Care Sister hands a tabloid to a staff nurse. They're talking about 'that Acid House' craze. I've been hoarding flyers, looking for numbers, listening to pirates, hunting any scrap that will lead me back to last weekend. To have it all over again. It's suddenly clear that I've become an outsider.

My first taste of serious clubbing was back in the early 80s. Friday night, me and the crew would go dancing in the Horse Shoe on Tottenham Court Road — Funk in one room, Jazz in the other. Paul Anderson would be DJing a wicked set, then he'd leave the decks to join the boys on the floor — he was a wicked dancer. In those days people would take an extra set of clothes to change into after the club. You would be DRENCHED. There'd be queues in the toilets for those new hand blow dryers, people trying to dry themselves off before facing the long walk home. Wednesdays and Saturdays it would be roller-skating at the Electric Ballroom, Camden Town where I was a marshal.

Paul Anderson would be there, DJing a wicked set, leave the decks to join the boys on the rink — yes, he was a wicked skater. At its best, the Saturday night vibe was comparable to the heat of a Jungle Fever. I'd hear about other clubs where it was also going off, the Embassy, Le Beat Route, the Royalty, Mud Club, the Camden Palace and The Wag. In trendy style magazines I read about American clubs like New York's Paradise club and the Warehouse in Chicago. I left London and drifted out of the club scene for a few years. When I returned, the places kicking it were the Boilerhouse, Raw and, of course, the legendary Soul II Soul at the Africa Centre in Covent Garden. Jazzy B famously berated sedentary clubbers saying, "If you're not dancing fuck off." Mates of mine were going to Westworld, Shoom and Enter the Dragon, name-checking people like Phil Salon, Nicky Holloway, Rene Gelston, Dave Dorrell, Steve Proctor and Danny Rampling.

I'd heard of some of the DJs which *The Face* said held sway in the 80s. Their list of fifty included Jazzy B, Jay Strongman, Jeremy Healy, Colin Faver, Pete Tong, Tim Westwood and Matt Black — Fabio, Grooverider and Jumping Jack Frost had yet to come to their notice. Producers Smith & Mighty in Bristol stopped messing with Acid, cooked up some heavy Reggae, drum and bassline grooves and started answering reporters' questions about 'The Bristol Sound'. The Hacienda had been going for years. James Brown appeared at the Town & Country. But the scene changed when the newly converted returned from Ibiza. DJ culture truly started to make its presence felt when S Express and Bomb the Bass hit the charts, all to a backdrop of rising house prices, low wages, Thatcherism, smiley faces and tabloid hysteria at a tenfold increase in Ecstasy use. Kiss FM came off air in search of a licence. By January '89, Acid House, so *The Face* said, was out. Maybe it was, but since the Summer of Love several strands of Rave music have proliferated. There was Acid House, Garage, Balearic, emergent Techno, Hardcore, Breakbeat, Ga*ridge* (sic) — but music like Soul, Rare Groove, Hip Hop, Ragga and Reggae also thrived. For some people, Rave was something different and weird. There was something about Rave that sucked people in from all over and created a kind of unity. But by '91, the Dance music scene fractured into subdivisions, including the Hardcore and Breakbeat crews.

We're in DJ Ron's car travelling North up the M1 to Bradford where he's playing out. The pirates on the stereo are fading into static. We're talking about JDB. You can talk about it forever …

Ron: So how did you get into this thing anyway?

B: I was a raver from time, but from mid to late '92 I started listening to Hardcore with Dub and Ragga samples, like *Terminator*. I always thought those dark tracks were wicked. The 'happy' tunes were good, but the dark ones really got you. I checked By Any Means Necessary at Brixton Academy at the end of '92. I remember the DJs were Grooverider, Frost and Mickey Finn. The whole night was dark. I remember dancing at the front, looking 'round and noticing there wasn't a smile amongst the people. Not one smile. But everyone was into it. It wasn't a bad vibe. I remember being off my head and thinking that I must remember this. This is different now. It's still good but it was different. It was serious now like a militant army. People were concentrating, no waving hands in the air. They were seriously concentrating. I don't know if it was billed as a Jungle rave – but it was.

BEGINNINGS

"We started in the fields, a lot of people joined the train and didn't know where it came from." GOLDIE

DANCING IN THE FIELDS, FOLLOWING THE MUSIC

On the ground as a raver in 1989, you'd ring the number, hit the meeting point at South Mimms service station off the M25, follow the 'pilot', join the convoy on motorways and country lanes and find x-amount of cars – horns blowing, suspension bouncing, stereos blaring, the whole lot rockin'. Crammed with your crew or any stranger glad of a lift, it took car-sharing into another dimension.

You'd be exchanging chat – "Where you goin'? What a get-up. D'ya get to that one over by … ? You was there?! Look at that geeza. What you got, trips, EEEs? Sniff dat … ! Everything sorted. Pukka!" – The circus had hit the road and it was instinctive to follow. One raver, MC 5ive'O, went everywhere, often on his own. Like many others, the only thing he cared about was the next party – Sunrise, Energy, Back to the Future, Perception, Confusion, Land of Oz, Breakfast Club, Raindance, Car Wash, Biology, Destination Unknown … chasing every Mystery Tour going. He

reminisces about the original Pied Pipers: "Paul Oakenfold, Evil Eddie Richards, Tony Bones, Paul Anderson, DJ Face. Big up … Dave Roberts, Neil, Jeremy Taylor, Tony Colston-Hayter, Ricky from Raindance, Paul Ibiza, Wayne – Genesis, 'nuff respect. I met some characters, Oh Mi Gosh! Remember one-eyed Gary and his trick with the cigarette box? Bwoy."

Like 5ive'O the vast majority of those now working at the forefront of the JDB industry were at those raves. Somewhere in the crowds you'd be dancing with the likes of DJ Brockie, MC Co-Gee, DJ Ron, Roni Size, MC GQ, DJ Ital and Rebel MC, who'd been tempted out of the inner cities to listen to what their friends condemned as 'That Devil Music'. They didn't care. Bare-chested, perched atop speaker stacks somewhere around the M25 you'd have found Daz, Chris and Jay, later to become World Dance. They'd be dripping with sweat on Saturday night and riding the first class carriages to work in the City of London's Foreign Exchange dealing rooms on Monday mornings. DJ Storm was wedged behind the seats of a friend's Spitfire heading to a rave in Cambridge with Kemistry. Down in the West of England, Roni Size ran through fields, chasing the beats of Bukem, Grooverider, Fabio or Jumping Jack Frost.

As GQ remembers: "You'd see it on the TV: ACID, HARDCORE, ECSTASY. People were getting intrigued man. That's what happened to me. I went and thought, right, this is the lick. My brothers and certain friends that didn't go to none of them parties, would be like, "Ya goin' to them parties 'n' taking them tings?" I'd be, "Well it's not all about that. It's the vibes, just bubblin' inside a field, with everyone on a level. Travelling 'round in a beat-up Sierra — boy we did some mileage on the motorway. No flyers, just meet up at some word-of-mouth petrol station. I remember climbing in some window to a rave with Kenny Ken. There was a lot of illegal warehouse do's. Beyond Therapy with Rat Pack at Reigate Lane was one. There were police everywhere, helicopters harassing people — loads of people. And they just weren't 'avin' it. It was like a revolution. They were like, "Fuck the Old Bill — Fuck da police dem. Fuck dem. We're 'avin' our party". And the police were like, "Alright then, have your fuckin' party". It was life. The government weren't making no money. We weren't paying no taxes and that's what really pissed them off. When the Rave scene went inside, it kind of killed it. Raves were a different thing and I was part of that and I'm proud to be part of it. That music was a class, an era. It changed my life. If I hadn't done that, I don't know what I'd be doing."

There were journalists, politicians' children, actors, burglars, lawyers, Sloanes, shop assistants, all the people that didn't usually fit together ... those that couldn't get into a club, might have had a row with their parents, hated their work, couldn't wear trainers, fancied dropping an E, doing a line, enfolded by a feeling of belonging. 5ive'O remembers, "There was nothing but love. Even the drug sellers who were Bad Bwoys used to come out and have a wicked time." This community was our own private sanctuary. It was also our escape.

STRINGS OF LIFE

I arrived at Sussex University in Autumn '89 with loads of the North London crowd who'd spent a gap year raving. This wasn't a crowd who sat 'round communal kitchens asking, "What A Levels did you do?" Their campus accommodation transformed into dens of camouflage netting and fluorescent wall hangings. They had a whole vibe going on. Unsurprisingly amongst their number were some of the most prolific dealers.

Weekend one arrives. A couple of guys organising a party pay me a visit. "Ah mate, a DJ from London? Safe. … Spin a few tunes? Wicked." Truth was I'd been clubbing for years but had only played hospital and house parties but "Yeah sure man. No worries." A House / Techno DJ called Damien from North London would also be playing. The venue was a long campus flat perched on a hillside called East Slope. The decks over-looked the high end of a split-level affair. Damien played Techno, I played Soul & Rare Grooves. Shoom versus The Africa Centre. It all went off till someone pressed a fire alarm and security plus fire brigade arrived clearing the building.

Days later Damien and I plan our own rave. We called the night Rare Ecstasy — me being the rare and Dee being the ecstasy. We found a venue and stood 'round photocopiers producing posters and flyers. Even though we didn't really know each other, when it came to setting up a party we lived the language of Club Culture. We'd instinctively fly post many a daring site around college casually handing out Rare Ecstasy flyers. The venue, Lancs House common room, had a low ceiling and was usually used for aerobics classes — much like Shoom back in London where Damien had been a regular. I contributed my Norman Jay / Soul II Soul heritage.

Party day sees Dee and me painting coloured banners and hauling staging into the common room to make podiums. We shifted the sound system from a campus club called The Crypt and people came offering help. Kate and friend Natalie offered to do the door which neither Damien or I had thought about. With afternoon turning to evening there was a steady flow of people asking, "What time are you on?" "How much is it on the door?" And we heard pre-match gossip like, "I've 'eard there's crews comin' down from London wiv bags of eeeeeeeees."

On the night there was mental last minute sorting out. Kate and Natalie on the door are asking, "Can we let 'em in?" They're insistent. We peer outside. A crowd of people stretches out the building and down the path. I wish someone filmed the night. Like I wish cameras rolled that first time dancing in the fields. Damien and I play three tunes each back to back. It didn't matter that Techno followed Rare Groove. We were all born of 80's Club Culture and mi word did-it-go-off. Pupils wide open reflect condensation trickling down cold glass windows. Feet stomp floor and podiums, jiving, sweat drenched bodies boogie double time; arms and hands joust the air. Funky fashions weave through clouds of dry ice. Strobes flash on swirling fluorescent stripes. *Blade Runner* plays in the chill out room. People sit, slope around chatting, skinning up, monging out, hugging tightly. The night is cookin'. In that DJ space behind the decks Dee and I look around, catch each other's eyes, knowing and feeling that this is a quality moment. For a few hours the strings of life play in a Sussex Uni common room.

Around about midnight security arrive to shut us down. They're befuddled and have obviously never seen anything like it. The music plays on whilst friends in the crowd spontaneously collude, doing their utmost to stall the uniforms. They're near deckside when Brooke a former Eton boy entangles them in diplomacy and promises. He gets them to leave. The authorities always fall for that one. But … In time … they return and switch the house lights ON. Though Dee manages slyly to mix in a couple more tunes, security made us stop. The hall resounds with

clapping, cheering and voices shouting the 'One more tune' chorus. Security get booed. I whack NWA on the decks and scratch out 'Fa, fa, Fuck Da Po-lice.' That was a night.

Back then some black people were getting knockbacks from West End clubs. The management didn't say it was about colour. It was your trainers, trousers, baseball cap or whatever else the bouncers or club runners suggested didn't fit. I remember The Wag Club that I'd supported throughout the slow Summer months, refusing me entrance when the massive — mostly white punters — returned from Ibiza. Jazzy B refused to play a Kiss FM dance there because of the club's reputation. Being black uptown in the West End meant that even if you did get in, it was like being tolerated. Trailing those outta town parties felt like home. Visiting your white mates in the countryside, where you and the crew could spend the day puffing and calling X-amount of mobiles, chasing the *Pied Piper* of rave. That was the one.

"Another reason I'm involved in Jungle music is 'cos it brought a lot of people together. Certain man a few years ago, they wouldn't dream of talking to a white guy and the same the other way around. But now, we're all under the same roof — raving, laughing and joking together." DJ KENNY KEN, ALL JUNGLISTS, CHANNEL 4, 1994

Between '89 and '91, Belgian and German producers evolved the Hardcore sounds from American House and Techno. The next wave of early '90s rave sound started to filter through, pushing out the older more classically uplifting music. The cycles of change were felt on the Groove Connection DJ roster.

"We started discovering our own Breakbeat sounds in 1991 - 92, so Fabio, Groove and them guys started playing that rather than Techno which caused a split in the agency. Frankie Valentine and Dave Angel, those guys wanted to stay with Techno, so we went our own way. They thought they could do better with Knowledge Agency who were more Techno-oriented. We started getting behind the British sound … I remember one particular Sunday afternoon session at Roast Turnmills, Fabio and Grooverider played, Cool & Deadly was on the mic. 5ive'O and all those guys were down there. We knew there was something different in the air. It started to kick through. There was a whole new sound away from European Techno, we were all going wild. There was a whole new energy."
SARAH, GROOVE CONNECTION

"I think it's funny the way it all split. I can remember when SS would be playing alongside Carl Cox and Keith Suckling. Those music styles were all under one umbrella and they have all splintered off. And now the splinters have splintered off." *TANIA, UMC*

Hardcore became the '89 sound for club Rage and new pirate radio station, Centreforce. During '90 and '91, distributors would drive over to Europe buying records, while punters in shops Black Market and De Underground would ask, "You got any imports?" "Yeah we got some more of that Belgian stuff. There's white labels someone brought 'round from a crew called Reinforced. Sort of like that Shut Up & Dance stuff or what's that other thing err, *We Are I.E.*, or there's this bloke Paul Ibiza from Haringey – it's all English stuff. Just 'ave a listen, some of it's wicked."

Late '91 and I'm still raving. It's the weekend rush and Rush FM's gone dead. Tune to that new one – Kool FM. What's MC Co-Gee shouting about? Some rave or other. Ring up the number, then the other number. Check out that one in West London, well, Harlesden. A lot of the time you'd never even find the place. But the journey's often worth it. I'll rave anywhere with anyone but this was strange – West London Rude Boys and Crusties. Don't know who was playing that night but it was something different. More beats than in Hardcore. My mate said to me, "This is Jungle, not Hardcore". I don't know who the DJ was that night but he played near enough a whole set of 'Jungle'. It was good.

History isn't carved in stone. It always seems that after every 'Official Story' is published, someone's contribution is omitted or negated. In my own short lifetime, the origin of humankind has been found at least five times, then someone else digs deeper. Perhaps it's down to poor research. More often than not it's the result of listening to those with the loudest voices – their stories become the 'Official History'. Just like the origins of humankind, JDB doesn't have a single 'Official History'. Listen to any pirate station as the MCs recite a mantra of DJs', producers' and MCs' names, returning to the oral tradition of storytelling. As far as history goes, it's both valid and flawed. Valid because *Mixmag* or *The Times* can't be relied upon to write our story accurately. Flawed because key developments in Jungle happened in small clubs and among tight crews, who had a sharp focus and kept their heads down, too busy to look up and notice what everyone else was doing.

At the time, in the midst of the mad nights and darkened studios at the heart of our scene, it's almost impossible to climb above it all with clear vision and God-like truth and say this crew were 'The First' or that producer was 'The One.' Life doesn't work that way. It's an organic process of evolution. Perhaps 'process' is shorthand for saying well there were 'nuff people making a contribution over a period of time. Just because they aren't at the forefront of popular historical accounts, doesn't mean that within the vagaries of Chaos Theory they aren't important in the whole scheme of things.

"Who was the first?" is a silly question. It's journalistically lazy. Things don't work that way. The scene has its own dynamics. Somewhere between Fabio and Rebel MC, it was the people, either at Rage or on the street, who gave the music the name Jungle. Collectively, they've named and described its sound, its essence. There are a few stories that are part of JDB's evolution. They're as good as any and all. In no particular order ...

ONCE UPON A TIME IN HACKNEY, EAST LONDON, THERE WAS SHUT UP & DANCE – SMILEY'S TALE ...

In '89 PJ was a stunt man, Smiley a cabinet-maker and both were professional contemporary dancers, but they couldn't find music fast, driving and hard enough to dance to. Based in Hackney and running their Ragga / Reggae sound system, 'Private Party' with DJ Hype, Shut Up & Dance went into the studio and came out with their first tune *5, 6, 7, 8*. Inspired by the success of Soul II Soul who were also originally on the North / East London sound system circuit, Shut Up & Dance hit the Top Forty with *£20 to Get In*. The musical hybrid was labelled Hip House but this hid where they were really coming from. They didn't know what they were going to label this type of music. They didn't care. They were specialising in heavy Reggae with Breakbeats.

Though instrumentals were all well and good, they really wanted a good singer to front their music so Smiley and PJ approached Deman Rocker who, with Flinty Badman, later became The Ragga Twins. They warned them that Shut Up & Dance were dealing with experimental music and people might laugh but asked them to come up with a lyric for the tune *Request to all the Trips and Es.* The beats had people jumping. But Shut Up & Dance were also sensitive to the needs of the predominantly white ravers down at the Dungeons under Hackney's Lea Bridge Road who didn't really know Reggae that well. Needing something more accessible with fewer patois vocals, they came up with *Hooligan '69.* Smiley recalls other producers using speeded-up breakbeats with EQ-ed basslines. Even The Prodigy put out an EP sounding very much like Shut Up & Dance. Call it proto-Jungle. One beginning.

Once Upon a Time in Forest Gate, East London, There was a Record Shop, De Underground, a Producer, Lennie De Ice and a Track, *We Are I.E.*, Often Cited as one of The First Jungle Tunes – Mikey De Underground's Tale …

"In Summer '89, the first label release on I:E Records was *We Are I.E.* by Lennie De Ice. There wasn't a contract, we just wanted to know how to cut vinyl and we cut five hundred records. We went all over England with that track. I got in the car with my older brother John of Reel 2 Reel, who did *Game of Love*, and a friend Para-Fabian. We were on a mission. It was always in us. If we could skive a day off school, it was straight down to Soho to check out the record shops. We were always adventurous. So when the pirates came along – same thing – it's something new, got to go out there and find them.

When we pressed the vinyl, we knew that if it took driving around England to sell the tunes, we'd have to go and do it. We were having a laugh. If we were lucky, we might get some change back on the tunes to pay for the petrol. We had to get rid of the tunes and we couldn't do the whole lot in London, so we hit the motorways. The rave promoters had got that big that they saved us half the work by putting most of the ticket outlets, like record shops, on the backs of the flyers. You'd hit the town, ring 'em up say "I've got this tune" and go and see them. You'd go there and that music is not on the shelf. Nothing like it is on the shelf. Soon as you hit outside the M25 it would be like, "Boy what are you bringing us?" This was the hard sell. "This is what's happening in London … You got pirate stations … this and that … take it … okay I'll tell you what I'll do, here's two copies sell 'em and call me for some more." We went all the way up to Manchester, Reading, Swindon, Bristol. Spent three weeks out there travelling England. A London man going outside feels dapper 'cos people say "You're from London!" You're *doing* it. They make you feel at ease, they want to know you. We made friends easy – people who sheltered us wanted to know more. Those three weeks were fun. Then you'd live off the stories. I got rid of the five hundred and must have got cash in my pocket for a hundred.

I had to leave them in the shops. We were out there and had to break the sound. About three months after we got home and started to get on with other things, it all kicked off. *We Are I.E.* was being played. Even Randall bussed it. Today that's an example of how the beats talk for themselves. It was made on a Roland 106 Keyboard, S900 Sampler and all put through a four track. The clarity wasn't there but the essence still stung. Every time I think about that track it wasn't the clarity, it was the essence of the music that done it. I took the track to a major A&R guy at Rhythm King. He said, "It's low cut, noisy rubbish. I can't do nothing with that." He called me again after it had all gone off … "Can we talk about this *We Are I.E.* track?" I was hurt by the way he put his views, decided to play the same game and told him to get lost.

People found out this tune came from an East London shop: it was built in England by a crew in Forest Gate. That just made more people want to get involved in writing beats. Before people were saying that they could never make a beat that's firing enough, it had to be from the States. That one tune proved them wrong, showing that an independent can make a tune and it can do the damage. It helped the scene grow. There were producers coming out of all parts of London and the surrounding counties."

Once Upon a Time in Haringey, North London, There Was Chris in The Record Shop Music Power, a Producer, Paul Ibiza, and a Couple Of Punters: Kemi And Jane aka Kemistry & Storm – Paul Ibiza's Tale ...

At Ibiza Records, Paul was tired of the foreign sounds running the British Dance scene. "Being a Londoner, I'd had enough of that sort of sound, the wrong direction, bringing us somewhere we didn't know where we were going ... That's when Ibiza Records started." Paul fused the bleeps and the breaks with Reggae B-lines. "The sound elements worked. The Reggae influence worked. And I said, I know what direction I'm going in, 'cos my dad's got untold Reggae tunes sitting at home."
Paul Ibiza, All Junglists, Channel 4.

DJ Storm on Paul Ibiza: "In 1991, Paul Ibiza was the first person I ever heard use the word 'Jungle'. I remember him bringing his first release on Ibiza Records into Music Power and we were all wondering what this weird bassline was. Chris behind the counter turned to him and said, "What you calling this then?" Paul replied, "I'm calling this Jungle". It had a faster bassline, with the depth that Reggae has. You can't have Drum & Bass without Reggae. If you understand Reggae, you can understand Drum & Bass. Paul explained it was about being deep in the Jungle, chilling out, smokin' spliff and listening to basslines."

Each of these stories was part of an organic evolution rising out of a wider music culture – the Ragga-Reggae-Hip Hop-Rave etc scene. They grew from a musically open multicultural society. To borrow from LTJ Bukem, it's all a *Logical Progression.*

Journeying from the margins to the mainstream, new music goes through the same tortuous route of ridicule, dismissal, tolerance and final acceptance. In the eighteenth century, Viennese Emperor Joseph II battled with Mozart believing that the young composer's music had 'too many notes'. At the turn of the century, Stravinsky, whose inspired classical mayhem changed the possibilities of the music, was disliked. In the Twenties there were criticisms that cutting-edge New Orleans Jazz was too much – musically, racially, socially and sexually – for the masses to handle.

Eighties House music morphed with a range of people adding different ingredients to the mix from their own musical roots. But shades of darkness hit the general Rave scene during 1990 - 91: the come-down. After driving for miles to meet the police and the neighbours who'd had enough of the outdoor revolution, we were driven back from the fields into the homes and clubs. Recession hit and there was less money about. But as in any recession, some of the best music is created and the word 'Jungle' started being bandied about.

And The Name Jungle?

Interview with MC 5ive'O, in his Hackney flat, June '97
B: And the name 'Jungle', where did it come from?
5: Moose was the first person I heard using the word 'Jungle'. It just came to us. Original Hardcore Jungle. Like you was in Africa. Like something Tribal. It just came.

Interview Sarah 'Groove Connection' Sandy, Groove Connection office, Brixton, June '97:
B: Going back to the term 'Jungle'.
S: People say I'm biased but the first DJ I heard playing Breakbeat was Fabio and it was early Reinforced and Kick Down Records, experimenting with breaks. We suddenly realised there was a really good basic Jungle sound coming from London. We loved it even though it was very unsophisticated. You could tell it was made in bedroom studios but there was a new sound. It had different energy. I heard it at Rage for the first time. Grooverider got onto the same thing. Techno faded more and more [at Rage]. We would all just shout "Jungle Jungle" every time a Breakbeat came on.
B: Where did the name come from?
S: I remember a guy called Danny Jungle – he is the first person I always quote. He's around to this day. As soon as the Breakbeat started he was calling it that. There was also Rebel MC and those guys back in 1991 - 92.

Sitting with Rob Playford in Moving Shadow's Soho offices, July '97
B: And about the name 'Jungle'.
R: I thought everybody knew. I've never heard any other stories really. It was on a Dreamscape tape with Top Buzz and Patrick the MC. He said it was 'Hardcore-Jungle-Techno'. It was known as 'Hardcore-Jungle-Techno'. It was 'Hardcore' before that, or 'Techno-ish', and it was

the way the music moved into early Breakbeat stuff. Everybody had the tapes at the time, and when you keep playing the tapes ... that was the first time anyone can remember anyone saying 'Jungle'. It was known for that for several months ... just dropping off all the other words. We'd had 'Hardcore' and 'Techno' ... but this was 'Jungle'.

Interview with Kingsley Roast, June '97
B: Where did Jungle come from?
K: I don't know. Someone said that Moose chatted about "Jungle, the new phenomenon." When someone asked us as promoters what sort of music we were dealing with, we said, "Jungle". Back in '92 we had a backdrop with "Roast Jungle" on it. Our tapes and flyers for the SW1 mention Jungle."

Interview with Grooverider,
The London offices of Sony UK, January '97:
B: And the name 'Jungle'?
G: Fuck knows. I don't know. I just picked up the articles and said, "Oh is that what it is then?"

Congo Natty's Rebel MC believes simply that it was "the people dem who called the music Jungle."

Happy? Not all the ravers were happy. They saw their happy exclusive scene being infiltrated by forces they did not understand. They called it darkness. Paul Roast recalls this initial split. "As the music progressed into Jungle, the scene changed. Everyone who was on the House scene moved away from Roast. They left us. They said, "You're not gonna do nothing, you're just promoting darkness."
PAUL ROAST, ALL JUNGLISTS, CHANNEL 4, 1994

Publications like *Ravescene*, *Mixmag* and *DJ* have been criticised for putting the Jungle scene down, "saying 'It doesn't exist ... let's forget about it ...' What they don't see is that there's people in this scene that are making music far better than anything being made in the UK."
PHIL FROM BASEMENT RECORDS, ALL JUNGLISTS, CHANNEL 4, 1994

Rebel MC described some people's view of Jungle as the Ragamuffin of House, full of racist connotations. He felt that they were probably afraid of the scene's real multicultural nature.

"It's not just music, it's a culture and a way of life. For people who haven't got open ears, it can be really hard, aggressive and quite a harsh-sounding style of music. At the same time, it speaks to people in different ways other than the speed of the Breakbeats or who's singing or chatting on that particular tune. I think that's more important than anything else."
LORNA CLARKE, KISS 100 FM, JUNGLISM, ZONE UK, 1995

A number of key tunes generally accepted as representing the best of the emergent Jungle / Drum & Bass included: *We Are I.E.*, Reinforced's *Internal Affairs*, Mark Evans' *Just 4 U London* and Gerald's *28 Gun Bad Boy*. The '94 album *Jungle Book: Intelligent Minds of Jungle Vol. 1* featuring Peshay, 4 Hero and Nookie was an early, though important, compilation. These tracks weren't the definitive best, nor were they born in isolation. But they were representative of a wider emerging underground. Other developments continued in parallel and DJ's careers grew with the size of the raves. However, when the Jungle explosion of M Beat and General Levy's tune *Incredible* hit the charts in Summer '94, the media focus distorted the scene's true nature. [see *Media*, p.161].

RAGGA BEATS

Electronic Dance Music is in a process of continual and fairly rapid change. As access to the technology increases, new people are able to make music, helping the scene to grow and develop in different directions. One consequence of this is a proliferation of styles. Jungle was part of this splinter movement, breaking away from Hardcore to create a new sound. In turn, Jungle too has been subject to musical digressions – usually a reflection of the people involved in creating the sound. So, you have Jungle which has elements of Jazz, Techno, Hip Hop, Swing, Garage, Pop and so on. The crucial difference tends to be the sample or piece of music used over the bassline. In 1993 - 94 it became 'trendy' to use Ragga samples. Though it must be noted that during the height of the Ragga period, not every tune played on radio or in raves was Ragga-dominated. Remember *The Helicopter Tune* and *Spiritual Aura*, to name just two popular tunes. However, five years later, it's arguable that no other samples have affected the music or the scene to such a degree. Ragga, itself a spin-off of Reggae, was particularly popular amongst young black British kids from '87 to '90. Originally from Jamaica, Ragga was younger, brasher and faster than Reggae. But its lyrics were also more homophobic, violent and sexist. Ragga stars like Buju Banton's lyrics created a mild ruckus worldwide on MTV and global Pop shows, with his infamous 'batty bwoy' phrases.

In '94 *Incredible* by producers M Beat with British Ragga star General Levy broke into the national charts. On the one hand, it took the industry to a new level attracting a huge number of followers. On the other, it may have helped to fuel a split in a once-united Jungle scene.

Producers and DJs often mention the time-lag between when tunes are made and the moment when the public finally celebrates them as dancefloor stompers. The volume of music produced each week means that producers may have already moved on to a new sound even as an older one is at its height. Potential Bad Boy – the 'Roni Size' of the early days and A Guy Called Gerald were amongst those who sampled the heaviest of Ragga Dons in their tunes way before the 1993 - 94 explosion.

"It was kinda part of a rebellion. Every now and again, I'd go to Ragga do's depending on what mood you were in. I grew up around it, went to sound systems and built one in my house. My sister was into Lovers, brother into Shabba Ranks 'n' all that. I'd get tapes from Jamaica. Some people in the Rave scene couldn't understand what it said but that's not my fault. It did build up barriers. I remember in the press when one of the guys from 808 State said they didn't understand what the music was saying. I wasn't on good terms with them and thought "cool". I like music where people can't quite understand it. They have to listen to it and it makes them think. It spurred me on. It was part of the build-up of what it is today 'cos there would have been no heavy B-lines. Without the B-line it would have been like what The Prodigy is today."
A GUY CALLED GERALD

The Ragga infusion was extremely entertaining, which may have contributed to Jungle's problems, as it was around this time that the media began to turn its attention to the scene. People already within the scene became more than a little confused by their portrayal, not recognising themselves in the media screenplay. For one thing, the racially biased views in publications like *The Observer* described Jungle as a 'black' phenomenon, excluding its white, Asian and mixed-race followers. DJ Zoe Richardson, a single white female

who'd been raving since the nights of Rage, was slightly bemused at the angle of the press coverage; though at the time she was happy that the music was receiving any attention at all. But, the media did focus on Jungle's stars, who at that point in time were mostly black. However, there were legions of important people working and partying in the scene, like Peshay and Mickey Finn who were not [see *Media*, p.161].

Press coverage also acts as promotion and it was all part of the excitement of the times. However, the early Ragga samplers had become bored and already moved on, whilst other producers were attracted by the vibe or the cash registers ringing from those highly successful sounds. Shy FX and UK Apache entered the Top Twenty and went Europe-wide on MTV with *Original Nuttah*. Theirs and General Levy's *Incredible* success can't be underestimated. *Incredible* did more to raise the profile of Jungle than any previous track. But something wasn't right.

Hardcore and Ragga attracted negative stereotypes. Companies outside Jungle's core like Reggae label Greensleeves junglised tunes in its back catalogues. Distributors handled hosts of Ragga compilations with titles like: *Jungle Explosion*, *Junglism* and *Ragga in the Jungle* – edited and compiled to cause *Maximum Eruption* – which, mind you, was exactly what many fans and artists wanted. Street Tuff Records, distributed by Jet Star, acknowledged on the *Ragga in the Jungle* sleeve notes that, as a music business concern, they were responding to a huge demand.

EVERYBODY SING 'COS WE DON'T GIVE A DAMN ABOUT A THING ...

In 1993 - 94 Jungle blew up Big Time. 1993 was the year of the MC, with The Ragga Twins, 5ive'O, Navigator, Moose, Det, GQ and Stevie Hyper D chatting from peak to peak. The raves were mental. If you missed out, you really missed out. Gutted, like only a raver left sitting at home without a ticket knows. On nights like that, even the pirates seemed to mock you. The 'Junglist Massive' had the time of their lives, raving madly in a proliferation of designer labels. However, cracks started to appear in the scene.

MC 5ive0

PHOTO BY ANDY COTTERILL

General Levy tried to grab the crown of the faceless movement. Signing an autograph in '94 "Maximum Big up, From De Oriogional (sic) Junglist – General Levy". Though he later apologised in a letter to *The Face*, his initial attitude caused great offence to the real hard workers of the scene who weren't too happy.

"There was nothing wrong with the tune [Incredible]. The tune was a bad tune. It represented for real. What was wrong was the fucked-up way they went about doing it. 'Levy's King of the Jungle ... Him run tings.' – He didn't know the real players." MC 5ive'O

"When that thing blew up, it blew up for the wrong reasons. General Levy came in and gave Jungle to the wrong people. It wasn't the people who initiated or instigated it. It was people who didn't have a clue what Jungle was ... Obviously some of the DJs were playing *Incredible*. And before you knew it, it blew up as the face of Jungle." SARAH, GROOVE CONNECTION

Politically, there were moves to restore the direction and ownership of Jungle. DJ's refused to play *Incredible* and in late '94, Rebel MC was amongst those who called a meeting of Jungle's founding crews including: producers, artists and promoters. Under the banner of unity, there was an attempt to tighten the control of Jungle by its family. One of the objectives of the foundation meetings was to remove General Levy's influence. But the meetings had some unexpected results. The 'unity' banner was soiled when not everyone who felt themselves to be key players were called to the meeting. Amongst this underground meeting of minds, seeds for the future were planted. Goldie's manager Trenton rose to say that he'd seen it all before; the politics and all the wasted energy. He felt everyone would be better served by concentrating on what they were doing. They took stock of themselves, each other and left Levy behind.

Some problems were still unresolved. Jungle producers busy using Ragga samples had actually begun to work with the music's stars. The collaborations had reached a point where Jungle threatened to become a poor Ragga hybrid, run by Jamaicans. Matters were brought to a head in Manchester, Winter '94, at the city's first Jungle event in the club Sankey's Soap, organised by Dave Stone of label Sound Of the Underground Records (SOUR). Jumping Jack Frost, GQ

and 5ive'O stood staring at the stage with disbelief, as the likes of Reggae star Tippa Irie performed over a Jungle backing track. There was a strong impression that things were slipping. When had artists like Tippa Irie moved into Jungle? GQ recalls a vexed Frost urging 5ive'O to "sort things out. It ain't about this. 5ive, tell 'em it's not about this". With Smiley Culture in the audience, Frost grabbed the mic. "Listen right. It ain't about this. Jungle ain't about this." He flung the mic to the floor with a resonating 'kooung' and left the venue. After that event, the core Jungle posse went their own independent way. Dave Stone learnt a very important lesson that night. "To have success in this scene, with this music, you have to have the support of the scene itself." A few months later, he became involved in Jungle Splash at Bagley's. With PA's, all the usual MCs, DJs and seven and a half thousand ravers. Filmed by French TV crews, it was one of the year's most spectacular events.

For the original ravers, the Ragga beat caused problematic undercurrents. The Reggae samples of love, peace, togetherness and Jah were replaced by sounds promoting *Bad Bwoys* who were *Wicked in Bed*, on their way to *Burn the House Down*. It was divisive and alienating. Many of the English audience, whatever their colour, couldn't understand the lyrics. Some people who could understand the words weren't down with sexist or violent lyrics. To be fair, Ragga isn't only about sex and violence. But those elements were there. Andre, a Metalheadz punter, described how having liked Ragga, he could see that the same lyrical problems which had driven him from Ragga, were now infecting Jungle. As DJ Storm said "The Ragga thing was talking about things we didn't actually do."

There were complaints that what was understood as MC's Bad Bwoy lyrics added to the problem. During the first weeks of BBC Radio One's *One in the Jungle*, broadcast Summer '95, a listener near the Welsh Brecon Beacons faxed the show with a complaint. How could he persuade his friends that the Jungle scene was 'safe' when MCs chatted about 'Bad' and 'Rude Boys' either on stage or on the radio? MCs Moose and 5ive'O who saw a copy of the fax at DJ Ron's warehouse flat argued passionately for several hours. They didn't feel they were promoting a gangsta lifestyle and explained how Rude Boy was actually a street term of endearment.

Back in the dance, people more concerned with keeping their labels and trainers pristine than raving exuded Attitude beyond the point of pushing and shoving. For a time the jeans and hooded top ravers of old didn't seem welcome.

WHAT AM I GONNA DO, WHAT AM I GONNA DO?

Some people were sick of it all. Many artists didn't like the monster they'd help to create. People had welcomed the Ragga / Reggae influence and the new crowd and influx of talent which it brought, but were sick of the Ragga / Reggae ethics. Deeper underground, some of those genre's shadier characters had also begun to move into Jungle.

In early '95, there was a conscious decision by the DJs, not to play anything Ragga-oriented or with a full vocal. Senior DJs like Grooverider, uninspired, almost lost their musical way. DJs like Kemistry & Storm lost work because promoters didn't think they were 'in it'. They weren't. Punters like Andre were left out in the cold with nowhere to rave and long-time producers kept their heads down, developing their art as they always had, but with nowhere to play their music. Others walked out of the Ragga Jungle arenas looking to build their own piece of heaven elsewhere.

At DJ agency Groove Connection, Grooverider, despite his reservations, and Mickey Finn championed the Ragga beats whilst Fabio and Bukem took to playing a new underground sound. The agency was instrumental in trying to build a new corner for a whole raft of music which wasn't getting a look-in. There were also stories that when certain named DJs were on a flyer the 'dodgy' crowd and their bad attitude would follow. Dissociating themselves from the Jungle sound, Fabio and Bukem, whose names didn't draw a problem crowd, moved into club Speed.

"However much I can say I totally loved the energy of that Jungle sound, we knew we had to keep moving forwards otherwise the thing would stagnate."
SARAH, GROOVE CONNECTION

Speed opened in the West End featuring Bukem's and Fabio's mellower beats. AWOL moved from the Paradise to the SW1 Club, where DJs played more Hip Hop based Jungle. A new metallic sound was emerging from the Metalheadz Sessions at the Blue Note. And Roast, Telepathy and a host of others, featured mostly Raggaless Jungle.

CALLING NAMES, FINDING MEANINGS

From '95 through '96 everyone in the scene seemed to be arguing over, muddled by, or purposely not caring about what to call British Breakbeat. But it seemed difficult to escape the mesh of labels. Some DJs, producers and punters dissociated themselves from the name Jungle and adopted the Drum & Bass tag which was free of any negative connotations. People trapped in muso-political labels behaved like fundamentalists. But it's not surprising: for some, music is a religion and this church split.

Producers making Jungle continued to borrow from a wide range of music. However, as Jazz, Ambient or Techno hooks were used by producers, the media and marketing men trumpeted it as a new direction in Jungle. Label subdivisions proliferated. Aside from British Breakbeat and Hardcore you had Ambient, Ambient Jungle, Jungle Techno, Artcore, Intelligent, Hip Hop and Jazz Jungle to name but a few. It created confusion in some quarters and within the confusion, there were glimpses of racism. During an *Open Forum* (Kool FM's seasonal debate show), MC 5ive'O described a flyer he'd been given which boasted, "Intelligent beats for the Intelligent few". It didn't take much reading between the lines to understand its assumptions or implications.

JUNGLE, DRUM & BASS OR WHATEVER YOU WANT TO CALL IT ...

It's debatable what the music should be called. Rob Playford uses the term 'Jungle' in the scene, with people who know the score. Otherwise he'll use 'Drum & Bass' to prevent Moving Shadow's music being mis-marketed. Cleveland Watkiss remembers the week when all the record shops started calling the music Drum & Bass, but noted that there was all kinds of JDB on the shelves. Rebel MC really dislikes the phrase, 'Jungle / Drum & Bass or whatever you want to call it' explaining that if you have a child and call it Jungle, it's disrespectful to have it called by any other name. He believes that those calling Jungle by other names have alternative motives.

Those labels became so important. It was hard enough going into a record shop to get tunes if you felt intimidated. Now, you had to nail your colours to the mast and ask "have you got any of that *Intelligent* stuff or any *'Ard Step*?" Being on the right tip could make the difference between getting access to the under-the-counter-tunes or the fillers on the shelves.

By early '96 the prominence in the media of clubs like Speed and Metalheadz at the Blue Note and of producer / DJs like Bukem, promoted a new direction, with the sounds of the Drums and the Bass. Drum & Bass wasn't any more real than Jungle but it became subtly important in marketing terms. Drum & Bass = Good, Jungle = Bad. That's the way the name 'Jungle' in 1995 - 96 seemed to drop. One Nation and World Dance were among those rave organisations who changed the wording on their flyers in an attempt to discourage any anti-social customers. Others clung religiously to the name, refusing to abandon their music because it was Jungle.

"I think there was a subtext with Drum & Bass meaning white, friendly, middle-class. Jungle meaning 'A bad boy ting.' There is an element of truth in that, but I think people waved that flag too much."
BRET, *TELEPATHY*

MC 5ive'O compares the split in Jungle to Hip Hop and it's "East Coast – West Coast bullshit, with people making Drum & Bass to accommodate the white man". He also smells racism in the development of the Drum & Bass side of the industry and its new media focus. "Drum & Bass is a white bwoys' bizniss. And it seems like they got certain coconuts involved … Any music that comes to this planet, the white bwoys and record companies are in it and that's the way it goes." The essence of difference had been there before but before it didn't seem to matter. It wasn't so overt. And there were no big money record company contracts flying around. By the time Goldie had been signed by London Records, the differences really did matter.

The names roll on … "I'm dealing with 21st Century Soul." Cleveland passes a CD across his flat. Roni Size on Talkin' Loud, *21st Century Soul* – 'A collection of music that takes soul into the next millennium and beyond'. "When I'm talking about Soul, I'm not talking about …" (he sings a soulful warble) "it's about freedom of expression. With artists having the courage of their own convictions and seeing that through, come hell or high water – Jungle becomes 21st Century Soul."

Elwood: What kind of music do you usually have here?
Lady: Oh we got both kinds, Country and Western.
THE BLUES BROTHERS, *UNIVERSAL STUDIOS, 1980*

There were those who went to great lengths to quell any Jungle / Drum & Bass musical division. Adverts such as those for the Jungle Fever Shop explained, "We sell all aspects of Jungle / Drum & Bass". After all the passionate disputes about titles, ads like those were quite refreshing. Never mind the bollocks, here's the music.

"My show on Kiss FM is called *The Circumference*, 'cos I do the whole circle. That is what we've got to keep, otherwise we start getting fractions and that's when it starts getting complicated." *JUMPING JACK FROST, JUNGLISM, ZONE UK, 1995*

Rising above the factional squabbles, DJs Hype and Nicky Blackmarket were also among those describing the 'full circumference' of Jungle / Drum & Bass. "It still doesn't bother me what the music's called. I'm classed as a Jungle DJ, then I'm classed as a Drum & Bass DJ. I'm reading a magazine today, 'Hype's 'Jump Up'. What's 'Jump Up'? I'm 'Jump Up' Bukem's 'Intelligent', Doc Scott is 'Dark'. We all play a bit of everything. I've always called it 'British Breakbeat' because that's what it is, whether it's jazzy today or fucking 'Ambient' I play it all."
DJ HYPE, NOVEMBER '97

The word Jungle can be made to mean what anyone wants it to mean – including the Drum & Bass tag. Terminology falls into and escapes politics, isms and marketing. Until whoever makes up a new umbrella name for this music, the industry will continue to work – business as usual. When the name is reinvented, they'll still be working – inventing and reinventing their music and the name will only matter as a marketing tool. The beats will continue to speak for themselves.

SOME JOURNEYS THROUGH THE MUSIC

"Your roots depend upon where you came into the music. That's where you understand it from."

JUMPING JACK FROST

For those on the outside, it may be difficult to understand how senior DJs or serious punters have arrived at the point where JDB is their day-to-day existence. It becomes more confusing during interviews as the senior and the serious cite different descriptions of the origins of JDB. But everyone who's made a journey into the music has their own story. The most common, though not exclusive path which many have followed is through the siphon of the Rave scene. People just get pulled in by some musical tractor beam on different stages of the path, being drawn to the source. That's the theory. These are the histories of some of the people on the scene.

ANDY C – DJ / PRODUCER

"I was totally caught up in the whole Rave Acid House and Hardcore sound. That's all I was listening to day and night. Where I lived you could pick up Centreforce and Sunrise Radio. I used to wake up in the morning, get ready for school and have that on in the background. And when I was 13 my sister took me to my first illegal rave in a barn in Essex."

A GUY CALLED GERALD – PRODUCER

"I was doing my own thing but I got my fingers burnt, with Voodoo Ray, then with 808 State and a little bit with Sony. What I always wanted to do was release records but I couldn't do it in Manchester, so I had to go down to London. The scene in Manchester was over-rated. It was mad, but not that mad."

Gerald was bored of it all. "I'd go upstairs in the Hacienda, Graeme Park would be there and I'd go in the lighting box and mess about with that for a while, look around to see if there was anyone there I knew, then I'd go home. That was it. I wasn't really enjoying myself or getting anywhere.

Goldie and Navigator came up to Manchester and I was thinking I should be down in London working and seeing what other people's angle was. I was missing things. Goldie called me, I think he got my number from the distributor. He phoned a few times sounding like a crazy man and he was totally into the stuff I was doing. I'd done this track called *Crazy Man*. I'd had feedback from London but nothing from Manchester.

There was some people taking an interest in the scene and going down to London occasionally but I started to go down every week. I'd stay over at Goldie's place and he'd introduce me to different people. You'd go to the Paradise, then hang around a bit and go to Roast. If there were parties, I'd just go not realising that there were all these different camps, like a stranger in town."

DJs Kemistry & Storm

One of the reasons Kemistry was enticed to London was that a friend had been to a party and returned to Sheffield telling her about this mad music, with everybody doing this crazy dance — enthusiastically demonstrating 'the thing with the arms.' Promising to invite Kemi to the next one, they travelled down to one of the rave boat parties on the Thames in '88. "It was really mad and someone offered me some drugs and I thought, "Oh why not enter into the spirit of it all". It changed my life. I was going to come down to London anyway. I was a make-up artist and wasn't really getting much work up North. It was time to come down and get some proper work. I moved to Finsbury Park where I knew some people. I got into clubbing straight away.

When I heard the music and everything I just wanted to go and seek it out, find out whatever the scene was." Storm had been studying in Oxford for the preceding four years with friends who hailed from Putney. "It was all about drink, money and 'Hey-ho, what a ball we shall have this week'. You get shoved a bit sideways when you live in a place like Oxford. What's always been good about our scene was that it didn't matter what your background was or what colour you were. Once you were into the scene and did what you did, you could be whatever, it didn't matter."

Cleveland Watkiss — Musician

"I started listening to Kool in '92. I'd be listening to the bass and the beats thinking, "Wha … wher … woa". That was the inspiration. I started to make the link. When I really made the link was down at Roller Express in '93. I saw the whole thing, MCs, a sound system. It was a modern day sound system. That first Jungle rave explained everything. It was as clear as light after that. I'd been searching for an outlet, that kind of link with sound. It was what I wanted to hear and be involved in."

Clayton — Trouble on Vinyl

I was born in South London. When I was nine I moved to America with my mum and came back to England when I was 17. I started DJing Rare Groove in early 88 / 89. You'd go out and everything would be under one roof. There wasn't such segregation of music as there is now. You would hear Norman Jay, Paul Anderson. Remember Shake 'n' Finger Pop, Soul II Soul and Mad Hatter Trevor? That was my in-roads into Dance Music. When the Summer of Love came I went to a rave. I got dragged there cos I was a purist. But I popped a pill and next thing you know I was like, "Yeah". The good thing about the Rave scene was that it brought the colours — black and white — together. Before the Rave thing black people would only want to mix with themselves. When the Rave thing came along everyone just wanted to get on. I started going to more and more raves; Rage, Land of Oz and all them sort of places. I used to go out religiously. I remember a party in King's Cross. It was some illegal thing. Probably started at about three in the morning. I remember being around thousands of people and everyone's happy and there was this big Mutoid Waste robot — it was quite a sight man.

Hype — DJ / Producer

The thing with Hype was he was a white Hackney boy who'd grown up with black music and friends both black and white. He doesn't try to be black but DJ Ron's brother MC Strings once commented that 'Hype was Caribbean anyhow.' Hype had two groups of friends. The black guys and the white. They'd meet on the streets but never go out clubbing together. Then … "Well, there was people from the office in the warehouse where I worked who were going to raves and saying it was bloody brilliant and I've got friends who were Ragga-to-fuck that had gone and everyone was saying it was wicked. They were loving it. I was used to going to things where everyone's screwfaced, whether there was trouble or not. But at these parties there's people going, "Do ya want a fag? Do ya want some of my drink?" I was like, "I don't want none of your drink … who're you mate? Oi, that fuckin' geeza's offering me some of his drink!" " But with time, Hype settled into the people, music, vibe and loved it.

Speeding late up the motorway, we swerve into a service station. Another stall, this time for petrol. I open the passenger door spraying Jungle across the forecourt. An empty beer bottle clatters onto the concrete in full view of a family of four in their Volvo. Two guys, a red Audi, the beer bottle and that Jungle. We crease up laughing, thinking how bad it must look.

We fill up, stock up on motorway junk food, pay up and start up. Already too late to contemplate, Ron checks his money and returns to cuss the assistant for short changing him. We're back on the road and the speedometer strays into uncharted territory. Talking racism, politics, wimmin and Jungle gossip …

CREWS

"Crews — There'll always be crews …" GOLDIE

Of the original party posse, some would always be happy raving. Others decide that they'd like to take things further, get a bit more involved. Some will explore completely different avenues. But your crew will always be your crew, whether it involves your MC, DJ / Producer, computer programmer, barber, carpenter or the guy who's always on-call with the weed. JDB's tight but interlocking crews, though historical and geographical, are also based on musical styles.

Crews can work like personal Venn diagrams. Goldie has his Wolverhampton and Miami crews and connections with various labels and stables, like Reinforced, Moving Shadow and the Metalheadz family members, who wear the label's exclusive emblem around their necks. On his '95 album *The Cutting Edge* on Sony, Goldie showcased the music of over eleven producers including: Lemon D, Dillinja, L Double, Rob Haigh of Omni Trio, J Majik and 4 Hero. They're all friends whose music he respected and wanted to involve.

MC GQ also has his home crew but he gets around, mixing with Metalheadz, Peshay Drum & Bassists, as well as DJ Ron and MC 5ive'O of the Jungle tradition. Newcomers can join crews, yet some rare types like Grooverider and Fabio manage to distance themselves from any distinct group, going it alone or slotting in with different teams as necessary. In this respect, they are free of the problems created by internal loyalties and external segregations.

Crews can be restrictive, informally dictating who you can or can't deal with. They feed directly into the scene's politics. There are many ways of analysing the Autumn '96 debate between DJ Ron, Goldie, Shy FX, Deman Rockers and 5ive'O on Kool FM's *Open Forum*. It had several subtexts, including those laced with crew politics and musical territories. Goldie was challenged to defend his concept of the Metalheadz Sessions whose choice of DJ / producers was seen as fostering elitism. On the other side, Brockie was among those who called in to slam Deman and MC 5ive'O for not defending their part of the scene properly. After the debate, in corners of both camps, there were vibes of satisfied just-triumph or angry unjust-defeat. With crews acting almost as the basic organising unit within JDB, Congo Natty's Rebel MC was noted by his absence. Many felt he should have taken part to represent the label's important contribution to Jungle. But he preferred not to get tied up in the semantics.

The closer you are to the streets, the more you rely on your crew. It's about survival where survival is a way of life, especially if you're dealing with the wrong side of the law. Relationships are based on a different level of trust. You'd need your mate to stand up in a fight, lend you a fiver, watch your back or put food on the table. In an age of family breakdown, they've become family. And they are 'De Man Dem.'

There were groups like the Arms House Crew, The Original Run Tings Crew, with names like Yella, Fabian, Sean, Luke Skywalker and Nightmare Freddy Finch. Between raving down at Roast, with grooves and champagne, or at Blues parties on their own East London Leytonside Grove Green Road turf, they helped build the connection between Rave and Blues / Ragga culture. But most importantly, up in the place, they were the vibe and soul of the party.

Interview with DJ Storm, November '96

B: So what's this about the Inta Natty Crew?

S: I'm not telling you.

B: Sorry?

S: It stands for: I'm Not Telling You. Legend has it they are bonded together by some dark secret, probably about women.

Their idea of a good night out: travelling with Grooverider, drinking loads of champagne, smoking Sensi, alternately nodding or firin' off to the beats and going blissfully home. It was always guest list business. They even had a football team and their own line of merchandise.

Crews are about supporting and representing. "De Underground Vs The Inta Natty Crew, home and away we beat them. I think that was something that developed when we went out with Randall", reckons Mikey, De Underground.

"We're West Ham boys, so us and Upton Park moved as a crew. Everyone was trying to get in with us. Our homeboys were supporting something. It was like going to a match. Twenty, thirty of us on the guest list, bigging up Randall."

ONE TIME THE WORD WAS, "REACH BIRMINGHAM".

The line-up was Grooverider, Mickey Finn, Frost, Randall, Fabio. The crew let off so much noise every time a tune dropped you could see we had the DJs buzzing. It was like a competition thing. You had to have brought your best Dub Plates that night otherwise you could forget your set. Grooverider went on there and pulled out the best of. That started the ball rolling. Man was getting bottles banging on tables, blood pressure going, Navigator's running up and down, the promoters going, "Who's that crowd up there. I want 'em here every time". The crowd is looking up, getting on it. Grooverider's done his thing, hour and a half, ripped it up. Man's sweating it out, lungs sore – gone. Then silence. There was silence between each man. Randall went on, ripped it up for an hour and a half. Blood pressure and everything. Frost came on, ripped it up – hour and a half, heart attack – all that kind of business.

Then it was Fabio. From the silence he knew that first tune wasn't the one. So he's gone in his box quick time, run the next tune and it was like, "Yes Fabio". It was really that kind of night. Best night ever. Man had to show his form. That's the good thing about having that little crew, that little posse. It was the spice of the whole damn rave. The whistle posse. The raves need that posse. You had one big posse jumping together in the middle of the hall or a few spread out and jumping, people just joined in. That was what carried your night."

BACK IN THE DAY

On stolen study periods when the youths slipped
    into streets which screamed for their souls.
Back in the day with the youths sharing a sodden
    cigarette in rainy Dalston waiting for the
                243 bus to nowhere.
    Back in the day sitting in someone's yard,
        dreaming of fame, fortune and glory.
    Back in the day crammed in someone's banger
        without enough cash for a bag of weed.
    Back in the day when your spar goes out to DJ
    in some forgotten club with De Man Dem up in
            the place, radiating support.

        Back in the day – up in the dance
    a nervous young producer approaches the stage
        and De Man Dem, gives his test press to
                    your DJ.
    Back in the day, when you had that McJob,
        he had a scam, we all had a hustle.
            Have you got a draw?
        The meagre money circulated.
Knew each other better than our parents knew us.
    Friends of the heart to the core, a family.
    Me an De Man Dem, writing street history.

    Me an De Man Dem, checking the women.
            Breaking out at the dance.
        Bussing through the air waves.
            Grabbing up the mic.
        Orchestrating the crowds.
    Drinking champagne with our DJ on the decks.
    Flying the World to party for the people.
        These are our nights – the rest's a
                long hard fight.
    That's my life with me an De Man Dem.

(LOOSELY BASED AROUND DJ RON, HIS BROTHERS MC STRINGS & LENNY, MCs GQ & 5IVE'O, DUBBS, SMUGGLER, BART SIMPSON, RUSTY RANKS, DJs SL & SPOONIE, AND FRIENDS – THE LONDON SOME 'TING CREW.)

GIVE UP THE DAY JOB

Some in the scene didn't ever really have a steady job. Before he became fully occupied with Kool FM, Eastman did all sorts of building work and security jobs for his father's clubs including Telepathy. Some did. After being released from prison, Kenny Ken worked for London Transport and DJ Ron worked as a plumber fitting everything from domestic central heating to industrial sized pipes for Pentonville prison. Gerald worked in McDonald's. Shy FX had been hired as a tape operator at SOUR. He was fired when he wouldn't clean the toilets. He left, but returned with his first track.

Randall's last non-DJ job was as a messenger for a City firm. A good laugh as ever, the City boys often invited him out on sports outings, even taking him abroad to boost the scores and banter. Randall began to think more seriously about his music and started to 'disappear' from work for hours on end. This combined with him being adopted by the white-collar workers, was enough for the office manager to take a dislike to him and fire him — as he simultaneously quit.

Before setting up flyer firm Design Asylum Ltd, Damon worked for Robert Maxwell designing pages of memorable publications like *Cranes Today*. Either happy or suspicious about the long hours he was putting in on the computer, his boss checked Damon's PC and found files full of flyer designs and "he weren't too 'appy". As Storm recalls, giving up work as a radiotherapist was a difficult decision. Apart from anything else, "If you're not working, you can't buy tunes." But as standards in the National Health Service began to slip, she was off.

One top MC was best occupied stealing high-powered motor bikes and pukka cars. "When I first got on a moped, it was a real experience not having to walk anywhere. You could just get on and be there, travel far. Getting into bigger bikes, we'd speed along, weaving between cars chased by the Ol' Bill, lights flashing. When we could see our estate, we knew we were home 'cos they couldn't get through the bollards or know the place like we did. Yeah, it was a buzz."

Qualified with an HNC in Electronic Engineering — the hardware side and trained at work in software to go with the hardware, Rob Playford's mind was not on his work. He programmed his computer to do his day's work with the touch of a button, leaving him free to acquire a suspiciously long list of mobile phone numbers on the firm's telephone bill. Having a mortgage was a sobering thought. His job plus DJing had paid for most of the studio equipment in his house. But giving up the day job to make tunes and go raving at weekends wasn't easy for someone who exudes common sense. It took four years, two Moving Shadow hits and boredom at work — plus some questions about those mobile phone numbers before he word processed his resignation one Summer's day and joined the party full-time.

"It's made me look at life in a different way.
When I was younger, I wanted things quickly.
I wanted my car quickly.
I wanted my bike quickly.
I wanted them clothes quickly.

But now, 'cos I'm involved in something
constructive,
for the first time in my life,
I'm prepared to wait.
I'm not in no hurry now,
'cos it's not going away.
It's there to stay.
And, as long as I don't mess up,
it'll be there for me.

Before I started DJing
and before I started working with
London Transport
I was always in 'n' out of prison.
I never had a future.
But then the last sentence I done
I came out in 1986.
And I thought to myself
I can't go back to jail again.
I'm a big man now.
I've got to try to sort something out.
And lucky for me
the Rave scene started.
I got involved with that
and made something of myself."

DJ KENNY KEN, ALL JUNGLISTS, CHANNEL 4, 1994

"I didn't kill, maim or rob nobody, I just hustled." For 5ive'0, hustling was part of survival, living on and off the streets. It used to be called 'living off your wits'. That probably sounds more romantic than it ever was. And 5ive had to get out before it dragged him down permanently. "I'd done a prison term already. I said, 'I don't want no more of that'. I had three children, I had to change my tings. I'm still in the Hood. But I've got out the ways of the Hood." MC 5IVE'0

"I tell you the truth as I sit here now. I would never, never like to do a nine-to-five. I looked at my mum — she worked so hard for the money that she'd get. This country is so hard. It's hard. She'd go out at 6am, get back six in the evening, still have to do the washing and cooking. You'd hear her talking about 'this country' and I was thinking, 'Boy, I could be like my mum or the average person. I wouldn't be able to handle it'. There was a stage when I never had nothing. I sold drugs, everybody does — Hackney and the way everything was before. You do what you do to make a little bit of cash. I did photography, went to college and did a business course. I was working and the music thing, Acid, happened and it just took me. That's the buzz. Living life, enjoying what I'm doing, getting paid for it. All the rest. What they want to pay you in this country for a job, it's just ridiculous and I'm just glad I found this music." MC GQ

GQ isn't alone in having something constructive to do with his life and future.

Sarah Sandy of Groove Connection and Creative Source studied Film and Cultural Studies at Goldsmiths College and started raving in '88. Initially checking Energy and Enter The Dragon, she couldn't believe the scene's excitement. By '89 Sarah was already underground in Brixton. She'd met Frost, Bryan Gee, Fabio and Grooverider and wasn't about to leave the party.

"I couldn't stop raving. I had finished college and was supposed to work for the BBC or try to do a Director's course or something like that. I couldn't do it. I was raving too much and couldn't get my head together. I didn't want to do it ... I thought, I'll just float for this next Summer or whatever and see what happens." Sarah went on to set up the premier agency, Groove Connection. In the early stages, it's difficult to earn a wage large enough to buy both food and records. Balancing the day job with DJing is an ideal. Many people can't or don't really have the desire to do that. Grooverider, the former accountants' clerk and computer operator, got the sack coming in bleary eyed after another night playing out at a Wednesday after-hours club with Fabio.

You can't survive in London on the dole trying to be a DJ, the financial hardship is crippling. But it can be an incentive to go out and push for work. A carless Kemistry & Storm would hire transport to get them to the venues and there'd be times when they'd end up earning only about twenty quid each. Storm emphasises, "It was worth it. We didn't care how much we earned. It got a bit bad when you couldn't buy any clothes for about two years, that was depressing but we just had this drive that we were gonna take any work. Even when people said, "You can't play there or there," we were like, "We'll do it." Then you'd be off driving like crazy somewhere. To us that was how it was supposed to be. That was the job and you do have to make

sacrifices which didn't really bother me." Apart from earning some money, that kind of drive will get your name around the promoters. If you'll play anywhere, you can fill a gap in the market. Kemistry & Storm caned it up North when most of the South's DJs were boycotting the area because of the violent antics of some travelling Manchester crews.

Aside from the self-imposed poverty, you may have to explain things to your parents. Storm, who qualified after four years as a radiotherapist at Oxford's John Radcliffe Hospital, told hers that she was giving it all up to become a DJ. "They were horrified and I got to that stage when I thought, what have I done? Radiotherapy was a career I really believed in." You find yourself having to justify your choice ... It must all seem very abstract to them. There was the notion that you're heavily involved in 'Rave' and 'drugs.' You have to convince them and perhaps yourself what it is you're doing, why and how you're going to support yourself. Even when you've reached the top of the tree, you might still hit some crisis and ask, "What the fuck am I doing? Tonight I'm going to play records to crowds of people, and that's how I earn a crust." It wasn't on the Career Officer's list. It's a dream and the reality seems unreal. Perhaps it's a passion that transcends vocation. Perhaps not. The career structure is so informal and semi-tangible that you can't expect anything but ridicule from superiors and peers alike. You may never earn a crust and have to return to that death of a dream, nine-to-five prison. But then again, you might make it.

"It's not easy. You've got to have qualifications to fall back on if you can't cut it in this. You're supposed to do what you feel is right. You've got to go for it. You've always got to go for it. If it doesn't work out, you've got something to fall back on. It's hard work but you've got to juggle it, 'til you're at the stage when you say, this is working for me and say yes, let me try that ..." GROOVERIDER

At the end of the day it takes a leap of faith.

MC GQ

Photo by
Cleveland Aaron

THIS IS OUR MUSIC

"It's weird, 'Oasis is the biggest thing since The Beatles.' I want something new not something John Lennon did."
A GUY CALLED GERALD

"As Navigator says in his lyric, "The Jamaican man big up the Reggae. The American man big up the Hip Hop. It's about time the British man big up the Jungle." "
MC 5IVE'O, JUNGLISM, ZONE UK, 1995

The major difference between JDB and Soul, Hip Hop, Ragga or Reggae is that JDB is British music arising from a unique mix of energy and culture. There were those of the MTV generation who became bored with foreign sounds. British Soul and British Hip Hop were poor cousins compared to their American superstar relatives though Soul II Soul had actually created a different sound. And not to do the British House and Techno crews an injustice, it should be recognised that there was the essence of a British scene in the early days of Rave. Local producers checked their tunes at raves like Confusion which featured the likes of Kid Bachelor and MCs E-Mix and Bullet. But the flood of Dance music originating from the US and Europe left some producers like Paul Ibiza cold. It failed to make that spiritual and musical connection. Perhaps searching through faceless piles of expensive imports, sporting far flung geographical references, proved too alienating.

When home-grown labels such as Reinforced and Shut Up & Dance began to make their own music, it did make a difference. It was inspirational knowing that London crews in Dollis Hill, Hackney or Leyton had made the tunes being played in your club. Producers would be inside the same club doing their own audience research and quality control as the tune dropped. Local producers were able to make music reflecting the shared musical experience of the DJs and punters in the dance. Geography and demographics have also played their part. Lemon D and Dillinja are neighbours, as were DJ Ron, MCs 5ive'O and GQ. GQ and Det were in the same class at school. MC Det and DJ Brockie lived across the road from each other. There was constant room for cross-fertilisation between friends. Dave Stone points out, "There's a lot of strange loyalties which bind the scene together. Loyalties that you'd never think would exist. They don't make sense in terms of business but are there because people have history. For these people, history counts for a lot."

The inclusivity of British Raves, coupled with the introduction of MCs, placed a stamp on something unmistakably new, and definitely home-grown. Perhaps there was something uplifting, feeling an industry growing with the support of money which, rather than being exported, be circulated around the immediate community. It stayed in the pockets of people you knew, even allowing you the possibility of earning a livelihood. Roni Size donated £15,000 of his '97 Mercury Award to the Bristol music project which first encouraged his musical interest.

Comfortable middle class journalists often tire of what they see as 'the same old sad story. Poor person born in the inner cities making something of themselves.' DJ Hype rounded on one foreign writer who failed to understand that the 'shit' is still out there and people have to live in it every day. Hype could only remember five friends from Hackney that weren't mad, bad or in prison. He acknowledges that we're not living in the 1920s and most people aren't starving to death but there's still the 'shit' to live through.

"You got to remember that 99% of the people in your book were destined for nothing. Nothing and nobody in life. At best they're gonna be in a nine-to-five job, Mr. Average. And that would have been termed good round this area (Hackney). But we're all businessmen now, man. I'm sitting there with Sony Japan in this big hotel up West and I'm sitting there like this (jeans, sweatshirt and trainers) and it's bare suits in the place. And I was thinking, "Fucking hell, five years ago I wouldn't have got in the building, they would've called the police." And now I'm here negotiating with Sony Japan. It's mad." *DJ HYPE*

Though there are financial rewards which can help Hype to do small things like replace his mum's 20-year-old sofa, he isn't complacent. "When you're in this scene, most people who work in it, DJs, Producers, MCs drive a nice car and every day, they've just come back from here, there or wherever. You think it's the norm. But it ain't the norm is it? Some people dream of going to somewhere like Japan and never get there. I've been there three or four times, toured the whole place. This music was my ticket from the shit, out of the shit. I'm a miserable git as a person but I couldn't thank God enough." *DJ HYPE*

"Political things won't stop at my own rave. I've used the toilets and walking out I've seen this young white guy go in and my sixth sense has said, 'Trouble.' I have seen these youths go in. I've taken blows to my head to save this guy and get him out and then deal with them. And their vibe is, "But this is OUR thing. This is OUR thing and it's the only thing we got." You hear that and it's deep, but you can't condone that sort of thing. Music is for everyone. Music really and truly brings people together. Anyway I see it, you wouldn't be talking to me if it weren't for the music. I wouldn't know you. I wouldn't be the guy I am today. My formative years were not the best years but I can honestly say, through entering into this thing it's made us different people. I didn't know about the arts. I didn't know social skills. I didn't know about talking to people. It's all

through becoming a promoter, driving 'round the country meeting people of all different persuasions and getting to see that the world is bigger than London, Tottenham, Hackney, Brixton. People are different. The Internet, I didn't know about no PCs. It's only through doing events I've had to learn. I think it's a good thing. I think it's a positive thing if it turns you life from a negative existence one." *BRET, TELEPATHY*

"I could see the whole picture, I wanted to do a British thing with Rave Jungle Techno, learning from the mistakes that I'd seen. It wasn't important that it was a British thing, more that it was a home thing. Keep it real, supporting pirate stations, the clubs, the Jungle Fevers and everything. I liked the community working together. It's about our generation, we were the kids who watched *Grange Hill*, it's our era. We finally have an identity. This is us." *A GUY CALLED GERALD*

It was important that Jungle / Drum & Bass was made here, it was our own. Rather than trying to get your head around another language, different names and unfamiliar geography, it was all here. That's why they've been able to keep hold of it and keep the music true.

But 'Ours' is a loose definition since JDB belongs to anyone who comes to contribute something positive. We give you the blueprint and see what you can come up with. The indigenous urban London phenomenon spread rapidly to the shires and abroad, where it also now proliferates. Its adoption by overseas producers, like Japan's Ken Ishi, is a reflection of the quality of the format. 'Ours' also means out of the hands of the majors. Producers like Roni Size and DJ Hype have developed their craft out of sight of the major record companies. The non-exclusive contracts have been signed later down the line. As the quality and credibility of JDB has become established, it is wise for the majors to adapt new strategies which cooperate with, rather than dictate to the producers [see *Majors*, p.56].

"We own everything. We own the whole industry.
That's why we haven't got any cheesy Jungle Records."
GROOVERIDER

Cleveland Watkiss takes time out to respect the history of
Jungle / Drum & Bass, born of the spirit of improvisation.
"We could only have got here because of our history. If you
break that down, Electronic, R 'n' B, Reggae, Rock, Fusion.
But the home is the Motherland, Africa."

Roni Size acknowledges the influence of other music in the
Reprazent album, *New Forms*. But he goes beyond praising
the music. "This album sums up how excited we are by the
technology, the music and the whole Hip Hop culture. We
saw how they built their own empire. I think that this
music is capable of doing the same thing ... For me there's
a new music in town and it's called Drum & Bass Jungle.
And that's me, I'm a Junglist." *BBC 2 OCTOBER '97*

*"Jungle means to me something that came from the
street. It means that people who were born with
nothing have found something they can relate to.
Something they can believe in."*
KENNY KEN, ALL JUNGLISTS, CHANNEL 4, 1994

*"Jungle is a feeling. It's how you live, it doesn't matter
where you come from. Junglist is a way of life, like
dem Hip Hop man. It's not the music, it's the way
you live. You're dealing with the deepness of Jungle.
Colour has nothing to do with it. You can have Mexican
B Boys. It's a religion."* MC 5IVE'O

TIP OF THE ICEBERG: SUSSEX UNIVERSITY, SUMMER '94

After the Easter break, the usual gaggle of
trendy Acid Jazz, House and Techno students
greeted each other in the library foyer. Two
mates catch up on vacation tales and more
importantly - what tunes they'd been listening
to. Moving away from the scrum, scoping
furtively, they both admitted to being infected
with the passion of Jungle. But they knew
instinctively that any mention of the J word
amongst the trendies and they'd have to defend
themselves against the derision of their peers.

Junglists in 1994 - 95 often had to defend their music
against a sea of enemies, who came with closed ear
prejudices. That's how it was outside the core of Jungle /
Drum & Bass. Isolated souls dotted around. Patriotic
conspirators fighting a cause in which, even getting a
handful of tunes on a mix tape played in polite company
was a victory.

Those sitting on the edge of the scene contributed to its
growth in any way that they could; especially punters with
jobs who'd use their firms' telephones for DJ business,
photocopiers for their mates' flyers and extended lunch
hours to pop down the studio. It continues today. There's a
host of people working for the music through their day jobs.
Not everyone wants to stand, up front on stage. They can't
all be named, but recognise that they're here, there and
everywhere ...

PRODUCERS

"Why do painters paint? Why do boxers box? Michelangelo used to say, "The sculpture was already there, all I had to do is remove the stone." "
DR SUNG, STAR TREK – THE NEXT GENERATION

Producers are the backbone of the JDB industry. They make the beats. Like artists in their studios, they're surrounded by an array of coloured paints, aerosol cans, brushes and pallet knives and sit before an empty Cubase canvas. Motivated by whatever internal / external inspiration fires them, they fill the space with music.

At their most creative, producers scour the planet capturing sounds which, when woven into the technological fabric of JDB, unite and transcend the senses. Shy FX, A Guy Called Gerald and Rob Playford cart around Digital Audio Tape (DAT) machines and pocket memos like electronic fishing nets. Urban streets and underground trains are in the mix. All sounds are sacred. If not in this life, then the next – looped, time stretched, reborn and primed for detonation as they pass through the next set of speakers into the defenceless cerebral cortex. They developed an auditory landscape in which hearing links with vision links with emotion links with imagination.

The home studio revolution at the root of Dance music culture is a relatively new development. Around 20 years ago, electronic music was seen as the poor cousin of real instruments, be they in a band or an orchestra. Remember *Fame* and new generation musician, Bruno Martelli, who was forced by Professor Shorofsky to do traditional orchestra practice? Martelli was ahead of his time.

PS: Lift the bow Martelli!

M: Mozart wouldn't do all this today.

PS: Do what?

M: All this bowing business. He'd just plug his keyboard into an amp and he'd have string quartets and symphonies coming out his fingers.

PS And who would play these science fiction symphonies?

M: He would.

PS: All by himself?

M: Of course. He'd over-dub and mix – he wouldn't make the same old noise exactly … He'd sound electronic – have spacier strings, horns and computerised bassoons.

PS: One man is not an orchestra!

M: Who needs orchestras? You could do it all with a keyboard, amp and enough power.

FAME, *MGM*, 1980

The professor is shocked, but 'new age' producers continue searching for ways to explore their creativity, developing their artistic musical expression. The fictional character Martelli didn't stand in isolation. Musicians have made use of technology as soon as it became available. The Beatles messed around with tape effects in the late 60s. There's of clip of Stevie Wonder on Soul Train playing Superstition on a very funky synth to even funkier dancing posse. There were the 70s German crews Can and Kraftwerk. And the telephone exchange type synthesiser instruments of Emerson, Lake and Palmer. Rick Wakeman held mighty synthesiser concerts. Roger Troutman and Herbie Hancock used their vocorders. Without synths and samplers there would be no New Order, Depeche Mode, Jean Michel Jarre, The Art of Noise or Paul Hardcastle. The influence of Hip Hop DJs isolating breaks and remixing in the live context cannot be underestimated. The Sugar Hill Gang, Afrika Bambaataa & The Soul Sonic Force and Mantronix, to name a few, exemplified this.

"Electricity has always existed and it's not just a phenomenon of this century. It's always been in thunder, lightening, Iceland — Thor's Hammer. Acupuncture has been around for 2,000 years. Electricity and the equipment are just tools. Instead of wood or leather or metal and all the things we so far make music out of like stroking strings — now we're using electricity."
BJÖRK, THE SOUTH BANK SHOW, *LWT, NOVEMBER 1997*

The real difference with 90s British Breakbeat producers is their multicultural environment and influences. Coupled with their access to cheap, sophisticated equipment is their ability to compose and record alone at home and the ease with which, without the help of major record companies, they can have their music 'performed'.

Producers generally emerge from five directions. Gifted technological musicians like Dillinja and Shy FX got their hands on, and made sense of, the electronics and software as soon as they were able. DJs like Mickey *Bad Ass* Finn, DJ *Spiritual Aura* Rap and MCs like *Heartbeat* Moose, who've been around the music day and night for years are committing their own sounds to vinyl. Actors often become directors or producers; DJs and MCs are no different. For working DJs and MCs, producing is an escape from playing out all weekend, every weekend, until they're forty. Studio engineers also become producers. Matrix's brother *Grey Odyssey* Optical, worked for several years as an engineer on other people's tunes, before being recognised in his own right.

And then there are the pure musicians like singer / songwriting, sax, bass guitar and keyboard-playing Adam F, who was responsible for the devastating track, *Metropolis*. And 'former' Jazzman, Cleveland Watkiss, coordinated Project 23.

Finally, there's the fifth group, the co-productions between producers and engineers — the silent partners. Even before the news broke that Goldie's classic tune, *Timeless*, had been engineered by someone else, there were whispers. "So what did Goldie do then?" The answer's simple, he was the artist and the inspiration. Trenton, Goldie's manager recalls meeting him on the street in Camden Town. "He kept talking about this tune he was gonna make. How long it was gonna be, how it was gonna sound. A complete version existed in his head." It's difficult to separate the artistic from the technical. Lines in the studio blur with the smoke and the hours. However, tracks like *Timeless* have one inspirational father. It's doubtful whether *Timeless* either musically or commercially would have become the track it did without Goldie. He's driven by an almost overwhelming barrage of ideas, tempered by a need to see perfection in their execution.

Goldie's choice of Rob Playford was itself an inspiration. Rob Playford had no contact with black music till he left school in '86. He had found his home listening to the sounds of Black Music on pirates Kiss, LWR and anything else he could pick up from Hertfordshire. The indigenous suburban Rock music left Rob cold. He preferred to catch up with Electro wherever he could and began DJing on the Soul-oriented Charisma sound system. Mixing had raised DJing to more of a skill and as an eccentric 'Whiteee', Rob got away with playing faster Disco and Rave music. In 1987 - 88, he'd make frequent trips to London's record shops just to buy tunes two days before everyone else. By night, he left the Luton-Letchworth-Hitchin home of the 'All-Dayer', for the emergent all night raves of London's warehouse scene. There began a chapter of meeting key people like Paul Ibiza, setting up parties and dodging the police.

Above all, Rob Playford wanted to make tunes. Left to mess around in a studio, he took some first steps in understanding how the gadgets made the music.

"We came from that Hip Hop style of making things. We didn't have a clue what we were doing. We were just gonna have a muck around, see what these boxes do. You were coming from the whole style of engineers making music, as opposed to musicians."
ROB PLAYFORD

PHOTO BY
TRISTAN O'NEILL

Rob
Playford

He was the engineer who made real the bizarre visions of music that swarmed around inside Goldie's head – you could imagine the ad in Melody Maker, "Musical visionary wanted ... No studio experience necessary." Rob explains, "It helped that Goldie didn't have any knowledge of the equipment because that can be inhibiting. You go through a thought process where your brain dismisses something straight away because you know you're gonna be sitting in front of this box trying to create this thing for the next six hours and then you don't know if it's gonna come out exactly as it is in your head. As an engineer, if someone asks you to come up with something, you've got an incentive. You can prove to them that you make the bizarrest ideas real. That's the exciting thing."

B: How did *Timeless* work?

R: Goldie had this idea that he wanted all these strings ... [Rob searches for words to bridge the technical and the artistic, to describe Goldie's vision of interweaving-flowing strings, each treated with different effects – taking different directions.]

R: It's fairly easy, putting the same sound on four completely separate midi channels, you can control each one and they're all separate and won't interfere with each other. Before, if you wanted to do a pitch bend on a sound, you'd do it on a keyboard and it would affect everything on the keyboard, which isn't what Goldie wanted. [When Rob showed Goldie how it could work, it opened up more possibilities.]

R: You're limited by what you know exists. Once you know more exists, it broadens your imagination. That's the two sides. Complete understanding, complete un-understanding and when you knock the idea about – between the two – it gets bigger. It's an upward spiral.

There're a lot of artists who are not *au fait* with technology but hear the sounds knocking around their heads. The engineers make those thoughts a reality. Engineering for Ed Rush and Trace, Nico has admitted that he couldn't have produced the same tracks on his own. Collaborations between artists and engineers are a legitimate way of making music. It works. Access to cheap, relatively easy-to-use technology, has given rise to an increasingly large stable of JDB producers. The modules of a studio can fit into the corner of a small bedroom. Shy FX's new software, Cubase Audio VST, incorporates all the compressors, samplers and a large mixing desk into his Apple Mac. In effect he has a desktop studio. Many producers can still work at mum's place or around a mate's house, avoiding the overheads of rent and studio construction. For talented artists on the dole, or those who are still students, this accessibility is a vital part of the JDB industry.

The basic ingredients of a Jungle / Drum & Bass track are: a drum pattern, bassline, a hook or break, mixed with a range of samples and other electronic sounds. With the aid of computer software, samplers, compressors and keyboards that can treat and manipulate all the sounds, the whole package is arranged and recorded onto studio quality DAT.

You could write a whole book on music technology. But a starship load of Rolands and Akai S3200XL samplers won't make any difference to someone with little talent or imagination. Original music comes from the heart, soul and a very creative ear. In choosing the artists to contribute to his compilation album, *The Prototype Years*, Grooverider's people were all original in their musical production. Most importantly, they all made good tunes.

"The producers watch each other like dogs. They watch each other close, close, close. And man always has to keep up if he's in it. They're perfectionists. They'll sit there together and tell you whose breaks are out of time, think about where this comes from, where that comes from. It's tight and it makes the music good." TRENTON, NUR

Amongst the industry's producers, competitive quality control is almost tangible. Perhaps peer group pressure plays a part, but rather than make a poor track, producers will go back to the computer bringing every last beat into focus before the final pressing, since others in the industry judge them by their quality, not their quantity.

SONIC INSPIRATION

The question, 'What inspires you to make the tracks you do?' often elicits shoulder shrugs or barely adequate verbal answers. The producers speak best with their music. Still, what they do say can be quite insightful. Inspiration for tracks comes from various directions. For Goldie, it starts on the street. Looking at heavenly constellations has inspired Gus, of Reinforced. Then there's the machinery, which, with a twist of a knob, accidentally hitting the wrong button, purposely tweaking the right one, will sing its own song and suggest others. Ed Rush recalls the inspiration behind his track *Locust*, featured on Grooverider's *Prototype Years* album. "It's a track of madness created by the music's technical internal loop. Imagine an intense *Old Testament* swarm of locusts, growing in a room, spreading out over cities and forests, wreaking utter devastation – and you've got it." By way of explaining DJ Trace and Ed Rush's beats, they have been described as 'angry men'. Their music expresses the emotion of wanting to have your say and ripping your hair out when you can't. Sometimes the inspiration is simple, like Lemon D catching the vibe of the city lights when he first moved to central London. Shy FX once claimed his inspiration came from a bowl of breakfast cereal. After that, he's ready to bang out beats. Inspiration can take place on the dancefloor. Adam F wrote *Metropolis* specifically with The Metalheadz Sessions and the Blue Note vibe in mind. "I wanted to get that same sound out my speakers."

Fabio and Grooverider have inspired legions of producers to create work of their own. "If you speak to some of the guys on our label they didn't know what they were going to make until they sat down at Speed, heard Fabio and found their heart." SARAH, *GROOVE CONNECTION*

Sometimes inspiration filled a gap in what people believed was missing from the music as it stood. Producers like Wax Doctor started using chords over basic Jungle in order to create something more musical. Some producers gain inspiration when they hear two tracks in the mix. It's something that can be taken from the live remixing arena of the dancefloor and recreated on vinyl, to be remixed again by the DJs.

Remember the darker tunes with hard beats and eerie strings, aided by, or inspired by those Gangsta / Sci Fi, Kung Fu film samples? To work on a Dance level they still had to have the Funk. In the same way that you can have a well-stocked art studio, in the music studio, a good creative producer stocked with experience and heart can compose a proppa tune. Pouring money into studio equipment won't be enough in itself. Mainstream record company-backed producers are unlikely to add anything greatly significant to the core of the music. It comes from the vibe and you have to feel it, live it.

A GUY CALLED GERALD, JUICE BOX STUDIOS, NOVEMBER 1996

By early '94, Gerald had changed his creative approach, trying to make his breaks sound different by reversing the drums and stretching sounds, not just by adding a B-line or speeding up the breaks. He tried to build a sonic picture comprised of a background covered with different textures, colours and shapes, in a sense using graffiti sound. In the same way that Dali or HR Geiger draw you in to their paintings so that you perceive something more, Gerald draws you into his soundscapes.

"If you put the tune on headphones, you can hear it going off at tangents behind you, with high-pitched sounds elsewhere. It's like an artist creating deceptions. The first time I got proppa stoned listening to some Jean Michel Jarre with headphones on, there were these sounds like drops of water. Every time I heard a drop I felt really cold ... I think hearing is stronger than seeing. It can take you further."

Gerald does sound exercises with his ears. Walking down a street he concentrates on the sounds of buses behind him, actually trying to hear how they move. Taking that into the studio, during a mix he'll put a bit of reverb on the left and as it passes, it gives you the growing impression of sound travelling horizontally and diagonally. Using a Doppler and an EQ, he creates 3d dynamics.

Shy FX

Shy FX Mum's House, October '97

A house near the Angel — Edmonton that is, not Islington. Shy as always apologises for the mess. "No, it's *really* bad." He's being polite as ever. The door opens only part of the way before it jams against something. After squeezing through the gap, there's a few seconds pause before we both collapse into uncontrollable hysterics. Even an estate agent would blush at calling this a box room. Record sleeves, Dub Plates, press releases, labels, cables and vinyl are everywhere. The only free floor space is directly in front of the mixing desk and between the Technics turntables off to one side in a corner. Thank God he's moving house soon.

For now his studio is an organic technological boy's room with Shy, the cut creator, at its centre. As he fires the equipment to life, his laughter gives way to gentle but intense concentration. A near-finished tune loops continually through an Apple Mac. If you're not used to it, the constant repetition of the loops can be maddening. You just want to hear the tune roll out. But that's just it; it's all part of the rhythmic gestation.

As he gazes somewhere in the middle distance between two powerful, crystal clear monitors, his fingers dart across the dials, fine tuning the bassline which has become one of the most recognisable sounds on the international dance-floor. The tune, a remix of the *Telephone* track, was runnin'. Treating each segment of the music with a slide of the faders, the Telecom woman slips through saying, "Please hang up and try again," to be nurtured in the mix to the right level. An organic technological boys room, with twenty-one-year-old Shy FX at the heart of the Jungle. I'm lost in the musical loops, dreaming pictures of the Confusion stand at the Notting Hill Carnival, bouncing on the B-line as he presses the Mac space bar bringing the tune to an abrupt halt. "That break's not right." He plays with the compressor, trying to get the right balance. A two second drum burst. "It still ain't right." An hour passes as he connects and reconnects the snakes from the desk.

A call to fellow producer and friend T Power around the North Circular in East London and Shy finds out that he's pushed his sampler to the limit. Somewhere else in North London, his purpose-built studio is on its way to completion. For now, he clicks off his walnut-patterned mobile, and rethinks the problem. Stepping on and over those piles of tunes, jamming in a final phono connection, he dances his Wu-Tang style dance with enthusiasm as the *Telephone* remix bubbles to a perfect finish. The tune is a VIP mix; a 'special' and only three copies will be made. One for DJ Brockie, one for DJ Ash, the other for himself. That's the way it goes. Exclusive circulation to De Man Dem. Even Grooverider, who first heard the mix at Music House and asked for a copy, would be denied membership to this club. This was Wednesday, by Friday night, "B- with the R-O-C-K-I-E" as MC Det intones would be playing the tune to the public. "They won't like it." "Sorry?' "The people dem won't like it." "What d'ya mean?" "Like when I done *Wolf* and Brockie played it out, the people just stood and stared. Sometimes it takes time before the people can get with it." It seemed doubtful, the tune was jumpin'. "Trust me. I know."

When Shy was eight years old, his mum bought him a BBC computer. By the time he got to school, he was bored and a bit disruptive, waiting for teachers and other kids to catch- up to his level. A trip to school by his mum failed to persuade the teachers to put her son in a higher group. What did she, a social worker, know about Shy's education? More than a proud mum, she knew potential when she saw it. As Shy became world famous, his music delighted Junglists everywhere and the cash rolls in, one wonders if his teacher at Enfield's Bishops Stortford school is happy in his work.

Photo by
Andy Cotterill

DILLINJA'S APARTMENT, DECEMBER '96

We meet in his glass and steel reconstructed residential oasis, a stone's throw away from Bermondsey. Grooverider has dropped by to share the new beats on a clutch of DATs he's been given. A collective of appreciative heads nod to the creations of producers – known and unknown. Deep, warm rhythms from the speakers drown out the sounds of builders, hammering together Dillinja's new home studio. He's only just moved in. This sanctuary, overlooking a tranquil, sculptured pool, belongs to him. Which is probably just as well, since he's been evicted from rented accommodation a few times. That'll be the excessive noise for which he's sacrificed more speakers than he can remember. The apartment is tidy, warm and deliberate. There's no clutter. With Lemon D as his next-door neighbour, Dillinja has built himself the perfect set-up. He's a person of few words to strangers. He speaks with his music and leaves the talking to others.

"Dillinja and Lemon D are Jazz musicians ... If you talk about Dillinja, you have to talk about Louis Armstrong. Dillinja's from that whole line of artists that can improvise, creating within the realm of the moment. Using different tools but the same concept."
CLEVELAND WATKISS, SEPTEMBER 1997

Bass always fascinated Dillinja. At the age of sixteen, he designed and built scooped sound system bass bins, striving forever deeper and warmer basslines. Originally a Hip Hop devotee, Dillinja spent little time DJing but moved into creating beats as soon as he could get his hands on the technology. He doesn't go out partying that much, except to the Metalheadz Sessions but he knows his music is out there. His output on several labels is prestigious, working under a myriad of cover names he's responsible for eerie, devastating tracks like *The Angels Fell*, *Silver Blade*, *Friday* and *Deadly Deep Subs*. He also remixes domestic and international artists from as far afield as Japan. One of the first of the '96 producer albums was Dillinja's *Suspect Package*. During the same year he signed with Sony.

Dillinja's music is deep, with layers almost Classical in their complexity. What does he think?
B: If you wrote your music down next to Mozart's, whose do you think would be more complicated?
D: I don't even think you could write mine down.

Before leaving, I lean over to scribble down the details of Dillinja's electronic boxes of tricks. "Nah man, you can't do that – that's my sound," he warns with uncharacteristic agitation. Without realising it, I'd stepped right in the middle of his trade secrets. By the way, his B-lines come from ...

DJ / PRODUCER HYPE'S BMW, THE BACK SEAT, OCTOBER '97

It's a grey afternoon in Hackney. The romantic summer gloss has disappeared with the sunshine, and wind and dry brown leaves usher in the darkness of winter. Across the road from Casablanca's – Caribbean restaurant and purveyor of food to Jungle's All Stars – a group of workmen stand 'round a huge hole that's been there since God knows when. *Paah, paah.* "Brian, Brian." I clock the B4DET number plate and the voice sinks in. "Alright Det." "Been shouting at you B. What you under?" "I'm waiting for Hype." We talk about checking the next Telepathy before he drives off in his BM. The car bounds up the road with the same energy with which he MCs, casting the other vehicles by the wayside. Guess Det hasn't heard the average speed of traffic in London is slower than in horse 'n' cart times. Hackney life passes by; the rotund Hassidic Jew in black Homburg hat and blue Volvo, two double-parked breddahs chatting about some-ting-or-other – completely unconcerned with the plight of an exasperated lorry driver trying to negotiate their obstacle course. A Rasta's singing and talking to himself. People do that 'round here, walk about, stand at bus stops, sing and talk to themselves ... *Paah, paah, paah.* "Oi Brian – over 'ere." It's Hype in his BM. He parks up over the road near a newly gentrified residential block. "You coming in Casablanca's?" "Na man, I've got the dog wiv me." Snoop, the Jungle Dog, pops his head over the passenger door, pants, pricks up his ears, turns around and settles back into his padded basket on the front seat. Guess I'll sit in the back then.

PHOTO BY
COURTNEY HAMILTON

Hype and
Snoop

It's weird, whenever you rub shoulders with these characters, there's a different energy around. We're parked up, he keeps the engine running. It feels like we're going somewhere. Suppose we are — back in time.

H: So I did these tunes with Scientist called *The Exorcist* and *The Bee* ...

[They always do that — jump in at the middle.]

B: Can we rewind a bit? How, when, did you learn to use all the equipment?

The short story — he got into production through The Islington Music Workshop and the National Association for the Rehabilitation of Young Offenders. "It was a one-day-a-week thing. They'd take you to this recording studio and you'd just have a fuck-about." Hype took Smiley there — before he was in Shut Up & Dance. Working with a drum machine and a sequencer, Hype scratching on his decks, someone rapping, all put through a four track, they entered and won a competition, landing £1,000 worth of studio time. They were featured on TV, *Thames News*, Hype, the young offender, who'd found salvation through this project and music sort of thing. He was on the right road, even started a music engineering course.

H: I walked straight out. Couldn't get my head around it. I wanted to know the basics. I was at a recording studio going, "I want that 808 Boom, Boom bassline like the Def Jam records." They were like, "Err, that's awful. You don't want that."

He bought a studio a piece at a time, a four track and two turntables. Hype would mix the breaks, cutting not scratching into a pre-computerised loop and record it all on tape. He got hold of a Casio SK1 that had a one second sampler on it. He'd hold it up to a speaker and record the samples. If it was a long sample, he'd speed the record up to 45 rpms. He'd put acappellas on instrumentals, all pretty basic. Some of the things, which can be done in seconds, now, took all day then. But he did it. He's one of humanity's foresighted people who believe in the potential of something — then work at it. An ethic of this scene — Just Do It. In '89 Hype was asked to listen to some tapes in an A&R role. He didn't think much of any of them, except for one guy's music. It was good but there was something

missing from the track. Hype also felt there was something missing from his own stuff. The guy, Scientist, was from the electronic, Kraftwerk, Depeche Mode side of music and Hype from Reggae, Hip Hop sound systems. Combining their equipment and knowledge, they produced their first tune within a week. "Fusing the two together, we made fucking good music."

A German magazine called Hype the 'Boy next door', which is the way he likes to be. "My music has to be big but that don't mean I've gotta be this big personality." He only started to show his face as a producer to gain recognition for the tunes he produced with Scientist. Though they were jointly involved in *The Exorcist* Scientist seemed to forget that fact when he fronted the PAs and gave interviews.

Sometimes it seems as if Hype has a Golden Touch. Perhaps it's an exaggeration but as a producer he's had so many unexpected successes, it's difficult to fathom. *The Exorcist*, one of British Breakbeat's first tunes, sold around 50,000 copies. Hype produced three or four releases through Suburban Base, to support his DJing. His first single *Shot in the Dark* on that label went to number 68 in the national charts. Then he started Ganja Kru — it was just supposed to be a little project. The releases, *Ganja Vols. I, II & III* were recognisable only by the Ganja Leaf on one side of the sleeve. There were no artists' names on the records, except for Vol III, when Hype made up a name, Dope Style, so he could remain anonymous. Despite his faceless approach, everyone seemed to know the music was his. The first release, *You Must Think First*, with its Wu-Tang sword samples, was another track which helped to change Jungle's direction.

H: I went through a few releases to the point where it was all taking off. I was like, "I don't want this to take off. I'm not trying to build this thing".

Working with Pascal on Face and Frontline Recordings, they started to collaborate with producer Zinc who had been taking tunes around for Hype to hear. Their first tune together, *Super Sharp Shooter* sold 13,000 copies. Hype finally accepted that they had a very successful label on their hands. Still, they stopped pressing after that. Hype hates rinsing tracks to death. They also won't put out a tune which was a bit like the last one ... apart from them being successful.

B: Can we talk about the *Fugees Or Not* track?

H: Ahhh no. Do we 'ave to?

He hates talking about the accidental / potential hit — smash the whole thing was unintended.

H: It was a 'knock-up' Dub Plate, made with no heart, with obvious samples and breaks. People heard it and went mad.

Hype pressed five hundred and pulled it before the Fugees record company sued him. However, someone had already bootlegged the tune and made it more widely available.

H: Yeah, it was a good tune though. It had its place. Mickey Finn and Mampi Swift rinsed it at Jungle Fever in Mannheim, November '96, to screams, lighters, rewinds, sing-alongs, hugs, the whole thing. (He said it was a 'knock up'. Wonder if he'll give me the formula?)

Now in his eleventh year of production, Hype's approach to making tunes is still DIY. He buys equipment bit-by-bit and learns what it does bit-by-bit. He doesn't know about frequencies or waveforms but he knows how music sounds. "If a qualified person came and watched me they'd probably tear their hair out and go "What da fuck is this geeza doing?" But it works. I just go with my own vibe." In the last year, Hype has produced remixes for The Prodigy, Armand Van Helden, Bally Sagoo, Jay Z and Foxy Brown. He's humble but confident enough to go with his own style.

SAMPLED

On their way into the studio, a couple of young producers ask Shut Up & Dance to autograph their CD. The youngsters then spent the session ripping out all the best beats for their own track. It was a sign of the times and everyone seemed to be doing it. The new producers didn't know or care about paying dues to the Mechanical Copyright Protection Society (MCPS). The white label economy provides few clues to enable officials to trace underground artists.

Problems arose when the original artists and the formal record industry machine began to trace their music to independent Junglists. When Shut Up & Dance's *Raving I'm Raving* blew up, people took to the *Walking in Memphis* melody. With thousands of units pressed up, ready and waiting in the warehouse for distribution, the original artist Mark Cohn, via his company Warner Brothers, served them with an injunction. As the distributor called Shut Up & Dance with the news that they'd gone to number one, another of the posse was on a plane to LA, striking a last ditch deal, giving the entire profits of the tune to charity. After *Raving I'm Raving*, the MCPS hit Shut Up & Dance for their use of uncleared Prince, Terence Trent D'Arby, Riuichi Sakamoto and Eurythmics samples. They were stung for an undisclosed amount in out-of-court settlements. Less formally, when the Reggae guys came to Jungle Don DJ Ron for their money, with a crew of raggas waiting outside in the car, he also paid up — though, when they visited Frost, he allegedly told them to get lost. According to Goldie's manager Trenton, the Fugees were unhappy with Zinc and Hype's hugely sought-after remix of *Fugees Or Not*. Goldie who'd met the group and built up a rapport with them, was commissioned to remix *Fugee La*. He feels there's no substitute for going right to the source and collaborating with the original artist.

With many JDB tunes lacking vocals after '95, there's been much discussion about their use and whether or not they can improve a tune. They aren't essential. If you take away the vocals, the track should still work on its own. The beats come first. That, according to Grooverider, is what Drum & Bass is all about; *Share the Fall* being a case in point.

Producers are always on the hunt for new sounds to incorporate in their tracks. Gerald recalls Paul Hardcastle's *Na Na Na Na Nineteen* Pop tune and The Art of Noise's *Closely Closely*, featuring samples of car engines and vocals. The *Star Wars* light sabre sound which comes from placing a mic between a speaker and the back of a TV allegedly makes a wicked bass sound. — *but no one would ever copy that.* "If you're an artist you have to defy the categories, be left of field otherwise there's no point. But the essence of the music is the most important thing." *JUMPING JACK FROST*

Though Jungle / Drum & Bass is based around breaks and samples, originality is important. JDB has not stagnated like some other music genres in which the same sounds are constantly reproduced in some hit-making formula, though it may have come close during the Ragga / Reggae era of 1994 - 95. Rebel MC and his Congo Natty posse were among those who used Reggae samples creatively, others did not. Some producers felt that people who didn't understand the Jamaican Studio One samples were driving Jungle into a rut. The sheer volume of records produced with unimaginative samples threatened to derail JDB's original music direction.

There's an avalanche of music released each week. I was once given hundreds of JDB records to flog at a record fair. It was clear that only a small percentage stood above the rest. The discerning customers put most of the formulaic tunes back in their sleeves. The road to making that classic tune is pitted with musical clichés. Even the samples get sampled. But some things go too far. The Hardcore version of *Sesame Street* (*Sesame's Treet*) was generally regarded as a musical low point. It may be difficult for a producer to come up with an original sound. Producers new to the game need to take time to find their own voice. T Bone dissuaded some guys on their first project from stuffing every possible sound, break and beat into their tune.

DJs sometimes complain about poor quality 'made-for-rave tracks,' which rapidly fall away with the crowd's enthusiasm after the jump-up drop. Or the dominating, cymbal-driven Amen tunes with little depth, which work simply because they're noisy.

ALBUMS

"The future is in the artist album. That's where you'll get to know how good the producer is and what he's all about ... There are so many producers out there. Albums will show the true producers from the fly-by-nights that are just producing the stuff and flooding the market." LEMON D, JUNGLISM ZONE UK, 1995

Albums give producers a chance to experiment with a range of music. They can delve into Jazz, as with *Adrift* on *Timeless*, ballads and Trip Hop as with DJ Rap & Voyager's *Intelligence*, or stay entirely within the JDB format as Adam F did on *Colours*. It features many of Adam's influences including Soul, Jazz, Funk and Drum & Bass itself. Albums are often seen as the test of a producer's real creativity. Listening to *Colours* on a Walkman, the track *Jaxx* struck me as music to fly a Stealth Bomber by. I mentioned it to Adam during a photo shoot. "Funny you should say that ..." Positiva / EMI, his record company, had already received a call from the filmmakers of *Starship Troopers*, a '98 Sci-Fi blockbuster, asking permission to use *Jaxx* for an aerial attack sequence.

Within Jungle / Drum & Bass, each of the top producers comes with a different style. When Roni Size came into the picture in 1993 - 94, he brought with him a fresh influx of talent. Hailing from Bristol, the city which has already given us Massive Attack, Tricky and Portishead, Roni is known for his hard work, intense dedication and prolific output across a range of Jungle / Drum & Bass. He was awarded the '97 Mercury Music Prize for his Reprazent collective's album, *New Forms* – something which no previous Jungle / Drum & Bass producer has achieved. Beating off competition from Suede, Primal Scream, The Chemical Brothers and The Prodigy, Reprazent's success was described by TV presenter Tracey Macleod as "probably the most radical winner in the history of the Prize". With Roni on BBC 2, flanked by a cigar-puffing Jumping Jack Frost and funki-dreaded Bryan Gee, Macleod went on to acknowledge that, "though Drum & Bass is still very much an Underground movement in Britain, it really goes overground as *New Forms* wins Album of the Year." Weeks later, Roni Size also won the Music of Black Origin (MOBO) award.

DUB PLATE PRESSURE

Access to the best music can be a struggle. Music is the hard currency of the scene and Dub Plates are harder to get hold of than fifty pound notes. When Ray Keith walks into a rave, he's carrying over two grand's worth of acetate in his boxes. Brockie, like other professional DJs, can spend hundreds on Dub Plates each week. Cut in places like Music House, directly from the producer's DAT, each Plate costs around twenty five quid and usually only lasts thirty or forty plays when bashed about in raves.

DATs containing music are circulated by producers amongst their select number of DJs. The choice of DJ is crucial. They are the shop front for the music. Shy FX only gives his tunes to DJs Brockie and Ash. Brockie gets tunes from everyone including Metalheadz. As a DJ who travels the world and plays the premier show on Kool FM, Brockie has one of the largest shop fronts in the scene. But first and foremost the beats have to be runnin'. They have to pass that spontaneous head-nodding test.

Dub Plate transactions can be a crew or loyalty thing. There's often huge dissatisfaction about tunes being given to the 'wrong' people or too many Plates being put into circulation. The lack of exclusivity somehow devalues the beats or the DJs playing them.

There's the limited edition stuff like the 500 copies of Zinc and Hype's *Fugees Or Not*. You have to have your ear very close to the ground to hear about a tune like that in the first place and be very quick to get hold of it. Because of their rarity, these tunes climb in value extremely quickly. Within three weeks of *Fugees Or Not* hitting the streets, the last remaining vinyl copies were going for thirty quid a piece.

Next down the scale are the test presses, the under-the-counter stuff which some persistent punters / professional buyers may get hold of and DJs get as standard. They're circulated free of charge by the producer to help vibe up the tune. They'll go to friends, other DJs (especially if they're on the radio), journalists and record shops who sometimes charge punters for them without paying the original producers. It all helps give the tune exposure.

The small change in the business, in terms of availability, are the vinyl tunes which punters get readily over the counter. Some Dubs are designed solely for the DJ, like the intro Plates which Grooverider, Mickey Finn, Brockie and Shy FX play. Shy has recently taken to playing punters specials that not only announce his set but name the venue he's playing at. The promoters of Heat were so chuffed with Shy's Dub announcing his arrival at Hastings Pier that they gave him a residency.

The quality and freshness of the Dubs help make top name DJs. It is also a measure of their stature on the scene as a whole. Eastman, not known as a top DJ, was still able to draw from a heap of serious tunes when he played the Blue Note at Cleveland Watkiss' birthday party, November 1996. His special access to music is a consideration.

The DJs and producers will pack out cutting houses during the rush hour on a Friday or Saturday afternoon, cutting tunes to play later that night. Even though cutting houses have existed in London since the Reggae days, the whole rush on Plates really took off in '94 when the word spread that you could get a tune cut that very day. Since then the culture has escalated. The music on Plate is the freshest you can hear. But because of the length of time music is in circulation, it's often out of date or gets played to death before it is in the record shops. In some cases as with DJ Krust's *Angles* or Adam F's *Metropolis*, it took about six months. Sadly sometimes, the tune never reaches the street.

Eastman describes the scene at Jungle Fever's shop after Brockie plays a Dub on his Sunday night show: "Monday, Tuesday morning when the record shop opens you got three or four people with tapes in here going, "You got this tune?". We say, "Sorry, it won't be out for three or four months". They're saying, "I've gotta 'ave it, gotta 'ave it". And we have to tell em, "Honestly, it won't be out". Then you get phone calls every week asking for it."

People generally have two views about this point of musical stagnation. Kemistry & Storm feel that, "The Dub Plate thing is something we have to live with. It won't be going away". Nicky of Black Market Records thinks there's both up and downsides to the situation but agrees that it does help the exclusivity of the music. Kenny Ken praises it as a quality control safety net. Producers have the opportunity to examine segments like the all-important bassline in a cutting room before the crowd hear it and may decide to go back to the Cubase. Even when a track is obviously a blinder, it still takes a significant time for it to reach the street. In this musical bottleneck, producers have to be convinced that a track will sell before they'll make the investment to get it into the shops. Consequently, some tracks never make it.

"More releases would help the scene but it wouldn't be so exclusive, would it? Imagine if you could go everywhere and hear every tune, you won't want to go near Brockie or Frost especially. Certain man's drawing out what Frost is not going to draw. Rider is drawing out what they can't draw. That's why it's good when they're on a rave together and they're all doing they're own individual thing. That's what keeps the buzz going." EASTMAN

The downside of the Dub Plate culture is its effect on record sales. Punters are as passionate about the music as the DJs but find it far more difficult to get hold of some of the best tracks. That's the way it is with Jungle / Drum & Bass. Mikey De Underground describes the shrug-of-the-shoulders attitude of many DJs and producers. "Listen to Kiss tonight. Man will say, "Here's a Plate, don't know who it's by, don't know which label it's on, but it's wicked." "

Dego at Reinforced finds the restrictive Dub Plate culture intolerable and doesn't condone it. Moving Shadow's Rob Playford won't hold tunes back. From DAT to vinyl, they meet a twelve week production turnaround. He hates not being able to get hold of tunes and feels that the Dub Plate culture can be abused, especially if precious DATs are given to everyone. "I can think of so many huge records that have come from this scene that have been left far too long. By the time they've come out, everyone's heard it to death." It makes little economic sense.

Maybe the Dub Plate culture is "something we have to live with," and it's not about to change. But for the sake of the industry, it would be wonderful if producers and their crews could work harder to get their music on to the streets sooner. If greater effort was made to meet earlier release dates, producers would probably sell twice as many units. Record shops would make more money and be places where punters could get the tunes they wanted rather than settling for "sorry, it's not out yet". Still, it's difficult not to get excited about the vibe around Dub Plate Pressure and what is a DJ without their specials?

MUSIC HOUSE

November '96. Somewhere in North London in a place with no address, on a cold Friday afternoon, a steady stream of top DJs stop by the cutting house. This is the place where a range of producers and DJs arrive clutching piles of DATs and come out with valuable musical currency: the record, a DJ-friendly Dub Plate. There are other cutting houses in the country but there is only one Music House. Artists crowd into this underground palace of music. It's the kind of den where the entrance opens straight into a backroom set-up. From floor to low ceiling, the walls are covered with posters and record labels: tributes to King Tubby, Yvonne Curtis and Gregory Isaacs, Jonathan Butler, Jah Shaka and Overlord X alongside Grooverider. It's the kind of place where anyone drops by to cut their tunes, every day, any day. Garage producers, Reggae, Soul, Pop, Swing, Jungle / Drum & Bass crews pile into its cramped innards jostling politely for places in the queue. Music House is an autograph-hunter's and trainspotter's dream. Some days it's Shy FX, others Rebel MC, DJ Rap, Kenny Ken, Randall, Swift and Ron. Heads nod to the multitude of beats pumping out from the two small cutting rooms. In the breaks you overhear snatches of conversation "What equipment do you use? ... Are you using vocals? ... Where's the nearest bank? ... Man, I've only got two to cut? ... Gotta reach Coventry by eleven ... Gotta fag? ... You won't like that, it's a bit ambient ... What's the DM27? ... Feels like I've been here all day."

People dash out to the alley making calls on the mobile and dash back in to advise on the quality of the beats as they're cut into pure gleaming black acetate. Each person steps up, delivers their DAT to Leon, Paul or Chris who feed it into the Fostex player and tend the controls of the mixing desk. Monitoring the beats from the dark Tannoys, the music and the dream flows through the VMS 70 George Neumann lathe. In the process, human thought, electrical energy, becomes mechanical energy, becomes sound waves in the grooves of a record.

Brockie nods, DJ Bailey leaves with some Plates, DJ Sabel shoots out the door on a mission to Heathrow, then Berlin. These are the tunes which will be on the turntable at the dance tonight. For many years, this type of London cutting house was only really known by Reggae producers and DJs. Then Rebel MC spread the word around 1992 - 93 and the whole Dub Plate culture came into Jungle.

The name Music House appears so often on Dub Plates, many think it's a record label itself. Music House is more of an institution than a cutting house. If ever a place deserved an award for services to Jungle / Drum & Bass, it's this one.

METROPOLIS MAN

I'm running late down West London's Chiswick High Road. Running – unfit, panting, distracted, counting street numbers and rummaging in my bag for a phone or tape or pen. The numbers and my pace give way to a courtyard where I'm dominated by an impressive Metropolis-like building. Metropolis by name, by nature.

The Metropolis cutting and mastering complex is based in a building which once supplied the electricity for the London Underground. Now engineers craft all sorts of music inside. This redesigned power house with its skilled operators is the top end of the market for the Jungle Dons precious breaks and beats. Surrounded by plants, wood, glass, stainless steel, stone and light in airy symbiosis, secretaries chat seriously about expensive cold cure remedies, Mo' Wax and Peshay's DAT.

Stuart Hawkes saunters back from lunch and we do the quick tour 'round the pukkerest yard on the JDB scene. Off the atrium two floors below there's a couple of orchestra sized recording studios, behind and above us, the then ahead-of-its-time DVD something or other area where they do Sensoround Sound – the next lick in home entertainment. Walking past restaurant, pool table and video room, we stop staring through our reflections into one of the many darkened mixing suites and their sound-swallowing upholstery. Someone's head bangs my shoulder rhythmically. It's one of those occasions when I'm conscious of time. This man's time, all the equipment is money – the meter is running and at £120 per hour I'm glad I'm not paying.

The amiable, relaxed Stuart Hawkes is a key person in the industry. Many producers can't afford him but they need his talents. He's invaluable yet you've probably never heard of him. But Peshay, Grooverider, Roni Size, Goldie, Photek and Adam F trust him implicitly with their music. Aside from countless 12"s, he's worked on all their albums.

Between the producer and the DJ there's the mastering process where the jeweller polishes the diamond. A producer brings in the DAT, Stuart plays it through a mixing desk, experienced ears and hands treat all the tracks with EQ and compression, loads them onto Sadie computer software – edits as required and cuts the tune onto 10-inch acetate for a Dub Plate or a 14-inch lacquer disc on the way to becoming the vinyl. At the day's end, he'll record the music onto tape for clients to hear with a spliff in the comfort of their own car or homes.

Seated in his studio, Stuart takes a call from Peshay. They try to resolve a technical problem with the quality of the recording. Assistants bounce in to borrow, download and enquire. I wander 'round the polished wooden floor scoping everything, slightly awed by the brooding quiet of this organic sound system. Across the room on a large Apple Mac screen there's 'Track: Peshsam1' – Peshay's music. In a side room there are amps from floor to ceiling, alongside a gleaming Georg Neumann cutting lathe with boxes of pristine black acetate discs at its base.

In the main suite, separated by a giant arched window over-looking some greenery, two seven-foot, narrow, black columns with their sub bass modules stare silently across the control desk to the seats running along one wall. It's hard not to admire £20,000 worth of speakers. I day-dream about sitting in the room with my eyes closed, facing the beasts, asking Stuart to access the latest Dillinja and crank the volume right up. But he cradles the phone and his story begins.

Four years ago Stuart Hawkes worked at Copymasters, mastering and cutting Dubs for a whole range of artists. As Jungle producers began to understand the various parts of the recording process, they turned their attention to the post-production phase. If two records are played at a rave or on the radio – it's very obvious which has been correctly mastered and which is an autopilot knock-up. Early on the case, Peshay and Bukem desired the quality but found paying around £100 per plate undesirable. As always in this scene, there are deals to be done under the table or 'round the back which makes things possible and keep things rolling. And Stuart kept rolling from his 10 till midnight job, through the night cutting x-amount of plates for a crowded room of Jungle DJs. He remembers when the fleets of BMWs and Mercs started parking up outside, the times when any DJ could cut anyone's DAT. He remembers these producers' nocturnal lifestyle, their living, breathing Drum & Bass existence and floated along with it until he stopped in hospital – for three months. A case of overwork and a fucked-up body clock.

The last few years at Metropolis have been a little less hectic. His day is a 'normal' ten till midnight shift, though as JDB producers are not generally known for their good time keeping, Stuart accommodates by cramming the schedule into those shrinking hours. It takes him about a day to finish the average fourteen track album, though this always varies. Grooverider's album took three days, but Stuart points out, the Grooverider album was a whole different business. The day would often begin with a hectic producer showing up late flourishing a bag of DATs. If they're making an album rather than a twelve inch there are more DATs, perhaps a track listing has been scribbled on a scrap of paper. But the main thing is getting the producer to arrive. After that all Stuart has to worry about is cutting the track onto a disc.

ENGINEER, MORE VOLUME PLEASE ...

Now that is a worry. And Stuart worries about his equipment when the Jungle crew appear – especially Dillinja. It's the loudness. The Jungle producers always want the loudest possible cut. Stuart has worked with many different artists but confirms the Junglists to be the most demanding of the bunch. Insisting on quality and demanding loudness. They know that DJs don't play quiet records, anyway the beats sound better louder. Producers will even drop a third tune from a disc since one track per side allows for a greater loudness factor. Ever noticed that album tracks are so much quieter than those on a DJ friendly 12 inch? Bigger grooves mean louder music. So the producers hover at Stuart's shoulder hassling him to push his equipment to the limit and Stuart rides the dials hoping not to hear that tell-tale electronic scream which could mean a blown recording head. After the scream and the silence – sometimes the equipment can be reset, sometimes it takes a serious refit. How serious? It used to cost over £22,000 to recoil a recording head – now another firm does the job for a bargain £8,000. And no, the recording heads are not insured. So Stuart does worry when Dillinja and his DATs come through his doors.

But his next appointment today is Bryan Gee who appears early and bowls in zestfully chatting ten to the dozen, dumping down his plastic bag and searching around for a place to plug in his mobile. The chat – either Peshay's or Grooverider's album is the best thing to come out of the scene so far. "Yeah" Bryan's saying, "All that proper Jazz stuff ... I tell ya, after this, Peshay's gonna get calls from Grover and Herbie an' all dem man, trust me". I leave them, their banter and Bryan's over-flowing bag of DATs behind. Leave them in the Powerhouse to continue supplying the Underground.

LABELS

Labels, like studios, can start in someone's backroom. They can be a way of sharing the financial load when buying equipment and getting music played in public, before being bought on vinyl. It's part of the process of getting the tunes from the studio onto the shelves, getting paid and receiving recognition for your art. It's a way of organising the range of music and tight crews. Informal becomes more formal. As they step up in the marketplace, people become sharper and more organised, like an efficient corporation.

Starting a label is one way for an artist or group of artists to maximise the earnings from their work. Typically, artists composing tracks on a regular basis get tired of taking a smaller share of the profits when they pass their music on to other people's labels for release. Both Ray Keith and Shy FX were in similar positions before they set up their own labels, Dread and Ebony Recordings respectively. Owning a record label even for non-producers, can be very profitable. The prerequisites are a good ear for music, access to a stream of artists, the capital and organisation to get tunes into the shops.

Labels provide a cohesive force against pressures which drag down artistic dreams. Life on the street is a constant hustle not much different from the deals of The City or Wall Street. Many of the same lessons apply. It's a battle and some labels just don't make it. In September '99, with bailiffs and creditors beating a path to his door, DJ Ron was forced to do a runner, leaving behind London Some 'Ting Records and thousands of pounds worth of debts.

A label like Metalheadz soon becomes a stable of DJ / production talent. A stable is a group of artists or can be a group of labels which provides artists with different outlets for their talents. Metalheadz and Congo Natty have a musical corporate identity with a recognisable sound. But producers are free to make tracks for a range of labels. And there seems to be no end of people announcing that their mate is about to or has just started a Drum & Bass label. Easy access to cheaper technology, abundant role models and the prominence of JDB in Dance Culture have all fuelled a rapid proliferation of labels. Even Nicky Blackmarket could only skim the surface as he gestured at the growing numbers of labels on his shelves. "Metalheadz, V, Philly Blunt, Dope Dragon, Full Cycle, Ebony, K Power, Dread Recordings, UFO and Penny Black. Then on the Intelligent tip you've got: Creative Source, Basement Records, Reinforced, Moving Shadow, No U Turn — all types of Drum & Bass."

Reinforced
Dego & Mark

REINFORCED
[www.reinforcedrecords.co.uk]

Reinforced celebrated their 100th release in October 1996. It all started in 1990 with *Rising Sun*, sold out of the back of the producer's mum's car. The Reinforced crew revolves around Gus, Nookie, Marc and Dego. Goldie has been part of their stable as has DJ Randall. With their second release, the classic *Mr Kirk Your Son is Dead*, Reinforced established themselves as a label to watch. Their output has been as prolific as it has been influential.

The core producers all fulfil the label's other roles. Gus is the label manager and handles administration. He sees Reinforced as an experimental trend-setter. Dego, the A&R man, has collaborated on Reinforced's sub-labels / imprints, 4 Hero and Jacob's Optical Stairway, and produced the ground-breaking *Internal Affairs* EP. He feels that Reinforced stands for consistency, quality and innovative Drum & Bass. He loves to incorporate different B sides using House or Hip Hop. As one of the pioneers of JDB, Dego believes they've often brought artists forward. Investing in the future, Reinforced are always trying to find the new kid on the cutting edge. Dego prefers underground projects where the financial rewards may be small but for him that's where the buzz is.

Marc Mack is 25% of the crew working under the 4 Hero, Tek 9, Manix and Tom & Jerry titles. Like many producers, Marc finds working under several names musically emancipating — "If you're known for producing one sort of music, people start to screw when you deviate from that." All the aliases give you the flexibility to produce different music. Within the Reinforced stable, artists are free to collaborate in numerous combinations. Goldie's second EP for Reinforced, *Dark Rider*, featured proto-Drum & Bass. Nookie has been with Reinforced for about four years, producing tracks including *Sound of Music* and *The Return of Nookie*. He's found a home with Reinforced and feels they don't need the majors. "Reinforced are unique in that it's not all about business. I hate the music business but love working with people." On the independent tip, Reinforced is one of the best labels for artists who are personal about their music.

"We've always striven to use original breaks and ideas. When Goldie came along, he enhanced it, made us think of things we weren't doing."
Gus Lawrence, All Junglists, Channel 4, 1994

DJ Randall is one of Reinforced's main supporters in the scene. Chatting on MTV Europe, he feels Reinforced are the future and beyond. "They've got so many individuals on the sound — everybody's got their own style and they represent each other from back in the day." Reinforced are and will continue to develop music in new directions.

MOVING SHADOW
[www.movingshadow.co.uk]

Moving Shadow's Rob Playford made the first four tracks for his label by himself. Between his day job, DJing and raving, he'd test his new tracks on his mates through his powerful car stereo. They thought his music was runnin', which was fine but what do you do next? A natural inquisitiveness led him 'round the corner from Groove Records, Wardour Street, where he bought his tunes, to Charing Cross Road and Foyles, where he bought a book on the music industry. Not too long after, he pressed up a thousand copies of his tune, *The Orbital Project* and began hawking them 'round the same shops where he'd bought his records.

He's apologetic, almost embarrassed at being so sensible. "That's my problem — being sensible." Sensible enough to get a computer education, to work at his craft, fund it with a daytime and DJ job, then be rewarded with two stonking hits. There's something about being sensible that can land you in the right place at the right time. The Moving Shadow tracks, *Waremouse* and *Bombscare*, with over 60,000 unit sales to their credit, provided the kind of capital of which other labels dream. Yes, a one person label can get by on sales of 2,000 - 3,000 per release, every six weeks, but get yourself a *Waremouse*, a *Bombscare* and a *Helicopter Tune* and you're in a position to make significant money. Aside from paying the artists, initially operating from Rob's home, Moving Shadow had few overheads. Rob calculated the company's worth and tied that in with the release schedule while engaging more artists. Very sensible.

At their Soho base, the studio is purpose-built and they do everything bar press the records in-house. Tony Mirror's stylish merchandise hangs on the walls, while efficient staff have time to sing and dance around the office. Gavin, their runner, slips down to Music House to cut a clutch of DATs. He's passed by Goldie arriving like a marathon runner before entering the stadium. *Timeless* a done, dusted memory, he's scheduled to finish his second album alongside Rob Playford — a smooth operation? (At the time of writing, Goldie and Rob Playford were no longer working together.)

Sound of the Underground Records (SOUR)

"We were dissed by the scene. They were saying, "Who are these people?"" Dave Stone, SOUR

Depressed with the state of England's music scene in '85, Dave Stone and Norton Blue formed a band and headed off to Thailand. By '88, friends were sending them Rave tapes and tales of the Summer of Love. By the time they returned from the beach in '89, the tabloids were full of smiley faces and Acid House hysteria. They'd missed the party but did get a song-writing deal with Virgin. Dave and Norton's luck really came in when Virgin was bought out by EMI and they were left with enough money to buy their own studio.

Dave Stone had been impressed with the growing Jungle scene and its self-sufficiency. It was important that people seemed to be in control of their own destiny and were running the scene they loved. "They were talented, made the music and could create a certain amount of hype about it." In '92, Dave and Norton set up the label DJ Only with

vocalist Elizabeth Troy and producer T Power, hoping to sell two to five thousand singles each release. This core personnel went on to become SOUR in the same year. Shy FX had joined as a tape op. He was actually fired within a week for refusing to clean a toilet, but returned to present SOUR with *Disease*, their first Jungle tune. When Dave Stone asked where the kick drums and 4 / 4 structure were, Shy explained about the breaks and beats.

SOUR made a conscious decision to take Jungle further, both in terms of different musical and geographical directions. Shy FX's and UK Apache's *Original Nuttah* took Jungle into the national charts for the second time in '94. SOUR signed deals with Avex Japan and Warners Europe. *Nuttah* gave the label a substantial boost, netting around £120,000 in licensing deals. SOUR took every opportunity for their artists to perform PAs at Jungle raves abroad. At their first gig in Berlin's mega club, E-Werk, the power was switched off at 8am when people refused to leave. They took Det's mic away and he still carried on. SOUR, including DJ Trace and the dance group A Tribe Called Jungle have performed in Tokyo, New York and at the '95 Berlin Love Parade. It's a label shaped more by its artists than an in-house sound. Though SOUR's first hit was on the Ragga tip, T Power continued to represent the Drum & Bass side of Jungle. His album was one of the first artist albums released in '95. When the album *Tech Steppin'* was released on their imprint Emotif, it was generally heralded as a new direction in the music, featuring the dark-metallic, angry sounds of *Mutant* and *Skyscraper*. Doc Scott, Ed Rush, Grooverider, and DJ Trace contributed to the album. SOUR also released Shy FX's *Formula* and the first MC-led album MC Det's *Out of Det* [see *MCs*, p.148].

Towards the end of '95, SOUR's release schedule of an album plus three singles per month, coupled with strained artist relationships inside the company, made the whole thing too much hard, unhappy work. UK Apache, Elizabeth Troy, Shy FX and T Power left the label. The second wave of artists including Tonic and Blim were now producing records. After x-amount of releases and footnotes in JDB history, SOUR personnel split amicably and went on to other things.

"When we started SOUR, the idea was to put out the sound of the underground at the time. So, taken to its logical conclusion, we should be doing Speed Garage now. Sorry, over the last four years the music has developed in such a way and I've become so attached to it that music was more important than money."
DAVE STONE

Though Norton has gone off to produce House, imprints Emotif and Botchit & Scarper are being managed by long-time SOUR co-worker Vini (RIP) and Dave Stone has stayed with JDB. He and his engineer have already released notable tracks like the jazzy *125th Street*. And Dave, alongside Bryan Gee, continues to run the club Movement. After the chart success, international travel and deals, album releases, offices and staff, Dave Stone's going back to basics – running the Click 'n' Cycle label from home with low overheads and a manageable release schedule. Next time around people won't be asking, "Who are these people?"

METALHEADZ
[www.metalheadz.co.uk]

Metalheadz started late '94 with their first release *Rider's Ghost*. Goldie had produced with Reinforced and been signed to Synthetic, but he wanted his own label. So Goldie and Doc Scott set up Metalheadz with tracks from Wax Doctor, Alex Reece and Dillinja. He'd met J Majik a while ago, along with Dextrous and Devious D on Planet Earth and Infra Red. Although Goldie signed them, he didn't have much time to put into the label. So Christian, who originally signed Goldie to Synthetic, became the Label Manager. Kemistry & Storm came into Metalheadz, doing all the day-to-day running like liaising with artists and organising the mailing list – which Storm does with an iron grip, but Goldie decides what's released.

Metalheadz' status as an independent label is important. Christian remembers days when majors would dictate to artists how they should make their tunes, literally ordering a catchy vocal hook in the first thirty seconds so it would sound exciting on Pop stations. Christian doesn't want to work in an environment where credibility is lost to commercial considerations. Metalheadz nurtures its artists. Rather than taking tracks from one-hit-wonders, they insist that new producers are able to supply at least two decent B-sides with their main track. In that way they ensure longevity, not only for their producers but also for the label. The contractual arrangement between Metalheadz and its artist is informal – that's to say, there isn't one. They are free to record for other labels, including majors, under their own name.

Like so many others in Jungle, Christian hates being pigeon-holed and feels Metalheadz' image as the hard, metallic label is not wholly justified. In Summer '97 Sci-clone put out *Melt*, a seasonal jazzy track. Going back further, on the flip side of Adam F's *Metropolis* is the far mellower sounding *Mother Earth*. Originally, Metalheadz wanted to acquire *Circles* before it was released elsewhere.

They, like SOUR, have been at the forefront, taking JDB on a tour of club nights around the world. Aside from the British circuit, their DJs have been to most of Europe, the US and Brazil. They always travel with Troy, the sound engineer from Eskimo Noise. Troy drives a van with the registration R4KET and has been known to rearrange other people's sound systems to boost the night's decibels.

As part of a new promotion, Metalheadz will release a video, mix tapes and CDs featuring the Blue Note Metalheadz Sessions, as well as a documentary called *Talkin' Headz*. This time around, no-one wants to miss out on capturing the magic of a special club. It's all part of the quality package that is Metalheadz.

Eye-catching logos can help sell tunes. Punters in record shops need only point to a graphic brand name. Moving Shadow's logo was inspired by Rob Playford seeing dancing shadows on the wall during a rave at The Astoria. People have tried to read many things into the famous Metalheadz logo. A friend suggested it was ripped off from some comic character he couldn't remember. There was even a suggestion of demonic undertones from another. Back stage at the '97 Essential Festival, Gus, Goldie's quasi-stepfather explained. Goldie had brought him a sketch he'd drawn based on a famous photo of an African boy sitting in the bush with headphones on – the link with Goldie, a product of the DJ culture. He says, "I'll die with my headphones on".

V Recordings

Jumpin Jack Frost + Bryan Gee

V RECORDINGS
[www.vrecordings.com]

Bryan Gee and Jumping Jack Frost don't spend much time in the office, preferring to run things from the road, with two part-time workers, Shirley and Tracy, providing back-up. Bryan and Frost have been described as proper 'road men'. They know the streets. In part that means doing everything yourself rather than trusting others to do it for you. It's a way of keeping direct control. It also means very, very hard work. But they rise to the challenge every time.

Bryan sits after-hours at the distributor Southern Record Distribution (SRD) talking artwork and packaging for the V Classics album, before going off to mix the CD. Frost mingles with early morning commuters at Seven Sisters tube on his round of meetings, press conferences and artist liaison before joining the queue at Music House.

V Recordings was set up by Jumping Jack Frost and Bryan Gee in '95. They also founded labels Philly Blunt and Chronic to cater for different sounds of JDB. V Recordings has a strong pedigree and is a powerful presence on the scene. It is a stable of many top DJs including: the legendary Jumping Jack Frost, who's graced many a Rave stage from the dawn of the scene and also had a show on the Kiss network, Bryan Gee who plays out on the DJ circuit and presents his premier Sunday night show on Kool FM, the Bristol posse DJ Die, DJ Krust, DJ Suv and award winning Roni Size. Ray Keith also moves with the V massive.

All are excellent producers in their own right. They exude maturity of attitude and sport an impressive collective history in the business. The V producers are militantly serious about the quality of each and every beat. At the first Jungle Awards in 1996, V won Best Label which was no small feat in the year of the Metalheadz. There was a serious buzz around the V Recordings album launch party at Mr C's club, The End, in Spring '97. It seemed that everyone from all corners had turned out to toast V's success. So strong was their sound that after the party people talked about the V Funk. Their artists are so innovative that, by Autumn '97, Bryan Gee was talking about a new JDB drum pattern, the 'three-step-lick'. When their album V Classics appeared, it spelled class, from the DJ-friendly packaging, the guest producers, Dillinja, Lemon D, Bill Riley and Goldie, and, above all, the music. The album went to the top of the Music Week charts.

V Recordings like many other labels are making good use of the Internet. Once a week, they broadcast the V Recordings Show from a London Internet cafe. There's incredible drive at the centre of this operation. Even before the V Classics release, Frost had another dream. "I'm going to Miami and setting up V America. I'm starting a scene there." No doubt he will.

TRUE PLAYAZ
[www.true-playaz.co.uk]

Hype, Zinc and Pascal, signed with Parousia / RCA as Ganja Kru, but still retained independence as their alter-egos, True Playaz. One of the scene's biggest releases, Still Smoking, was produced by Hype and Pascal. They were one of the first DIY labels, along with Reinforced, Moving Shadow and Surburban Base, to release a self-financed album. Their music is known for its accessibility.

True Playaz, along with V Recordings and many other labels, are one of the many labels to have effectively exploited the Internet. It's perhaps the fastest, most immediate way to receive specific information on Jungle / Drum & Bass. Just log on and type Drum & Bass, click on 'links' and you are surfing. Pascal is the brains behind True Playaz' user-friendly site which includes biogs, a label discography, release news, funny travel diaries and even downloadable samples. Their regularly updated pages are very popular.

"Someone sent me an article from the papers in America. There it was, from some little, hill-billy, nothing-to-do-with-Jungle place and our site was "web site of the week" in their local paper. It's amazing 'cos you forget this thing goes everywhere, doesn't matter where you are. That's why we need the web. You gotta 'ave that man." DJ HYPE

MAJORS

Remember when you were in school and you'd made a pact with friends not to do any revision for those exams. Come the results, you realise every other bastard has secretly been on the case. Many independents claimed they weren't interested in the majors, but when they started getting calls from companies like BMG dangling tempting deals, there were those looking over their shoulders checking who'd been offered what. They couldn't bear to miss out. In music, when the record companies are after you, they'll always tell you that a partnership with them is the best possible step you could take. They certainly have enough cash to buy you up. But sandwiched between the forces of the street and monolithic corporations, there should be one consideration, "Will the move benefit me as a producer, as an artist?" Even the greats like Prince and George Michael couldn't escape the clutches of the clauses.

But the underground wasn't going to go quietly. They weren't naive. The old rock days when bands hankered after any old contract are gone. With JDB, the majors had to throw out old contracts and bring in non-exclusive deals. The interesting thing about these signings is that they leave the artists free to work for other labels using their own name. Roni Size continues to work under his own name on Full Cycle, V Recordings and Dope Dragon as well as for Talkin' Loud. It was a case of the majors adapting to the underground. One of the things producers fear the most is any encroachment on their artistic territory. In the new relationship with the majors, artists are held on a very loose leash. This isn't as unusual as it may seem. The

Jazz Cafe's Simon Rawles describes how Jazz musicians in the 60s and 70s on Blue Note were free to collaborate with artists on other labels. Those artists were notoriously precious about the quality of their music and its progression. The freedom to 'cross-pollinate' in this way creates a healthy artistic environment which is especially important to those used to producing JDB for a number of different labels under a range of pseudonyms.

A Guy Called Gerald's early experiences with Sony left him unhappy. He felt artistically compromised and destined to spend a life under contract, producing remixes, until he was a forgotten, spent force.

"I don't think I could work with Sony UK. Maybe if I drew up a non-exclusive contract saying that they weren't gonna stifle my creativity. Everything that they have, from the Spice Girls to whatever, is somehow linked to the Street and that's still the safest place for me. It's where I'm coming from. If it's created out of nothing, when you look down and there's nothing there, you've got no foundation. There are lots of artists out there with nothing to stand on. I found that with Sony, the best place for me to be was in the Underground. I could keep my feet on the ground. When I tried to move into their world, they didn't know I existed. I think I existed as a name to a few people but you're really not recognised. If they want to get involved in what I'm doing, okay. But if they say, "Come with me," I don't think it could ever work that way again. For a couple of years with them, I didn't know where I was going. The charts thing with *Voodoo Ray* was an accident. It wasn't what I had my eyes on." *A GUY CALLED GERALD*

A few years down the line, some things have changed. Sony's roster now includes Dillinja, Lemon D, DJ Rap and Grooverider. At the age of 30 Grooverider has achieved most of his life ambitions. He's helped build a scene and wants to keep on building. He's not leaving the underground, just taking things further.

B: Do you see your relationship with Sony enabling you to achieve that?
G: Definitely. They're helping me. They can get to places that I can't get to on an independent label.

At the same time, he remains free to produce tunes for different labels including other majors. Grooverider's 'Jeep Style mix', *Share the Fall*, which went out on Talkin' Loud, could be bought in 'all good records shops' and was played by pirates and legals alike. Share the rise.

THE GREAT SIGN-UP

One employee at a major record company, who preferred to remain anonymous, broke it down for me. He described, "the unmistakable-unmissable street vibe which followed the rise of Ragga beats in Jungle. In the media, in the clubs, this thing – don't care what it was called – was selling, creating a buzz, and everyone wanted a piece of the action. By the time some A&R men really were on the case, the DJs had already moved the music onwards. Acts like Kemet Crew, who signed early, were put through the album production mill and by the time their Jungle record was released, it dropped – crashing right through the Drum & Bass floor. People didn't know where Goldie was coming from, where he was going, what he represented. Then came a switch of focus from Jungle to D&B and the worrying question of whether the independent artists could really keep up the pace and on the case, after they'd been signed."

Perhaps with the exception of RCA / Parousia's Kemet Crew in late '94, Goldie's deal with London Records was signed just ahead of the flood. Trenton remembers the traipse around carrying the *Timeless* DAT. "Loads of A&R men get bored listening to your stuff, so people end up giving them edited versions. Taking *Timeless* around, they'd bang the DAT in the machine and it'd have them hooked for the entire 22 minutes. They wanted to meet Goldie as soon as possible. He'd arrive and give them the low-down in intense two hour meetings. A few people have been sacked since *Timeless* did the rounds. Like the man who said no to The Beatles, either they didn't get it or failed to pass the tape upstairs for a second opinion. By the time they'd caught themselves, the deal with London had been done. Goldie had offers from everyone, all the majors beat a path to his door, some without even hearing the track. *Timeless* created such a buzz that he was offered silly money. For a time every A&R man wanted something like *Timeless*. In true record company fashion, they'd eject artists' tapes from the machine, drop in *Timeless* saying, "We want something like this." It was a good position to be in. Goldie had been around the companies before, being told his music was too fast, could never be programmed, would never sell. They should have been on the case two years previously, supporting the artists, developing the music. Instead, they pushed out one compilation after another making easy money." *TRENTON, NUR*

DJ Hype remains sceptical. "I signed for a number of reasons. I was looking at people who signed. I remember talking to Roni and he's saying, "I'm signed but it's wicked 'cos I can still do my own label." I was like "you're 'aving your cake and eating it too." I'm paranoid. I wasn't confident with a major. I thought, they're gonna sign me up and spit me out. A year down the line, I'm gonna be in the shit again. But I was watching artists who had been signed and they were getting the right attention." Hype was also afraid that by the time he made up his mind, the majors could have changed theirs. So he signed, without being tamed, to BMG's Parousia imprint. Parousia can get Ganja Kru the international media coverage and Hype is free to talk about his other label, True Playaz. The majors open doors but Hype is still sceptical, viewing them as banks. But even if the Parousia project was foreclosed tomorrow, he, Zinc and Pascal could continue – making both accidental and intentional hits.

With the early signings of artists whose only output had been a series of twelve inches, there remained the question of whether or not they could produce albums which is where the real money in the music business is made. After *Pulp Fiction*, Alex Reece was put through the fast-track production route. Many thought his album wasn't very good.

There are those like Sarah Groove Connection who believe that the majors don't really know what they want. "The record companies switch very quickly from wanting to make Jungle to Drum & Bass. Like George Kelly, Moose, they all got signed to record labels and before you knew it, before they even had time to make their albums, the label wanted Drum & Bass. They didn't want Jungle anymore. Now they want – the "Roni Size sound". They're scared of the Metalheadz sound now but in '96, they wanted anyone who could make a "Metalheadz sounding" album. I'm just scared 'cos they're so fickle and they don't know what they want. Now they're wanting "something more accessible", they're regressing to what we had in the first place."

Over the past four years a range of top DJ / producers have signed contracts with major labels. They include Goldie on London FFRR, Roni Size on Talkin' Loud, LTJ Bukem on London for his one-off *Logical Progression* project and Photek on Virgin's Science label. Hype, Pascal and Zinc of the Ganja Kru, DJ Ron, MC Moose, Reinforced projects, George Kelly, and Maximum Style all signed with RCA / BMG. While Grooverider, Dillinja, Lemon D and DJ Rap went with Sony, Adam F and the F Jams signed under EMI's label imprint, Positiva. 2Bad Mice are with Aritsa, 4 Hero Jacob's Optical Stairway with R&S and Peshay is with Mo' Wax. There are rumours that Shy FX, Mickey Finn and Aphrodite are also about to sign major deals.

WORKING WITH DRUM & BASS

On *Open Forum* in late '96, Goldie noted that there was still a wide gap between the majors and the independent artists. As the majors cross the street, there are little irritations to get right. Goldie remembers trying to play a set for Polygram US in NYC, only to find that the decks had been set up on a bass speaker. Storm feels that The Metalheadz album *Platinum Breaks* wasn't really well supported with any deep commitment by London Records because Goldie's name wasn't all over it. "There was a "Who are these other people?" approach from the label."

Perhaps this was one reason for the relatively poor sales of Radio One's album release of *One in the Jungle*. Apart from asking DJs to select the tracks, they never really got the street strategy right. *The Scene*'s Terry Turbo remembers Radio One's rather snooty attitude when he called the press office offering advice and asking for advertising. Matt in the Unity Records shop put the low sales of the album down to poor advertising. "It's got some blinding tracks, but no-one seems to know about it." He shrugs, looking at the bulk of records in the rack which would probably be returned rather than sold.

The merger between the Jungle scene and the majors has yet to produce consistent financial success. The *Incredible* bonanza is still to arrive. And the accountants won't wait forever.

PHOTO BY TRISTAN O'NEILL

Goldie

THE WIRELESS

PIRATE RADIO

"Everyone has the right to freedom of opinion and expression; this right includes freedom to hold opinions without interference and to seek, receive and impart information and ideas through any media regardless of frontiers."
UNIVERSAL DECLARATION OF HUMAN RIGHTS, UNITED NATIONS, 1948, CITED IN REBEL RADIO BY HINDS AND MOSCO

"Pirates represent the underground. Without the pirate scene, London wouldn't be what it is."
DEGO, REINFORCED

Pirate stations are the lifeblood of Dance Music in England. Without them we would still be trying to persuade the Radio Authority (RA) of the validity of JDB against the accountants' balance sheets suggesting that stations playing specialist Dance formats are not viable. In spite of the government's 1990 Broadcasting Act, which should have liberalised the airwaves, Britain has some of the most restrictive, conservative regulations in the world. Kiss 100 FM's Gordon Mac agrees that present regulations mean the accountants call the tune. As stations need to be what the RA calls 'commercially viable', there's little room to be passionate about the beats and lots for lowest common denominator – commercial music.

"Without the pirates, I don't think there'd be a scene. The rest of the scene reviled Hardcore. They looked at it as speeded up chipmunk kind of bullshit. There was nowhere interested in representing it. But a whole section of young people were really into this music. So the pirates formed as a natural need for people to hear this music".
DAVE STONE, SOUR

And people who are passionate about their music don't hang about. *Pirate Radio Then and Now* tells how, in June 11 1972, the Rev. James Paterson, minister at Palmers Green Pentecostal Church was charged with operating a transmitter without a licence. Radio Odyssey played 'hot Gospel' music throughout North London.

In Britain we have near on a forty year history of pirate or unlicensed broadcasting, from Ronan O'Rahilly's Radio Caroline in '64 and 70s land-based pirates like Invicta, to Kiss, Fantasy, Centreforce and Kool FM. All giving exposure to new music. The book *Rebel Radio* describes the impact of the Dread Broadcasting Corporation (DBC) in 1981, with Londoners hearing Reggae presented by rootsy Jamaicans for the first time. A Hip-Hop jam funded by the Greater London Council in September '84, promoted by Tim Westwood on LWR, attracted 30,000 partygoers. Radio is central to a community. London Greek Radio is an example of a former pirate that became legal meeting a local need. There is a Dance Music community and British Dance music is our greatest contribution to the global youth market. Yet the very heart of the Dance Music scene is under constant attack.

Kool FM's Guvnor General Eastman is not alone in recalling the authorities' groundless allegations that pirates must be organising a huge percentage of the capital's drug trade. Call me prejudiced but when you see the average councillor or Radio Authority executive, you really have the feeling that they could never possess that same passion for music that drives all pirates forward.

April '96 in the basement of GLR studios, Eastman in baseball cap and dark glasses takes part in a live phone-in discussion with a former Head of the Radio Authority, Lord Chalfont and Howard Rose of the *Radio Magazine*. The old arguments circulate. Drugs, big earner for organised crime, not enough support for the music, not enough space on our (comparably empty) FM band and the 'Who knows how long this fad will last?' rationale. Not understanding the religious devotion to Dance Music and mooting the involvement of 'Mr Big', they're left speechless when Eastman asks, "How many Giros does it take to buy a transmitter? 'Cos that's what your dealing with." A level of commitment where even the normally work-shy might get a part-time job, bringing their few pennies to start or keep a station on air. Whilst politicians sound off about the New Deal or community pond clearing projects, they keep missing the point. How do you get someone up at any time, day or night, make them perform obstacle courses, stand around in the freezing cold in a four-by-six foot room for hours and pay them sod all if anything at the end? There's teamwork, dedication, camaraderie. Sound familiar? Replace militarism and nationalism with a love of music and you can begin to understand some of the motivating forces behind British Dance music and the unlicenced broadcasters who promote it.

"You had to be the kind of person that felt your station and your music was more important than this or even last year's labels. Stations, as much as the raves they promote, are central to the living scene. Whilst artists produce the music and promoters put on raves, there is a passion to get the music on air. That was when the Department of Trade and Industry (DTI) started to come heavy and only the strongest survived. You had to be dedicated. It became more important than going to football." MIKEY, DE UNDERGROUND

Centreforce and Sunrise were among the first pirate stations to hit the capital's airwaves, playing the new Dance Music of a House Nation, featuring exactly the sounds that the fledgling Rave DJs spun. They were essential to a weekend's raving. Before flyers, they provided the word-of-mouth link to warehouses in and around the M25. Without leaving your house, they put you in the centre of the rave, or that's what it felt like. And back home on the come down, after the dance, they were still there providing that buffer between Utopia and the Real World.

The list of pirates stretches right into the past, with many older people on the Rave circuit today searching for ancient tapes featuring Invicta, LWR, Horizon, Kick, DBC and the original Kiss FM. Some like Kick played Pop tunes. Invicta played a range of Soul, Funk, Jazz Funk and pure Jazz, which blared from beat boxes, entertaining Sunday street skaters in Hyde Park, and people in flats who'd erect all kinds of makeshift aerials to catch the signal. Kiss FM, under the dedicated stewardship of Gordon Mac and Rosie Lawrence, kept the likes of Jazzys B & M, Norman Jay, Paul 'Trouble' Anderson, Danny Rampling, Trevor Nelson, Colins Dale & Favor, ColdCut, Manasseh, Max 'n' Dave, Steve Jackson and Judge Jules on air for three years, only to come off air in December '88 in search of a licence, just as Rave hit hard and Centreforce began broadcasting.

People really into their music wanted to know how to get on one of these stations. It was a bigger dream than wanting a car or getting a new pair of strides. As more and more people got access to the technology, knowledge and music, the scene grew. Back in 1990 - 91, there must have been a good seven stations broadcasting from East London, three of them sharing the same ground in the decaying tower blocks of Leyton's Oliver Close Estate. In the 80s these estates were like grey, slow death with burnt-out car wrecks on the ground, muggers above, piss-stenched busted lifts between them. Reeking of external financial deprivation, damaged by internal vandalism, they were areas that local councils and the police had effectively abandoned. For residents of the hood, boredom reigned above all. Then along came pirate radio. It didn't change everything for everyone. But it offered a purpose and an outlet for some.

Early '92, with the towers of Hackney Downs looming behind him, Rush FM's The Gaffer addresses film maker Nigel Finch's camera with clarity. "If they cut pirates then what we going to do? We'll all be sitting 'round the flats again. No one's doing nothin' — it'll be back to the whole thing. Hackney crime rate goes up. People get burgled, people's cars get robbed, people get mugged in the lift. It does happen; I'm not saying everyone's turned golden, but not as much. Before it was people you knew who did those sort of things, now it's no-one you know."

Whilst pirate stations were a pain for some of their unwilling neighbours, others welcomed the homegrown invasion. DJ Brockie remembers with affection how people living on Hackney Downs Nightingale estate unconnected with Kool FM would watch out for and warn them of the approach of the DTI. Even the caretakers would open up the lift shafts so the engineers could hide their transmitters there.

Pirates weren't exclusive to East London estates. Nicky Blackmarket playing 'a whole selection of everything' on Star Radio based near North London's Harrow Road. Kemistry & Storm with their MC Goldie recall arriving at a squat in Kentish Town and shoving their decks through a hole in the wall at Touch Down FM. Allegedly their transmitter was once housed in Goldie's high rise flat. Grooverider, Fabio and Frost all did apprenticeships of varying lengths on South London pirate stations. But, many people recall Rave and Breakbeat music resounding from the towers of East London. They'll recite the roll call: Friends, Centreforce, Fantasy, Sunrise, Juice, Don, Chaos, Dance, Pulse, Rush and Eruption, to name a smattering.

Centreforce, founded by Andy Pascher and Fantasy, gave way to a new wave of stations that coincided organically with the overlapping rise of Hardcore and Breakbeat in 1989 - 90. During this era, one thing was clear. DJs on the legal stations weren't interested in the Underground, with the exception of Steve Jackson who played the odd bit of Hardcore on Kiss 100 FM and Radio One's John Peel who, as always, had a taste for the fresh and musically dangerous.

Neither the music nor its artists waited for an invitation to the legal stations. Everyone just got on with it. In '92, a punter named Charissa who used to regularly call Rave FM was finally invited down to meet the lads. Mikey De Underground picked her up from Walthamstow station and Cool Hand Flex taught her how to spin the vinyl. The girl was in it. From raver to riches, DJ Rap's career began. In '98, the next generation continues to entertain London.

I'LL BE IN TIME FOR MY SLOT

20.00 Tuesday, the call came through.
"You've got a slot. 4 till 6am starting this Saturday morning. Is that alright?"
"Yeah man I'll take it. Wicked, I'll take it!"

23.55 Sunday
Bam bam bam bam
"B with the R.O.C.K.I.E. Brockie. My DJ Brockie. Brockie. Rewind Friday 'n' come again."
Kool FM, Brockie and Det, last stop of the weekend. Can't sleep. Won't sleep.
Yes Det. Rewind Friday night / Saturday morning just before my first show.

02.30 Saturday morning
I tune to the station and call in. Studio sounds pour through the receiver into my bedroom.
"Yallright? This is DJ Zy:on, I'll be in time for my slot."

The shout comes back at me out the radio, "Hold tight the DJ Zy:on next up at 4 till 6 after me the DJ Plex. Stay locked."

The reality of the words coming out the radio deepened my growing stage fright. Panic introduced the option of calling the management and ducking out. Suppose the station got raided. How does the ad tape work? Which fader is the mic on? And suppose I clang out London Town?

03.30 Alarm call
I wake with a buzzed sense of detachment, dress and stuff the pre-selected tunes, some notes and headphones into a shopping bag. Reaching the door I turn and grab another handful of tunes. Glancing back at the silent practice decks, I in DJ mode, have a show to play. A friend, Kate — the posse starts the car.

03.45
Feeling like outlaws with no tax on the car, we criss-cross dead backstreets, heading for the inner city spires of the studio somewhere through the early morning fog. Parking a couple of streets away from the tower blocks, we walk silently in the dark oppression of unfamiliar territory. I contemplate my motivation to the max.

03.50

The 'graveyard shift'. For this or any shift, there was no big money. Irresponsible broadcaster? No, even the DTI had admitted that the better pirates did seem to know what they were doing. Taking on the authorities? That's the last thing I wanna to do. If they made us legal and let us carry on doing what we're doing, yeah I'd do it tomorrow. 'Til then, this is me. And taking on the law is just part 'n' parcel.

Finding the back entrance to the block, the redhead and the funki dread called the lift. The door crawled shut as the light in the aluminium box flickered. In the corner of the lift, I noticed chicken bones and a Kentucky box floating in a pool of piss. My mind lost somewhere in the zone, I didn't notice Kate telling me that I was standing in it.

Creaking towards the 18th floor, this was 2000 AD elsewhere land. Weird pre-show nerves. Somewhere in between buzzed calm and dire panic. Between lawful and unlawful. I wondered if this was how it felt in a car just before a firm did a bank job.

03.55

The unlikely couple left the lift on the 19th floor, so high in the air, so deep underground. In the gloomy fluorescent overhead lights, there was nothing to distinguish the studio from the identical portals.

03.58

Knocking on the door and still lost in unreality, the nervous knot in my stomach threatens to unleash an adrenaline rush into my hands, causing a horrendous case of the shakes. Fugee opens up onto a tatty squat. A doorway opposite reveals a bedroom too dark and nasty for anyone to sleep in. Wires hung along the hallway ceiling, disappearing around the corner into the living room. A small posse of bodies rocked and nodded on the sofa. Stars of amber light glowing in the dark, illuminated the over-sized T-shaped aerial propped against the lounge window. Fugee pulls back a mattress blocking the

kitchen entrance and pours light across the room, and a moody DJ clutching his records makes to drive back to Croydon. Turns out he'd missed his slot three times running and hadn't bothered to call the management to explain. So he'd been turfed.

"Last one coming from DJ Plex, next up you got DJ Zy:on." Piano tinkles of the *Lighter* flow out of the Technics resting on a kitchen cupboard. Everyone remembers the *Lighter* tune from '94. That was where I came in. It's a good omen for the show. I chat to DJ Plex about tunes, the microphone and the mixer. Unpacking the records, headphones and notes as the ads roll, there's little time to skin up. "So if you want to book our DJs or MCs to rock your party, call 0585 …" Sitting on a kitchen chair, Kate works the phone line. Fugee watches and waits by the door. He's seen it all with first timers. Like the ones that lose their bottle and stand bent double over the mixer, sweat dripping, shaking their heads as they clang out every mix. Zy:on at the decks, vinyl on the turntable, fader to 9 … "0585 …"

… Line 1 to phono, cross-fader to deck 2, hit the start button … spin 'round to grab the mic off the cushion on the draining board, count the bars … *Share the Fall*.

"Good morning London. You got the DJ Zy:on taking you through the next two hours … This one goes out to Rider, the inspiration."

… Replace the mic, headphones back on, cue the next tune, work up the mix, come with the cross-fader bouncing the mix across London, beats on beats on beats. Just like back in my room, except it's not, except it is.

04.15

Contented, Fugee disappears to find a spliff and get some kip.

04.40

Apart from the mistake with the station's frequency and phone number, it was alright. I play Roni Size, *You're Not Alone* and realise there's been no calls. That's the way it is on the graveyard shift. I can never be bothered to ring up at this time. Suppose not one person in London is listening? Wouldn't make no difference. Still gotta be professional 'n' do my ting – *Just 4 U London*.

05.53

"Wake Fugee 'n' find out who's doing the next slot." I was down to my last tune, even played the B-sides. Stuck in the shopping bag was one last tune. Kate pokes her head 'round the mattress. "Fugee says he'll sort something out." "What's that supposed to mean?"

05.54

"This is DJ Zy:on. I'll be back next week 4 till 6 'ere on the Rude FM. Not sure who's up next but we'll keep rolling thru the weekend. Keep it locked."

One last tune. Run the whole version from the outside edge. The all-DJing, all-MCing, DJ Metro appears grinning and bubbling with pre-match excitement.

"I've gotta cut 'n' run. I'll leave you with this. It's the one like the Roni Size and Nuyorican Soul 'n' *It's Alright*."

Coming down to earth in the car park outside the tower block, there were no crowds cheering or fans wanting autographs, just early morning mist and empty streets. No Old Bill or DTI. And the show? "It was alright you know."

01.00 Monday morning back in bed

Kool FM, Brockie and Det, last stop of the weekend. Pirate radio, a rite of passage. Brockie, back-to-back with the Shy FX plays that tune. *It's Alright*. And you know that.

STREET

A Centreforce street soldier used to running all kinds of skanks and schemes spotted an empty car brimming with aerials in the street below. It was obviously the DTI. He dashed down the Oliver Road tower block, figuring the boot of the car must be stuffed with x-amount of taxed rigs and records. Working the lock, dreaming of the spoils of war, he clocked some bloke who he figured lived on the estate. It was a rough place and he was rougher. He didn't know or remember that when doing a raid, the DTI travel with a police escort. In this case plain-clothed. Irritated by the approaching stranger who was just about getting in his face, he worked the lock harder. The geezer whispered, "Want a hand?" "Nah Nah, you're all right." The Old Bill just stood up there watching and finally says, "You're nicked".

In the early 90s, between the masses of pirates, competition between the stations didn't limit itself to who had which tunes. Devotees from all sides battled it out on tower block rooftops, stealing each other's aerials and mashing up their transmitters – doing the DTI's job for them. When the DTI did hit there would be short truces during which the unlicensed broadcasters would unite, getting to know each other, even sharing aerials and personnel.

But stations went to the wall. There was in-fighting, poor organisation, low morale and those who just couldn't take the pace. It takes a lot for a DJ or MC to get the night bus out to the studio to do a graveyard shift, especially if there's little heart, cohesion or family spirit at a station. Corruption can also be a problem. On Don FM, one-time home of Trace, Ed Rush and G Force, DJs had to pay for their slots. But their money was allegedly invested in the Don FM BMW. The DTI busts, wars between the stations and unprofessionalism amongst station personnel took their toll. In '91 Eastman came along. That's when people cleaned up their habits. That's why Kool survived. Everyone needed one strong person to organise, motivate and say, "You shouldn't do that. You're risking it too much. You're out."

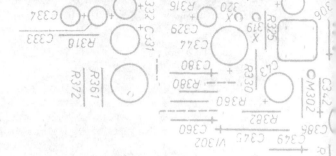

Kool FM

Kool FM, now one of the most famous pirates in the world, celebrated its eighth birthday in November '99. The station started as Eastman and Smurf's own venture. They, like so many others, wanted first and foremost to get on air.

For a station which is still illegal over eight years after its first broadcast, Kool FM are as important as Radio Caroline, which became the backbone of Radio One and Kiss FM, later to become the legal Kiss 100 FM. Bristling with a serious rosta of talented DJs and MCs past and present, Kool has survived where many others didn't.

After Rave, Sunrise and Centreforce had disappeared into static in 1991, Rush, Pulse FM and a few other stations flew the Rave flag. The pirate wars were at their peak. Before Kool FM installed their first rig, Eastman, called all the stations to a meeting and laid down the law. "I told them, "We're a new station coming on air and we don't want anybody touching our stuff ... We won't be going on other people's wavelengths, sabotaging them. So I don't see why anyone should trouble us. And I don't want anybody caught on our roof". "

It started from there. The fledgling Kool FM had the engineers and contacts to get their equipment made and core personnel who could keep the station on air. It was a question of luck, being in the right place at the right time, all underpinned by a certain amount of respect on the street. It all fitted into place.

Their core crew was more mature than many others. Eastman fits together the pieces of a successful puzzle. "Not dissing anyone, but I found that a lot of younger stations, when they earned their money, they just blew it all. Whether it was drugs or weekends out raving. We weren't into none of that. When we had money, we just bought spare equipment. I just did a bit of building or whatever. Brockie was doing youth work. Everyone had something they were doing but nothing really full-time." After a test transmission in the early hours of November 28th, transmitter, decks and DJ Brockie were ready to go on the dot of twelve noon, November 29th 1991. Broadcasting 24 / 7 for eight months, they stayed in the same ground floor council flat on Amhurst Road a short distance away from Stoke Newington police station for two years solid. Until one day they came back to find the place all metalled up.

A few of the crew had known each other when they were kids. Eastman had known Brockie, DJ Ron and MC 5ive'O for about twenty years. He also knew The Ragga Twins and Navigator from time. In the early days Kool had DJs playing a range of music plus a few commercial radio-type presenters but there weren't any MCs apart from Cogee who used to chat over (rather than really MC) Brockie's show. Originally there were about twenty people involved in the station including: Red Alert, Pepsi, MC ID and DJ Buzz. As DJs on Kool became less focused on Hardcore and more on the emergent Breakbeat Jungle, the station moved from location to location. Many of their bases are still in use and must be kept under wraps. But some studios have been grand enough to have a pool table for off-air recreation. Though more fearsome than the police or DTI, they were once discovered by one of the crew's 'mature' uncles who, none too pleased at the discovery of a 'disgraceful disco-jockeying pirate radio station' based in the back room, cast them out with much kissing of teeth, arm-waving and a right old West Indian raging lecture. It was in these formative years, that the 'stamina massive' was born. With listeners being fickle, Kool's staff felt duty-bound to stay on air, come what may – it was sleeping bags in the studio and engineers up all hours. MC Navigator remembers getting the wake-up call, performing hour after hour, then, when someone couldn't make their show or was too tired to play, he was on again. Those who couldn't take the pace fell by the wayside. Only the stamina massive survived.

During 1993 - 95 Kool FM's unceasing dedication to Jungle undeniably helped move the music from the underground to the mainstream. With a front door on the street, Kool FM provided a platform for the artists and an outlet for the music. During the summer of '94, every car stereo and open window in London's estates seemed to pump out Kool.

Brockie

PHOTO BY ANDY COTTERILL

Like Kiss FM in its heyday, Kool is an impressive stable for DJ and MC talent. The station included stars like DJ Brockie and MC Det; Ron, SL, Moose, Strings and 5ive'O aka the Supreme Team; Bryan Gee, Nicky Blackmarket, Stevie Hyper D, Digital, Tonic, Rema Dee, Trace, The Ragga Twins, Navigator, Mampi Swift, Funky Flirt, Footloose, Shabba, Younghead, Marly Marl, Pugwash, Ash, MC Co Gee and Cool Hand Flex to name a few. The station always had its friends – Hype, Shy FX and Andy C – who'd supply the DJs with Dub Plates or play the occasional guest slot. From the mountain of demo tapes they receive, Kool has continued to introduce up-and-coming performers who've then progressed to stardom in their own right, like MC Skibadee and their only female DJ, Wildchild. They have invited a range of DJs including DJs Kid, Frenzic, PM Scientists and Kemistry & Storm to play on the Super Sunday afternoon sessions.

Kool's Jungle Fever raves are legendary. Always major events on the Jungle calendar; they were the public forums of a secret station. In '97, six years after its inception, Kool was still picking up award after award, even gaining a following via mix tapes sent as far afield as Australia. In line with their mission to spread Jungle they've taken dances outside London to Coventry. In November '96 they held a successful rave in Mannheim, Germany and have a monthly residency in Dublin, Ireland. They are also linked to Kool FM, Birmingham. By mid '97, Kool released its first album *The Fever* featuring contributions from many of the station's in-house DJ / producers, and are now broadcasting on the net.

BACK IN THE COMMUNITY

Pirates feed directly back into the community. The police realise that unlicensed broadcasters reach sections of the population that they have little chance of speaking to directly. On more than one occasion, officers from Stoke Newington police station have taken part in their own bit of community policing from the studios of non-Junglist pirate Station FM. Kool has launched fund-raising events for local causes. As role models, DJs and MCs have visited local schools with positive messages of empowerment for the pupils. In their record shop, they tolerate victims of the 'Care in the Community' schemes, who come and dance around or MC to everyone. But kids who think they can hang out in the shop bunking off school are sent straight back to class.

"The police and the local council have ignored us or allowed our ways. Certain things don't get said or get left. But I think they know we have a positive intention. If they thought we'd had anything to do with drugs or if we were doing harm or getting into politics, they'd be down on us one hundred percent. But they know we have a positive, mature attitude".
EASTMAN

One of the benefits of true community broadcasters is their ability to help local businesses target the right people with specific advertising. Ads have included firms offering car insurance, fashionable clothing, hairdressers, mobile phones and studio facilities. Based on an ability to pay, this need not be prohibitively expensive as some people on a limited budget find is the case with the legal broadcasters. Spritz, a young teenager putting on a rave, asked Kool how much it would cost to broadcast an ad. They did it for nothing. Eastman remembers, "He's like Brockie and me when we were fifteen, getting into the music. We try to encourage that." Their label K Power invites tapes from new producers hoping to release tunes.

Dem a call us pirates
Dem a call us illegal broadcasters
Jus' because we play what the people want.
PIRATE'S ANTHEM, SHABBA RANKS ET AL, GREENSLEEVES

Those are lyrics from the first track played by Gordon Mac on the day Kiss FM became legal. Away from all the politics, financing and static, the message remains the same. Illegal broadcasters, especially of the quality of Kool FM, provide an alternative form of community entertainment.

The Jinx

Sunday post-rave approaching midday and I can't sleep. The music is still running through half-awake dreams. Give up and hit the tuner button. Radio Four's *Desert Island Discs* with yet another old bore being fawned over by Sue Lawley. Glide down the dial to the sounds of The Jinx. One of Kool FM's finest. "Wakey wakey. Rise 'n' shine. It's time to get up, open those curtains, and get to the bathroom and whole afresh. Clear away last night's mess." The track rolls. The calls come in. It's time to get up and join the rest of the family.

He's always there – never seems to get the booking on a Saturday night which stops him doing his Sunday breakfast show. It doesn't matter. If others rule the dancefloors, this is his lick. Jinx rules the Sunday breakfast shows and the massive tune in en masse. No Tarrant-type tomfoolery. Here, the music comes first. You feel you know him and when you do meet him in the flesh, he's warm, amiable and polite. You remember his day job as a garage mechanic, and in a nest of viper-mechanics you feel you'd trust him with your prize BMW. Jinx is the ultimate community DJ, rallying the massive to attend fund-raising events for Hackney's Brookfield Boys Club or organising the toddler's Chelsea Thake's appeal, collecting money to ease her fatal cancer. He chats "You've all had good times in your years. Now this little girl hasn't got long to go. So all of you dig deep in yer pockets and give this girl just a little of the life you've had." It's strange to turn on the radio and feel there's a friend talking right at you. Big up the Jinx!

Mid-October, a magical sun beams through the windows. For a moment you feel you've hit the wrong station. How ya mean? Pure 1989 House-Techno tunes from back in the day. Jinx voice comes in "We're going back to some old-time

business". Strains of the *Chime* and Richie Rich flood the airwaves. Your memory darts back to the ecstasy of raves and fields and warehouses and a small cloud of confusion sets in. Then you realise as Jinx tells it: we were all there together. Back in the day – we share a common history. Across the kingdom we raved with the joy of childhood. Tears of nostalgia well up. Midday Sunday and we're up, out of bed – dancing.

The calls pour in. It's a wonder he has time to mix. "Debra in Surrey and Baby Face Ragga, say big-up Jinx, you're rinsin'." Others arrive at the studio, I have to ring in, "I want to dedicate this tune to my best mate Damian". As each old tune drops you shake your head in remembrance. Endless calls for the rewinds that they didn't do in the old days. Even Brockie rings in for a rewind. The excitement is tangible in the virtual community. This is pure entertainment. This is radio. This is illegal – and that's the crime.

Last Caller Try Again

Calling a radio station seems an odd thing to do. Stepping up in the public arena, it's like writing to your MP to express your views. But ringing your favourite pirate station to bawl for a rewind is so natural. Interaction confirms to the pirates that they're doing the right thing. Nothing establishes a sense of community better than regular callers.

The committed dialers: Anita from Charlton, The Brown Brothers, Kelly from Harlow, Blacka, The Soldier Man, Ole from New Cross and the B.I.T.C.H., are the most boisterous bubblers on the telephone line, like the crew next to you at the rave, blowing horns, mouthing MC's words and screaming for the rewind. They are all part of the family environment that Brockie and Det enjoy about radio.

MC Navigator remembers: "Sunday afternoon, sun blazing. Kool FM blazing across London. A geezer rings up from Brixton. He goes, "Yeah mate, listen. I just phoned up to tell you, right, that I turned up the bassline on my speakers and I've blown out all the windows ... Got the police out here 'n' everything. It's all goin' off". I was killing myself. Then there are people phoning up saying, "What's happened to that geezer in Brixton?" Windows blown out!" *MC NAVIGATOR, ALL JUNGLISTS, CHANNEL 4, 1994*

DJs and MCs take time out to mention those who can't call back. The HMP Massive. At least those in prisons around London can still hear new sounds on pirate radio.

BUREAUCRATIC AIRSPACE AND THE MEN FROM THE DTI

Branch Four (formerly Five), of the Department of Trade and Industry is responsible for policing Britain's airwaves. You could see its role as Quality Control or as the Radio Communication's Agency puts it, "Monitoring and Quality Assurance." It keeps the frequencies clean for legal users. From the Radio Authority's (RA) point of view, the DTI protect, if not its investment, then its official corner of the technological market place. With breathless astonishment, the RA Press Officer stated of the air waves, "Well, it's not all free you know" coming like they're the kind of people who'd charge megabucks for a bottle of water at a rave. So, anyway, there's the Home Office who issue broadcast licences, the Radio Authority who decide who gets the few available licences, and the Department of Trade and Industry who police the airwaves. Oh, and there's the MCPS anxious to collect money on behalf of the producers. Producers, by the way, don't want the cash — they do want airplay for their tunes and wish the pirates the best of luck. Right then, so on the ground when a pirate station is actually being raided, the DTI gets back-up from the police to protect the property of the Radio Authority who *allegedly* have backroom meetings with the BBC and the Military who eagerly protect their bandwidth within the airwaves — *allegedly.*

Branch Five — sorry, Four — the men from the DTI are quite nice chaps really. More technicians than actual police, teams of two drive around the streets working in tandem with the Government's listening post just outside Baldock in Hertfordshire. Driving around the South London streets in a red Rover, with a BBC film crew in the back, a foot soldier from the DTI confessed a sneaking admiration for the pirates. "It's not easy to put on a program. It's not easy to transmit. It's not easy to build a transmitter but they achieve it." Even at the police station or in the courts, they like to shake hands with the unlucky broadcaster who returns the compliment. "It's all quite gentlemanly really," he confides.

Quite gentlemanly considering their huge resources. Baldock is their base, resembling an ominous cold war complex with a forest of aerials and over-sized satellite dishes, surrounded by a high fence topped with barbed wire. Inside, like Brains in *Thunderbirds*, shifts of technicians monitor the input of a massive desk, scanning the nationwide myriad of Ragga, Soul, Garage, House, Techno, Reggae, Jungle, Drum & Bass pirate stations twenty four hours a day, seven days a week.

The rather droll Mr Barry Maxwell, Head of the Radio Investigation Service based in Hertfordshire, doesn't feel they're killjoys. They have a job to do. They receive complaints of interference from the emergency services and legal broadcasters. He also claims interference to aircraft landing systems. When two Birmingham stations, Radio Hamdarad and Radio Sangam, affected ground to air approach signals at Birmingham airport in late May '97, the stations were promptly shut down and had all their equipment seized. There haven't been any air crashes yet as a result of pirate radio interference. Barry, a loyal civil servant, doesn't tell you that mobile phones pose more danger to aircraft landing systems. But for the benefit of the cameras, he whips out a range of transmitters including the dodgy cake tin, crammed with market stall Walkmans, a hairnet of wires and crude circuitry stuck on the bottom.

There seems to be a grey area of tolerance. New stations are often taken off air but those that do gain a positive track record might be left alone for a while. 'Til it's their turn to be hit each and every time they switch on. During one Winter '97 weekend at least eight stations were hit. The DTI pack some very considerable powers. Rush FM's Gaffer remembers one spectacular occasion when a helicopter pinned down two guys on the roof of a Hackney tower block. The three-hour operation to arrest them and remove their aerial resembled a terrorist siege.

They can confiscate and destroy anything deemed to aid transmission including records, decks, mixers, aerials and even mobile phones used for advertising. During 1994 - 95 the DTI pushed the boat out a bit too far, targeting several records shop owners whose businesses were even mentioned by a DJ or MC on the radio. They tried to prosecute them for giving financial support to pirate stations through advertising. All the cases were thrown out and the judges were none too pleased with the waste of time and public money.

The maximum penalty for unlicensed broadcasting is an unlimited fine or two years in prison, roughly equivalent to the penalty for having sex with a minor. Anyone charged with unlicensed broadcasting will receive a criminal record and be banned from working in any electronic media for five years. So it's a risky strategy for anyone wanting to use pirates as a route into formal broadcasting. But during 1994 - 95 total fines nationwide only amounted to eleven thousand pounds. In reality, the Magistrate's Association admits that their members can only impose realistic fines based on the defendant's ability to pay. So fines tend not to be huge. Organised stations have various means 'round the back' to get back on air as soon as possible. However, confiscation of the tunes burns a DJ deeply.

Call To The DTI, December 1997
B: Do officers follow unlicenced broadcasters to their studios?
DTI: I couldn't possibly comment.

Aside from their massive technical back-up, the 'local' DTI men have a range of tactics they employ on the way to finding their studio prize, from following DJ's cars, to guessing the approximate studio location from the direction an aerial is pointing. There are occasions when officials receive tip-offs or the police just happen to stumble into your studio ...

"WE GOT NICKED ONCE" DJ CHILLUM SMILES "YEAH ..."

... The squat somewhere in Hertfordshire was a sweet location. The darkened upstairs room was nicely full of crew and vibe. But the elderly couple arriving downstairs to collect their mail wasn't too happy with the occupation and the sounds of Drum & Bass vibrating through the floor. Flexing like Bing from *Brookside*, deducing that Jungle obviously heralded an illegal drugs party in the property, they scurry away to raise the alarm.

Chillum, with his back to the door was deep in the mix ... "Going out to the Lady like Sam, this is Ru ..." The MC swallows his words. Chillum's distracted by the big light on the wall inches in front of his face. Turning around he clocks the uniforms in the doorway. Pleased with themselves, the Bill try to book them for burglary. Pleased with themselves, the crew point out that with eight hundred quid's worth of their own stuff in the room, burglary wasn't on their minds ...

"So they nick the lot of us and cart us all down the station. Rude FM locked up in the cells. DJs shouting, MCs chatting. A fourteen-year-old MC – his mum going to the Desk Sergeant, "Pirate station! You cyaan tek ihm haway an' lock ihm bak up." We were banged up from eight till five next morning. Well it took time to book all nine of us. Got all the gear back. Well, all except the transmitter. Munch asked for it back as it goes. Cheeky is Munch. "Yes Sir, that piece of equipment" says the officer. "If you'd care attend an interview with a gentleman from the Department of Trade and Industry who's on his wa ..." "Nah, nah you're alright mate"... Munch disappears down the station steps on his way to dig up another box."

THE STATION TECHNICIANS

It's difficult to talk about the techies without causing them huge legal or strategic difficulties. Often working in tandem with the management, they're the quieter, more cautious members of the family. On stations that are all about musical and professional promotion, their names will never be on any flyer. A person like Smurf over at Kool FM is what every station needs. They are the people prepared to keep going up on top of that tower block plumbing in the rig and devising ingenious ways to keep it out of the clutches of the DTI men and other crews. Wrapped in sleeping bags, keeping an eye out 24 / 7 while the massive are raving in the studio, winter, rain, snow or fog. If the rig gets nicked or the DTI take it, they and the management will get everyone's heart together on the matter, rinse out their pockets, go and get another transmitter and set it all up again. Sometimes it's a buzz. More often it's hours of hanging around. The DJs just want to come and play their music. Generally, they don't want to know about climbing tower blocks, carrying sand, cement and scaffolding poles up twenty-two stories, plumbing wires into the rig and messing around with electrics. It's hats-off to guys like Smurf and Fugee.

Then there's the Rig Doctor. The bloke who builds the rigs, fine-tunes them to the frequency and keeps it there. These people are deep under cover. Let's call him Dodger and suppose they're underpaid BBC technicians, ex-employees of Her Majesty's Signals Corp or out-of-work Marconi engineers. He's just doing business and doesn't really care who he's building it for. Good luck to them. Around early '97, after lots of busts, there were unconfirmed rumours that the DTI were hitting a few known Rig Doctors who'd had to shut up shop and take an away day – abroad. The Rig Doctors and the techies keep the whole thing rolling, getting reception reports from listeners and taking the flack when things break down. And despite operational difficulties, some DJs battle through without dissing the techie.

Remembering DJ Marly Marl, Kool FM … his one-man operation was hectic at the best of times. But one particular occasion was classic. The show began well enough with Marly Marl in his usual ebullient mood. Then one thing after another collapsed. The mixer played up. Then a deck went down as he chatted the details over the mic in a 'why me?' voice. Furiously fishing out records and slamming them down on the deck with one hand. The other answering the shouts on the mobile stuck under his chin. Oh mate. You had to laugh.

The technical back-up staff deserves the medals. All in the course of duty, they get broken bones and sprained ankles installing aerials and escaping from the DTI.

"There's been a lot of trouble in the last six months. We had to go and see a few new stations and ask them to behave themselves. They get excited. It's a new thing for them – a lot of the people are really young. They don't have proper engineers looking after their equipment. They bleed on us and mess about, but it's been all right for a few weeks now. We've even gone to give them a hand. Tuned up this and that, checked their site out. We help when we can."
EASTMAN, WINTER 1996

STATION SECURITY

Other members of the family are out scouting new locations for the next studio or rig. A good studio space is hard to find. Pirates are always on the move. Centreforce's studio shifted around Leyton, Stratford, Isle of Dogs and Rotherhithe Tunnel to a tower block near St Catherine's Dock that Kiss FM also used previously. Flex remembers, "That was one of the best places, you could beam quite far out. We had a nice rig there, a tower block that was kind of tall. Yeah man, you could get a good broadcast from there." Some places are just too hot. Everything threatened to come on top when Kool had rented a hideout on Dalston's busy high street. Saturday shoppers were quick to recognise Jungle's rising stars, stopping them in the street as they tried to get to their shows.

This isn't some mess-around business and youngsters on the case can screw things up for everybody broadcasting irresponsibly or attracting the wrong sort of attention. Grinning all over their faces, members of a younger Happy Hardcore station in South London had been blabbing about the tricks of the trade on TV. They were well happy. The DTI was listening. The DTI always listens. Radiomen from Luton to Brighton were screwing. Because of that exuberant indiscretion, crews all over had to rethink their technical strategies. Out-thinking the DTI boys is part of the whole business but the techies really don't like the publicity. Over at Kool FM, Smurf remembers the weekend after the station received positive publicity from the BBC *First Sight* program, *Radio Renegades*, when there was static across the FM dial as stations all over were hit. Maybe they would have hit anyway but TV publicity usually only brings trouble.

As the station organiser, you've got someone to handle the technical side and you've found a room for a studio. Then there's your greatest asset and biggest liability, the DJs, the MCs and crew. On many stations the pattern is common. When the first meetings are called, it's discretion all the way. Don't bring your records to the station in boxes or record bags. Don't hang around the entrance. Don't park outside the front door and don't get taxis to pick you up or drop you off at the studio door. A few weeks pass and people are bowling in with record bags and getting cabs to the door 'cos they're late for the show. Before you know it, man will be parked up outside, station blaring on the car stereo and people skinning up on the dashboard. Then, when it all comes on top and there's a studio raid, everyone's going, "Well it weren't me."

SOMEWHERE IN LONDON ...

"This is the DJ Zy:on awaiting the arrival of the next DJ … don't know who it is but we'll keep on rolling throughout the weekend. Keep it locked." Bleeep. Bleeep.
"Yo Rude FM. How ya mean, where's the studio? Who's this? … Right you're up next. Well I still can't tell you where the studio is." Click.
Who was that guy? Mix the next tune. Call the management. Peel back the mattress blocking the window, look out hopelessly at the police station across the way, wondering if the place is about to be raided.
"This is DJ Zy:on on the Rude FM. Cause for the calls 0585 8 …"
Bleeep. Bleeep.
"Yo Rude FM."
"I'm outside the door."
"Right."

Click the flap shut, wander to the door hoping that it wasn't all gonna come on top. No spyhole to check the guy out and he's knocking loud enough to wake the dead. Slide back the bolts and pray.

"Sorry man. Got held up at the rave."
I've never seen him before. The guy breezes into the dark hallway. Headphones 'round his neck. Silver box in each hand and a silver record bag emblazoned with his DJ name in fluorescent green. He's definitely not DTI, even they wouldn't be so obvious. Still, he might as well have worn a flashing blue arrow on his head saying, "The studio is HERE."
Talk about hot.

Remember Cool Hand Flex at Centreforce and Kool FM? "Yeah, we had studio busts, it happened but not to me, thank God. If man was caught behind the decks he'd have his records taken, he'd have to take a court case, a fine – whatever. The station is like a family but if you get caught, you were on your own. At the end of the day you were working for the people but you gotta take what's coming to you."

It's really time to split. I pack up my records, sign off and leave him to it.
He rolls his tunes and grabs up the mic.
"This is the DJ Fly-By-Night rockin' ya to da ma-ma-ma-MAXimum on the ten forty tr …"
I'm heading down the corridor, thinking about the guy who's broken every security rule in the book. When we get busted, I can hear him saying, "Well, it weren't me!"

Other people take station security a little more seriously. DJ Kemistry wore a large hat-and-coat disguise when she realised that her station Defektion FM, tended to get raided every time she left with her distinctive locks flowing.

Some outfits are just too street to survive. DJ Zoe once played on a small station broadcasting out of someone's girlfriend's Housing Association flat in Hoxton. "She looked about twelve, thought it was cool and had obviously been completely taken in by all these ruffnecks. They had such a shit transmitter, they could only get as far as Shoreditch, less than a mile." Zoe and co-DJ Marcel played tunes for about a month noticing that every week the whole station was more fucked up. "One week there was all these videos and stereos in the studio and the following week there were dodgy dealings in the kitchen – and crack smells coming out from under the door when we were trying to do our show." As a woman, Zoe felt safe with Marcel alongside but the people hanging around the station were off their heads most of the time. She moved on before the place got raided big time.

Rude FM November '96

DJ Psychic shuffles off down the stairs in mellow mood after his chilled Sunday session. As the ad tape rolls, DJ Syras squeezes into the small studio, ready to play her tunes to the waiting massive. Broadcasting to London and the home counties (from the bathroom), this is Rude FM. MC Pedro syncs up with DJ and the show grows its own rhythm. Way down in the mix the tuner crackles, instantly mashing-up the vibe. "Someone's playing with our rig," explains Syras, taking off her headphones and disappears to find another member of the management. No one's about, so they persevere through the static. Another enthusiastic MC is held back from messing with the transmitter, with a polite but stern warning not to touch the box unless he absolutely knows what he's doing — authorised personnel only. The one like Chillum arrives cradling a box of supplies from the local 7-Eleven. Squatting with his back to the room, Fugee makes the necessary adjustments to the transmitter. With Syras and Pedro battling through with true professionalism, Chillum moves away to deal with some other matters.

Rude FM has had problems like any unlicensed broadcaster. First there's been the usual occupational hassle with the DTI. Then there are the other crews who've been messing around with their transmitters. Worse, someone broke into the studio and cleaned everything out, including the rig. Asking the perpetrators to behave themselves was no good. Their pleas were answered by pulses of noise, as the rig thieves bounced Rude's own pre-set signal back at them Morse code stylee.

Pausing only to build, Chillum rummages through a box to find a soldering iron to repair the mobile and restore the strangely silent phone line. "0585 …" chats the MC over some Metalheadz business. The flat bubbles constantly with activity.

Syras' last tune comes to the end, and Pedro slopes off. The entry phone buzzes with the voices of the next team. In the post- and pre-show banter of the chill out room, MCs joke about new lyrics. Another tries to change his slot complaining that 4pm was an early start for a man on a Sunday.

He's generally cussed. Someone asks if everyone heard Hype's show on Kiss. "Serious. I like Hype, he's got personality." – The babble of male voices continues – "We should get some proper jingles – yeah like with Navigator or Ian Wright. Yeah, check this, "My Name is Winnie Mandela 'n' whenever I'm in London, I listen to Rude FM!" " Shuffling into the bathroom / studio the MC checks the DJs' game plan for the show. "Yo Chopper! You gonna roll it out slowly or going flat out?" Selecting a tune from a ragged plastic bag, the amiable dark-skinned Chopper D grins, "Flat out man. All the way."

Rude FM first switched on in '92. The management remembers back then: "Originally, it was a matter of just switching on and having a party every weekend with people drinking loads and whatever. There were guys passing the time with girlfriends – it's good pulling power saying that you play on a radio station." They weren't looking at the radio as a serious career prospect. In '96 there were some complications. One of the owners had to leave for a short while on her Majesty's business and Chillum automatically offered to help Fugee with whatever needed to be done. It was all new to him. It began with the basics of helping to switch on. As they began to get hit and they needed to buy new equipment, it became a financial thing, which meant going to work. Chillum proved his worth and when the other owner returned he was made a partner of the station.

Rude have DJs as good as their cousins over at Kool FM. With Smokey Jo of Smokers Inc, Magistrate of Eastside, Kendall of True Playaz and Dylan from Droppin' Science, they have their own stock of producers. MCs like Pedro are stepping out on the international circuit. And they've introduced guest slots with Berlin's DJ Sebel, Genotype, Stakka of Liftin' Spirits and vocalist Kirsty Wilcox. Rude FM has become such a reliable station that there is a long queue of aspiring DJs and MCs waiting to join its rosta.

Like Eastman and Brockie, the management listens to demo tapes, eager to help the up-and-comings. It's important to give everyone on the station motivation. Especially if they think it's all a dead-end. Living in the shadow beyond one hundred on the FM dial isn't easy. There was the thought that Kool was where all the big name DJs were, that depressing feeling – "Everyone listens to Kool, no-one listens to us." But the feedback from the street is good. Now it's, "Wow. You're on Rude FM." After three years they've passed an important stage, realising the first lesson is taking yourself seriously.

Listening to your regular station is like checking your favourite rave. It sometimes takes a lot to change habits. But you might be pleasantly surprised by stations like Rude whose DJs continually reach in their boxes to draw different flavours of Jungle / Drum & Bass. You may not hear as many upfront Dub Plates, which Kool's finest play, because much of Rude's music comes on test press or vinyl. But the chances are you will be able to get the tune next day in all good record shops.

Staying on air is one problem for all unlicenced broadcasters. Arranging the station format is another. Like legal broadcasters, Kool and Rude all have occasional, long and loud, democratic meetings to sort out finance, station policy and direction. Schedules are altered. Sometimes people are kicked off, usually for repeatedly failing to make their shows or exhibiting the wrong attitude.

In July '98, due to artistic differences, Rude management split and Ruud Awakening was formed and Rude continued to broadcast.

EASY FM

Outside London where there's less competition, any DJ with the right connections can practically turn up with his tunes and get a slot on a station. That doesn't mean the quality is any poorer — only that there is a huge pool of very talented DJs out there. In '96, when the one like The Wizard enrolled for college in Brighton, he tuned up and down the wave band in despair. It seemed amazing that a place like Brighton, teeming with dance, ready youth and a huge club culture, was only served by BBC Southern Sound. Daniel Nathan and Eugene Pereira's excellent Festival Radio was never given more than a twenty-eight day licence. Eventually, they started the successful Kiss Manchester FM. The Wizard hated the gloomy radio silence that cradled Brighton beyond the South Downs. So he and a mate from his hometown set up Easy FM. At first they didn't really have any DJs so he broadcast Rude FM Christmas tapes.

Back in London Chillum couldn't understand why their phone lines started going mad when they weren't even broadcasting. Brighton's streets now have a soundtrack adding to its Bohemian vibe but Easy FM came and went, as did Pure and Kamikaze FM.

Some are less enthusiastic about pirate radio's contribution to the scene at present. Grooverider, with his own successful show, acknowledges pirates' contribution in the early days of Jungle but he's less impressed in '97, citing style and content as problems.

INTERVIEW WITH GROOVERIDER, JANUARY 1997

G: Pirate radio was important then. More then than now, because everybody trusted their professional judgement. Now they ain't professional. They're so much shit — Joke bizniss.

B: What is unprofessional?

G: The presentation of shows. Half of them don't even speak English. What the fuck's going on? If you're trying to introduce people to this music and they've never heard it before, if they switch on the radio and hear *that*, they'll switch it right back off again — 'cos I switch it off and I know about this music. They've got to get more professional.

B: How much is down to the MCs?

G: A lot of it. But it's not even the MCs, a lot of it is down to the DJs. It's down to them to say to the geezer, "Now just hold that off. I'm going to do my thing." I blame the DJs not the MCs. The MCs are only doing their job. That's what's they're there for. If that's what you want, that's what you call for. You need to present it in a professional manner, so that someone who doesn't know it will want to listen.

B: Is that why Kiss has no MCs?

G: Yeah, and why not? When I listen to other stations I don't hear people MCing down the place. There are people presenting the show and the music, telling the people what's going on. I don't hear people shouting down the place, talking a load of shit. I don't care about this, 'my bredren' thing. I don't care about none of that. 'Cos I'm professional, if I need to say something I'll say it. Don't get me wrong. Some MCs are good. But there's a place and a time for all that and the radio isn't the place for me. Some DJs like it — cool, that's their thing, but I'm not like that.

DEAL WITH THE MATTER

The Selector at Yard FM studio clicked off the mobile kissing his teeth with irritation and twisted around to face his bredren. Some likkle Junglist had the cheek to ring him about Yard FM stealing their frequency. Fe true, they had to borrow the rig that one of the breddahs had found on the twenty-second storey roof last weekend, but de dyamm Junglists cyan juss move aside. Turning back to the single deck, large gold-ringed fingers pushed up the volume of the stark homemade amp. Ragga beats rasped the air. He grinned with satisfaction through the dim smoky light. The orange tip of the Toaster's spliff glinted in the cutlass leaning against the table opposite.

The meeting had been the usual loud but unanimous affair. Bass FM couldn't put up with it any longer. Everyone had their own frequency. They'd been responsible, even rung 'em up. Now Bass would have to deal with the matter.

In spite of the truce of '91, it happened occasionally. Better than back in the day when the DTI or some crew would always be on your case confiscating, stealing or mashing-up your rig. It was urgent, listeners were fickle, you couldn't afford to be off-air for a whole weekend. Press the workers to empty their pockets, hustle for cash or tax someone's rig. Just get back on air. Things had been calmer. Usually it was just a few kids getting over excited at being on for the first time. But this outfit was older, harder and Yard FM was based on that Forest Gate estate. It wasn't a confrontation thing, just a question of manners, proper tings and *their* frequency.

They had to take two cars. Roly insisted on coming along, all 16 stone of him. Roly and that poxy Fiesta. Didn't want to diss the guy, he was part of the crew 'n' all that. Bass FM rolled through heavy late night streets, Yard FM's signal growing stronger as they neared the towers of the estate. Park up. Entering by Exit C, Level 1, the motley crew of six soldiers climbs out the lift on the 22nd floor. The studio could be anywhere. In any one of the flats behind the identical corridors of doors in front of you − or it could be five miles away.

The MC and his girl rub-up in the corner of the studio. The Selector's huge head bounces inside Ragga pulses. Building a spliff, gold teeth, chat through the mic to the Lady from Peckham. 'Wheel & Come again.'

The roof was cold, windy and nasty. Beneath the trap door, Roly had been persuaded to keep the doors of the lift open. Above, three Bass FM boys scanned all points below as two pairs of frozen hands pumped the car jack between the D-lock and the bar holding their rig to the side of the lift mechanism. The brown co-axial cable was the last link between Yard FM and London. Roly's between the lift doors, the lookouts as happy as they could ever be.

Hands on the rig and fingers around the cable. They could be downstairs, they could be five miles away. Bass FM on the case and shitting themselves.

Skanking to the rhythm of his lyrics, string vest sticking to his chest, the MC's hand bangs the table with wine-up vibes. Yard FM pours into kitchens, cars and backroom dens around town − they were runnin'.

Cold metal jaws close around the co-ax. They could be downstairs, they could be five miles away. Deal with the matter, deal with it proppa. Snap.

Static bursts through the studio. Vexation follows the one thought every pirate has when they hear static − the rig. Gold-ringed fingers grab the cutlass from the table as Yard FM bundles out the door. Dead transmitter box in hand … The lift takes ages to descend. There'd been an argument about which floor to get out on and Roly's fat finger had mashed into the fifth button.

The long leather-coated Toaster, big dread-head Selector and Cutlass man arrive at the lift to see it descend past the fourth floor. Breathing settles as the light hits
3. Time to sort out those dyam rig thieves.
2.
1.
The doors open and they steam in flexing like some Kung fu, Tiger Cage business, cutlass flashing, fists flying – inside the empty lift. Five floors above, transmitter box in hand, trainers squeak squeal, running left right across level three walkways, Exit C, Level 3.

On the roof, gold fingers snatch at the broken D-lock. Selector bawls over the edge of the building at the escaping Junglists push-starting a broken down Fiesta. Cutlass and his retribution disappear through the trap door. Too late. The rig rests on the floor in the back of the car as the engine splutters uncertainly to life and Bass FM melt back into the forest of frequencies.

A RUDE AWAKENING: THE RAID

Green digitals blink 05.50
Arrive at studio to find there's no one home.

06.50
Waiting for the management, I try to sleep in the front seat of the car off a dingy back street dual carriageway. Paranoia increases with the headlights in the rear view mirror and diminishes as the sky over the breaker's yard turns from black to grey. The location in the back room of an end of terrace house was safe. But the cul-de-sac was too hot to be sitting around for hours on end in a steamed-up parked car. Neighbourhood don't watch this!

07.09
The management finally arrives and it's still dark enough to mistake the lift shaft's mud and grease for SAS night camouflage. Anyways they were covered from head to foot in the stuff. We unload the studio from a van – monitor, mixer, mic and decks – set up, switch on and I roll out the beats till the next crew slips into the schedule. Shouts come in from a buzzing Potters Bar posse to a mate in the same house.

11.15
Three young lads dressed with pre-rave neatness take their turn to broadcast to London and the surrounding counties. My four hour set done, I leave in the sunshine trying to ignore the twitching net curtains and a guy washing his red Astra looking pointedly in the direction of the house, soap suds slopping down his front. Driving with the stereo on, my man is playing some new sounds – his set is runnin'. I reach home, bell the station to call for the rewind and 'Big up the one like Mellow D.' Saturday morning February sunlight shines through the yard, the weekend shifts into second gear, then … Silence … and terminal static.

Rewind sixty seconds with Mellow D deep in the mix, one MC on the mobile, the other on the mic.

27 minutes after I'd left, the street door splinters against a metal battering ram, and six pairs of grown men's feet stampede up the grungy squat stairs. The crew are too stunned to move as a guy in a suit bursts into the studio, shouting "Everybody stay exactly where you are", his long arm zigzags a badge in the faces of the lads. Backed by uniformed police, the man from the DTI pushes past the DJ, his fist pounds the Technics' stop button and listeners hear static as he reaches behind a cupboard and wrenches out a cable from the link box. On the landing, a second door gives way and another Branch Four man enters carrying a T-shaped ariel. As if reality wasn't stark enough, Mr Stone-faced DTI Man rips out the mattress blocking the window, flooding the room with harsh daylight. A camera fires rapidly at the evidence assembled on the floor, taken along with names, addresses, studio

equipment and records. Calls to the phone line bounce back. And the management announces via the back door connection "We've been hit." Later there'd be rumours about the DJ being thrown into the back of an unmarked van, blindfolded and dumped in the middle of a Hertfordshire field – after he'd spilled the beans. The reality is much less dramatic. No-one tries to barge through the officials, jump or throw records out the first floor window. The DTI gentlemen had done their research. The warrants even had the correct address of the studio. They'd tracked, arrested and charged the crew – a rare collar. But it's all part of the same cycle. And as one DJ retires from the station another steps up to fill his slot.

A Rude Awakening: The Raid – Part Two

8.30pm … News Just In.
DTI and police raid Ruud Awakening Seven Sisters studio. DJs are helping police with their inquiries … I don't believe it – 20 minutes after I left – Silence.

You know when you have a premonition? I remember glancing at the door behind the metal security grid dismissing rising paranoia as just paranoia. During our Friday night *Kick Start* show we'd mentioned a forthcoming Stephen Lawrence Special – Chillum worried about provoking controversy and bringing hell down on all our heads. I remember strolling into the shag pile carpet front room where the management was chilling on the sofa. The home computer screen flashing crucial station details. On the floor a mixer bounded by two Technics 1210s. And the stacks of records in the front room and bedroom. The precious acquisitions of two long time DJs. It's their entire collection. I remember not warning the management again. For once I'd left quickly after the show with Sage and Ron Danger. For once I didn't go on at somebody about making sure all the security was locked down tight.

We were comfortable. We were making an impact and achieving something new in quality pirate radio. I loved that station.

So when the silence came – and it was silence not the static of a rig raid – the horror of the premonitions rolled forward. No answer from the studio mobile. Try the backdoor number and walk straight into, "Yo Chillum …" "Call me back … We've got the DTI here." "You're joking." "No." "As in no? Shit … Later."

The men from the DTI asking, "Where's DJ Zy:on and MC Sage?" In the silence of my Tottenham front room I did the 'How did, What have, What will, What now's?' Confiscations, fines, records made, records destroyed. I felt sick. I feel jinxed. 20 minutes after I'd left.

It is illegal to listen to pirate radio – as if we care.

Inside The Law: Kiss 100 FM

Late '93, early '94 – on stage in front of collected radio bigwigs at a Radio Academy Music Conference, Gordon Mac clicked off the tape spewing Jungle into the hall. He commented, "This is the music of the streets. This is what people are listening to. And none of the networks are playing it – or have the guts to play it."

Emerging from the turbulent years that marked the loss of pioneer DJs like Norman Jay, Kiss 100 FM was realising itself as less of a former pirate station and more of a commercial operation. But the word on the street was that Kiss was losing touch with its listeners. There were allegations that Kiss had an unofficial anti-Jungle policy, though Steve Jackson played the occasional tune. Kiss's own research indicated that they weren't reaching a major part of their potential audience. Behind the scenes, Sarah Groove Connection had been petitioning both Kiss and Radio One with proposals for a Jungle show.

S: I did speak to Lorna Clarke at Kiss. She wasn't interested at first.

B: So how did the Kiss show come about?

S: Well, they'd already seen it was working well for Innovation and seen there was a major market for it in '94. We got a slot on Wednesday night. Ten months later they realised it was doing so well, they got their listening figures and gave us another slot.

Finally, legal stations were acknowledging Jungle. Very much under Groove Connection's guidance, the show, hosted by Grooverider, Fabio, Jumping Jack Frost, Kenny Ken, DJ Rap and Bukem on rotation grew in popularity such that it warranted an additional Friday slot. It's rare for listeners to take the trouble to write in about shows. Kiss received sack loads of mail for the Jungle DJs weeks before they actually broadcast. This was unheard of.

"Listeners to Jungle are a lot more enthusiastic and a lot more active. And they really do take notice of what we're doing, down to every single track."
LORNA CLARKE, KISS 100 FM, JUNGLISM, ZONE UK, 1995

Under the guidance of Lorna and Wilber Wilberforce D&B on kiss FM grew. The tight *crème de la crème* crew, which grew to include Randall and Hype and increased their audience when they started broadcasting across the UK on the Kiss Network, including a live link with Manchester and Yorkshire. In the second quarter of '97, Rajar figures showed 83,000 Londoners listening to the Wednesday 9 till 11pm show and 11,000 listeners for the midnight till 2am Friday slot. DJ Hype's show is extremely popular. One of the reasons that his show has won so many awards is his down-to-earth presentational style. He's always looking for a new audience and his accessibility helps: "I want your mum to laugh and your dad that don't even like Jungle butt will say, "I like that one." It's music for everyone."

The 1990 Broadcasting Act came into effect just as Groove Connection was established. From that point their DJs made a conscious decision not to appear on any more pirates. Knowing that, however much they wanted to, it could seriously complicate matters if they planned to do any legal radio. It was about that time Sarah Sandy sent her first proposal to Radio One.

"I did a whole study and read all the reports – being a bit of a media student. So I wrote a proposal about multi-cultural Dance music, the whole concept. And got back a letter saying, "Nice proposal but we don't really know about Dance music." This was in 1991 - 92. They were really far behind. They didn't have a clue."
SARAH, GROOVE CONNECTION

In fact it took a further three years before Radio One was ready to present the new sound of the Underground.

ONE IN THE JUNGLE

"I thought it was a fight", commented Andy Parfitt, Radio One's Managing Editor. He'd been passing through Crouch End one day when he spied a scrum of youths on the street. Andy stopped and realised the boys were bubbling around a beat box pumping out Jungle. It was early '94, he knew this was the sound of the street – and Radio One should be playing it.

Change in large institutions can take an eternity, but Parfitt was aided by the climate of revolution led by station controller Matthew Bannister. As he initiated a radical change in direction, criticism of Bannister in tabloids, broadsheets, music press and broadcast media mounted. "Poor Old Radio One" (*The Daily Star*), "Listeners Continue to Switch Off" (*The Independent*), "The Great Switch-Off" (*Today*) and "Radio None" (*The Sun*). Everyone reckoned that the national youth resource had lost its way. With few exceptions like John Peel's show, not listening to Radio One was a definite mark of street cred. Perhaps the necessary speed of change alarmed some of the station's more conservative listeners. However, sixteen-year-old Hannah Mummery, youngest member of Radio One's Listeners' Advisory Board, urged them to, "introduce more music like Rap and Dance from outside the charts to broaden the station's appeal." Nigella Lawson writing in *The Times* hit the nail on the head, "I think it should just get people on who like playing records." As the station haemorrhaged millions of young listeners, Bannister moved to employ high-profile youth presenters like Lisa I'Anson and Chris Evans.

Bannister appointee, Trevor Dann, invited suggestions for new programs from the radio pluggers and an idea for a Jungle show was floated. But Andy Parfitt's Jungle fever, discussed at a planning meeting, was still on hold. There was a desire amongst some of the staff to get Jungle on Radio One — indeed, there were plans for a documentary, *Now That's What I Call Jungle*, to be produced by Matt Hall. But no one at the station seemed to know how or where to start when it came to broadcasting an actual Jungle show. How should it feel? What should it be called? And how would the British Broadcasting Corporation contact The Street?

SATURDAY AFTERNOON, WOOD GREEN LIBRARY, SPRING '94:

Next to the cake shop, *Militant* and *Socialist Worker* sellers jockey for position, their slogans interrupted by streams of Jungle Breakbeat booming from yet another BMW bass-bin cruising the high street. Downstairs in the library a tramp, sheltering from the world, holds a Greek paper upside down, hawking up thick globs of phlegm as a disapproving old lady waited to return her large print books. Upstairs the revision crew crammed every table with a spread of files and textbooks. GCSEs, HNDs, BA Hons loomed large as the conscious massive worked to face the final exams. I read the past papers. "Discuss the proposition that modern developments require us to approach the study of International Relations … And, *Was wird aus der Familie?* Translate and précis." It was easier to pick up the Walkman and scan the dial.

Between the crackles and cheesy presenters, over snatches of Ragga, Techno and Lovers Rock, an MC described the scene below on Wood Green High Street. The vibe in the headphones warped space and time. Live performance over sampled sounds, "Where's Ricky? I don't know he just got shot!" intoned voices from a gangsta film. Londoners with weird street names called in to request rewinds. This was some interactive business.

Summer, autumn and winter of '94 were lost in a rush of Jungle raves. Desert Storm, Jungle Fever, World Dance, AWOL at The Paradise,

Telepathy, and Thunder & Joy, with the pirates locked day and night. By January '95, as the papers and BBC Radio Four's own critical program, *Feedback*, continued to be filled with reports of Radio One's decline, a long letter to Matthew Bannister seemed in order. My letter developed into a proposal asking, "Will Matthew Bannister dare to be different?" I'd thought of the title, *One in the Jungle*, listening to Kool FM at home in Tottenham.

Weeks later I was asked to see Andy Parfitt at Radio One. The meeting was short. He was amiable. I / we had a result. A professional raver with the unbelievable dream of putting together the first national Jungle show — *One in the Jungle*. In surreal mood, I met Westwood along Portland Place then stopped outside Top Shop thinking, 'I don't actually know one single DJ, MC or promoter on the Jungle scene.' But I knew the music.

The concept behind *One in the Jungle* was to give a national platform to a range of Jungle / Drum & Bass artists including DJs and producers. I tried to balance regional, musical, even gender considerations. I'd either been blown away by their performance on the Rave scene or heard their music on pirate or mix tape. My list was adopted in its entirety at a second meeting where I was introduced to the other 'team' members, including Trevor Dann and Kate Marsh — two smiley music-executive-types that one instinctively didn't trust. The wider the toothy smile, the less trust. Still, we had a show to do.

The vibe at Radio One was acrid with mistrust. The streets, in contrast, smelt of freedom. There was a slight complication. By this time, I'd become a Trainee TV Researcher at BBC South, so much of the early work setting up the radio show was done via secret calls from my mobile while I was standing in the *Grange Hill* playground at the Elstree studios, or via faxes and letters disguised as research. It had to be done.

I traced DJ Rap through a Ton Promotions ad in ravezine *Prestige*. Rap and her agents, Traci and Nikki, were warm and extremely helpful with contacts. Then there was the process of getting used to speaking to people like Goldie's manager, Trenton or Susie G, the woman who keeps the Fever office running or the DJs themselves and trying not to feel too knocked back by Grooverider's agent, Sarah Sandy when she turned down the show on Groove's behalf as she left for the West Indies.

The format was Kool FM's. The choice of DJs and producers was mine. There was criticism in some quarters that the rosta included non Rave DJs. But I felt that there was more to Radio than Rave. Perhaps the idea of including producers, such as Goldie, Shy FX, A Guy Called Gerald and producer / DJ Roni Size was slightly before its time. It's now extremely common for producers to play out on the DJ circuit. The DJs chose the MCs they most wanted to work with. Goldie and Kenny Ken drew for MC GQ, Brockie and Shy FX for MC Det, Rap for Moose, Roni Size came from Bristol with Dynamite and A Guy Called Gerald insisted on Navigator.

The best part of *One in the Jungle* was dealing with the DJs, MCs, agents and cutting-edge Jungle / Drum & Bass. The worst part was working at Radio One. I had to wise-up very quickly, thinking my way through every aspect of the show and laying awake at night developing the next idea. We needed a chart – call the record shops on the flyers. We need a nationwide gig guide – down to Unity, Black Market and Jungle Fever shops for more flyers, check the 'zines, call the booking agents. We need publicity – a photo shoot, a launch party and what the hell were Radio One's publicity office doing for us? Not a lot. The new Assistant Publicity Officer admitted she knew little about Jungle. As she was sucked deeper into the corporate fold, her initial enthusiasm seemed blunted and I detected a palpable 'hands off' vibe. There was a telling moment when she beamed at me, relishing the prospect of travelling to Glastonbury waving a press pass from Matthew Bannister's Range Rover. My mates and me would be going over the fence. Much of the real administrative support for *One in the Jungle* came from a fellow raver working outside Radio One. There was to be no launch party, no money for further research and Kate Marsh had no problems in announcing that *One in the Jungle* was to be a program made on the cheap. The feeling that 'my baby' was being neglected made me rage in a positive sense. When the going gets tough ... when Jungle stepped up in the national forum, we were gonna come correct. My friend and I began calling every fanzine and music mag for the photo shoot. Everyone bar A Guy called Gerald, who was abroad and Roni Size and Dynamite, who got stuck on the motorway, showed up outside All Souls Church, across from BBC Broadcasting House – Goldie, GQ, Moose, DJ Rap, Kenny Ken, Shy FX, Det and Brockie. The Underground up in the place, standing where Radio One's first wave of pirates had once stood. It felt like history.

Temporarily released from my TV contract, I ran around like a thing possessed. I suppose I was. I gatecrashed the heavyweight intellectuals of Radio Four's *Start the Week* to persuade Melvin Bragg to record a jingle for the Jungle show. He didn't do that sort of thing, "There'd be no end to it." But he was so impressed by my enthusiasm and cheek that he did it anyway. Chasing a veneer of middle class credibility, I dashed up to the *Woman's Hour* office and persuaded them to do an interview with DJ Rap [see *Media*, p.161]. I even tried Radio Four's Arts program, *Kaleidoscope*. But was told by a producer in a rather apologetic whisper, "Our Editor is a bit old-fashioned ... Sorry." No opportunity to raise the music's profile could be missed. Though I did stop just short of persuading an *Archers* producer that Kate Aldrige would spend her time listening to Jungle on pirate stations – just.

Back in Radio One's Egerton House, the arrogance and petty insecurities amongst the station's Production Assistants exemplified the worst elements of the music business. It was wearing and difficult to deal with and so unlike the relatively genteel, civilised vibe that flows through the rest of the Corporation's employees. Though it was amusing to watch Soul Show producer Ivor Etienne dash out the building one day to prevent a Disc Jockey decking someone in the street below. The best time to work in the place was at night, often running into the delightful Annie Nightingale, who'd long since discovered the same thing and also enjoyed the peace and quiet.

I shared a claustrophobic office with Ivor Ettienne who'd been appointed producer of *One in the Jungle*. The planning for the show continued but there were to be problems. Despite the Jungle artists being seasoned professionals with Brockie, Det and Kenny Ken having their own slots on other radio stations, the shows were to be pre-recorded and then broadcast 'as live'. What did that mean? You record it, get the vibe right and do the 'live' as a lie. I wasn't comfortable with it, especially for the kind of show it was to be. There'd be consequences for the punters. During one show, a girl stood in a phone box in Milton Keynes for most of Goldie's set, pleading to speak to her friend GQ. In the corner of the studio the tape rolled – GQ having left a couple of days previously. Though shouts would be taken and given to the MC to read during the next recording, Julie, a punter from the Orkney Islands, who prided herself on being the most northerly Junglist in the British Isles, was amongst those who ended up on the edit suite floor. It didn't seem fair to the listeners.

Kenny Ken

PHOTO BY COURTNEY HAMILTON

Recording each of the original sessions was a memorable, exciting experience. Even if it wasn't always for the right reasons. Within seconds of Goldie rolling the first classic Dub Plate of the first show, calls flooded in from BBC engineers across the country complaining about the distortion. It was the sub-bass wot done it. Shy FX did an impromptu back-to-back with DJ Ash. And Roni Size's session was so good that, dancing 'round the studio, I failed to notice MC Dynamite's voice in the monitor getting louder and separating from, rather than nestling in, the mix. Roni weren't too 'appy.

Rap and Moose

Rap and Moose arrived with friend Archie, Royston (the VIP Champagne Bash calendar designer) and the rest of the posse. The producer Ivor disapproved of the number of people hanging around outside the main studio. He didn't seem to understand that having a crew was important. It's near impossible to build the vibe of a live pirate show in a sterile BBC studio. You definitely need your crew. As the session progressed more of Rap's friends arrived and the intensity of the vibe deepened. The energy flowed through the glass and monitors. As Rap and Moose bashed out a solid set, the room seemed to inhabit some other plane of existence with Oxford Circus a million miles away. The session ended all too quickly.

Wishing for just one more tune and buzzing in the adrenaline afterglow, I noticed Ivor pounding the control desk. He was swearing like a mutha. "What is it? What's wrong? Ivor, what the hell's wrong? That was wicked!" Ivor emitted an anguished sentence. The quarter-inch reel-to-reel tape had flicked over half way through the session — we'd lost the second half of the show. Rap was speechless, Kate's head was in her hands, Moose looked sympathetic and concerned, the crew just looked, I felt like throwing up and Ivor alternated between swearing, pounding the desk and burying his head in his hands. Someone had to take hold of the situation. "Ivor" I said, "Let's go again. We can't let everyone leave, we'll never get the same vibe back." "No we can't," he replied, "the studio is being used for a live show in ten minutes." That previous Saturday I'd been chatting to John Peel in his studio on the floor above. "What about John Peel's studio upstairs?" "No we can't. We can't, we just can't ..." "Okay Ivor, explain to me exactly why we can't move upstairs." Finally sitting up from his head on forearm position Ivor explained, "It's the gear, there's too much gear." But De Man Dem were in the place. "Right Ivor, we've got a studio full of blokes. Royston,

Archie — you grab the decks. Moose — you take one of Rap's record boxes. Big Jason, you take the other. Kate — get all the paper work. Ivor, I'll take the monitor and see you upstairs in John Peel's studio." He followed clutching cables and another reel of quarter inch tape.

With Ivor recovered enough to run the equipment, Rap belted out another session — the crew, especially Big Jason, nodding and dancing in the place. Moose sent a shout of thanks to John Peel for the use of his studio. As we left the building via the underground tunnel between the Radio One building and Broadcasting House, the posse noisy as hell, buzzing with high-five slapping energy, we bumped into Westwood in congratulatory mood. One underground crew met another; The Jungle Massive was moving in. The uniformed security guards in the marble foyer were incredulous but the noise only increased as we left through the giant brass and glass doors. Perhaps it wasn't much in the grand scheme of things but elated outside the BBC, it meant a hell of a lot. Jungle / Drum & Bass on national radio. We'd left Ivor in the building and he didn't look too happy. John Peel's shout never appeared in the broadcast program. I wonder what happened to it Ivor?

IRRITATIONS AND DAMN IRRITATIONS

A warm June evening, Egerton (Studio) One, Radio One FM. Goldie sits with MC GQ recording their biog for the first session of One in the Jungle. Ivor Etienne puts the questions. "What inspires you when you're in the studio?" GQ sighs, shooting a bored glance towards the heavens. Goldie almost snarls at the mic with irritation, "I don't get inspiration when I'm in the studio. I get inspired by things outside, that's why I go into the studio." 'You BBC fools understand nothing,' he might have added.

Kenny Ken and GQ

Thankfully, the middle managers stayed out of the studios for most of the sessions — except during the final recording with Kenny Ken and MC GQ. Squeezing precious studio time in Egerton One, Kenny and GQ arrived to do their set. Kenny's daughter was in the place alongside two fans Juli and Susan who'd made the coach trip up from Dover and sat buzzing outside the studio. With everything ready to roll, the mixer suddenly developed a fault. Minutes ticked away as the producer, then technicians, appeared to re-plug, unscrew and cajole the persistent buzz into submission. With Kenny and GQ growling, "This is supposed to be the BBC", the girls rapidly coming down and the rest of us gutted, the session was postponed until Wednesday, a few tight hours before Kenny's live Kiss FM show.

Wednesday arrived as did GQ and Kenny Ken carrying his own mixer and decks which had *never* left his house before. The two were in a mood to do some serious business. Relying on a table barely big enough to accommodate the equipment and with time passing rapidly, the sound check began. For the first time during the recordings, Executive Producer Wendy Pilmer entered the control room and things took a turn for the worse. As the beats rolled out, GQ couldn't hear himself in the headphones. Pilmer pressed everyone to get on with the session regardless. Struggling to make the best of an impossible situation, GQ finally pulled off the cans ... it wasn't runnin'. The man, who within twelve months was to be voted the industry's Best MC and the 1994 Jungle Sound Clash's DJ Champion were quietly fuming.

Kenny stood arms folded over the decks as the Exec was told that nothing but nothing was going ahead until the problem was sorted." This is supposed to be a national radio station for fuck's sake." As Khan the studio technician worked furiously to rectify the fault, Kenny just about restrained himself from packing his things and leaving the building. Plans to get back home and drop off his daughter before his Kiss show dissolved with the ticking clock. Khan achieved some semblance of an output through GQ's cans but it wasn't enough for him to roll with his usual fluent style over the beats. It seemed that a host of pirates persistently achieve what One FM couldn't. The artists felt compromised. It wasn't a happy experience. On hearing the broadcast show, Kenny, GQ and those of us who'd been involved were saddened thinking about what could have been.

A Guy called Gerald

A Guy called Gerald's set was perhaps the best. Gerald's label manager Craig had worked hard to get him back from the States for the session. Perhaps wisely, they opted to record the session at their own Juice Box Studio near Hammersmith's Riverside Arts Centre. They'd invited Navigator to MC their set that didn't begin until eleven at night. Because there weren't any real shouts before the shows were broadcast, Kate wrote much of the program at home in Tottenham, weaving in names from her imagination, London's pirates and faxes from a few in the know like Louise and Paul at *Eternity* Magazine.

As the session rolled into the night, Navigator skillfully freestyled his own words with those penned in large letters on sheets of A4 stuck to his mic stand with masking tape while Gerald mixed in Doc Scott's *Far Away*. Nav, brow-mopping 'kerchief and mic in hand, strolled around the studio and came with some wicked, spontaneous lyrics.

Leaving the studio after three, gliding East over an empty Westway before turning North through Camden for Tottenham, the raw cassette of the show in the system was for our ears only. 1am, a few warm Summer nights later, we ended up pumping up the sound, windows open and dancing in the back garden ... *Far Away*. The combination of Gerald, Navigator and Doc Scott's tune went down on my secret *Desert Island Discs* list. Retaining the magic, it made you feel above the law with no thoughts of coming in to land. We did land. There was a technical fault. No-one's fault really but *Far Away* was excised from the broadcast version.

Brockie and Det

Kool FM's DJ Brockie and MC Det recorded one of the first pilots. Though I'd heard them on the radio and on endless mix tapes, there was a worrying pause when they first entered the studio. Could they do it? Did I believe they could do it? My mouth went dry as Brockie rolled the tune. Det opened his mouth and it was all over. As the pair unleashed pure demons in the place, anxiety turned to another fear – could the BBC studio take the pace? Oh Mi Gosh. Ten minutes into the session, Ivor began to nod his head as he monitored the levels. It was runnin'. That was the pilot. When their show was recorded for broadcast, two special guests sat in the studio as Brockie and Det performed. Ivor didn't know who Eastman or Susie G were.

The invitation was my way of saying thank you to Kool FM. I scheduled Brockie and Det's show for the last slot in the first series. After they play, people always want more. But at that time, I didn't realise that Radio One wouldn't want more of me.

Despite many problems, *One in the Jungle* had its friends at Radio One who supported the show to the max. Lisa I'Anson read the chart and gig guide, Presentation producer Eddie Temple Morris and sidekick Chalky, obviously buzzed by the artists, enthusiastically made trails for the show. Chris Evans bigged us up on his breakfast slot, DJs Tim Westwood, Mark Tonderai and Annie Nightingale were amongst those expressing enthusiasm for the project and the music. The two most valuable people were John Peel, who gave me moral support and provided much-needed publicity in his weekly column in the *Radio Times* and the doorman Gerald, who really knew the score.

The day arrived, mid-production when my purposely short-term contract came to an end and Ivor asked for all my contact numbers. I was effectively being pushed out before the series I'd helped initiate was concluded. I offered to finish the show for free. But one dark morning, Wendy Pilmer came into the office with a proposal to bar me from the building by implementing Health & Safety regulations.

No one without a BBC contract could stay in the building, which was curious since a daily trail of contractless record pluggers and artists kept the place running. Naturally, I was angry. Though I managed to squeeze in a couple of sessions answering the telephones during the broadcasts, the atmosphere exuded by the production assistants became so odious that my soul was in danger of contamination. This was typical bad Music Business — people who love their positions more than the music. It was time to leave.

Matthew Bannister and Andy Parfitt encouraged me to put in a proposal for a second series. I did, working with professionals from outside Radio One. Live producer AJ Lyons and Kiss Manchester's Daniel Nathan, who'd taught me the radio craft on Brighton's Festival Radio when I was a Sussex student, were to be the team. We wanted to produce a Friday night two-hour live show, free of the Radio One environment. We recorded a pilot with DJ Ron, MCs Strings and The lady Chickaboo. They didn't choose us. Andy Parfitt later apologised to Daniel Nathan. Apparently, the

decision to produce the show 'in-house' had been taken for political reasons. Radio One, the young people's station, had all its cutting edge Dance shows produced by external production companies. What did that say about the regular One FM institution? Heavy with disappointment we accepted the decision, but it was curious to note that the majority of DJs and MCs we proposed appeared in the second series. The format remained generally unchanged but does include outside broadcasts. Wilber Wilberforce arrived to produce the second series of *One in the Jungle*. The show continued to give a range of DJs, MCs and producers a platform to play out nationwide. Though there were remarks from some fans that the show had fallen into an 'Intelligent' trough … *One in the Drum & Bass?* Mickey Finn, DJ Kid and MCs 5ive'O, Stevie Hyper and Fearless also stepped up. Veterans like Reinforced's Dego as well as DJ SS provided some excellent entertainment.

SUMMER '97

Click on the radio Friday night to *One in the Jungle*. DJ SS's intro Dub Plate drops through the speakers. Dash out of bed and the haze of some spliff, frantically tearing at the plastic wrapper on a blank tape. Damn those beats are runnin'. Fine tune. Check the levels. Press record. Turn down the sound of *The Next Generation* and get transported to the rave. DJ SS an alchemist in the mix, just like that time at Telepathy. This is the SS that Goldie and Grooverider praise to the very echo. Don't know the MC. But it sounds kinda ruff, just like a pirate …

NOVEMBER '97

As part of BBC radio's re-organisation, *One in the Jungle* was moved to 2am Saturday morning. There is an argument that the new slot was good for listeners outside London who tend to get home earlier from the clubs. But with nine hours of House, six hours of Hip Hop at peak time and only two hours of Jungle in the early hours of the weekend it seems that Radio One's commitment to Jungle is minimal. January '98, Groove and Fabio leave Kiss 100FM and join Radio One. Now Jungle rests in safe though exclusive hands.

RECORD SHOPS

"The majority of youth today listen to pirate stations. It's like a network. You got the label, companies, you got the radio stations plugging the stuff. They all come into the shop."
NICKY BLACKMARKET, ALL JUNGLISTS, CHANNEL 4, 1994

Aside from the rave itself, record shops are the only real public face of the industry. People pass through not only to buy tunes or mix tapes, but also dance tickets, record bags, sweat shirts, turntable slip mats and bomber jackets marked in the colours of your favourite rave organisation. The outlets come in all shapes and sizes ranging from the designer finished Black Market Records or the labyrinthine Unity Records in Soho to Horace's surprisingly well-stocked market stall, Camden Tunes. All display an overwhelming number of flyers and 'zines; they are an active information centre.

BLACK MARKET RECORDS

The soundclash of softer House beats and Jungle / Drum & Bass starts as you hit the entrance leading down to Black Market's inner sanctum. Punters – Japanese, Germans, Canadians as well as locals pass through, almost as much to pay homage to the beats as to check the latest tunes. No one ever asks for the volume of the twin eighteen-inch JBL speakers to be turned down. It would be sacrilegious to disturb the roll of the B-line. Hand signals and mouth-to-ear shouting are by far the best way to communicate specific enquires. Whenever Ray or Nicky, Clarky, Clive or Ash-a-tak mix in a long awaited dancefloor stormer, interested parties raise their hands or nod their heads like bidders at an auction, staking their claim. Midweek, ravers in suits and ties spend their lunch breaks and the salary they've earned that morning on music that has to be had. There's Balz, an eccentric Swiss distributor buying boxes of tunes for Get Records in Zurich. DJ

Mellow D discerningly stocks up with tunes for his first show on Rude FM. Another punter comes in saying, "I want to buy some tunes. I don't know the names or anything. But, err well, how many fit on a 90 cassette?" On Fridays and Saturdays the heavy atmosphere is even more special. It's the weekend rush and the massive turn out in force.

The scene is the same in shops up and down the country and a variety of tactics, conscious or unconscious, are used to persuade the punters to part with their cash. First there's the sound system: even if it's only one speaker, it's pushed to its sub-bass limit. Then the tune is enhanced in a skillfully cut-up mix as the selector's head nods. And if that hasn't worked, the bass on the desk or amp may be pushed up. If you're still undecided, staff may *even* bubble enthusiastically. As a very last resort, they'll draw a tune from under the counter. "I got one left. I was keeping it for DJ So 'n' So but you can 'ave it. Trust me. It's so baad, you don't even need to hear it first." It's all in good fun and honest enthusiasm. You've had a good shopping trip but sometimes when you reach home, the tune somehow doesn't sound the same.

Soho's Black Market Records is central to JDB history. Nicky Blackmarket set up its Jungle section. "About '92 Hip Hop wasn't working downstairs in the shop. The raving thing was getting so big we decided to move Hip Hop upstairs. Me and Ray Keith, who'd been working at City Sounds, moved downstairs to concentrate on the Breakbeat thing. City Sounds weren't interested and we had people coming down the shop asking for that kind of stuff. It was getting very popular. We were on the same vibe and wanted to concentrate on it. I'm a realistic businessperson and wasn't supporting a charity but we were in it. It was something we could call our own. You had House and Hip Hop coming from the States but this was our thing. It was important. You knew all the people, we were all doing it. There were loads of people like Goldie and his Rufige Crew, all the Reinforced Crew. Seduction was smashing it with his thing. Shut Up & Dance – they were smashing it. In 1992 - 93, you had all the big raves, Telepathy, In the Name of Love, Raindance, Elevation. It just blew up." *NICKY BLACKMARKET*

Ray Keith & Nicky Blackmarket

PHOTO BY TRISTAN O'NEILL

For the employees of most record shops being behind the counter is an excellent place to practice your mixing. Every shop spawns its own crop of DJs, lower rankers, would-be stars or DJ / producers. In the course of a day, they mix their way through a full set of everything that's available. Everything that's runnin'.

In spite of the restrictive Dub Plate culture, for the professional or occasional record buyer the huge quantity of tunes available each week is enough to break most bank accounts. And DJ Ron warns people to be realistic about what they can afford. Music addiction means that you'll buy tunes before putting food on the table. There's been a few times when I've sheepishly had to face my girlfriend Kate, plastic bags full of DJ SS and Dillinja rather than Tesco's own brand. The range of precious tunes is so good that sometimes you have to take your money and run out of the shop before they play yet another gem. For those sensible spenders who can afford it, the record shops usually provide an excellent, deeply knowledgeable and enthusiastic service.

It wasn't always this way. Some underground record shops were citadels of dismissive arrogant aloofness that put off many potential customers. Some found that if you didn't know your stuff, you needn't bother entering. But things changed. Nicky Blackmarket explains as he stands next to the punters award for Best Shop '96, "You can't run a business that way." Especially during a recession. "Most punters don't have huge amounts of money to spend, but a person with a fiver here or a tenner there ... it all keeps things ticking over." Recession or not, the huge proliferation of tunes on sale demonstrate the health and diversity of this underground scene. Though there are seasonal and musical variations in what's available, with over thirty labels selling well one wonders at the sense of any in-fighting between factions of Junglists. Nicky is positive.

"Loads of different people buy tunes which is wicked. I like to see all the different people coming. You can see the trend, Hype, Shy, Goldie and Ray are selling as much as each other. But they're not selling as much as before because there's more choice. I'm very optimistic about the future moving with the times – a *Logical Progression*. This scene will still be here."

HORACE'S MARKET STALL, CAMDEN MARKET, THURSDAY AFTERNOON

"Hey Du Komma Here. Deutsch ya? Komma. You like zis Record?" Horace calls over the trendy blondes. He makes them smile as the tunes rolls, blasting the other semi-frozen market stall owners. A guy in a dapper suit wanders over. "Yo geezer" shouts Horace "haven't seen you since Mannheim. What's happening? Got those tunes for me? Es is guud ya?" The blondes aren't sure. Instantly, Horace draws a tune from another pile, slamming it on the deck before they can answer. A couple almost slip by in the silent hiatus. In that calm before the drop, Horace captures them with a blast of MCing, jigging about for extra effect. The blondes giggle beside themselves. "Tis gut neh? Yeah man, da Bukem tape is blindin'. A fiver to you. So I'll see you Saturday with the tunes." He hands everyone a flyer for some not-to-be-missed night. The blondes depart with three tunes, the couple, with Bukem and Hype tapes and the guy in the suit will get those tunes on Saturday in time for Horace's trip to Berlin's Love Parade.

Visualise a tall, black, boisterous, cheeky chappy, MC / DJing, irrepressible East End market stallholder and you're half way there. Horace, the guy who always seems to be backstage at every major rave started trading in '89, selling tunes at parties like Rage. Over the years his business Camden Tunes has sold music to punters and stars alike including DJ Rap, Goldie, Mickey Finn, Bukem and Frost. Producers would bring him boxes of tunes that he'd shift quickly. The stall was responsible for helping to break tunes like *We Are I.E.*. Boasting a following from Australia to Zimbabwe and with connections in Frankfurt, Berlin and London, the European Union would be proud of him. Horace can speak East End in three different languages. He and his self-professed 'skinny little white' trading partner Olie, a Canterbury undergraduate, are the living sales men. And bwoy do they love their music.

Aside from being points of sale, shops are often closely associated with recording studios, with producers on site making the tunes that weeks, or usually months, later will find their way onto the racks. A nod and a wink from professional buyers and the staff will part with special under-the-counter packages of records best suited to their playing style. Some shops like Re-Run in Bristol take the trouble to write colourful descriptions of each tune on the record sleeves. Promoters pass through to check the resident DJs' diaries, trying to squeeze bookings. Hopefuls pass through to give tapes to the local named DJ behind the counter; perhaps this gives them the start they all so crave. Just as important, shops are an excellent place to hang out.

Forest Gate's Mikey De Underground used his shop to support their record label De Underground. Hype remembers the days when there was a studio in their backroom. It was a special place frequented by guys like Randall and Fats. With people banging on the walls to the freshest of beats, it was like making a tune in a rave. Outside London there's a nationwide network of independent record shops including, Nookie's shop in Hertford, Eastern Bloc in Manchester, Red Eye in Ipswich and KMC's shop in Jungle's most northern foothold, Edinburgh. As well as running Southampton's Tripp 2, its owner Neil also promotes raves around town including one on a specially chartered boat that steams punters around the Solent.

Across the water in Berlin, Ulli Gueldner, known as Rambo because of his ever-present headband and upstanding hair, has managed to stock his shop Downbeat with an incredible selection of records, many of which can only be found with difficulty in England. An excellent idea from Germany's Goa records is its twenty-four hour mail order operation. Tokyo's three shops, Cisco Techno, DMR and Tower records are so well stocked that Japanese visitors to London find few surprises in Black Market, as their suppliers are only two days behind.

Justin's Lucky Spin on London's Holloway Road in association with DJ Pat Brodeur's Mystical Influence helped the launch of Toronto's firin' Jungle / Drum & Bass scene. And Englishman Alan Stevenson with his crew John E and Michael Stein set up X-Static, Toronto's premier record shop, stocked with a mass of UK rave merchandise and not forgetting NYC's Breakbeat Science.

DISTRIBUTORS

Back in '90, producer / DJ Rob Playford carted his boxes of tunes around various shops like many other producers. In one place he spotted a guy with piles of records, leaving some and taking others back. Rob asked what he did. "That'll be the distributor ..." After a few crosschecks with other shops and those in the know, he joined up with Southern Record Distribution (SRD). Producers need to be in the studio, not carting records around, endlessly chasing

cash and stock. Between the large distribution companies and the individual producers hawking their wares around, there are a few independent distributors. They collect tunes from the producers or pressing plants and transport them in small vans, cars and even the tube. Sometimes, their warehouse may be nothing grander than their own front room. Distributors fill the gap between the producer's record label and the shop shelves. For the DJ / producer, they are the major contact with the market place. To any ardent record buyer, a distributor's warehouse, stacked high with vinyl, is heaven.

SRD

SRD was founded in '87. John Knight and John Loder worked out of a box-filled house in Wood Green, supplying tunes for the growing Rave scene. In response to a demand for the music, Southern Record Distribution acted between the shops and the labels, selling the tunes to retail outlets dispatched by parcel post. Five years ago SRD moved to an industrial estate in Tottenham. They now use reps and a fleet of vans to distribute the mass of tunes piled high in their prodigious warehouse.

A distributor's role is not restricted to that of musical postmen. Emma (DJ Wildchild), Label Manager at SRD has responsibility for around eighty labels including Ram, Trouble on Vinyl, Dope Dragon and Full Cycle. She is in regular contact with producers and knows the territory and its players inside out. It's Emma's job to handle the paperwork, inform the labels of the release schedule, acquire DATs of the finished tunes, coordinate artwork for sleeves and labels and persuade the major high street shops to stock JDB.

VINYL DISTRIBUTION

Phil, Lance and Arthur founded vinyl Distribution in November '92. It started as a record shop in Reading before moving to Slough. As distributors of hits like, Alex Reece's *Pulp Fiction* and Adam F's *Metropolis*, alongside SRD, Vinyl Distribution is central to the JDB scene.

SHERI

Sheri, a one woman show, came to Britain from the States in '91, got a job in Mash, Southampton and joined the party. Moving to London, she became more involved in the scene working with a distributor from Stratford. Sheri started to get to know London's independent record shops like Black Market and Lucky Spin. Carrying boxes of tunes on the tube and later by car, she went solo in '94. Horace connected her with Vinyl Distribution and she became another of the foot soldiers getting records into the shops. In January '97, Sheri opened her own shop called Trix Trax.

A PUNTER FROM HASTINGS CALLS LONDON SOME 'TING RECORDS

You occasionally get punters ringing up asking for tunes. But this guy was desperate.
L: 'Allo it's Mr Lee 'ere. Sorry to bother you but 'ave you got *Just 4 U London* or any of them old tunes? They're the ones mate. I'd give me right arm – sell me mum …
B: Sorry, we don't. Have you tried your local shop? How about Vinyl or SRD? Here's the numbers.
L: Ah thanks mate. You dunno 'ow much this means to me.

A few days later …
L: It's Mr Lee 'ere again. Look mate, the distributors won't deal with the public. Sorry, but I've got to 'ave them tunes. There's nothing like 'em. Local record shop? Nah, they can't be bothered. They don't understand. Sorry to hassle you but someone must 'ave them tunes.
[This guy had the Fever bad. He was deep in it.]
B: Okay, I'll give you these numbers but you never got them from me.

Two weeks later, a call from a very excited Mr Lee …
L: Allo, Mr Lee 'ere. No, I'm not phonin' to hassle ya. It's just that … well that number you gave me, well it was Susie G and she spoke to Eastman who gave me Smurf's number. I couldn't believe it. Eastman and Smurf man! I got Smurf out the bath – thought 'e was gonna 'ave a go

at me. What a safe geeza. 'E can get them tunes. I'm comin' up to London this weekend – can't believe it. Jus' wanna say fanks mate. You dunno wot this means to me.

BACK CATALOGUES

With records, it's supply and demand: producers generally don't have the cash to keep boxes of their own tunes around on the off chance that someone will buy them. They have to pay production, artwork, pressing plant and advertising costs up front. But Dance tunes are around for such a relatively short time; the window of purchasing opportunity is narrow.

Would-be customers can find it difficult to get hold of records that are more than a few months old. Though independent producers find it difficult to stockpile huge numbers of records, there are some occasions when tunes are forgotten deep in a distributor's warehouse. Because distributors won't deal with the public directly, punters have to rely on their record shop to place orders for them. There are times when shopkeepers can't be bothered to chase orders and the punter's left out in the cold. Worse, the sought-after tune languishes on someone's shelves.

Perhaps there's a niche for someone to deal exclusively in back catalogues. Some producers like Bukem on Good Looking do very well with their back catalogues. Larger labels like Moving Shadow still keeps the back catalogue rolling. Deep Blue's *The Helicopter Tune* released in '93 is still selling.

People can pay to join a label's mailing list but that can cost a lot of money. There's no guarantee that you'll like all the tunes that producers make for that label. And they don't necessarily have the older tunes which some people want. SRD's John Knight suggests that making connections with your local shop or one in the next town is essential.

Looking to the future, the artist formerly known as Prince has turned to a new flex, further avoiding any kind of economic slavery. He intends to sell his tunes via the Internet. Also, David Bowie's most recent album has been released on the World Wide Web and is downloadable from any computer in the US.

RAVES

*"Nothing's ever given me so much excitement.
No man's given me so much excitement."*
SALLY WOOD GREEN, RAVER

"I'VE BEEN IN IT SINCE THE BLEEPS!"

The doorbell rings as the telephones goes.
The bathroom is road-blocked. The bedroom,
strewn with clothes, is more like an end-of-
sales changing room. The front door opens,
spraying the terraced houses across the road
with the sounds of a DJ Hype mix tape. Pre-rave
mayhem in a two-up, two-down Dover council
house. "Don't you come 'round my 'ouse and tell
me about Breakbeat", Juli yells as she dodges
through her raving posse, slamming the bathroom
door with satisfaction. "I've been in it since
the bleeps!"

Balancing on the side of the bath for full-
mirror effect, she adjusts her white micro mini.
A gold ring through her navel glints in the
stark light against her exposed midriff. Her
red, little-to-the-imagination top clung in all
the right places. Juli gazes into the mirror at
her own growing pupils, her thoughts flittering
and flying. "The little un's wif Mum till
Tuesday … well it's not fair to 'ave kids around
when you're on the come down. Besides, I'm 21,
single, it's Bank Holiday weekend and our own
Kent rave World Dance at Lydd Airport, is down
the road. My 'oliday."

The bathroom door flashes open. "Right everyone,
ready? What's 'ee mean, 'ee's left is ticket at
'ome. Ah, for fuckssake."

Is it arrogant to suggest that Junglists have the best
parties on the planet? Not at 3am in the Jungle tent at
Tribal Gathering, at Heat, Hastings Pier '97 or Champion
of Champions in a downstairs Dalston club.

The parties are hot spots, filled with crucible like intensity,
heat and excitement. The hyper vibes build with people
looking stush, wearing less, spending more, partying harder,
raving to excess. Here the beats are faster, records put
down quicker, x-amount of MCs large it up. Plates on Plates,
champagne, whistles, horns, rewinds, Oh Mi Gosh!
Everyone's on the dancefloor trying to dance and there's no
room to dance. The head nodding, foot-stamping, physical
grinding extends to all corners of the gaff. The heat and
sweat generated by so many bodies is sensual, the music
utterly visceral.

The Lighter tune drops and at the back of the
arena, two girls, different races, same lace
dress, dash down the stairs onto the dancefloor
and jump up with all the innocent enthusiasm
of children.

Raves, dances, parties, call them what you will, are at the
heart of the Dance music industry. Rave is an institution
almost totally reliant on its greatest assets – its people.
Jungle raves are arenas where devotees can go and seek
out the sound of their Dance music. They are places of a
musical coming-together of minds. Jungle is our corner of
a large world. There are other raves to go to, other music
available but it isn't the same as here.

THE CHURCH OF JUNGLE

This is our house … Where did you used to worship? At the Temple of Rare Groove? At the Ministry of Hip Hop? In the Chamber of Techno? In the Mansion of Heavy Rock? The thing with the Church of Jungle is that it allows you to come – needs you to come, with previous musical baggage.

Something brought you here to this spot on the dancefloor, this spot in the box. Perhaps it was a previous affair with Bob Marley, Kraftwerk, Public Enemy, Miles Davis, Buju Banton, James Brown or Rage Against The Machine – you're here now. And it's to do with the kind of energy we produce.

You'll dress smartly if you're part of the pride, a card-carrying member of the tribe. It's part of the ritual. Get on those glad rags, dance till the music stops then baawl for one more tune. Forget the past week. Forget or find yourself.

Sally, Wood Green: "Jungle was like Darth Vader's light sabre going right through me. The music was an expression of what was inside of me, except it was out there in sound form. I could identify with it completely. It was my own little discovery. Jungle freed me." Transfixed by the beats, Sally even found it difficult to leave the arena to go to the loo in case she missed a tune. "I don't know if it was finding Jungle and Es at the same time but it made going out so thrilling. I had the best fun I'd ever had in my life."

Each of the individual raves had their own flava. These regular club nights provided platforms for DJs and MCs alike – Fabio and Grooverider at Rage; Brockie, DJ Ron, Moose and 5ive'O at Telepathy and Roast and Randall, Gachet, Kenny Ken and GQ at AWOL at the Paradise.

There's been several generations of raves since the dawn in 1988 - 89. Rage, Telepathy and Roast in legal venues were shadowed by the original World Dance on the warehouse circuit. There was Dreamscape, 2000 AD became Desire and Biology reformed as Desert Storm. Raindance was granted one of the first licences. And after 1992 - 93 the massive followed; AWOL at the Paradise, Thunder and Joy, Jungle

Fever, VIP Champagne Bash, Roller Express, Champion of Champions, Carnival, Stush, Run It Red, Voodoo Magic, One Nation, Pure X, Heat and a host of others. The related Elevation, Ravelation and Innovation parties bubbled around the edge of the Jungle scene, as did Rezerection and Helter Skelter, initially known more for their Happy Hardcore contribution. Speed started by Autumn '94, opening the way for Bukem and Intelligent Drum & Bass. Hardcore, Jungle / Drum & Bass has been pumped out on the free warehouse circuit since Jungle's inception. After that, everything spread like wildfire.

THE NIGHTS OF RAGE

"When it came to clubs, Rage was the place. Thursday night, Grooverider and Fabio WHAT!! Man dem buck-up riddim like a muthafucka in the place. The wickedest B-lines in Rave. Man, the floorboards were shaking … Clean, kriss, bass." MC 5IVE'O

It's difficult to analyse or know exactly why certain clubs have the magic ingredient – creating a special vibe. But over a Hardcore Breakbeat soundtrack, Rage at Heaven had it.

Grooverider and Fabio had already played through the early hours to ravers looking for an after party at a club called Mendoza's and at Sunrise on the large rave circuit, when they were invited to play a back room at Rage based in club Heaven, central London. As their slot took off, Grooverider and Fabio moved to the main floor. Many industry people around today blushingly remember dancing on podiums, learning about mixing by watching the two at close quarters and screaming, "Jungle", whenever they heard those strange drum beats which had infiltrated their sounds by '91. Rage was the only place to be. People occasionally drifted to different clubs, checking the scene elsewhere but they always seemed to return. It continued from '89 till '92. The atmosphere of Rage was like nowhere else. Musically, like Farringdon's Sunday Roast and East London's Telepathy, the DJs now concentrated on playing Breakbeat Jungle.

"And This One Will Put You in a Trance ..."
AWOL at The Paradise

"I used to go to AWOL religiously from '93-'95 and hear all the DJs: Randall, Mickey, Kenny, Gachet and Darren Jay with GQ MCing all night. That was school for me. You used to get two hours of each DJ. You'd be exposed to all the different wicked styles of music and you used to hear some mad mixing; especially at 10 o'clock in the morning. Some weeks it didn't finish until one in the afternoon. It was definitely inspirational." ANDY C

It's easy to put people's fond memories of certain clubs down to nostalgia. But with AWOL at Islington's Paradise club, there was definitely something special. The place had all the right ingredients, perhaps growing beyond what Jay, the promoter and crew, had expected. Together they built a home for Jungle / Drum & Bass. A range of DJs including Trevor Fung and Richie Fingers played before the rosta was distilled down to Kenny Ken, Darren Jay, Mickey Finn, Dr S Gachet and Randall. If one DJ played a tune, it wasn't repeated by the others. The club was intimate, the sound system phat and the DJs (resident MC GQ) and audience contributed to a one hundred and ten percent atmosphere. Regular punters included a guy in a wheelchair, rocking, waving and absolutely drenched in sweat. Customers and artists alike remember just visiting the club, staying immersed in the vibe as deeply as possible, for as long as possible.

"You weren't going there to hear the same beats. What we was doing was about education. If you as a DJ weren't going off, the crowd would let you know. Not by booing or anything. But if you was goin' off, Mi Gosh you would know. We went from the front of the club, right through to the back. All the DJs would stay there after their sets. Groove and Fabio would pass by. Goldie would be there with his head in a speaker – Randall would be tearin' the arse out of it. Kenny Ken would snake through the club and plant his hand over the edge of the DJ box, stopping the record for the rewind. No matter what there is now, and certain clubs like Metalheadz and Movement and all the others that are going off, you'll never get that vibe again. There was no politics 'n' shit. Everybody would be there. I'm just glad I was involved with that era. You'll never get that again."
MC GQ

Jungle Soundclash

"Back in '93, most Jungle events at the time were a thousand plus. They were always an event. And spectacular in their execution every time ..."
DAVE STONE, SOUR

The Jungle Soundclash at Roller Express, Edmonton was a case in point. An exercise born of the best excesses of the Jungle massive – a hangover from the sound system days. It was loosely billed as a competition to the death between the best DJs who'd rise to the musical challenge. The crowd's votes measured in decibels were registered by screams, whistles, horns and rewinds.

"... It was fucking amazing. The decks in a boxing ring, Moose and 5ive'O wearing dickie bows – ringing a bell. The crowd controlling the DJs – screaming for the rewinds and getting them. It certainly was a spectacle. Rap got death threats on her answering machine warning that, if she played *Incredible*, she would get killed. The BBC had been told to stay away. Rap started her set with *Incredible* and finished with three rewinds of *Nuttah*. Kenny Ken went on to win drawing freshly cut Congo Natty Dub Plates. The atmosphere, the vibes. I've never felt such togetherness."
DAVE STONE, SOUR

Colours

"This is the only music format that I know that's ever brought so many races under one roof. Hip Hop's never done that. Reggae's never done that. Rock and Pop's never done that." MC 5IVE'O, JUNGLISM, ZONE UK, 1995

There is a perception that few black people attended the early raves although a World Dance video shot in '89 clearly shows a crowd as ethnically-mixed as Wood Green, well almost. The racial make-up of rave audiences depends mostly on location and demographics.

Eastman remembers his friends Brockie and MC Cogee raving in '89. "They used to tell me how great they were. People loved you, give you their water – I used to tease them and we'd laugh about it."

There was a media-fuelled perception that Jungle was a 'black thing.' Back in '88, when black people were getting knocked back from certain West End clubs, they found the embryonic Rave Culture far more inclusive and colour was less of an issue.

"It didn't run that there was a race thing involved in the scene. Andy Swallow at Centreforce was rumoured to be with the ICF (Inter City Firm) lot. I would shake Swallow's hand without a thought, 'cos he brought my brothers in. He heard what they was dealing with and said come. There was a minority of black people in the raves at that time. When we went, we couldn't believe white people coming up to us saying, "How you doing mate? Do ya want some of this? You alright?" We couldn't believe it. We couldn't walk into certain pubs without asking for trouble. Then to go amongst a few hundred of them in a warehouse in the middle of nowhere and be welcomed, greeted. We never experienced anything like that. It was NICE. I found a new exclusive lick where I could mingle with people from this land." *Mikey, De Underground*

Steve from Dover didn't feel himself to be racist but feels there is a difference in the way in which people grow up. "That affects the way people party." He talks about the quality of the vibe in a rave like the Laserdrome in Peckham being different to his local rave at Lydd in Kent. There were black people in both but in greater quantities at the Laserdrome than at World Dance. "When *It's the Way* dropped, big guys were going mental, screaming for the rewind. Jumping up and down, banging the walls, horns and whistles going off." Being British without the reserve. Englishmen raving and going insane.

"No denying it. The way I see it is this. I'm just gonna talk it real. In '94 I'll never forget standing outside the Astoria and this young black guy was trying to get in and they said, "No you can't come in." He said, "But you're playing my fuckin' music in there." That resonated with me. The thing is, there's no getting away from it. There was an element where it was a bit dangerous in terms of the racial mix. You've got to remember that people live on the road, live by their wits and live a very tough hard existence. And then you've white people who may live in Essex or Kent. You push those two together ... You can't put the wolves in with

the lambs. I do believe it had got a bit bad and a lot of violence was kicking off in Jungle raves. I've seen a lot of violence at my own raves and others. And I think there was an element that said, "I don't want to be involved in this." So that's where a split came. *Bret, Telepathy*

For many it was a process of multicultural education. Raving is about coming together. In being and dancing together, all sorts of changes are possible. But you've got to do the work to make a real multicultural society that understands the nature of its different elements. Perhaps in the end, all the separate ingredients in the pot will melt together. But Smiley of Shut Up & Dance feels the Rave scene changes nothing. Remember Stephen Lawrence.

SERIOUS JOY

There was danger, real or imagined in the music. Militancy in the beats — hyper intensity. It felt fresh. You had to like this new music a lot and be brave enough to go and seek it out. It was truly underground. The energy levels were different, perhaps because of the music or the people, or the inner city areas were you'd have to seek out. The edge present in Jungle raves created a different level of hectic, wild, uncontrollable, militant energy. And dancing was very serious. Exuberance without the gaiety, pleasure without the grins.

Initially, it was go out and rave in any space you could find. Everyone was in it together. Part of the magic arose from transforming an often derelict space into something for which it was never intended. The Ebeneez were good. It had all been so special with ravers feeling they were members of a community. Then it went mainstream. When the CJA (Criminal Justice Act) pushed the Rave scene indoors, it became increasingly institutionalised. There was also rumoured to be a lot of shit E around — Not to mention crack and coke. Clubbing became more exclusive and the scene more fractured. The mood also became darker. During 1993 - 94, as the Ragga crowds flooded into Jungle, problems of race and Attitude became more of an issue when the Dance Hall mood barged in. New music but with the old club rules. "Don't step on my trainers. What da fuck do you think you are doing? Don't talk to me. Don't look at me. Are you chatting to my bloke? Is he chatting to you?" The too-cool-to-move brigade made a come back. The press also turned its focus on the scene around the same time. Troubles in the dance weren't something the Jungle family wanted to discuss in public and they were slow to deal with it. Punters, black and white, shied away from certain venues or events, feeling they were more trouble than they were worth. A million miles from the fields, sporadic fights broke out. They tended to be a territorial thing, just as much present in the after-hours violence of a small town on a Saturday night, as it was on the dancefloor. Grooverider remembers that there's always been punch-ups at raves. But these problems seemed to be more severe.

Some neighbourhoods are rough. You get excited young people, who aren't going to stand in the queue waiting patiently for their turn to party. They want to take the place by storm and end up bum-rushing everyone, aided by those queuing and holding onto that English reserve, not saying anything, 'cos you don't like to.' There's also a human fear that being vocal will lead to a fight you can't possibly win. These youths come from further down the street and have more Attitude than you. Best say nothing. After all, hanging on in quiet desperation is the English way.

FULL ON, HANDS OFF

Some women have experienced sexual harassment in the dance. Completely lost in the music, dancing to the tribal vibe, Sally, eyes closed, would move within the beats dancing on her limbs. Some people would clap or smile, seeing the ecstatic expression on her face, and say, "Ah bless her." But when the 'Dance Hall' vibe overwhelmed Jungle arenas, opening her eyes, she really had to check herself and ask, "What have I just suggested to these boys with their tongues hanging out? I'm a physical person. But I was getting the wrong attention. These boys are really thinking I mean, "Come and get me". "

IT'S THE WEEKEND RUSH

The rush — let's not play this down. At its best you're in the sixth dimension. Music carries you up, flows through you creating images, shades of light and dark. Synethesia — you're seeing sound. Making love on a thunderstorm-ridden coastline. Another form of energy, as pure as light and heat. The essence of life, ethereal fire.

The intensity subsides but the waves remain, diminishing in their force to carry you with them. Decide: do you catch the next wave which will take you to an almighty crest again? "Christ yes. A cheeky half? Oh go on then. No, I've seen the other side. I'm not ready for it yet." The music just swaddles you in its arms. Bwoy it jus' tek you. It's time to pump up the sound and metamorphosise with the world, gwan. We're all in cars, living rooms, bedrooms, screaming for the reeewind. "Come again Selecta, come again. Engineer, more volume please."

All participate, all perform. Dance close, groin on ass, groin on groin, look wicked but don't touch. A complex, contradictory, honest moment we won't exchange numbers but hey thanks, that was wicked. "Mi Gosh come Selecta, Brockie, Andy C, over to the Skibadee."

The last tune is a ritual. The DJs and the crowd are one as you come face-to-face with the authority that tells you to turn the music off. It's the same stage — cut to World Dance, cut to the Confusion Stand at Notting Hill Carnival — the slow motion pleading with security, the police and the awareness that the end of heaven is nigh. The DJ makes a pact with the crowd and slips a hidden record into the mix under the eye of the law. And the crowd respond to that sweetest last tune. Thank you for this moment which melts into glorious digital memories. The selector drops *Circles*, the notes express the joy of life itself. It's the new *Fanfare for the Common Man*. It's only when the last DJ is rinsed out that you say person-to-person, alright mate, you can get your records and go home with your crew and our love.

It's Britain today, as real as John Major's genteel lady cycling through a country village to the sound of church bells. The reality is that we found reason to come out of our inner city boroughs. We may sit in our motors listening to Drum & Bass, Techno, Hardcore but in coming to see your reality it became our reality. We can begin to understand our heritage. MC 5ive'O shouts, "Meeting people from Blackburn, Glasgow, Brighton, Bristol – we discovered the Shires, man."

Was it the tape, pirate radio stations or all those mobiles causing us to home in? Determined as heat-seeking missiles fully tuned up and hungry to party. Oh, and I'll be back on Monday, meeting at 10am, honest.

STYLE

The class of '93 brought in a new dress code, with the old hooded tops finally giving way to big designer labels. Paul Roast remembers the changing attitude among ravers. "They'd do themselves up like they were going to an old style dance." Perhaps it was a backlash against the practical rave gear, or just a different cultural attitude displayed by the new crowds going out in all their finery, celebrating to the max.

"Style has always been a major part of the black community. They weren't wearing no beat-out trainers and baggy t-shirts and say they're going out. They brought in labels." MIKEY, DE UNDERGROUND

The new styles went right from elaborately curled, sprayed and razor patterned hair, brightly-coloured matching designer clothes with prominent branding – for you and your mates – to patent leather, knee high boots and training shoes. Big sunglasses obligatory, gold jewellery desirable. Picked and mixed designer, made at home, market stall and off the back of a lorry gear. Go out and large-it-up in clothes as loud as the music.

DANCING

Upstairs in the circle, on the stairs, 'round the bar, in the aisles, by the toilets, on the dancefloor, dancing everywhere, the Techno raver of old turned with awed disbelief to her friends and says, "My God, people do love their Jungle." JANE, A PUNTER AT METALHEADZ FORUM, HER FIRST JUNGLE RAVE

"Dancing isn't everything but it can help you understand the music more deeply ..." JUMPING JACK FROST, 1997

In the early days of Rave it didn't matter how you danced. It was just get right on one matey, blow your horn and let off. People still dressed for comfort especially in the heat of a long night. But gradually, fashion and dance styles developed and people started to check each other. Looking around the crowd you get snapshots of people raving. The bredren spars dancing opposite each other, hankies, lighters and horns waved aloft, lines of women strutting confidently, the couple grinding in the middle of the floor and individuals brockin' out on the stairs, stage or podium.

One of the first comments you hear from someone new to the JDB scene is, "How do you dance to the music – it's so fast?" To the uninitiated, Jungle can seem hectic and the thought of furiously jumping to the pace of the hi-hat all night is somewhat daunting. DJ Zoe recalls, "When Jungle emerged from Hardcore there were the early tunes that had the half time basslines and you'd dance differently to it. The first place I remember with lots of people dancing differently was at Spiral Tribe." The second comment you hear as the new club-goer watches the people around him or her is, "Oh, but you can dance really slowly." The key to Jungle is that you can choose your beat, dance at a pace to suit yourself, follow the bass, the drums or combinations of both and ride the riddim.

When you're abroad, breaking new territories with the DJs and MCs, you can often judge how long the music has been around by the progress of the dancers. On tour in Berlin with Sour at the '95 Love Parade, some of the new punters were clearly having difficulty coordinating their enthusiasm with rhythm. A year later, at the Kool FM rave in Mannheim, though some German ravers were overheard asking their British cousins to show them how to dance, the vast majority had obviously got it. They'd developed their own dance language, a different accent from the UK home turf but it was alright. That was how they were dropping it. There's flexibility, everything runs from crazy legs to break dancing, Rave-yer-hands-in-the-air stomp and rub-up-inna Reggae stylee. In the States, DJ Ron played to a floor which was less of a heaving mass and more a clump of circles with people breaking in their midst.

A sign of our increasingly multicultural society is that no one can confidently generalise, "White people can't dance." Times have changed.

ALL THAT'S FINISHED NOW ...

In the TV production office of Goldie's Channel 4 pilot, *Fereala*, Summer '96, a couple of researchers view the rushes from the previous night out with Randall. In the office overlooking Brixton High Street, the energy of the dancers still radiated powerfully from the screen. As the camera pans across the AWOL crowd dancing to Metropolis, the male researcher asks, "What happened to all that 'white girls can't dance as well as black girls' business?" "Na," says Eulenea, the black female researcher. "Naw, naw, all that's finished now." "Yeah. Too right!"

Ultimately it's about enjoyment. You should just do what you do – it's about you. There are movements which a lot of people find best express themselves and the music. But copying informally choreographed steps can be limiting rather than liberating. At the end of the day as MC Det often says, "If you can't dance, just nod your head." Express yourself. "You come here to dance. Just drop the whole week. The whole thing that happened in the week. Just drop it off and rave."
AWOL PUNTER, ALL JUNGLISTS, CHANNEL 4, 1994

Sitting comfortably crossed-legged on the grass at the '97 Green Gathering, Amritar, an Anglo-Buddhist monk and former raver, explains that, in Western society, intellectual ability is prioritised over the physical. It has consequences. "I found on the whole that people's ability to live in their bodies – inhabit their physicality, is quite poor. Low self-esteem, paranoia, reflects the way people actually live in their bodies. With dancing, people get out of their minds into a much more physically grounded, immediate way of being. It can be very liberating. Which is why I think dance is very important. It changes one's patterns of thought, by being more grounded in one's physical experience. The whole energy of dancing, moving, getting your energy up, chest open, smiling, making eye contact, gives you a much better sense of your self."
AMRITAR, FRIENDS OF THE WESTERN BUDDHIST ORDER (FWBO)

DESPERATELY SEEKING SOMETHING

Humans need entertainment. We're easily bored, perhaps even empty without it. Raves provide excellent entertainment for all those people who've always felt that it wasn't enough to sit in on a Friday night, watch the box and go to bed early. In the dance, you become the participant observer. Rave meets our needs for collective ritual. "Human beings have a deep need for ritual experience. They need to come together and confirm our world view of what we're doing with our lives." Amritar feels that with the advent of Rave Culture, festival culture actually moved into the city. People met, networked, swapped information, ideas and contacts. Perhaps, even the physical taking of the 'sacrament' E was in some way part of the whole ritual. In a godless society, this is where people wear their Sunday best. Aside from being a bloody good laugh, does the whole thing have a purpose? In the midst of the mayhem, DJs and punters alike can catch themselves experiencing an existential crisis. "I'm being paid to stand here for an hour and play music to this hall full of people and make them dance." Or alternatively, "I've spent x-amount to be here now dancing with all these other people who've done the same."

Throughout the world, societies past and present have recognised the need to dance. "We've seen man heavy with the weight of the world come into our raves. Boy he's gonna be trouble, we think. See the same man at the end of the rave skipping, skipping." STING, TELEPATHY

Jungian psychology and American Indian philosophy recognise three levels of consciousness. The first, 'consciousness', the second, the 'individual unconscious' and the third, the 'collective unconscious'. When we reach that third level, they say, it is then we feel at peace and one with others and ourselves. The American Indians use dance in ceremonies to reach the collective unconscious.

Fabio

Then there's the guy who gave us 'Another E please Bob' – Alexander Shulgin, scientist and modern godfather of Ecstasy. He and his wife Anne believe that, "one of MDMA's assets is a partial passport to a night's freedom. It dissolves paranoia. One of the great fears that everyone has is that the 'essential self' is a terrible thing. This is a basic unconscious fear and E replaces it with a tremendously peaceful acceptance, not just for yourself but of other people." *ANNE SHULGIN, BIG ISSUE, JULY 1997*

LOOK DON'T TOUCH

You know it's a good one when it hits you in the groin. Just as well it's look don't touch or you'd screw your way through every woman in the place. Shit! Does everyone feel like this? They sit on the stairs near the back of the venue. While they share water, innocently or not, Mickey Finn slams downs the Dub Plates, somewhere in the distance through the lasers. They chat, innocently or not, throughout the set locked in the mix of some other journey.

It's look don't touch. That beautiful face which hovers close to your ear. Look don't touch. The curves of her body in that minimal white dress. You fall into her saucer-sized pupils. Time and again you incline your head to hear her speak and you're looking down a perfect cleavage. Then break away and dance like a bastard with the World Dance massive.

Look don't touch plants a kiss on your lips, tongue tip pushing half a pill in your mouth. The ghastly bitterness – expectation of ecstatic sweet. She's cheekily nuzzling her body against your crotch. Writhing with pubescent-like energy.

Lost in Randall's beats, snogging to *Black … And I will always love you*. She takes your hand and leads you out to the shadowed row of Portaloos beyond the fairground. Her bare shoulders are up against the plastic wall. The white dress crumpled around her waist, you pound

frantically, gently, the loo roll holder banging against her hips. Go on till you can't – without end, without orgasm.

Turfing the condom, adjusting your clothing, you walk back, paranoid, past giggling ravers into a throng where the beat goes on and on … *I was a fool to let you love me. I was a fool to let you in.*

SPEED

Leo opened Speed in October '94 through his connection DJ Nicky Holloway. After visiting the club in its first empty weeks, Kemistry & Storm helped with some ideas. They established a large guest list by constantly phoning members of the Jungle family across the board. Sarah Groove Connection joined suggesting the move from a Monday to a Thursday night and a change of DJ line-up which brought together Fabio and Bukem and took Speed to a new level. Sarah & Fabio had been looking for a small West End club where they could promote the huge numbers of tunes which producers gave them. No other clubs were playing what people now know as Drum & Bass. They also hoped to exclude the 'dodgy' crowd.

Based in the West End's Mars club, Speed offered small, casual, safe mid-week clubbing where the music was mellow in comparison with the hyper vibes of the traditional Jungle rave arena. On the first night, there were only five or six people inside the Mars Club. DJ Zoe and a friend Anne remember being the first on the dancefloor. At the time it was unusual to have a Jungle dance in the West End. But it was a welcome addition to London's club scene for those who did want a different sort of Jungle. In due course, the club was filled to capacity. Though Goldie and Trenton still went to the Laserdrome, Speed was the place where they could chill out. DJ / producer LTJ Bukem & MC Conrad made their names there and producers Source Direct and Photek found somewhere to hear their tunes played. It was a fertile environment in which Drum & Bass grew. Interested record companies and their A&R men soon went down to catch the new sounds. It was around this time the term 'Intelligent' was used to describe the less rugged style of music, with far reaching consequences for the rest of the scene.

"The music was good, spacey. Not what you'd want for a Saturday night but this was good. We went quite a few times and it picked up by the end of '94. That was the split from Jungle. But I just thought it was different kinds of styles with a different kind of energy. It was the first time that you could hear whole sets of Drum & Bass." *DJ ZOE*

Some Jungle artists who dropped by found it too tame. Brockie and Det were bored. Sally from Wood Green found it musically light and the crowd "too officey". But Speed and its DJs attracted a lot of favourable media attention. Journalists seemed to feel more positive towards the gentler sounds and chilled out punters. To them, Speed represented the safer face of Jungle.

Sarah Groove Connection denies that Speed was a media club believing that their crowd came from a total cross-section of punters. Though she agrees that the media did attract the 'trendy.' Sarah feels that the hugely popular club met its demise when journalists meddled and things became too big.

"The media started coming down and tearing it apart. They were talking about deep separations. Leo started reading all the magazines and believing them more than what we felt was happening to the music and it caused a rift between us. In my opinion, it was working because it had such a strong identity. But Leo and I started falling out because he didn't really understand. He was really caught up in the media and we'd seen it all before. They liked causing confusion. So we had to be careful. The atmosphere between Leo and myself was so bad that he kicked us out when we were on holiday. So we left and it fell apart. That was June '96." *SARAH, GROOVE CONNECTION*

In the Jungle / Drum & Bass debate, Speed was definitely Drum & Bass. It was the clubbing precursor of the Blue Note Metalheadz sessions. Perhaps it was Goldie's personal energy, the heavier selection of beats, together with Grooverider's touch on the decks, which made the difference between Speed and the Blue Note.

THE METALHEADZ SESSIONS AT THE BLUE NOTE

"The whole purpose of the Blue Note is to hear something new. You have to make that environment for yourself." GOLDIE, OPEN FORUM, KOOL FM, 1996

December '95 and Winter has set in good and proper. Outside the Blue Note the queue of fatter than phat puffa jackets stretches around the corner. Guvnor commands the guest list and Goldie's Merc sits outside the front door bristling with Attitude. Sunday night, 10pm. There is a tangible buzz in the air. Even with work the next day, you're drawn in. You weren't going to hear this music anywhere else. And Mi Gosh did it set you up for the week.

In the early part of a Metalheadz evening there are breakdancers spinning on their heads as Goldie plays the first set. By the end of the night, every cranny is filled with the jump-up massive. Upstairs, people sit talking, nodding, eating, drinking in an old school atmosphere. Frequent bouts of mayhem burst through from the floor below and people are dragged downstairs by thunderous rewinds. The punters are a mixture of students and Tottenham boys, Soho trendies, celebrities, industry and tourists. Swaddled in Eskimo Noise's sound system and swathed by video artist Justin Keery's dense visuals, they're dancing in the alcoves, breaking out on the stairs and losing it on the stage. The Metalheadz Blue Note Sessions had all the elements of an intimate classic rave. With Sunday after Sunday of serious nights, one wonders if this is what it felt like to party at Rage or the Paradise?

Founded in July '95, every week, the Metalheadz Sessions felt like club history in the making. It was based in Hoxton Square's Blue Note, the former home of London Jazz club, the Bass Clef. In Jazz theory, a blue note is an off-pitch sound common to African — but not European — music scales and rhythms. A distinct sound. The Blue Note was a distinct place.

MOVEMENT

In '94, Jumping Jack Frost and Dave Stone decided to co-promote a club event. A year later, along with Frost's label mate, Bryan Gee, set up Movement at club Embargos, Chelsea, relocating to the more central Bar Rumba in the West End. Another night which can't wait for the weekend, the emphasis is on quality music and vibes. Bryan Gee and Dave Stone see the club as an extension of their record labels. The tunes played in Movement clearly reflect the wider circumference of Jungle / Drum & Bass. Dave and Bryan take a hands on approach to the club, actually handing out flyers themselves. The night is another in the more intimate mould, with a good mixture of tourists, industry and faithful punters enjoying an exceptional Thursday night roll out. The MCs, who include Det and IC3 have managed to achieve a harmonious balance with the DJs.

A club in the right place at the right time, it became the focus for post Mercury Award celebrations, when around fifty of the guests including prize winner Roni Size, continued to party on at Movement's home ground. Like Rage, Roast, AWOL, Speed and Metalheadz, there is a feeling on the dancefloor that this is a ground-breaking place.

FEVER GOES TO MANNHEIM – WINTER '96

Most of the DJs and MCs had flown ahead. In typical style a third of the ravers failed to make the coach even though Susie G had wisely conned everyone into turning up a full hour before the real departure time.

The coach reached Dover too late for the early ferry. Punters milled around the dockside as distinct from the grey-haired day trippers as from a well turned out school party. But their uniform was designer kriss with sharp coiffure, curled, razored hair and bright fabrics. As the morning mist cleared above the white cliffs, talk was of Grooverider, Goldie and the Jungle Awards. Patois mingled with East End / North London chat as the second bottle of Napoleon Brandy was passed liberally around the coach. Black, white, Asian, multicultural junglists, with those cliffs towering behind us. This was home. And we were all as English as they come.

The Jungle Fever crew were taking Jungle to Europe, except this time they'd be waiting for us, waiting to party. Riding the crest of a wave, you could feel Drum & Bass growing.

"Driver 'scuse me. Mind if we stick this tape in the system?" One of the uniformed Geordie drivers clunks the cassette into the machine unleashing MC Det in full flow at Telepathy, "What's gwaning" and calling for the engineer to "Boost the volume." By the time Skibadee joined the mix, the mature Geordie drivers were swaying to the music in spite of themselves. It was 9.15am.

Stepping further into the Jungle, talk went deep. MCs' styles, DJ flexes, the state of the station, and all to a soundtrack of DJ Brockie, MC Det, Flinty Bad Man and New York City's TC Izlam.

When you reach a clearing in the Jungle, clarity and understanding descend. We've all reached this point from different paths. Anita from Charlton, the Rewind Queen, is originally rooted in Heavy Rock, DJ Swan-e original Hardcore man, now rolling out the Drum & Bass beats, MC Det a Hip Hop man, Susan from Dove, a Stone Roses Indie kid.

Russian was one punter who didn't make it to Germany. In a sea of ravers, a few stand out, Russian was one of them. A big mutha of a guy, often seen sweat streaked, dark skinned, bald headed and straight faced on many a pumping stage. Resplendent in string vest and Ray Bans, he alternates between rock solid stances and bounding, jump up madness. Sporadically, he points people out with a knife-like jab and beckons you over with a commanding 'SAS' wave of the wrist. After he releases your hand from his vice of a grip, you're free to go. Relocating your shoulder in its joint, you realise that for a few seconds you'd shared a moment of extreme warmth. As he saunters or bounces through the crowd, mopping his head with a 'kerchief or blasting his horn, you could tell he wasn't just enjoying himself, he was having a blinda. It was a shame he hadn't made the trip. But it would have been weird to see him in broad daylight, even exchange a few words. He along with others are the best supporting actors on a bass blasted Jungle Fever, Telepathy or World Dance stage …

And Mannheim …? It such a kicking party that I was too rinsed out to finish my notes. It was one of those … sorry.

Under-18 Raves

Under-18 music events go way back. Bands like Lynx gave matinee performances in the late seventies at the Hammersmith Odeon. But raves are another matter. On the illegal underground circuit, children of all ages with or without their parents, often arrive playing and dancing amongst us 'old uns'. They're welcome. For us 'old uns', raving with children feels like such a natural thing. In the 1997 Brighton Dance Parade, organisers put on a float especially for children, allowing them a space in the celebration of Rave Culture, in recognition of their present and future contribution.

Kool FM are amongst promoters who run raves for under-18s. Alongside Evolution at the Sanctuary in Milton Keynes and New Generations, Options in Kingston, they provide a forum where young people can enjoy the same entertainment as their older siblings or parents. Grooverider, Mickey Finn, Brockie, Det, Skibadee and Shabba are amongst those who play teen raves on regular basis. The kids themselves have embraced the clothes, dances and music wholeheartedly. Though Lennox, New Generations promoter, feels they prefer Jungle's Jump Up vibe to mellower D&B.

Lennox is conscious of wider aspects of Rave Culture, like drugs, which young people could be drawn to along with the music, mistakenly believing that the two have to go together. Like many parents and teachers he is aware that kids will do what they want. But in acknowledging the gap between home and school, Lennox provides real life education, aiming to prevent early drug casualties. With the cooperation of local education officials and councillors, New

Generations is able to fly their events in schools. On their club nights, there are displays of the usual recreational drugs and young people have a no-pressure environment in which they're free to ask questions in their own time.

Generations of ravers move in and out of the music. "I notice how a lot of people saying, "such and such a dance didn't feel right, 'cos all these new people were in it." You can't knock that. Back in the day, the same thing happened with us. We got this music." *MC GQ*

Manchester April '97

B, MC Strings and Scott, professional ravers head up the M1 in Scott's Porsche for a spot of mid-week partying. We're moving with Foxy Brown booming in the back. Mobile to mobile motorway traffic we hear, DJ Bryan Gee is already on the road, half an hour ahead. Too far behind us on the North Circular, MC 5ive'0's driver has been "Excuse me sir, would you step out of the car?" and us at 120 mph, a crumpled local address on the dash, flying with no map and just a vague idea of how to get there.

Driving up the M1, M6 and the M62, we get lost in the town centre. Thankfully, cab drivers always know the clubs. Right, u-turn, left turn, right around and past the Mancunian accent. Outside Top Nosh Indian Cuisine "serving chips, burgers and pizza", we're lost again. These dark streets and buildings feel like East Berlin.

Our destination, the medium-sized arty not glitzy club with unisex toilets, the unlikely-named Sankey's Soap, is marked by an island of gleaming motors and the echoes of an MC announcing 'JUMPING JACK FROST'. 5ive'0 is still on some carriageway. As we enter the club between the beats an MC announces the arrival of "the Porsche posse all the way from London". MC Strings takes the mic and raps out "Listen to the style …" A couple of babes strut amongst the dancers near the front of the stage.

Familiar from the Blue Note, familiar from the Rocket. From Wood Green to Manchester Sally and Maddie are up for a good night out. Jumping Jack Frost on form across the stage, cuts in Dillinja's *Silver Blade* as the massive 'Watch the ride.'

5ive'O flies in, puffa and headscarf with mic in hand, his vocals are on point. The tableau on stage is runnin. As De Man Dem bounce to the beats alongside the decks, appreciative lighters flare and bottles are banged in applause. "Give it Up for Jumpin Jack Frost!" Let's go deeper – a deeper dimension in sound. In steps funki-dreaded Bryan Gee spreading rhythms like Marmite in the place. A Roni Size Doppelganger stares disturbingly from the stage through the smoke, as 5's anglepoise mic grooves with his lips, with the limbs of the clubbers. "Sounds of the Philly Blunt – V Recordings …" You're riding the rhythm to a different headspace, the music provokes more shouts for the rewind, more bottles banging. The impossibly long helter-skelter of an intro that's brought you so far into the tune explodes at the drop of a *Warhead*. All that's left is to cheer, to dance, nod heads and lyric it off. Amidst the smoke and the strobes … the onslaught continues … "Mi Gosh, how ya meeeen." Sally screams through the melee, "Who's that MC?" "Everyt'ing is everyt'ing, I'm the one like Papa Strings …"

We've hit that level deep in the night, within the vibe, beneath the grooves. For the next dimension ravers it's all too much … It's never too much. "Roll the bass. Big up the Younghead insiiide …" It's a special dedication. The dancers shapes are different and all are one. Baseball caps and bra tops move between t-shirts and oversized puffa jackets. From within an Amen break, Sally and Maddie hit the floor with a spliff rolled in some dark corner. Deep in the heaven of strobes, smoke and beats, this moment is all. Forget the Marmite. Rhythm pours like molten lava from the hands of Bryan Gee. "Come again, Selecta." The flashes of faces Japanese, Spanish, Asian, Black British, blonde bobs,

beautiful bodies rebound from speakers emanating sounds like a Hackney manhole cover hitting the deck. That *Warhead* track rumbles the earth beneath the floor's foundations. Earnest countenances scream without words. "Bring That Beat Back." In the depths of the dance, even the Hilfiger-clad Jack Frost hits the podium. This joy is serious.

The beats penetrate the glare of the house lights that threaten the end of heaven. The massive rave on through the false daylight of this journey's end. People emerge that have been there all night. "Check the blonde in the yellow bikini. Mi word – she been dancing like that all night?" The youth with a spliff buried somewhere in his Russell Athletic hooded top breathes out smoke through the air as the last fragments of the *Warhead* rewind fall from existence. The faithful gratefully, spontaneously "Give it up for Bryan Gee." It's the sign of a wicked night when, as the last notes die away, no one leaves their spot. Telepathic whispers coalesce into screams, "One more tune please Bryan. One more tune." The amiable DJ obliges, stoking the smiles on the faces of the ravers as their bodies dance the dance of the very last tune, like there really is no tomorrow.

Screaming home through back alley Manchester with a promise to see Sally and Maddie somewhere on a dancefloor, we get lost after three blocks and ask two well tipsy, sling-back-clacking women for directions. The small loud one just about keeps hold of her can and shrieks, "Wha …?! You've cum all the way up 'ere a go te Sankeys." She can't quite believe it. "Sankey's! Shirl." Shirl's at an angle grasping some railings. "You 'eard that? Oi Shirl." We leave them to laugh, bent double, swagger and gaggle down those desolate night streets. Echoes of directions mingle with shouts; "You're mad you are, mad."

AFTER THE RAVE: 11AM

Saturday morning, post-Heat haze. A terraced
house in Dover. The telephone rings, doorbell
goes. Three raving mums join the cluster.
A late-90s coffee morning - without the coffee.
Trips to the off licence for more bottles of
cider, Bacardi, packs of fags and Rizlas.
Ashtrays overflow between the mechanic, teacher,
mothers and unemployed. Nicky Blackmarket plays
on the stereo and overlapping conversations chat
Jungle, Jungle, Jungle. Who played the best set.
Praising and cussing MCs. Your best DJ. That
last tune. The quality vibes, states of ecstasy,
state of the toilets. The double-dropped lost-it
tales. Rumours of fights, DJ no-shows. Popping
more pills. Comparing flyers, the pukka and
poorer raves. Talkin 'bout holidays in Ibiza
clubs, sex, and STDs. Times raving with angels
and that time tripping out in the ambulance with
death at the wheel. Dancing in the kitchen.
Rushing on the sofa. Everyone drinking, no-one
eating. Hating Happy Hardcore. Raving 'til the
last penny and pill. Mourning the loss of
heaven. Life is still on hold. Caned, still
caning it. Not straight enough to face the
parents. Hearing that *Warhead* tune every DJ
played. The photo to go in the before and
after rave album. Putting off facing the world
of normal people. Crash out, drift off, collect
the kids and plan for the next big one.
That's *This Life*

ONE RAVER - SALLY WOOD GREEN
SEPTEMBER '97

"I used to be very spiritual. Always there, strong for people.
When I started raving friends were like – "What's going
on, you're never there? ... When you're in your house, you're
asleep." Monday to Thursday, it was get through the week
for the next weekend. From Thursday to Monday there was
no sleep involved. Then you'd plan the next one. It was like
that for two years. For the first time, I found time for my
own enjoyment and it offended a lot of people. Maybe they
were worried about my health. They could see I was totally
homed in to this Jungle.

I'd be the 'girl with the bunches'. Everything that was
Jungle, I'd be there. Everything new had to be checked out.
Even GQ at the Paradise said, "Don't you have a home to go
to?" I split up with my boyfriend. Jungle was a big part of
it. He'd say, "Can't we listen to something else except
Jungle?" I twisted my diaphragm once through excessive
raving and couldn't even stand up straight. I lay on the
floor of my flat listening to Jungle tapes for two weeks
solid. I made myself stand up, just to get to Jungle Mania
at the Astoria. Mind over matter. There was no two ways
about it, I had to go.

In clubs, I couldn't keep still. I'd wonder off mid-sentence
to follow the beats. I was only there for the music. People
were of secondary importance. The Paradise was one of the
few places I'd go on my own. Friends would say, "You can't
go to Jungle clubs on your own." And I'd say, "Watch me."
I suppose it was cocky but I wasn't gonna feel a way,
where they were playing *my* music.

Then, you couldn't go out and just enjoy yourself. You didn't
know what would kick off. With the troubles Jungle
disappeared. The Laserdrome, Voodoo Magic, Paradise,
AWOL at SW1 all gone. I was like, "What am I gonna do?
Where am I gonna hear this music?" All these kids have
come in and spoilt my enjoyment. I've found something at
the age of twenty-seven that's made me feel brilliant and
they've creamed it.

I still wonder where all the old crew have gone. Has
everyone found somewhere to go and they're not telling
me? I know people went off to Garage, partly because
of the trouble. Jungle doesn't take over my whole life
now. Before, I'd get panicky if there was an out of town
wedding to go to. I'd be like, "Sorry. Can't go ... got to be
here raving."

I kept chasing a dream thinking, I'm gonna go out and
have a brilliant time and I'd come back at the end of the
weekend and think, "That was rubbish." But I'd try again
next weekend. The horns and whistles used to create the
vibe. The crowd were much more hyped. There's new stock
coming in all the time and you'd think they can incite the
same old vibe, but it's not true. Can it be the negative
effects of E? Going out over doing it too much? So the thrill
pales into, "Here we go again." I don't think it's just that.

My work and health suffered. Perhaps, before I became a
proppa raver, I was too entrenched in being a mother but
then I felt guilty about not spending so much time with my

son. I still listen to Jungle 80% of my musical time —
probably more. It gives you the pre-going out buzz. But
when you get there, you think, "I'd have been better off
staying at home. There was more excitement in my living
room than there is in this club."

POLITICS, WHAT POLITICS?

*"Rave Culture, what's that got to do with politics? Shit
loads of people getting off their faces. Just going out
and having a good time. Sod all to do with politics."*
JOE BLOGGS

Sure if you think political change can only be achieved by
joining one of the traditional parties. This culture of political
change is far subtler. And perhaps far more powerful. Yes,
drugs — some drugs have something to do with it, a lot to
do with it. After you've danced through the doors of
perception each and every weekend, life never seems to be
the same again. But they aren't the only ingredient that
pushes individuals along a path of personal revolution,
turning their lives into an ill-fitting suit.

Change isn't something that happens to everyone. There's
those who will say, "It was just a bloody good laugh."
Others who find it a nightmare of depression, loss of
financial and emotional control. They've caned it to excess —
crashing and burning in the wrong sort of chemicals.
They've been controlled rather than empowered. There is
justified concern for friends who have become casualties.
But others take something else away. Have you ever
revisited a field where you've raved after the party has
gone? Empty, slightly trashed asking what did it all mean?
All those people, half remembered friends for an hour a
night, the mad conversations, the proppa sights imprinted
on the memory? There was a sense of a community raving
against the machine. I came for a party not desperately
seeking anything.

Perhaps you didn't know what was missing until you
experienced what could be. Surviving day-to-day city life in
a personal cocoon, head down, Walkman on, avoiding any
eye contact. Living in a non-community, where you know
soap stars better than your neighbours. You're a dissident
for even thinking of not becoming the processed human,
happy to live the nine-to-five. Perhaps the thoughts are
already there. But after the rave, some people change their
aspirations, goals, the way they interact with others.
Sometimes, they're never the same again.

A ghastly caricature grows in my head, tall and
nasty, dripping black ink — a robed Headmaster
waving a cane — a besuited Boss swinging a watch
screaming a Pink Floyd lyric. "Welcome my son,
welcome to the machine." In front of me, the
queue of thousands with death behind their eyes
stretches on in the distance between towering
legs. I can't see the front. Where are they all
going? I'm not a lemming. I've cut and run. I'm
running like a muthafucka. Like my life depends
on it. Running with eyes closed, instinctive
overdrive, leaving Linford Christie behind.
My one chance to escape the prison camp.

The sound comes first. Then the trainers, bare
feet, sandals and boots. With eyes open, there's
others here and there. Different from me. All
cultures, races, ages. The strangers who are
friends. "What are you doing here?" "Don't know.
The same as you and you and you, I guess. Just
followed my instincts."

In life's chill-out room, there's time to
discuss the state we're in. Criticise that life
out of balance which sucks at our planet, our
being. Only one thing's for sure. It can't go
on. Analysing all the pieces that make up my
life — remember the time I was nursing an old
man in the stench of that High Wycombe geriatric
hospital? Thought he was completely gaga with
nothing to say. The morning I bed-bathed him,
reeling out the prepared script? … "And you won
the war sir." In a moment's lucidity, he fixed
me with his eyes. "No, young fella. Only the
arms dealers won the war." Retreating into his
last days, that's all he ever says to me. I
dress him in clean pyjamas, take the washbowl
to the sluice and pour the water down the
toilet. The words have hit me like a bullet in
the head. No longer can I blindly walk someone
else's treadmill. Subdue my instinctive values,
my essence of life. Back in life's chill-out
room, the party was wicked. I've danced a
thousand raves. But what else is there? Talk to
me friend.

Along with the booming beats, the lights and sights, grows the feeling that there's more to be gained from this Dance department of the People's University. More than just saying to the bloke next to me, "Alright mate." What else is in there? What else could our interaction be? How can we share the sum of our experience? What's our collective potential? Can we change things? Can we contribute to some sort of psychic critical mass?

I LOVE THE SMELL OF WOODSMOKE IN THE MORNING

I never thought I'd go to Glastonbury. I don't think I'm a 'hippy.' Wasn't into camping, being unwashed, dealing with the mud. Yet in Winter '97, getting to Glastonbury was all I could think of. Even when the tickets were sold out, bought up by ticket touts, selling through agents on Shaftesbury Avenue for £150 a time. Still had to be there "by any means necessary."

War films have their uses. Me and the Glasters crew were on a mission. We wandered 'round B&Q, buying the bits for a homemade rope ladder and practiced our climbing technique in a local park. The kids thought we were mad. No, just driven. Had to be amongst the festivalgoers. Learning, sharing our experiences with others who just had to be there.

By a campfire, I met a five-foot-nothing girl and her friends who'd used a grappling iron to get over the fence — sorry Michael Eavis. For a few days a year we've created a State with no flag, the City of Hedonism on Earth. At one end of the city, there's the Dance tent's raving posse, giant stages are in the middle and at the other end, the relative peace of the Green Fields — an alternative suburbia.

A further extension of Glastonbury's Green Fields is the Big Green Gathering, a festival based on the Wiltshire Downs a short distance from Stonehenge. The crucial thing about both these events is that they provide a forum for discussion, exchange and personal growth. Clubland and raves have lost some heart with their move into the mainstream, whereas the vibe in the Green Fields and more so at the Gathering is so thick you could climb on top of it.

The whole site is powered by wind and solar energy, the music goes right across the board. It's clear that JDB is in England's bloodstream. Bands like Spacegoat create rollers with an Irish fiddler, African drums and Aboriginal Didgeridoo providing the B-line. Festivalgoers party and talk till the sun rises, then catch a range of timetabled workshops, classes, and seminars. Want to know about road protesters, new technologies, the Big Brother state, permaculture, GMOs, water powered cars, the arms industry, meditation or anything to help combat life's real stresses? It's there. It's cynical to call the set-up a cultural supermarket, especially for those who collect experiences valuable for future life. You'll only travel that part if your instincts lead you there. People who think it's all a load of tosh will stay away.

Luton's Exodus Collective have created a permanent home on the back of their legendary illegal raves. They, too, realised that raving is all very well, indeed everyone deserves a damn good party and their DJs have been banging out Hardcore and Jungle from time. Largely comprised of local Luton people, they've established a permanent community around an abandoned hospice and farm. Utilising the collective knowledge of its family — former carpenters, mechanics, glaziers, soldiers, electrical engineers, estate agents, students, factory workers, train drivers and unemployed, they've built a home open to all-comers. Ravers in part, they have gained such valuable experience of community regeneration that they've been visited by a delegation from the European Union, eager to learn lessons. Children have been born into the Collective and they, like their parents, will learn to live as part of a greater family which values others, is non-exploitative, respects the Earth and takes partying very seriously. Dangerous? Oh yes, the authorities absolutely hate them. Exodus — Movement of Jah People.

PROMOTERS

"We're nothing without each other. Without the public there's nothing, without promoters there's nothing and without DJs and artists there's nothing. For that matter without people giving out flyers outside the clubs every fucking weekend there's nothing".
JAY, WORLD DANCE

After the lights, music, action and vibe has trickled away, very few people really think of the promoters, the people way behind the scenes, who've risked the shirts off their backs to throw the party. They think of them when they pay a hefty ticket price, when the queue gets out of hand, when things go wrong. But it's difficult for people to appreciate the planning, organisation or financial outlay involved. That's demonstrated time and again when novices leave a successful rave, thinking they could organise the same thing themselves and their attempts go pear-shaped. You're relatively lucky if people have just had a shit time. But suppose there's been a real public order disaster, punters have been hurt and it's your responsibility. And do you know what it's like waking up on Monday with people pounding on your door looking for their money? There's no substitute for hard work, expertise and drive. Sure raves are fun. But you need to have sensible people to look after the runnin's. Brand name raves have survived for a reason. Even then it's still a risky business.

IT'S TELEPATHY MAN

"It's weird because Telepathy is so much bigger than we think it is now. I got arrested once. I've gone into the police cells and seen on the wall, 'Telepathy is the one.' One time I was in an Internet cafe proofreading a flyer that I was doing. And a guy looked over my shoulder and goes, "Telepathy Man." It's down to all the hard work. We've always tried to be unique."
BRET, TELEPATHY

Telepathy's history harks back to the days of the early Rave scene. Like Jungle Fever, which came later, Telepathy's crowd and edgy vibe represents one of Jungle's true facets. More Street than World Dance they came from the other side of the tracks. And boy did we love them. They remain one of the few organisations that stood the test of time. So Bret what's the story?

"Me and Ken were doing custodial sentences at the time and I got released first. When I came out my friend Bowler took me to an event down Rosebery Avenue, Islington. It had Ratpack, Rob Eliot and was called The Window Smasher. We arrived around 1 o'clock and by half one we were gone. I was just like, "What the fuck are you taking me here for? Full of these people, mad people." Because my background up until that point was strictly yer Rare Grooves, Reggae events – your more Black orientated events. To be honest, I couldn't dig it. It was just a mind blower for me. I screamed. I screamed and shouted at him and his girl, "Get me outta here." We came out of there at 1.30 and went to Funky Express.

Next week Bowler's come to me again and says, "We're going out." "Where we goin'?" "I'm taking you to one of those places again." "Ah fuckin' hell." I was kicking and screaming. I'm in the car just moaning. He's driven down I think it was somewhere off the M3 Southampton way; one of these big warehouse raves. All I could see was loads of parked cars and everyone walking in one direction. We've gone into this warehouse; this massive, gigantic warehouse and it's going off in there man. There were thousands of people. And there was a massive heap of coal and people are dancing on it. Now I'm still cussing but at the same time the money element of me clicked in. I was thinking,

'There's thousands of people here ...' "Dave how much did they pay to get in here?" "£25. Some people are payin' £50 ..." 'Ching!' Something's gone off in my head. All I remember saying when we left was, "You know what? We are going get into this." That's all I ever said. This was '89. I remember writing to Kenny saying, 'Kenny don't worry, I am working on something. Things are happening don't worry.' Bowler comes to me and goes, "I wanna do a rave." And I said, "You know what? I'm up for it."

The very first rave we did was just crazy man. It was called Juvenile for the under 18's market. We were trying to hit the summer holidays, blah, blah, blah. We planned the event and everything was going to form. We hired a room in Edmonton Baths, done it out nice, did the flyers, got the tickets sent out and all the rest of it. Unfortunately a guy from Tottenham killed a guy from Edmonton. So the police have put two and two together and got six and they've gone to the venue, "There's potential of trouble, blah, blah, blah." So they cancelled the event. We didn't want to let all that money go so I hired minibuses, found another venue at Muswell Hill and tried to shuttle the heads there. We did it but the rave flopped simply because we moved the venue. If it had carried on it would have done well. By then it was me, Bowler, some other guys, my brother; everyone is gutted that money is lost and they're saying, "I ain't doing this again." I said to myself, 'I'm gonna carry on doing this.' Me and Bowler continued. We created an event called Freedom — That's what's life's about, which was like your typical Acid Warehouse kinda vibe.

We used to break into warehouses, cos the law then meant you could do that. We knew people that were electricians. Get them in, spark it up and you're on. Things were starting to go well. We started to make our name. We used to operate around Amhurst Road, Hackney. There was a place called Third Floor 'round Stoke Newington, the Pyramid Centre we used to hire as well. In them days it was a lot more serious to nowadays i.e. some heads that originally started this game were either football guys or men that had another side, if you understand my meaning. There was a slight criminal end to it. Things were serious in the sense of, you'd be doing your events and you'd have to secure your own event. You don't want anyone coming to rob you.

When Ken arrived I said, "We've got to start something else now." We were sitting and talking and I said, "We've got to get a venue." We got the venue off Eastman's dad Billy, cos we knew him very well. His dad and a guy called Cecil got us Marshgate Lane. We were sitting in some guy's bedroom in Hackney. Kenny's flicking through a magazine and said, "I like that." And he just went, "Telepathy." And I said to him, "Expand your mind." And that was it. That's how the name came. 'Telepathy — Expand your mind.'

We were planning to do our first event; I'll never forget it. November 19th, 1989. So we started promoting and Kenny said, "My God this is going to flop." I said to him, "It's like having a party and no one comes and you can tell that no one likes you." But lo and behold all the meeting points were jammed. And — boom! — that was the beginning of Telepathy. We just went on and were down there for six months. It was *the* rave. Friday and especially Saturday we would just get mobbed. It was definitely very much underground. Raw. I think it was a combination of the times. And the rave just grew from strength to strength.

The down side of things ... At New Year's Eve someone got killed. That was sad. It was real sad. We were doing two events, Freedom down at Lea Bridge Road and Telepathy at Marshgate Lane. About 5 o'clock I got a phone call asking me to come. I said, "What's up?" And he said, "You're not going to believe this. Some one's been stabbed and killed." "Shit man." So I've left Lea Bridge Road gone down there and the guy is actually lying at the entrance to the venue. Billy must have closed the guy's eyes. It was deep man. A man's died and what didn't make it too good, at that moment DJ Rap was playing *Mr Kirk Your Son is Dead*. She didn't know but you understand ... So New Year's Day we're dealing with someone who has died, the money and all the rest of it. And from then we closed for a couple weeks. We had police around asking people for information. They did get the guy. But when the rave came back it was rammed. It ran for six months then got shut down by the authorities.

We got the opportunity to do the Sobell Sports Centre. Me and Kenny went down Islington Town Hall to get the licence. And they were firing all these questions, "How much security? ... Parking?" I said to them, "It would be better if you let the event go on until eight because by then the tubes will be running. That would allow people to easily disperse and go home. Rather than 6 o'clock and they're milling around." Lo and behold we got the licence. What we wanted to do was fuse Telepathy and Freedom at the

Sobell. That rave, that rave was phenomenal. Phenomenal. Phenomenal. Phenomenal. In the sense of the numbers. We pulled 13,000 people.

Some of the high points for me, I remember Music Power down Green Lanes. Nick called me about ten on a particular morning. He says, "Bret, I have a young girl in here waiting to buy a ticket." And I say, "Yeah, yeah, yeah, I'll be down in about an hour." I arrived there 5 o'clock that evening she's still there. Nicky said to me, "You know what? We gave her a job as she stayed here all day just to get a ticket." On the day of the event a shop in Ealing called to say, "Bret we've run out of tickets." Me and Kenny dropped off about 70 tickets. On our way back the phone rings near Trafalgar Square. "We've sold out and need some more." Me and Kenny were like, "We just gave you more tickets." "Yeah they're gone." It was a mad one. Crazy one. We knew it was gonna be busy but we never thought it was going to be that busy. We never thought it was gonna create the madness and the hype that it did. Setting up on the night people are telling me outside the queue is going around and around and around. It was frightening bruv. We never thought that we were gonna have that effect on people. That was the power of the Rave scene at the time. That was the power of Telepathy at the time.

Telepathy's parties were often advertised by clever, catchy ads produced by Ken and broadcast on pirate radio stations. "A lot of thought goes into the Telepathy adverts, catching them with the hook, keeping a constant theme – so that the ads all have that, "Telepa, Lepah, Le Pah ..." cos that's the signature." They now employ MCs to voice the trails. It's another element which Telepathy introduced and has now become an industry standard.

"We worked really, really hard to create what we do. Today's promoters don't realise how much work needs to go in to make an event. Now if I'm promoting an event I might drive to Bristol. Some say to me, "You've come all the way from London?" Like it's a big deal. Where I'm coming from that's what you have to do. You have to go to the end of the Earth. There's a lot of work that goes into it. We are unique. We both come from West Indian backgrounds. We grew up here. The Reggae flavours we incorporated, things like the MC because that's what we were used to. Things that are industry standard now like rewinds – we created that at Marshgate Lane. We said, "Tell 'em "Stop the tune. Rewind it." We invented the back to back. A lot of people are unaware of that. We were innovative at the beginning

cos we were influenced from a West Indian background. I'm proud of that; we are both proud of that. You can't take that away from us. Someone will go, "Telepa, Lepa, Telapa ..." from the ads and you feel proud of that. Inside you think, 'Yeah alright we do things for money.' I'm not gonna lie. But to get recognition is good. We have got something we can do. We can make a difference. That's how Telepathy started."

THE ROAST CREW

Kingsley, Everton, Wayne and Paul Roast founded Roast in 1991 - 92. In the spirit of the after-party, it kicked off on Sunday afternoon, hence Sunday Roast, from 12pm till 4pm and extended till 8pm – based at Turnmills, Farringdon and Linford Studios. Regular DJs were Ron, Grooverider and Kenny Ken. Others included Dominic, Mickey Finn, Top Buzz and Tamsin. They weren't booked because the promoters thought they played in a particular style so the music changed with DJ's tastes. In '91 their original music was House or Rave. By '92 when Roast had moved to Linford Studios, Breakbeat and Jamaican Studio One samples were in. Wayne noticed more black people turning up at Roast.

"We weren't discriminating [against anybody] on the door. In those days with some other London clubs, if you were black or had a face that didn't fit, you weren't getting in. So we got a predominantly black crowd." Their ravers could relate to the music embroidered with Reggae sounds and Dance Hall style MCs. Their first MC was Moose "the original", from the Pirate Club who was soon joined by an enthusiastic 5ive'O, whom Moose trusted with the mic while he took a break. It was a groundbreaking era. The DJs and MCs took the music forward. Roast have a place in Jungle history.

Realising that the Dance industry is here to stay but that styles of music would change, Roast introduced a Garage arena back in '93. Under new management in '94, with Wayne, Kingsley and Everton, but without Paul, the new Roast crew continued to write Jungle history using MCs Navigator, Stevie Hyper D and Det. The Drum & Bass tag was viewed with suspicion. Kingsley commented, "People were trying to find a difference between Roast and Desire. And rather than come with a racial angle, they'd say, "That's Drum & Bass and that's Jungle." That's the easiest way to say, "that's for spades and that's for the other lot"."

They've seen clothing fashions come and go. The casual rave look of 1991 - 92 was followed by 1993's dress code explosion and the designer label crew strutted it out at the Astoria and the Hippodrome. Excitement and the size of raves have decreased since the fever of '94. Apart from the resurgence of festival events in '97, which have provided another platform for JDB raves, smaller club nights are more prevalent than the former mega raves. Perhaps the scene goes through cycles. Is Jungle on the come down? Not dying, just changing. Roast will carry on doing their thing. Perhaps it was the day I saw them, but despite holding a stonking birthday party in early '97, they weren't wholly positive about the future of large inner city Jungle raves. In September '97, Roast announced its last dance, but Desire resurrected itself. November '97, One Nation – The Island Ilford, people dance madly from the rear of the circle, to the stairs, to the front of the stage. The main floor heaved. Horns, whistles, lighters, rewinds – all the business. If Jungle is dying, the ravers didn't seem to notice.

WORLD DANCE AND AWOL AT THE PARADISE

Interview with Jay World Dance: "We can still remember when we were standing on top of the speakers with our shirts off in '89. I know it's a bit embarrassing nowadays, but fuck it, we were having a good time. If I dare say, it was during the days when the E was still good and us white boys got rhythm – you know what I mean?

In '89 I got involved in the first World Dance (WD) with an ex-colleague of mine. I used to work in the City as a foreign exchange broker. I was going to raves at the time and enjoying them, as were some of the other people who worked there. You'd be surprised how many people you'd bump into at raves who couldn't reveal at work what they were up to at weekends. We'd be reading *The Sun* in the first class carriage to work every Monday morning hoping we weren't in it. Before that I'd been a ticket tout for years. When I went to my first rave I saw people selling tickets there, I saw the light at the end of the tunnel. I said to a couple of my friends, "I think I can do this." And here we are ten years later. The first event was a long hard struggle. I had to take a back seat 'cos I was still broking. I put the first event together with a colleague of mine from the office. We put up the money. But we were had over by the people who were producing the event for us. Once I realised what had taken place I took control of World Dance

as a company. In 1991, once I was with Chris, we registered the name. We came back after a couple of years out of the wilderness to put on our second rave. People were asking if we were the original WD. Well, yes we're the people behind it, we're running it. I decided to leave broking as a career when it got to the point where the majority of calls coming to the office were for our events rather than the business.

The first event was successful; there were 8,000 - 9,000 people there, even though it was our third site. The police had battled us from county to county. In East Grinstead, the Sheriff runs us out of town with a helicopter. It was a "Junction six of the M25, down a few miles, turn right, there you go ..." kind of business. The show was fabulous, everyone had a great time. I mean, Adamski got signed there by his record company. N-Joi, Oakey [Paul Oakenfold] and Carl Cox were there. It was one of Mickey Finn's first gigs.

We did the Paradise, which is still reckoned to be one of the best club nights. We also did a gig called 'Beyond Therapy', which brought Harlow to a standstill. This was pre-Criminal Justice of course. We argued that the rave wasn't illegal, just unlicenced, and we didn't need it to be licenced 'cos it was a members event. How did you become a member? You bought a ticket and got free membership. It was real borderline stuff. Quite frankly, it was clearly anti-social as far the powers-that-be were concerned and they wanted it stopped.

We ran some stuff in the old Clink Street Studios where Shoom and that used to play. We also did a thing around the back of Club Labyrinth called 'The 3rd Floor.' It used to be Club Labyrinth and us. It worked well. We didn't disrupt Dalston too much and the police used to leave us to it, to an extent. Till one week. We arrived, sneaked in to set up under the cover of darkness and all that. We were on the third floor and Jah Shaka had set his system up on the ground floor. If you can imagine the impact of our lot, the Labyrinth and Shaka crowds all converging on Dalston at the same time ... The police soon showed up to put a stop to it. They moved us on, so we woke up Lou who ran the Dungeons in Lea Bridge Road, which had been shut down for a while. "Lou we've got a crowd and no place to put 'em. Will you open up for us?" Lou, never one to turn away a pound note, said, "Yeah alright." We had the show there. Next week we wanted to do the same thing but he said, "No. I'm doing it myself now." Our crowd went back and we were back to square one.

But that's how it was in them days, if you got a space and you got it open, you were going to be busy. Back then it tended to matter more whose event you were going to rather than the DJs or artists performing at them. The public wasn't as aware of the artists as they are now. If you were given twenty flyers, you'd drop nineteen of them if one of them was for Sunrise or Energy. It didn't matter what DJs were playing, you just trusted the promoters would put people on who knew what they were doing. This wasn't always the case, but it didn't fucking matter anyway. It was more about the promotion and the particular vibe they created.

People look now and say, "Oh you guys, you've really cracked it, you got this and that." But we risk almost everything we've got almost four times a year. Now if anyone else wants to do that, they're welcome. Remortgage your house, sell your car, borrow all your friends' money, put your money, your life savings, your sanity and your fucking life on the line and you may well come out of it with a smile on your face. People ring me up and ask me for advice. My advice is always, have the money, try and make sure it's your own, and be prepared to lose it all, because for every successful rave, there are ten that fall down on their arse. If you take the scene as a whole the odds are probably worse, twenty to one. This is a hard thing to do. If you're lucky you'll get your first show off successfully, then you're more likely to make the next ones work and as you go further down the line, you've got your profits from your organisation to put in the raves. But if your first one is a failure then you're pretty much pushing it uphill. The first World Dance lost a load of money. We've pulled it 'round since then."

Professional rave organisations have gained a good track record by considering all the angles: planning, finance, advertising, entertainment, security, public health and safety, insurance, venue and, most importantly, your customers. You're stepping into the heart of an industry where all the elements must come together. Of course you could just set up in a field as Jay World Dance did and watch the police come over the horizon in riot gear and smash up your equipment. Paul Ibiza had tussles with the law in the early days for his commitment to promoting raves. Some groups like the Exodus Collective, Advanced Party and Brighton's Positive Sound System still manage to put on old style 'convoy-to-secret locations', stonkers-of-

raves in fields. But they are among the few groups who escape the full wrath of the authorities. They, like pirates, do so only by tentative hard-won agreement with or tolerance of the locals. They have their problems and post-Criminal Justice Act, a legal venue is the safest bet to start risking grands of your own or someone else's money.

PLANNING

For a well-established Rave organisation like World Dance, whose dances regularly attract over 10,000 people, preparation begins months in advance. During that time you have to find a suitable venue, get a licence, draw up your DJ and MC roster (making sure they're available), negotiate a price, hire them plus sound equipment, lighting rigs, staging, Portaloos, barriers, drinks and sometimes marquees for extra space. There are funky extras including, dancers, fair ground rides and merchandise traders to organise. Getting a licence involves meeting local council licensing officials. They and the police have to be satisfied with all the public health and safety arrangements which include hiring paramedics, even doctors — Jay comfortably announces their medical crew, should it be necessary, could perform minor surgery on site. Choosing the right night to maximise the number of punters through the entrance, avoiding exams, mid-month poverty and clashes with rival raves is also essential. Promoters tend to liaise with each other, but Bank Holidays, the Notting Hill Carnival, Easter Sunday, Christmas and New Year, are free-for-alls.

There's one consistent thing. However early promoters start planning a dance, in the hour before doors open, the idea of them sitting around, having a quiet spliff, sighing and saying, "Shall we open up then? — Yeah might as well."... just doesn't happen. It's frantic — then the unexpected happens. Roast have had a lighting rig burst into flames three hours before their do. And during the night?

"You're lucky if you can get a half hour's dance. You're busy man, busy, you're running around and running around, then it's over. Saturday is a twenty-four to twenty-six hour day. Then there's the DJs (Ron), calling up to ask what time their set is, even though they've been booked a month before." WAYNE, ROAST

FINANCE

"Putting on raves is the easiest way in the world to throw away £15,000." JAY, WORLD DANCE
"Put my name right underneath that." KINGSLEY, ROAST

None of the promoters really wanted to talk figures although reactions from laughter to astonishment followed the question – "Won't the banks lend you any money?" Finance tends to come from independent backers, and you have to put more aside than you'd probably imagine. Some raves crash quite spectacularly.

"Frost, Brockie and a host of big names on a flyer won't necessarily fill a venue. Anyone can book a DJ. People think, "I've got a bit of money," so they print up a flyer, put 'em out and assume they're guaranteed a crowd. But when they don't have any people in the venue, they wonder where it all went wrong. A lot of it is down to how well you promote and your name on the street. You've got to have pedigree behind it. If we make mistakes, at least we can carry on. Some people lose all their money and have to go driving buses. That's their future." KINGSLEY ROAST

Some people go to a rave, see a thousand people and think there's three thousand. Then they start calculating fifteen times three thousand … It's only when they try to promote an event that they start to realise it's not that simple. Though you can start in a bedroom with a mobile phone as Roast did, it's a risky business. Jay, amongst others has learnt from bitter experience.

"I've had someone knock on my door on Monday for the money I'd lost them on Saturday. But I've got a reputation out there, I've got a brain and I know how to make money and I pay people back. There was a time when I didn't go on holiday for five years because I owed people money. I don't think you should be seen going on holiday when you owe people money. If you're prepared to risk someone else's money to make money for yourself, then you should be prepared to pay it back. Even when we set up again with auditors, accountants and tried to make ourselves as efficient as we could, the first three World Dances lost money. The first lost £60,000, the second £50,000, the third £40,000. That's £150,000. If it hadn't been for other things we were doing within the industry like AWOL at the Paradise, then we wouldn't have been able to pay our way.

You're only as good as your last show. If the DJ plays a bad set he still gets his money. If a promoter does a bad show, he ain't eating or opening his front door for three months." JAY, WORLD DANCE

The financial outlay is much greater than the old days when you could put on a rave for a few grand. But it's counter productive to scrimp. Ravers notice shoddiness, especially when they themselves have spent so much on a night out. It was never supposed to be an exploitative scene. "If every promoter said, "I'm gonna spend as much money as I can on the production", then you're caring about the raver." TERRY TURBO, ONE NATION

Punters have seen a steady rise in ticket prices over the years. People might grumble and feel they're being ripped off. But when you compare the cost of a seven-till-seven, all-star line up party, with other forms of entertainment, a West End show, football match, or Pop concert – Oasis fans paid £18 to see the group at Earl's Court in September '97 – raves compare reasonably.

VENUES

November '96, the Dalston club had been so cold that one punter had driven home a couple of miles past Stoke Newington to get his puffa. It still wasn't any good. One of the few places to sit in the club was on some stone stairs backstage and security soon moved you on. So much for government regulations stipulating chill-out areas. The whole night turned into a miserable endurance test, which a steady trickle of punters were failing. Outside on the high street, two dressed-to-the-nines ladies had had enough. Striding, shivering away, their Friday night tattered from within, they were vexed. "Fuck what a shit 'ole." "Yeah, well it's JUNGLE innit."

Back in the day, any old warehouse, barn or muddy field became a sacred space, because everyone was so grateful for the opportunity it provided to rave. That was before the final regulation of the Criminal Justice Act that almost ended the outlaw life and pushed the masses into the arms of some club owners whose commitment to ravers can best be described as minimal. In the name of profit, punters are put in danger. There are still allegations of deliberately depriving punters of cold tap water. Punters know when scouting a venue if the promoters or owners haven't bothered. Ravers aren't stupid. They know when they've been treated or cheated. In the case of the latter, they won't be coming back. In the fragile world of Club culture, exploitation doesn't lead to longevity. Kingsley Roast blames Jungle's down turn in part to the lack of venues. Many organisations have had to use the same venues repeatedly. Promoters have found themselves barred from some sites and there have been allegations of Rave organisations bad-mouthing each other to venue owners.

"All these venues what we use in London / England are mainly disused cinemas or old dance halls where you used to get three hundred people in evening gowns and all that. London venues are too small. They haven't got proper queuing facilities, proper security. It's no fault of the ravers. Every major incident has been because people can't get in quickly enough. That is it. It isn't because there's gangsters and people doing this or that." EASTMAN, JUNGLE FEVER

THEN THERE'S THE BLAGGERS ...

All the promoters have had them. Susie G at Jungle Fever wished she could install a camera at their counter to record the Oscar-winning performances. "I know Brockie's cousin." "I am Brockie's cousin." There's impostors faxing the Roast office with requests from Carlton TV and *The Evening Standard* on suspect headed notepaper. And people calling to say they're writing for the college magazine – "How many are you?" "Yeah just me, plus four." Roast have asked for faxed copies of the published reviews, only to be told it can't be done: "I'd like to, but the review's confidential." And callers to World Dance ... "Hello World Dance." "Yeah Daz put me on the guest list." "You're speaking to Daz." "Errrr." World Dance had a 'blaggers guest list' for known blaggers. "Yep right, you're on the guest list." After hearing the magic words, the unfortunate chancer would go down to Kent and then face the choice of paying on the gate or going home. Some people will try anything. A geezer turned up on site at Lydd with a box of bulbs saying he'd come to change the lights on the fairground rides. Another guy with a box of records, claimed to be one of the DJs. He was the wrong colour. Then there were the twelve travellers who fell out the side of a generator that they'd tried to use as a Trojan horse.

ADVERTISING

The flyer design must be right and you need to allow time for printing and distributing the flyers and posters. Ads must be on the streets a full six weeks before the event. If you are a long-running, well-organised outfit like World Dance, Roast or One Nation, you'll have a mailing list of thousands of faithfuls. This direct marketing provides remarkable access to your core customers and almost guarantees a sell-out before the tickets hit the high street. Almost. It is vital that the mailing list is updated at least every three years. There's no point sending post to people who have moved on, geographically or musically. There can be legal problems with advertising on pirate radio but nearly everyone does it. It's an opportunity that's too good to pass up. Wayne Roast understands all too well. "As independent promoters, pirate radio advertising is cost effective. It gets to our target audience. Besides ads on legal radio are expensive. When it comes to promotion, you can't use the major radio stations. Kiss charge silly money."

"Fly-posting. It is very much part of the standard. World Dance were the first to really do it, then we did it and it works. Certain other mediums, you're not reaching people, but if people are going out shopping, going to work, they will see it and it gets reinforced by the radio and the flyers." BRET, TELEPATHY

FLYERS

Saturday afternoon, upstairs at Black Market Records, teenagers (some with more front than others) elbow past the older ravers and stuff handfuls of flyers into plastic carrier bags. The large ones are especially good. Just like those their older brothers and sisters have kept on their walls from years back. The ones promising lavish productions, exotic technical specifications and a host of Rave stars all wrapped in otherworldly computer artwork. The promoter's brand name is the most important thing on the paper. The flyer is their shop window and their production and distribution is yet another vital part of the scene's cottage industry.

At the height of the 1993 - 95 madness, Damon Kroonsberg at Design Asylum produced a lion's share of flyers for events like World Dance, Desert Storm, Roast, Desire, Kool and Promised Land. Other promoters have their favourites. Malcolm of the Jungle Fever family produced a classic hand-drawn oversized number for Fever's second birthday bash, caricaturing the Kool FM crew with insightful detail. Like Damon's use of molten chromium, it passed the test by standing out from the rest. Design Asylum, updating their technology to remain at the cutting edge, has already been featured on Carlton TV's *Club Zone*. Damon and his co-worker Steve work long hours. The average time committed to a World Dance flyer is five to six hours. And they're very fast at what they do. With an avalanche of twelve inch and album covers, Design Asylum's workload increases as the industry expands in new directions.

Flyers — you need thousands of them. Five thousand flyers won't pull two thousand people into a venue. Promoters need to reach as many potential punters as possible, so they'll pay flying organisations like Turbo Promotions, The Flying Squad in the South of England and Oracle in the North to do all the leg work.

TURBO PROMOTION

Terry Turbo started out as a sales rep for a scaffolding company. The recession hit in 1987 - 88 and he lost his job. He started raving around the same time, checking out House and Old Skool dos, whilst labouring on building sites. Based in Surrey, he loved coming to London for a good rave and discovered a way of getting in free. He became a one-man ticket outlet, shifting two hundred tickets in Surrey at the first go. Terry worked with London flyer organisation the Flying Squad, moving on to start his company Turbo Promotions in early '92. By the end of the year, he was flying for most of the major raves, including, World Dance, Helter Skelter, Roast and Dreamscape. The task basically involved placing flyers in shops. It was a sweet job for Terry and his mates. They'd come to London for the day, hang around shops delivering flyers and go out raving in the evenings. By mid '94, after travelling around, working in and experiencing the scene, Terry Turbo launched *The Scene* magazine. Rather than approaching a publisher and facing any 'ravers don't read' scepticism, he decided to start the twenty-four page free magazine without backing. *The Scene* expanded to a hundred pages by Christmas '96. The entrepreneur also set up Rave organisation, One Nation to name a few. Terry started business driving a battered W-reg Austin Allegro without tax or MOT and with the bumper hanging off. Less than four years later he drives a XK-8 Jaguar with all the trimmings.

HE WHO PAYS THE PIPER

"I had a policy back in the day, that I wouldn't do a party without Fabio or Grooverider on the line-up. I just felt that it would be like having a cup of tea without the tea bag."
JAY, WORLD DANCE

Although promoters have their own preferences, if they want to remain successful, they have to adapt continually to the musical tastes of their punters. The initial separation of Jungle and Drum & Bass caused problems for some. Should they promote Jungle or Drum & Bass — should they include Hardcore?

Promoters have had to come up with new ideas for packaging and repackaging the same DJs and MCs. We've had the renowned Jungle Sound Clash at Roller Express, the Back-to-Backs, Back to '89s, Birthday Bashes, Dub Plate arena's, Designer Label Balls — with or without champagne, all female DJ line-ups and even a soundclash featuring Top Buzz Vs Grooverider with decks at each end of the venue. And, of course, old style novelty arenas like Heat on the pier in Hastings.

Most of the brand names have been offering ravers alternatives under the same roof, either by playing different formats in a number of arenas, and / or changing the music format in the same arena. The latter option has met with varying success. Full-on Junglists prefer undiluted Jungle rather than have the music altered from DJ to DJ. With the 'Back to '89' Stush rave in early '97, the vibe and madness increased with the hours / years and the number of punters who had entered the scene in that particular year. So the massive that had come into the music in '93 had to wait till around 1am before they could start firin' off. World Dance have consciously planned their customers' journey through the night's music.

"It's not for us to tell people what to play, but we're picking DJs who are becoming publicly known for their particular style. So for example Fabio and Grooverider have been a partnership from the earliest days but I think it's fair to say that Fabio is more known for the mellower, jazzier side of things. And good luck to him. There's still a place for him at WD, but not at one o'clock in the morning. Because then people are still full of energy and want to be hearing your Mickey Finns and your Hypes. But we also try to finish up with some of the mellower stuff, 'cos at 7am in the morning, do you want to be jumping up and down like a lunatic?" JAY, WORLD DANCE

Promoters still like a good night out and can be found dancing among the ravers. Daz World Dance never seems happier than when he's chilling at Glastonbury's stone circle catching the last night's vibes. There have been occasions when organisations like One Nation and Telepathy have staged so-called, 'pay back' raves, with scaled-down but quality productions at a cheaper price than the usual dos. They're an opportunity for the promoters to say thank you to their customers. In a sense, they are loss leaders. But, warns Terry Turbo, promoters with shoddy intentions can exploit pay back raves. "Some promoters, 'cos they can't pull the crowds put on cheap ones all the time and it fucks things up. People go to these raves and they see that there's nothing in there. A shit line-up. Half the DJs and MCs don't turn up, no lasers, no lighting. It's just a load of crap. And it doesn't do much for the scene in general."

THE DANCERS

Clubs have always hired dancers. They're another part of a full-on show, particularly in raves, with only a static DJ as the central character. They're a good way to liven up the stage. Sometimes the dancers are ravers who've managed to find a free way to party, sometimes, they're professionals. Most of the women, and they are mostly women, have other ambitions. Dancing is not all they do.

Sharon of A Tribe Called Jungle is at Kingston University in her second year of a Civil Engineering degree. She's a natural freestyler who likes to dance in the crowd to check the vibe before hitting the stage. Way back when, Sharon would take off with a rucksack and follow Spiral Tribe for days on end. Her first professional dance job happened when her MC brother invited her to dance on-stage during a rave at Edmonton's Roller Express. Although dancing is a great way of keeping fit and getting into raves free, her first love is still engineering.

Ambition's Terri was born in France and came to England when she was seven, moving to a village in the Midlands. She took dancing lessons and has been a professional dancer for several years. Practicing and teaching Yoga for the past fifteen years, she's also part-owner of the Soul Shack, a restaurant on Holloway Road. Describing her blonde dance partner Sarah as, "having the spirit of a black woman", they choreograph their routines in classes at Pineapple Studios and Dance Works, and spend hours practicing.

The UK Apache Dancers became A Tribe Called Jungle. Jennifer, Simone, Ukachi and Sharon danced with UK Apache on the *Original Nuttah* tour. They also toured with SOUR at the '95 Berlin Love Parade and in Japan.

On stage, groups of dancers perform in rotating sets. As work picks up the dancers take several bookings a night and have joined DJs and MCs on the rave-to-rave dash. Like the artists who present the nightly shows, they face their own share of problems. In one glorious moment, Terri remembers falling straight through a gap in the stage at Club UN. Preferring to stay out of the crowds because of a touch of agoraphobia, she dislikes punters crowding the stage, preventing the troupe from doing the professional performance a promoter has paid them to do, especially as blokes making lewd suggestions often bounce them into. Their dance routines could be sexually confusing but they are performing on stage. If any woman danced in the crowd like they do on stage, Ambition admits they'd be asking for trouble. The Fetish Crew's semi-striptease act at a World Dance event caught people's attention. But not all the female punters in the audience appeared happy.

END PIECE ...

"There's been a lot of focus on the DJs and hardly any of the producers or the promoters. The way I see it, if it weren't for the guys who say, "let me find some cash, get the warehouse, and get the DJs in there ..." It's the promoters and the producers have made the DJs, not so much the other way around."
MIKEY, DE UNDERGROUND

"Back in the day we were one; we were in this thing together. Nowadays, it's the promoters, it's the DJs, it's the producers, it's the agents, it's the so and so's and everyone's got there own agenda, which is fine. But people seem to have forgotten that we have a common piece of ground here."
JAY, WORLD DANCE

Somewhere past Leicester, we steam straight into a sudden, blinding rainstorm. DJ Ron on autopilot sits up and takes notice - Steering 'round the slowing vehicles, with hazards flashing and wipers at double speed. The car threatens to aquaplane, our lives get the rewind as the anti-lock brakes bite smoothly. On this road, you never know when trouble will strike …

WORRIES IN THE DANCE

"You just didn't know when things were going to kick off." SALLY WOOD GREEN, RAVER

With half an E still left in the fluffy corner of his trouser pocket, Curtis left the Rocket heading North along Holloway Road. The promise of dawn was reflected in his knocked off Versace sunglasses. It was time to check out Telepathy. The buzz in his veins bounced his feet along endless cracked pavements, spreading through his brain and out his eyes. Turning a corner, Curtis looked up to check the junction. Rows of traffic lights twinkled and changed obligingly to the beat he could still hear in his head. He shivered and rushed as the venue loomed closer. This was a good E. A swig of water unglued his mouth whilst he thought optimistically about getting into the rave without a ticket and only enough money for the bus ride home to Tottenham.

Crowds of people were still trying to get into the Sobell Centre firing blags like bullets at security, "My uncle works on security." "My brother is the DJ." "I am the DJ." "Don't care", said the bomber jackets on the door, "Yo muddah coulda indere, yo faddah coulda indere but ya nat goin' in." Some security were cashing in on the desperation, letting people in through a side door for a price, 'till it got steamed. A mean looking Rottweiler strained its chain, barking at anyone and anything. Then there was the odd Busy taking far too long to stroll past the place. Grasping in the gutter at a strip of

metal he watched a police car glide slowly up the road. It's funny how you can sober up suddenly - sort of - when the need is forced on you. "Rass Babylon." The cops stood chatting with security at the door. Kissing his teeth, Curtis went around the side approaching the venue from behind, sneaking along head down like some SAS business, he pulled up near a half-open window. Voices. Safe - the men's bogs. "Blood clatt!" One of the Busies stood at the end of the alley staring up at the flats across the road. Curtis froze. How long had he been standing there? This was serious business. Likely combinations of punishments flooded his head. He might just get turfed, he might have to turn out his pockets, worst of all, he might not get in. The beats were calling. Babylon still had his back turned.

Curtis found it impossible to know how long he'd been there - time warp again. He had to move. Reaching up, he slid a catch with the metal strip. Holding the water bottle in his teeth, grabbing each side of the frame, Curtis pulled himself up straight through the window. The cubicle was empty. His brain threatened to mess right up with a gravity rush, as he hit the deck landing in a Spiderman-style crouch. Between his outstretched hands on the cold wet bog floor was an eighth of hash - "Result!" He stood up,

shoving the gear in his back pocket as someone
from the next cubicle pushed his head 'round the
door. Eye to eye, the next man knew the score,
grinned and continued tearing a tube ticket into
a roach for his mate busy skinning up the last
of their weed with a well-ragged Rizla.

Minutes in the toilets stretched in warped time.
Curtis washed his hands and smudged off the
fluff from his last half E. Briefly thinking
that this should have been the larger half, he
shoved it in his mouth, wincing as he crunched
it, knowing the bitter taste was a small price
to pay for the rest of the journey. Washing the
taste away with water, he knew he'd come up
quickly. Good. He had some catching up to do.
Itching to burst out of the toilets he slunk
back to the cubicle knowing it was better to
skin up now than in twenty minutes when he'd be
too fucked to work his fingers.

Through the doors and down the corridors the
music was calling him … 5am and the crowd were
bawling for the rewind. He slunk into the
madness as waves of Ecstasy hit from all sides.
The change was so intense, so sudden. He thought
of *Mister Ben* dressed in designer suit and
string vest, opening the curtain of that
changing room. The heat, the mayhem, the fever.
5am and completely ram, everyone goin' for bruk.
Sweat-streaked skin, MCs chatted – hand to hand
business. DJ, head down, worked the mixer to
death. Underneath a pyramid podium he clocked
first a mountain of puffa jackets, then a couple
writhing their own way to ecstasy, releasing
thermonuclear energy in the place.

Suddenly the action went into slow mo and Curtis
saw everyone scatter. Stroboscopic flashes
caught knife blades and flying chairs. Persons
unknown slashed at everybody in the gaff. Bruk
up the rave – quick time. Music gave way to
screams and MC's pleas – "Security wanted up
front." Curtis climbed a lighting tripod.
Pausing at what seemed a safe height he stopped,
looked down, drew on his spliff and got ready to
stomp on the head of any knife man who might try
to juke him. Below was chaos.

Outside daylight was cold. Police and security
buzzed ineffectively 'round the venue as steam
poured out the exits along with stunned punters.
Screwing about their clothes, clutching
bloodstained handkerchiefs to cut legs, arms,
faces, ravers stumbled past the growing numbers
of police, who didn't seem too bothered about
detaining any witnesses.

Curtis fought to make everything seem all right
in his head but the mood on the top deck of the
bus was heavy. The Tottenham youts clutching
more blood stained 'kerchiefs were not happy.
No words or glances exchanged, just mutual hate
for the bastards who'd trespassed on their manor
and mashed up the dance. Curtis slipped down the
stairs at Bruce Grove, a few stops early,
leaving the bus with a nursing sister who'd
just finished night duty. Coming down, alone,
he walked slowly up the hill.

THE QUEUE

Ideally, apart from controlling the entrance, security should
have very little to do. At the larger raves, they generally
patrol discreetly, looking for dealers or drug casualties.
In smaller venues like the Blue Note or Dalston's Pier One,
they have time for a dance. Good security is about knowing
the customers and understanding its energy, not inflaming
or irritating them. It's a crowd control exercise. The
entrance to a venue is a potential hot spot with hundred,
perhaps thousands, of energetic people converging within
a few hours of each other. Ticket checks and searches can
create a bottleneck. World Dance at Lydd Airport processed
a commendable 8,000 people in less than three hours.
Everyone wants to get in. Everyone wants to know they
can get in. The queue is the customer's first point of
contact with the promotion. If the promoters and their
security don't work effectively here, the first public order
disaster will take place right outside the front door.

The September night is unusually hot. Kriss cars with stereos bouncing search for places to park up on the inside of the roundabout near Battersea Bridge. The air between the service station and Adrenaline Village is charged. The designer label foot soldiers pour towards the riverbank venue. Scores of ravers sit on an overlooking wall, scoping the queue. Near the entrance, there's a moment when the excitement turns into chaos. There's no barriers to regulate the sea of people. Any queuing system has long since collapsed. The place is ramm' and people are shouting, "Is this the guest list queue? When can we get in?" Others bum rush the throng and kissing their teeth, inflame the temperature. I'm clamped chest high, feet only intermittently touch the ground, all friends are lost. Caught in the whirlpool of people, gasping for air – this isn't fun, it's a nightmare. I squeeze 'round the side, sticking close to Jumping Jack Frost and his record boxes who seems curiously untouched by the surrounding havoc. The foyer of Adrenaline Village is strangely empty of people but full of panic. A couple of security men stagger into the main arena, coughing painfully, eyes watering pitifully. CS gas stings the lungs of all who rush forward to help. 'Round the side of the venue, a mob with or without tickets, push aside a fence, storming over those sitting on the stairs.

Juli from Dover sits on the wall across from the venue, her ticket well stashed. Buzzing, she takes in the only action she'll see that night. Along the way, MTV producer John Clements, there to catch Jungle fashions for a new show Stylismo, clocks a yout drawing out an axe handle. He's had enough and takes off with his three grand camera. For many of those who did get inside, the night is muted.

"When shit goes wrong it's always the promoter that will get the blame. Invariably we are the ones through our experiences and knowledge that tell venue owners how they should do an event. Some of them don't listen and

that's where the problems start. The reason why the crowd got so out of control was because the guy didn't listen to us. We said, "Have barriers. Have a dead man zone. Zigzag the barriers. Don't have the cloakroom as you go into the venue because that's going to cause a bottleneck. He never listened. And that's why we experienced those problems. At Adrenalin Village a similar thing. I said to the guy, "Make sure you've got x-amount of security. Make sure that 25 per cent of them are women. Have separate queues for tickets and payers." They never listened to us. They lumped everyone together – Boom – bottleneck, out-of-control, but it's us that gets the blame. It's unfair. 90 per cent of the time it's not the promoter's fault but when the shit is hitting the fan the venues like to shift the blame. You never can scrimp on security because when things to go wrong you need them to sort things out. They are the first people who you meet and that can set you up for the rest of the night. It's important that you have good security that can deal with things not just on one level. That can communicate and people feel safe to approach them as well. That's important." BRET, TELEPATHY.

Kingsley Roast said wearily of the other promoters' mess, "If you lose control, you never get it back."

That particular night in September '95 is perhaps one of the most well known debacles in Jungle history. To be fair, the promoter did apologise to everyone on Kool FM's Open Forum. But many people weren't convinced. They wanted more than a simple sorry, they wanted their money back. However, because of difficulties in authenticating ticket loss, customers were given entry to the next event, rather than cash refunds. The main issue here is that it should never have happened. The venue's security staff didn't understand the promoter's audience profile. No adequate provision was made for barriers, which calmly channel customers swiftly towards the entrance in an orderly manner – ensuring that heightened vibes didn't change into aggro. The small number of security carrying out searches slowly added to the frantic backlog. They didn't seem in control – didn't seem to know what was going on and could only shout at customers anxious for any information, and the 'what-the-fuck-is-going-on?' atmosphere fuelled panic. A backpacker described the same kind of disturbance outside a venue in Auckland, New Zealand when things became hectic as customers waited to see Grooverider.

Wayne Roast feels that using dogs for security is too intimidating for the customers. I remember TV pictures of the former South African security force's canine crowd control exercises in Johannesburg. Use of dogs is entirely inappropriate — especially as a prelude to a night's raving, for God's sake. Crowd control is a serious business. People write books about it, police attend courses on it. It's not something that should be left to chance. There are always unavoidable last minute problems. Keeping punters waiting is not a situation most promoters are happy with. Excited customers want to get into the venue as soon as possible. The cold, boredom, stress and occasional aggro can take the edge off the evening before it's even begun. The queue is one thing that reviewers tend to mention. Everyone remembers a bad queue. But it's not always the organisers' fault. Sometimes things happen inside the venue that delay matters outside. Sometimes punters' last minute decision slows things down. People who hadn't bought tickets mobbed Roast at Leicester Square's Hippodrome in late '96 and police were called to the disturbance. Anyone with a valid ticket who couldn't get in was given a refund that night.

"Tickets are on sale four to five weeks in advance of an event but some people can't be bothered. They prefer to get there on the night, waving 20 / 30 quid in the air." WAYNE, ROAST

One raver waited unsuccessfully for what seemed like an eternity, trying to get into AWOL at the Ministry of Sound. "Loads of people were in the queue and it looked like we weren't getting in. I started shouting, "Refund", and a guy came out with a big wedge and started giving people their money back, which we thought was fair. When people saw that there was something being done about the problem, there was respect for the promoter."

Terry Turbo's team has their own way of dealing with potential hooligans in the queue. "We do an attitude test. We've got a couple of people out in the crowd. If you see people pushing to the front. They don't come in. They get taken out the crowd and told to fuck off. They're just being rude. They don't give a fuck about anyone. They just want to get in."

THE SEARCH

Despite how precious we may all feel about the sanctity of a good night out, raves and dances are just a part of a wider society. Perhaps the shock of violence hits hardest when it happens during another of the best nights of your life. The search can seem intrusive and slightly ridiculous, especially when women are asked to undo their eighteen hole, knee high boots, and remove their jewellery 'cos it's driving the metal detector mad. But a proper, polite and thorough search at the door is essential.

"If you don't want to get searched, then don't come in. If the searches aren't done properly, you don't know how many weapons you've got in there. With drugs you've got a second chance to catch someone. You ain't got a second chance with weapons. The only time you know it's in there is when it's being used."
WAYNE, ROAST

Promoters have suggested that many problems which occur inside the dance are drug-related. A drug buyer is ripped off by a drug dealer. The customer won't say anything because it's illegal. A posse robs a dealer because he's got a lot of money and drugs and he can't say anything because it's illegal. It's difficult for security to control everyone, and mugging at some raves, including in the days of Rage, is not unknown. Terry Turbo, finds the criminal attitude inside a rave incomprehensible. "You pay fifteen quid to come out to a place that's full of nice birds, music, have a laugh, get off yer head, do what you want. What is the point of mugging someone for a gold chain or twenty or thirty quid?"

Ravers often blame security when trouble kicks off, sometimes with just cause. Arrogant and hasty treatment meted out by undisciplined heavies, barely in control of themselves or their dogs, can be a major source of vexation. Clever promoters know their security teams. A lot of people will hold a rave, rent a venue and not even take their own security.

"When One Nation put on an event we take ten. You have to think on these people's level. I'm not slagging off venues or their security staff generally but if you're a doorman working in a club, sick of the job, poor wages every week you get fed up. You start thinking of ways to earn money, all sorts of things can happen. Some doormen are a hundred per cent. Some ain't and you never can tell, so we never take any fucking chances. The way I see it, if people are paying out fifteen quid to go to our dances they've got to be safe. If it's not safe they're gonna tell other people it's moody. Security are troubleshooters. Ours are all martial arts black belts and professional boxers. I've got no steroid freaks on my firm. If you get people pumped up on steroids, they're aggressive, violent and want to fight everyone. If you've got people who are trained in martial arts or boxing they know what they can do to someone and they don't need to give it all that. They can be calm, polite and aware of what's going on around them. We've got some bodyguards who work for us as well. They'll go in the rave watching people and will spot things that don't look right. And you'll find he's got a bag of Es on him or a load of money and wonder where he's got that from and someone's just been mugged. If somebody gets mugged at a rave that's not necessarily the promoter's fault. Anyone who experiences a mugging should report it to the promoter immediately, otherwise the muggers get away with it. If the promoter has done everything that he can possibly do to stop people getting mugged and harassed, if he does everything he can to make the rave what I call a safe rave, well at least he's tried. There's not enough promoters out there trying hard enough. They're just there to rake in as much money as possible." TERRY TURBO, ONE NATION

Rave organisations like World Dance have learned to work with the police. Perhaps their presence doesn't bother young ravers as much as it does the old M25 crowd for whom the arrival of the Bill signalled the end of the dance.

As Jay World Dance points out, "Seeing the police standing there officially at the gates of Lydd or wherever directing the traffic is a lot fucking less oppressive than having them coming over the fields with riot batons in their hands."

TROUBLE IN THE DANCE

It's not so much the trouble in terms of violence. Trouble can also be subtle. Sometimes it's just a feeling. People are left trying to check the attitude, suss out the vibes and watch the body language. Without a psychological metal detector, people are left with their intuition.

One of the unfortunate realities of our multicultural society is that racial power relationships still exist. On the whole white people have the upper hand, but the dance is ruled

by predominantly black music. In raves on their home turf, black people, usually black males, are the only ones free to be the bad bwoys. White guys come in peace to dance, especially if they're in the minority. The majority of black guys also come in peace to rave but if some have got the front, they can exploit the bad-bwoy-in-the-dance niche. However, people should be very careful to avoid simplistic conclusions about racial generalisations. Depending on the circumstances, anyone can flex with Attitude. It's up to the raving collective to educate, ease and squeeze out the bad bwoy niche.

Violence is a distressing part of everyday social interactions. The Jungle / Drum & Bass scene does suffer from it. Let's face it, the last thing you want is someone mashing up the dance, bringing you right down. With few exceptions, problems which affect hundreds or even thousands of innocents are often set off by a tiny minority.

THERE'S ALWAYS BEEN TROUBLE

Eastman, who does what he can to deter any problems at his events, feels that there's always been violence in music and the media focus has made the problem seem worse than it is. "With Jungle, people just got worried. There's one thing you have to remember, Jungle is too popular for its own good. You can go from here to Scotland on a Friday night and you'd probably get three or four murders in some little disco where there's about two or five hundred people. With people cutting each other up, stabbing each other and that's just at little clubs. So all of a sudden, this music gets a lot of attention and the media try and slaughter it. In any underground scene you get trouble. I wouldn't like to tell you some of the things I've seen when I was young. If you think you've seen trouble at Club UN, you should have been at the Tottenham Royal every Sunday night. It was full and you used to get little crews from Hackney fighting Tottenham. Tottenham fighting Enfield. And then if anyone dared come down from Broxbourne or Cheshunt, they'd get bashed. I think it's quietened down. When I was younger in the sound system days, everyone had their things on them. Everyone walked with a knife. Everybody. But a lot of the youths nowadays are very respectful." EASTMAN

It's also well to remember how much events are exaggerated. I once sat upstairs at the Island, Ilford, nursing a friend back from a minor turn he'd had on the dancefloor and overheard a punter going on about a white bloke who had been stabbed and everyone just danced around him. Actually he was alive, almost well and sitting next to us. No surgery necessary.

In JDB there are highs and lows. At times a kind of gloom descends over the London scene and even the music seems off. In mid '95 many DJs like Rap talked about easing off on their London bookings. Navigator, 5ive'O, Moose and a host of other MCs chatted lyrics of peace and understanding, with a warning. If the bad bwoy elements didn't fix up, the artists would fill their diaries with dates in Toronto, Tokyo, Mannheim and Chicago. They didn't blame the massive, but they were tired of the destruction of a scene they'd worked so hard to build.

Eastman does have a point about the focus on violent incidents at Jungle raves. How safe is anyone, anywhere? After the Glastonbury '97 Festival clear-up, the police confirmed that a number of offensive weapons had been confiscated by officers and festival security staff. They also confirmed that during Glastonbury '95, festivalgoers were hit with rounds from a real firearm. What kind of people take guns to Glastonbury? Perhaps the focus on problems in Jungle has been too great. But some promoters have decided that a policy of absolute zero tolerance is the only way to combat troubles in the dance. Sure, there's violence in society at large and there's always been problems in clubs and raves but some promoters aren't going to accept it. They'll have none of it. No mugging, no moodiness – don't even think of entering their manor with a bad intent.

"There is a bad element and we have to deal with it."
GOLDIE, OPEN FORUM, 1996

COMBATING TROUBLE IN THE DANCE

Metalheadz at The Blue Note. Three bad bwoys barge their way through the packed dancefloor towards Grooverider in the DJ box. They lash out, with a hail of punches striking Metalheadz' label manager Christian on the head, sending him to the floor. Goldie and Grooverider clock the commotion. Groove stops the track dead and jumps out of the DJ box. Dealing with the matter, they eject the guys with a 'warning' not to come back – ever. The music stays off until Rider returns to roll the track, leaving the silence hanging as a lesson to anyone who still needed one.

"I saw some commotion, just got off the decks and flung him out. Anybody who comes with any Attitude like that goes straight back out the door. Simple as that. I ain't got no time for it. 'Cos when you've got time for it, more will come and more. You've got to send them the message straight away. We don't have no trouble down Blue Note. The only fights is between me and Goldie, when we're flinging somebody out. We're not having it." GROOVERIDER

Grooverider wasn't impressed that one of the ejected punters was a crack user. When it comes to drug use, ravers are usually tolerant. But, no other drug has been cited so many times, by so many people, as an unwelcome ingredient in the cocktail.

"A very large reason I like this scene is that, if you ever saw anyone in a club smoking anything chemical, you're gonna throw them out. You won't wait for the bouncer to do it. If you're the promoter or the DJ or even just a regular member of the crowd, you'll feel that person's taking the piss. Crack has the same kind of sociability as cocaine but has a complete psychotic reaction in people."
DAVE STONE, MOVEMENT

"People have to realise if they are going out for the violence thing it's not good because ultimately it will destroy the scene and it almost did destroy the scene." BRET, TELEPATHY

Cleveland Watkiss calls the dance arena "Church". "When you step in there seven till twelve, you're coming to Church man. You have to respect the Tabernacle. We're very vigilant at Blue Note with people that wanna cause trouble. We're not having none of that down there. It's just about music."

Aside from anything, it's about respect – doing the right thing. And that goes for everyone. Luton's Exodus Collective have an ethic that permeates through all those who attend their parties. Respect the space. Don't distress the dance. Leave all the negative energy outside or hard step it off to jump-up JDB. Although some of Exodus' security originate from Luton's baddest bwoys, disputes are avoided. Not by a show of force but through a code of personal / collective responsibility. Respect your fellow man. It's not a message they preach, it's an example people follow. The rave becomes hallowed ground. With crews who have travelled from as far as Manchester, Wales, Bristol, London and Northern Ireland, the Collective have more problems with the police than any of their own followers.

BOOKING AGENTS

A DJ arrives home with a vague memory of having to play out somewhere before they get to bed next morning. The agent has sorted it. They are the DJ's link with the next booking. They make sure you know where the venue is and tell you which slot to turn up for. Your agent knows the sort of places you like and which parties and crowds you love playing for. They'll call you to discuss money or to prioritise a World Dance or Desire over an unknown. There are judgments to be made about new names in the game. Hopefully, the new organisation is not a fly-by-night.

But with the experiences of the eighties when, after the excuses, DJs were the last to be paid, very little is left to trust. Back in the day, there were occasional articles in magazines about the need for a DJ union. Nothing of consequence came about. Friends continued to see their hard working, talented DJ mates facing last minute cancellations or being ripped off. Having to walk away without so much as a taxi fare, let alone anything to cover the outlay for their tunes. There had to be a halt to business deals concluded in back rooms and alleys with threats of violence.

SARAH SANDY, GROOVE CONNECTION

That was often the form when Sarah Sandy moved from being a raver friend of Fabio, Grooverider, Frost and Mickey Finn, and became Sarah Groove Connection — agent to the DJs. It wasn't any easy ride. After graduating from Goldsmiths, and free-falling through the raver's life, Sarah fancied the path of artist management. Bored with the inappropriate training ground in the accounts department of artist management agency, Chris Morrison Organisation (CMO), a door opened unexpectedly.

"I knew all these DJs and they were all getting knocked and ripped off. And I had a concept of what I'd like to do but couldn't put it into action. I didn't have an office. I didn't have anything. So I went to meet this woman and we kind of clicked. She was managing a Rock star and said to me that I could use her office as a base for a DJ agency and introduced me to Frankie Valentine and some of the other guys. Now as soon as I'd met Frankie Valentine we clicked too. He'd had an idea about trying to set up a DJ union. I'd had the idea of setting up a DJ agency. When we started there were no other DJ agencies. But about the same time I heard that Dy-na-mix had been set up. It was exactly the same time. I don't know who was there first."

Taking on an unwieldy list of over thirty DJs, Sarah tried to formalise a part of the informal Rave scene. In late '89 a number of hoax raves sprang up. And though Rider and the others trusted this enthusiastic, professional raver with their wages, things went wrong on the very first payday. "The worst possible thing happened. All the DJs cheques bounced. I found out that my business partner was a fraudster with huge debts. All the time I was working for my little agency thing, putting money into this bank account, she had a thirty grand debt and the bank were closing all her assets. I went down to the office and she decided not to let me in. Just tried to take over the business and not let me have any of my work — my stuff on the computer. I actually had a punch-up with her, the first I'd ever had in my life. A proper punch-up and walked out with my things."

Back in the cold, Sarah linked up with Caroline Robertson of Westbury Music who she met previously at CMO. Caroline liked Sarah's concept, and with a 'go for it' endorsement she set Sarah up with a cheap office near Brixton tube station. The name Groove Connection came to Sarah as she stood in the bank and needed a name to put on the business account application form. In January 1990, with a fine-tuned list of DJs she knew she could work with, Sarah began again to formalise the business.

"I got a really rude name for asking for payment up-front or no-one's coming. 'Cos Fabio and Grooverider were getting knocks. Getting paid twenty pounds or sixty pounds for playing six hours each at Sunrise or Biology. Sometimes not even getting paid for that. So I tried to implement this new way of working. Of course all those people hated us from day one 'cos I was really strict."

It seemed very irregular. In the past, deals had been done directly with the DJs. Now there was this middle class white woman, apparently calling the shots between promoters and the artists. Honest promoters didn't know what to make of it. The dodgy ones were vexed. She wanted money or at least a deposit up front. There would be contracts and discussions about working conditions. But business went well and the DJ / promoter bad old days mostly came to an end.

"As time went by, the promoters knew there wasn't a way around it. The DJs were totally loyal to us when they phoned them; it was like, "Well, phone Sarah." I know I'm rude but I can hold my own in any argument and I'm good at checking contracts. Ultimately, I'm protecting them."

Along with Kate and Jo in the Groove Connection office, Sarah works with a core of DJs from across the Jungle / Drum & Bass spectrum including Mickey Finn, Frost, Fabio and Grooverider.

CAROLINE, UNIQUE ARTISTS

Most of those leading the scene today are the hardcore posse who stuck it out right through to the after-after-party. Another of the crew who's been raving since the days of Energy, Sunrise and Biology, Caroline never wanted to leave the scene. She linked up with the likes of Randall, Fabio & Grooverider at Rage and ardently followed the music into a dream job, booking DJs and MCs for an emerging Jungle scene. Working for rave agency, Kryptonite, Caroline loved her Jungle and didn't really appreciate being asked to book

House and Garage DJs. It wasn't working out. Things like that spoil the party, make you want to leave. Caroline felt she'd been taken advantage of. She'd already done the dancefloor networking and, realising she could do the job herself, spoke to the DJs and Sarah Sandy about setting herself up as an agent. The professional promoters were also on her side.

Caroline started Unique from her bedroom at her mum's house in '93. DJs Randall and Hype joined her agency and others soon followed. The foundation work had been done in the clubs. At this end of the business, once your name stands for trust and reliability, you only need a telephone and a place to put it. She now represents DJs Randall, Hype, Roni Size, Andy C, Darren Jay, Cool Hand Flex, Phantasy, Marly Marl, Zinc, Probe, Ron, Krust, L Double and Doc Scott with GQ, Flux, 5ive'O and Strings amongst the MCs.

"There haven't been any problems with money recently. You get the money up front. If the DJ can't find the promoter on the night and has to get back on the road, you just have to chase the cash by phone. The DJs aren't really into the back-to-back business. The promoters say that the crowd are really into it but the DJs can sense the crowd and feel they're not."

Some promoters who stage regular events have a set price, as they book DJs for more or less every event. New promoters are always trying to blag the price down. The artist always has the last word as far as a booking is concerned. If they go somewhere and the system is crap they'll speak directly to the promoter. If the system doesn't improve they won't go again. A lot of work comes from abroad: Chicago, Belgium, Finland, Paris and Athens are all new destinations. Someone's always off to Germany. Randall's just come back from Japan and he'll be off to Australia in a few weeks time. Hype will be there next year". *CAROLINE, UNIQUE ARTISTS, NOVEMBER 1996*

Four years down the line, business is good though stressful. She's on call twenty-four hours a day. Promoters will ring up to ask for a booking for the next night. She even receives calls on the mobile when she's at the supermarket checkout.

Tania's Underground Music Collective

Tania wanted something more from life than working in a factory like many of her schoolmates. After leaving school and training Tania was employed by Social Services caring for pensioners in residential homes and also became a home help. "This is probably where I get this sort of mother hen thing from. The need to take care of my brood if you like." Part time hours allowed her to explore other avenues. She took a turn on the mic in a Jazz club and modeled briefly in New York. Returning to England her itchy feet led Tania into a two year training course as a croupier. Then she was off again, this time sailing the seas on cruise liners. Then DJ SS offered her an opportunity that she'd stay with. Tania started artists' booking agency Underground Music Collective (UMC). Her roster is impressive: Simon Bassline Smith, DJ SS, Bryan Gee, Shy FX, Donovan Bad Boy, Twisted Individual, Generation Dub, Distorted Minds, Jo Jo Rock, Frenzic, John B, The Mixologists, MC Fun, Skibadee, IC3, The Ragga Twins and MC MC. When Tania first started her agency few people owned mobile phones. Contacting artists could be difficult. "You'd have to go through all the information with them. "You are here at this time. Here's the name of the promoter. Here's his number. That's how much you've gotta collect." That is what it was like."

Tania organised quarterly agency meetings bonding UMC artists together as a family. She also wanted the agency to be seen as a collective exploring what they as a group of talented people could achieve. That's the ethos behind UMC. The meetings were originally held in Bryan's V Recordings office with everyone crammed into a small smoky room. They'd discuss whatever was on the agenda for a few hours, and then head off to Bar Rumba. "The meetings were a place to bring new ideas and ask, "What if we did this? What if we did that? Would that work? Would this work?" The meetings were a good place for me to find out what they look like. I used to see people at raves but that was the only time. I didn't want it to be like that. If I was going to represent them I wanted to have a better relationship with them. More than just waving at them in the DJ box."

The meetings were positive and many of the ideas presented by the Collective were later adopted. Tania would also relate to the artists how she wanted to run the agency and clarify what she expected from them. The artists could discuss any issues they had with Tania's management. "The meetings were a good thing until people started to abuse them. I started to get fed up cos I used to travel down to London to hold these meetings and only half the people would turn up. We had booked and paid for the room. It wasn't just a social gathering. It was to discuss important points in the agency"

Thinking about how the other agents perform Tania understands that they all have individual ways of working. "Sarah Groove Connection and Tracey Ton Promotions have very different personalities but both are very strong women. Jo who works in the Groove Connection office has been part of the scene forever. She handles people totally different to Tracey or me. Sometimes I wish I had the front to handle artists as Jo does. Jo's kind of, no flannel, no fuss, "What's your problem? Get on with it." Tracey is very tentative and likes to care for people's needs. I am somewhere in the middle. I would like to give them a good slap and say, "Come on get on with it." If they really push me to the limit I might bark at them down the phone. But that lasts for a minute. And it only happens with the ones that I am really close to. You look after each individual as an individual. They all need looking after in different ways. Some artists are very self-sufficient. You can send them information for their diaries and you don't hear from them apart from a reply to say that the gig was good, the gig was not good, whatever. Then you have the others where you have sent them their information and in half an hour they are on the phone asking, "What time am I going on?" and they have to admit that they are in the car having left the house without the information. They are known offenders. It's always the same people. I can guarantee that a Friday evening call will be from somebody who has missed their flight. It's a very small number of people, perhaps two or three. Bryan Gee said, "We should name and shame them."

"I think it doesn't take a certain type of personality to do this. Perhaps Sarah and Caroline are a bit more edgy than Tracey and I. We all have that care element because that is what we do but you have got to have a firm edge somewhere in there." All the agency ladies are excellent at multi-tasking. "I can coordinate someone's diary, be on the phone to Australia, cook dinner, and run a bath for my kids at the same time.

"Regular promoters have always got their bargaining tools. If they have artists that they put on every other event, they have a fixed agreed fee. That's not going to be the same as the next artist that they very rarely book or have never booked. The terms and conditions are going to be different. There's always room to negotiate. I would rather take a gig for an artist for less money with their permission, than turn it down completely. If artists can be flexible it's all the better for them. The people who do bargain you down and pay that little bit less than they should have, expect to pay that on every occasion. And that can't happen. There is still a promoter who calls to say, "I gave him his first booking and we paid him 50 quid.""

TON PROMOTIONS, LEABRIDGE ROAD, SUMMER '95

The burgeoning chaos of sorting out the professional lives of their MCs and DJs is a feat to organise. As is common everywhere in this scene, the telephone rings constantly, only here it seems even more manic. Tracey takes a well-handled list from the wall, whilst Nikki talks to a promoter about their DJ's cash. Kenny Ken's name and the date was followed by an impressive number of towns and cities. The first booking around 10pm, the last at 6am.

Winter '97 and Ton Promotions have moved their office closer to home in Leyton. Kenny will set up his studio nearby. Two years down the line it's clear that the burgeoning chaos is always part of the job. And Tracey Ton Promotions does a stressful job, without stressing out. Agents have an informal pastoral role, taking time out to chat to artists about their personal lives. Aside from the bookings, egos and artistic mentality – they're friends. Curiously, they're all women. And no, not all of them are DJs' girlfriends. Even if they are, as is the case with Sarah & Fabio, Tracey & Kenny and Tanya & DJ SS, that's not the point. Perhaps it's one of those gender division things but the agency women get the job done. They exude efficiency, dependability, an aptitude for clear-headed organisation and a sense for business. But they don't make everyone happy.

In the World Dance office, Jay fumes at the latest charges he has to negotiate with a DJ's agent. At Roast, Kingsley hands me a photocopy of an article from *Knowledge* magazine. The writer isn't happy either. In fact it's one of the most critical things I've seen published. One agent suspects the author's true motivation. That aside, the issue that warrants attention is higher fees. Jay feels the scene can't take it. The ravers can't afford it. As an agent who also has experience as a promoter, Sarah Sandy insists that she'll only negotiate what she feels the promoter or scene can take.

"Compared to DJs like Oakenfold, Fabio and Groove aren't making as much money. I know some DJs charge five / ten grand a set. We're nowhere near that. We still keep it real. I have to increase their money because of the demand. Otherwise they're going to look stupid." SARAH SANDY, GROOVE CONNECTION

Sarah cites the big Rock style agents as the real problem. They're the ones trying to entice artists with much larger wads of cash. She also reminds us that she works for her artists. "At the end of the day of course we do what we're told. If they want to do the job, they do the job. It's not like I'm making their choices or fucking up their business."

"Sara's comparison was right. If you look at House DJs' wages, and even Garage DJs, we are way behind. We're the poor relations." Tania feels that part of the problem stems from the way in which Drum & Bass promoters promote their parties in comparison with the House scene. Seems we have it all too good. "Drum & Bass punters are spoilt for their £25. They go in and see 20 DJs and a million MCs for their £25. Whereas your average House party goers will pay a similar fee and have maybe two headline DJs doing a three or four hour stint with no MC." One can see Tania's point. Drum & Bass promoters would be risking everything by trying to mimic House organisations. "People would look at the flyer and say, "What's that?! I'm not paying £25 to go there." TANIA, UMC

Then there are the agency tours. The agent takes a group of artists from their rosta and sets up nationwide promotional nights. In a sense, the agents turn promoters. It can be taken as agents encroaching on promoters' territory but we've yet to see a Unique Artists or Groove Connection night on a Bank Holiday Sunday or New Year's Eve.

As new promoters, even with phat rostas, success isn't guaranteed. But the transition is hardly surprising, and for agents who rarely see their artists perform, it's an opportunity to be involved in a 'family' event. DJs, MCs and agents also have the chance to stage the kind of night they all want to do. It's difficult to hold back this accumulated experience. Besides, it's the way they all started, by seeing a gap in the market and filling it. Unique held club nights, including an English and American tour, and produced a Unique Artist album.

If the artists didn't want to be involved, they wouldn't be. And the accusation that agents live off the backs of their artists? Well they're all consenting adults, with everyone working hard for their money.

The final straw for some is the verbal Attitude radiated down the phones by some booking agents. And Jay points the finger in one direction. Perhaps different people have different ways of communicating. But the promoters are collectively pissed off.

"Caroline You'll Never Guess What Happened ..."

DJs are always missing their flights. Andy C and Phantasy were off to Switzerland when they missed their flight. They booked another flight and went off to get some food. When they returned to board the second plane, they found it had left as well. So for the third time, they went back to the desk to sort another flight.

DJ Ron parked on the hill opposite Hastings Pier. When he left the rave, his car was gone. He asked some cabbies if they'd seen his car. "Yeah mate, the police had to tow it away to the compound." Ron had left the handbrake off and the car had rolled down the hill. When the police arrived, it was sitting in the middle of the main road. That night Ron and his brother Lenny stayed 'round a delighted raver's house and collected the car the next day after paying the tow-away charge.

"Don't know about doing those under-18 raves again ..." Andy C was at an under-18 rave and the kids were rough. When the sound broke down, Andy was shocked at the kids screaming at the poor engineer in a very un-rave-like manner, "Sort the sound out you big fat cunt."

DJ Hype on The Frontline ...

"There's funny things, mad things, bad things ... I've been in Canada DJing where they've been throwing spliffs at me. There was a power cut at World Dance with 10,000 people looking at me like I pulled the plug out. There's no soundman coming or nothing and I'm standing there, everyone's going "Wooa" and I'm like, "Well it ain't fucking me is it?!" Zinc was in Germany once when the warm-up guy was playing. Some raver's come and just freaked out. He picked up the turntable, threw it and started rolling 'round the floor. One time in Canada, there's me, Brockie and MC Fearless held at customs for nine hours – they were saying we were drug smugglers.

Another time I'm DJing and someone's going, "Stop the music. Stop the music." And I'm like, "What the fuck?" And there's this guy out cold on the floor and I'm like, "Shit someone's been stabbed or robbed or something." And it ain't. What's happened is, whilst he's raving, the glitter ball has fallen and knocked him out. Later that night, he's come back with a brace thing on his neck and he's still raving".

Management

If their career develops, a DJ / producer's life can become too difficult to handle. Aside from a mountain of contracts generated by new work, there's the media, record companies and yet more promoters to deal with. Some artists expand outside the Rave industry and their career paths need greater planning than a booking agent can usually provide. However in JDB, artists seldom allow one person to sort everything for them. Perhaps it's a fearful hangover from the Rock days when the 'manager' made more decisions about the artist than the artists knew about themselves. Many JDB players have opted to take care of their own DJ / production business, leaving the rest in the hands of those they can trust.

At A Guy Called Gerald's label Juice Box, Craig manages the record business and leaves Gerald to manage himself. "I've been through management teams. It didn't really work for me. They were going for themselves and I came to the conclusion that I was unmanageable so Craig does the label. Another reason is that when you deal with the majors, they want to deal with your management, not you. I'd have to have someone that would speak to me."

A section of the underground DJ / producer booking agents experienced problems when the majors started to move in. There are reports of Caroline at Unique fending off the advances of the big management agencies. Groove Connection suffered problems when Bukem came under new management. In a confusion of loyalties, he started to no-show for some Groove Connection bookings, including the '96 Phoenix Festival. "We had a real problem with the Bukem thing. I decided to cut my losses it was either he worked with us or with them."

Management agencies can offer artists the larger fees more common outside the Rave scene. It's this factor that Sarah Groove Connection blames for the real escalation in DJ wages, not the agencies. Sarah feels that with her experience as a promoter, she understands clubland economics and will try to negotiate with promoters who tend to talk prices down.

"The problem is the big agencies; like ITB and MPI who work with Rock stars and people like Paul Oakenfold, push prices up. They still like to sneer at us saying to the artist we can get you this and that price. Groove said when he signed with Sony, "Don't get me with a big agent. Sarah is coming with me." I'm good at what I do. They can't get 'round me. I don't think one of those agents could do what we do in our scene. They can't work fast enough and they charge too much. They don't have an understanding of the club scene and trying to charge so much money will break up our scene. I've argued with all these people and managed to come out on top. It's a struggle the whole way and I'm not going to give up."

But Sarah acknowledges that she can't do everything for everyone's career. There is a logical separation between the work Groove Connection do directly on the Rave scene and that more related to the record business.

Trenton Harrison manages Goldie and Trenton's world is the music business. Formally head of Hip Hop's Rush Management UK, he's also worked at the Chris Morrison Organisation and with artists Technotronik, Nicolette and A Homeboy, A Hippy & A Funky Dread. Trenton wanted to get Goldie in the studio to cut a tune. John Knowel who was managing him at the time saw Goldie doing other things and really didn't want him making records. Two years later, after Goldie had worked on over forty or so other tracks, Trenton and Rebel MC were driving through Camden Town when they saw Goldie. They arranged a meeting and discussed some of his tracks. Trenton remembers, "He was always going on about this track Timeless that was in his head, knowing its structure, exactly how long it would be. He got the track down within two or three weeks. It was totally out there. It was then that I started managing him." It would be Trenton's job not just to go out and negotiate a major deal, but find a company with whom they could really do business. He didn't just go for the most money.

It's a manager's role to get the best for their artists, raising their profiles with coverage in magazines, TV, radio, attending award ceremonies and staging promotional tours — especially when a new album is due. Anything that can maximise record sales. Meredith, Goldie's PA, sits in Trenton's office at his company, NUR, and sifts through the requests for interviews, TV appearances, photo shoots, DJ and radio slots. Trenton dealt intensively with Channel 4 Commissioning Editor, David Stevenson, during the filming of Goldie's pilot Fereala. Though Goldie, hands-on as ever, always had the last word.

Trenton has a knowledge and feel for the street, especially when it comes to where the punters buy the music. "If you ignore it, they'll ignore you. If they don't know the tune is out there, it won't sell." Sitting at the top of the pile, Trenton watches as companies grab artists without researching or investing in the underground infrastructure. "You could have Michael Jackson, but if you don't know where to put the records, if you ain't got good distribution, you won't sell the records." The same goes for publicity and marketing. "We've told London Records everything and they've been excellent in asking what they don't know. They've had to work with the smaller distribution companies and set up an account in Romford market so the vinyl could be sold there. We had to give them a list of four hundred shops — they didn't know half of them and didn't have accounts with another section. That meant forging links with all of those shops. The fact that 'things weren't done that way' wasn't runnin' ". Other majors would have to find a new modus operandi. London Records had to check out all those guys with the small distribution vans because they have a solid base.

In '96 Trenton took on Grooverider, Dillinja and Lemon D when they signed with Sony UK. With regards to all that 'DJ business', he doesn't want any part of it. It's a different world.

04.55am. We hit Bradford town centre, squeezing every red light. The number of mini-roundabouts connecting the empty streets doesn't tally with the faxed details. Pull a u-turn as a taxi driver points us in the right direction. Clock still ticking, we park up, grab record boxes out the boot, blur through security, punter's greetings, the promoter's "Didn't think you was gonna make it" shout, and DJ Ron steps up to the decks right on time.

DJs

"If music be the food of love, play on."
WILLIAM SHAKESPEARE, TWELFTH NIGHT

Peering through thick rimmed Ronnie Barker glasses, the shopkeeper's fat fingers stab at the keys of the alto saxophone. *I can't sell my baby.* "I'll give you one fifty for it," he grunted. *It's wrong to sell a musical instrument.* "Ah mate. I paid you two fifty." The sax rested on his beer belly paunch. "One sixty, take it or leave it." *Can't abandon Coltrane. This guy doesn't feel my sacrifice. I'm no good at this bargaining business, should have brought my mate.*

Shit it's now or never. "One seventy, I'll throw in the case as well." "Done." *I might well have been.* Shifting into fourth on the high street with the notes stuffed in my pocket, I don't really care. Cutting through the traffic from Edgware, homing in on Tottenham Court Road, I park up and practically run into the shop's glass counter. Voice shaking slightly with words I'd waited too long to say. "Yo mate. I'll take that Technics Twelve Ten."

Across the way I check the brother clutching his own freshly purchased Technics deck; Londoners and strangers, we exchange a knowing look, heads nodding to some hidden beat. My man was made up. A new dawn for both of us and fuck it, the bank could pay for the rest.

SO YOU WANNA BE A DJ?

How can I move the crowd? As a punter, it's not enough to be part of the crew, you want to be the captain – you want to be the DJ. You want to take your turn to rock da party.

The path to fame has many courses. This is the 90s. DJs, as is often said, are the pop stars of the 90s. In a sense this is true. There's money, groupies, flash cars, adoring fans, travel to exotic locations and in some instances for those who cross over to producing, large record company deals. DJs move around, have their times and places. They make a contribution that's meaningful for one person or thousands. They can break a new direction in music, as was the case with Fabio, Bukem and Intelligent Drum & Bass. They can rule the roost as Jungle Godfather Grooverider, Jungle Don DJ Ron or x-amount of awards winner DJ Hype. Others achieve a modicum of fame on pirate radio whilst many never leave the bedroom or mix tape circuit. But in the imagination of the youth, DJs are glamourous.

Back in the early eighties, for any of the names riding on point today, fame wasn't the goal. Today's household names were and are compelled by a love of music and entertaining. Nicky Blackmarket is known universally for his outright enthusiasm for music and DJing.

"Me and Clarky used to play Blues parties where we was the only two white blokes in the place but it was wicked. We loved it. We'd set up all the speakers with our friends. I checked Shaka. I'm into everything. I was playing all kinds of Dance music, Ragga, Street Soul, Funk – James Brown stuff. That was when a DJ was a DJ in terms of his selection. All the younger DJs don't really know about all that". NICKY BLACKMARKET

Rave folklore has it that, at the end of their 4am slot in some empty, back alley, old style club, Fabio and Grooverider were loading their records into the boot of the motor when they were besieged by some new style ravers – desperate to party on and on. Fabio and Grooverider stayed and played till the last of them dropped. The importance of the Originators, Grooverider, Fabio & Frost, cannot be underestimated as they provided a platform and focus for underground music. They had faith and saw potential in British Breakbeat where others didn't.

If you become famous through love and dedication to your art, it's an added bonus. But being famous can't be the driving goal. Premature ambition can cloud the mind. Musical perfection must come first. Sometimes you know you've got it. Honest mates are possibly the best initial judges. They'll compare you to the best that's inspired them last night. But they can be wrong. Sometimes it takes an expert ear. Sarah at Groove Connection receives around fifty tapes a week from people who either can't mix or don't have their own distinctive style.

It seems a long way from producing bedroom mix tapes to getting your name on a flyer and standing in the DJ box at Tribal Gathering, World Dance or wherever but there is an informal, albeit haphazard, career path. If you're lucky, you'll manage to get hold of a pair of decks. DJ Zoe remembers, "Some of the guys we knew had decks and went on holiday. They were some crappy Sound Lab things, but we had decks in the house." Getting used to manipulating the vinyl often starts with DJs like Ron scratching and rewinding his mum's single belt-driven turntable. Some people use slipmats made from newspaper and mess around with volume, bass and treble controls for extra effect. Anything that sort of works to get in the groove. If you can't afford the outlay for turntables, you might have to go part shares on a set-up or borrow the cash, as Kemistry & Storm did from Goldie. Hype learned to scratch mix through not being able to afford a mixer. Once you've got hold of the technology you can spend hours alone trying to mix two simple tunes, trying to remember what your school music teacher said about beats and bars. When you've cracked that, friends suffer streams of dodgy mix tapes in your quest for perfection. Some of the cassettes are destined for tomorrow's demos – when you get around to it. There's no time for slackness. Going out to clubs and observing other DJs in the box is your master class – you won't find many DJing lessons offered in *Floodlight*.

As you improve, friends will ask you to play at their parties. From there, you're in the public arena. With luck, you start playing bigger parties and / or pirate radio, depending on the people you know and the access you have to those avenues. Reaching this goal is only the first hurdle of the real training ground. It's here you learn about motivation, getting to the studio or the party in all weathers no matter the distance or availability of transport. Eastman of Kool FM took time out to big up all the DJs who've made their shows despite having to wait for night buses in the snow not knowing if anyone's even listening. Or going out to play in some 'God knows where club,' where you're lucky even to get paid. Mixing disk after disk, with no monitor or on a dodgy frequency, skills are inadvertently honed.

There's the stress. Even Randall admitted a pre-performance rush of adrenaline, which can make your hand jitter almost uncontrollably. In learning to concentrate and focus, you have to keep your head while all around you are off theirs. You get used to being under stress – without stressing out.

"I will admit I did turn off the wrong record at the Blue Note. I got so excited. I stopped the wrong record but luckily I could bluff it and pretend it was a rewind. We're always a bit nervous, under pressure to perform. But we put pressure on ourselves." *DJ STORM*

BETWEEN THE BEATS

It's a constant circuit. Living in record shops, listening to the radio, checking all that's fresh and new. Perhaps DJing seems deceptively easy but you have to put in almost obsessive groundwork. In the cause, you need to get about and get your name about. Blagging to become a producer as well as a consumer of the industry. Musically and aspirationally you start separating yourself from the crowd. At this point, amidst hundreds or even thousands of ravers, friends will always find their aspiring DJ mate – stuck by the DJ box. Some find the people who stand in clubs staring at the DJ's hands a little sad and trainspotterish. It's an unfair observation. Gazing over the DJ box is probably the best place to understand exactly what they are doing. You can observe how to mix and blend the tunes, change the pitch, cue the next record and get the rewind stylishly right without knocking the stylus abruptly across the grooves. That's aside from learning the tricks of the cross-fader. You'll muster the confidence to go beyond playing a selection of crowd-pleasers, heading deeper into the music, expressing your arrangement with the beats and the voice you sing with.

Coming with that B-Boy 'I'm gonna be the best' ethic, you don't have the right to step out of the bedroom until you're sure you've got something better to offer. That was the case with Hype in the early days, "There was all these DJs that were earning a fortune and they couldn't even mix two beats! That's what got me into this scene – I thought most of the DJs were technically shit."
DJ HYPE, DREAM MAGAZINE, SPRING 1997

The fast moving JDB scene is so tied up with the freshness of the beats that it almost seems that having the latest test presses, more so Dub Plates, is what it's all about. DJs can get caught up in the politics of tune acquisition, but good DJing is more to do with structuring your set and having a good musical ear.

Interview With Grooverider, January 1997

B: If you're Grooverider, you've got the best record collection in the world.

G: It don't mean that at all man, 'cos I make the most of what I got. It's not about going down Music House and spending five hundred pounds on Dubs. It's not about that. That's where a lot of people go wrong. They think that 'cos they got loads of Dub Plates in their box that makes them a better DJ. It doesn't do that at all. It means you're an idiot. You just spent five hundred pounds on a pile of shit and I could spend fifty pound on something that would rip out your whole collection.

B: I've got this theory that being a top DJ isn't only about technical skills it's about politics.

G: No, that's bullshit as well. You could pick out your best five records and I could pick my best five and then we play it to a crowd and we'd see who's got the best five. That's what being a DJ is about. D'ya get what I'm saying? It's about who has got the best ear. You could have the same tunes in the box as the next person if you're not structuring those tunes right, they ain't gonna sound the same. That's what DJing is."

Many DJs fall into the copycat trap. It takes something more to be different and stand musically above the rest. "I've got pretty much some of the most innovative DJs at my agency. Unfortunately, there's not too many innovators out there."
SARAH, GROOVE CONNECTION

IN THE MIX

"They're using tools. There's an art in mixing two records. Making them run in synch is just part of it. There's loads of other aspects like what part of the record is played." CLEVELAND WATKISS

Miles Davis talked about finding your own musical voice. It's the same with a musical instrument as it is with a pair of Technics. Taking the crowd on a musical journey goes beyond playing an informed selection of tunes, remixer', a tune in each hand with a mix to deal out.

After a workshop with Nicky Blackmarket, Gavin Hills suggested in *The Face* that there was nothing much to it really. He didn't see what all the fuss was about. But professional DJing is a difficult business. Like a martial art you're blending the technical, physical and spiritual. Hearing the beats on beats with clarity inside the storm. Riding the pitch control, nursing every note into the next socket. No clanging. No beats bouncing ahead of the field like so many rabbits. DJs call that 'sword fencing' through the mix.

"In the mix, you're in the zone. Your mind and body are elsewhere ..." DJ RON

"Mixing is like meditation." MISTER T, RUDE FM

"If the sound system is shit, I have to really concentrate and I'm in a world of my own. If you talk to me when I'm DJing you could go, "You're a cunt. I've just robbed your house." And I'd go "Yeah, yeah." "And I'm gonna kill your girlfriend." And I'd be, "Yeah, alright mate. Safe." When you see me after I've finished my set it's like I've done a workout. Try and talk to me then and it's like "Give me a couple of minutes to get my head back together". " DJ HYPE

They're all in a world of their own. Brockie's head bounces with every beat in the headphones. Rap and Wildchild bob from side to side, riding the rhythms. Roni Size, bent almost double over the mixer, works the grooves intensely – a vein running down his forehead throbs furiously 'til he draws the next disc. Ron screws up his face like a bass guitarist as he teases the funk out of the track with the faders, dancing as the beats fall on the one. Others like Mickey Finn make

Grooverider

mixing look as hard as the beats that flood out the speakers. Rider, Randall and Andy C stand impassively over the decks moving confidently from mix to mix to mix. Hype often looks pissed off as he matter-of-factly scratches his way through a set.

On stage at the '97 Finsbury Park Essential Weekender, MC Moose navigated any novices in the audience through the mix. As DJ Rap began to blend two tunes, Moose rapped out "Here comes the mix ... This is one tune ... Here comes the next ... Into the mix .... It's the *long dark tunnel*." This is the area where even the producers don't know what will happen to their tunes. Producer Boymerang described how after giving your tune to a DJ like Grooverider it becomes something else in the mix. There's occasions when, in that *long dark tunnel*, a 'third' tune is created which no one in the house expects.

They used to call Randall's mixing, 'double impact mixing'. He rolls the drops together. When both tunes drop, you get double the impact, double the bassline. The mix is another key part in the crowd's anticipation of a night built on expecting the unexpected. It's a curious thing though, when many DJs try to repeat the same mix at home, it never really comes together in the same way. If you can't prove an element of spirituality, at the very least, creative mixing is the point of art.

GQ remembers the combination of knowledgeable clubbers and DJs at AWOL, Paradise. "Everyone was very sharp, Gachet, Darren, Mickey, Kenny. Randall's mixing ability was different, on another level. The crowd would be goin' off because they'd understand what's going on with the mix. You had a man come running clean from the back of the club, everyone screaming, "Stop the mix! Stop the mix! Rewind the whole mix." I don't care what anyone says. We were the first people to rewind the whole mix."

As a DJ you can only do your best. You might have rocked the horns-in-the-air vibe to perfection, made someone's night unforgettable, impressed the promoters and your peers, inspired other DJs and had the phone lines runnin' red. At worst, you'll have clanged the place out, clearing the floor. If things are really bad, like for Scotland's DJ Kid, you'll be the only Jungle DJ in a sea of very Happy Hardcore punters. When they booed and chucked beer cans he grabbed up the mic, told them to "Fuck off" and left the stage. A tad unprofessional but who'd blame him? Try keeping your focus as Brockie and DJ Ron did in a Manchester club, where gunshots were fired for rewinds showering plaster down from the ceiling.

A SERIOUS ROAD TRIP

"There's a lot of people out there who want to be DJs, but they couldn't cut it on the road. It's really hard out there." DJ RANDALL

Dj Randall's New Year's Night, 1996 / 97
Everyone's prime night and for a top DJ, also the busiest:
Devotion, Cardiff 6.00pm till 7.00pm
Helter Skelter, Milton Keynes 10.00pm till 11.00pm
Euphoria, Wolverhampton 12.30am till 1.30am
Desire, London 4.00am till 5.00am
Moondance, 'Honour set' 6.00am till 7.00am

May '96 and Channel 4 follow Randall through a Saturday night as he plays four raves. Producer Cas Peacock and cameraman Dick Jewel settle into a specially hired Space Cruiser for a punishing night. Many's the time Randall would have to drive himself. Tonight it's my responsibility. We leave Forest Gate, East London, with producer T Bone and De Man Dem and reach Northampton for Randall's 11pm set at Pure X. The buzz sets in as you hit the parked cars and clock the ravers on their way in. Then blap. Randall's at work. Records out the boot, he's through security, finds the right arena, the DJ box, assesses the crowd, the vibes, the acoustics and has a few words with preceding DJ Hype who explains any quirks of the mixer.

Randall

PHOTO BY LU VU

Then it's head down for one hour of total concentration. That's your time to entertain, enhance or mash-up your reputation in that town, with that crowd and that promoter. You're only human but no one remembers that if you clang out. Randall didn't clang. Perhaps there's space for a smoke between the mixes. Hopefully the next DJ turns up on time from wherever, so you can track down the busy promoter, get paid and hit the road again with the crew intact.

Randall settles in for the ride back down the M1 to Central London and AWOL at Victoria's SW1. Same again, churns it out intensively, skillfully until Gachet takes his turn. Across London to Jungle Mania at the Island Ilford to play the three till four set. A brief pause at the Kentucky across from the venue before we're off around the North Circular for the fourth rave of the night at Innovation in Tottenham's Club UN, where Randall's booked for the last or honour set. It's been a busy night. The camera crew has been in his face all night distressing the vibe by turning the stereo down to record their interview. But Randall would be back on the road on Sunday night.

For the Top Guns, gone are the days of the clapped-out Ford Fiestas and Fiat Unos. DJs draw for the fast, stylish and reliable, whichever series of BMW or VR6. With all the stalling that goes on, picking up and waiting for mates or being stuck in the studio until the last possible beat, there's many a motorway journey that takes place at well over a hundred miles an hour – in all weathers. If you're lucky, there's the car crew who'll share the driving and keep the tapes, conversation and refreshments coming. They'll also keep an eye on the road. Randall seems to have a nationwide knowledge of where the speed cameras are and which ones are a blag. Having travelled in excess of 80,000 miles last year – he knows the roads. Brockie who loves the crowds and his work, is thoroughly sick of driving. Between 1996 - 97 he drove over 40,000 miles.

It's an odd existence regularly driving hundreds of miles through England's 'green and pleasant' in the dark, following vague directions to a venue where it's all going off, bang out a session and drive straight back again or off to another club. It's part of the job. Sure, hearts won't be bleeding but for the record, DJs wages don't include driving time or the petrol. It's usually only on trips abroad when the promoter covers flights and accommodation.

With car culture a necessary part of DJ life, there have also been a few accidents. DJ Hype spun his car *en route* to World Dance. "I was a mile away from Lydd and we was on a curve and I was like, "Look, there's the rave" and the car went into a spin." On Boxing Night '96, DJ Ron's Audi spun out of control on Hasting's frozen country lanes. The car, with MC GQ in the passenger seat, bounced upside down into a ditch, mashing the roof over the rear seat – which for once was empty of the usual posse. In April '99 DJ Kemistry was tragically killed on the road returning from a gig in Southampton.

Most people think that women DJs may consider their personal safety a real issue, especially starting as a fresh faced DJ, taking records to some well dodgy areas and hidden studios filled with geezers. None of the female DJs interviewed considered this to be a real concern. Many, like Wildchild, either travel with male friends / fellow DJs or just trust, like any raver, that things will be okay. Usually their concerns are more universal like, "Do they rate me as a DJ?" and "Will we get raided?" Interviewers often ask if there are advantages or disadvantages to being a woman on the circuit. It's a question they're either bored of, or hate. Unsurprisingly, just like the men, their music comes first. They are being booked because of their musical ability, rather than what they look like. "I could look like Pamela Anderson ... If I was crap on the decks, I wouldn't get any bookings and if you're not in the runnin' – don't even race." *DJ RAP*

DJ HYPE

DJ Hype joined the race when it dawned on him that many of the other runners were crap. Back in 1982 - 83 he learnt to scratch mix on one deck — 'cos he didn't have a mixer. He was a natural who put in the practice. In '84 he joined the Heatwave sound system. Like DJ Ron on TNT he played everything from hard Ragga and Rare Groove to Hip Hop, Michael Jackson and early House. Everything that makes up Jungle today. Hype entered the DJ Mixing Championships (DMC) between '87 and '89 getting knocked out in the South England finals. He and Ron were competitive in that Hip Hop sort of way.

"There was a time when me and Ron was on the same Youth Training Scheme learning design and photography. We were never rivals but we were friends. I'd be like, "Ron, can you do this new scratch technique?" and Ron would be like, "Yeah — of course. Can you?" "Yeah." And we both couldn't. Then we'd both be at home learning it." Hype jacked in DMC when he thought the judges biased. More importantly, he wanted to play to audiences. "As a scratch DJ, you don't have too much opportunity to do that."

Hype was still in the sound system working as a scratch DJ alongside rappers. He made flyers, speaker boxes and checked new pirates, Centreforce and Sunrise, whilst working nine-to-five in a Hackney warehouse. "I was listening to some of those guys on air and thought they were shit. They were just crap to me. You'd hear them going "You can catch me at x, y, z — a, b, c", all these clubs. I used to meet up with them in record shops and they're blagging their diaries. And there's me, £80-a-week Kev, down the fuckin' warehouse and I could scratch with every part of my body." Hype's first pirate, WIBS, was based in Tottenham. That's where 'Kev', sorry, 'Dr K' became 'DJ Hype.' The word was on a t-shirt he was wearing.

In August '89, pirate station Fantasy FM started around the corner from his mum's place in Hackney. He played several shows a week and loved it. "In 1991 - 92 I was with this agency from the Midlands. I'd played raves like Dreamscape. I was doing Orange at the Rocket on a Saturday with 2,000 people, Fantasy FM and the Astoria every Saturday. Then it all stopped. The agency fucked up, Orange stopped, Fantasy broke up and it kind of left me high and dry." He even lost

his warehouse job. Demoralised, but with encouragement from Shut Up & Dance, Hype started producing, almost casually making hits whilst looking for a way to further his DJing. He didn't want solely to be either a DJ or a producer but he did want to work in music. "End of '93, I was watching people like Randall and Bukem, wondering why they were doing so much better than me. Well, they were working harder." So Hype worked harder. He made mix tapes, produced more tunes, almost accidentally developed labels and stepped up on legal radio with his show on Kiss 100 FM.

He's a character. Mi God is he a character. You sit there — we're still in the car outside Casablanca's with the engine running — you sit there and he comes out with these things, unprintable things and you're laughing. He's the kind of bloke who says things and goes, "What's so funny? I'm being serious." "Hype, man." I'm catching my breath and drying my eyes from yet another anecdote or comment about people passing by. I sit up straight on the back seat and remember another question. He's a natural who works hard.

B: So how many awards is it this year?

H: The awards don't mean I'm the best or nothing, 'cos for every guy that says, "Hype's wicked," you got another saying "I'm into Rider or Randall."

B: So how many awards was that?

H: Two awards for my Kiss show and about six awards as a DJ. Germany gave me best International DJ — Det got best International MC. I've been awarded about 10. It was nice to be recognised.

Recognise him, you wouldn't fail to recognise this 'boy next door.' Just ask him to play a few tunes, and then you'd know.

A Tale of Two DJs:
Kemi and Jane, aka Kemistry & Storm

"We dreamt that one day we'd become these big DJs and be up there in Rage with Groove and Fabio on the same line-up. We knew Top Buzz to chat to and told them that one day we were gonna be up there and they said, "Yeah, yeah". When we see them now, Top Buzz are astounded, saying, "I can't believe it. You're Kemistry & Storm!" " Storm

S: Kemi was born in Birmingham to a Nigerian father and English mother. He was a biochemist. Kemi's her [shortened] name. The full name is quite long. I was born in Kettering, Northamptonshire, to an Irish dad and English mum. Kemi introduced me to raving and this music. I was classically trained but was into lots of different things like David Sylvian, Japan, Prince, a bit of Disco, Blanche, and Heaven 17.

K: I was into Spear of Destiny and Cabaret Voltaire. When I was in Sheffield there was a lot of those industrial groups around, Nightmares on Wax and Joy Division. We both liked Bowie.

S: I was going out with a sax player. I tried to learn the sax but it wasn't for me. I could never get my mouth 'round it. Did a bit of singing in a band and did a bit of dancing and singing when I was a child.

Kemi & Storm sang in a Reggae band — which failed. They joined a Jazz band — which failed. After that they tried a cool, trendy band that wrote their own lyrics — it failed too. Finally, somewhat desperately, Storm went into a covers band, which was fun, but only for a while.

K: I've always been caught up in music.
S: When you're around musicians for years, you can hear correct influences and you get to work out if someone is good at what they're doing.

S: Kemi had been doing this 'going out thing' and played the music at home all the time. It was in my head constantly. I had been quite cynical of it. It was '89 and Kemi went to Shoom. She would come in after a good night out and sit laughing on her bed. Being a concerned medical person,I finally asked her, "Where have you been, who are you mixing with, you're not taking drugs are you?" All the things you do for a friend.

Following the call of the rave, Kemistry, Storm and friend Nikki decided to check one out on Kemi's birthday. They wanted to do it properly. Find out about it on the radio, drive to a meeting point and follow the convoy. Three of them went to Andromeda in Cambridge, crammed into a Spitfire with one person lying on the bass bin behind the seats.

S: That night changed my life. We kept raving and just progressed from there. In late '91 we borrowed the money to go and buy the decks and paid it back in instalments.
K: Before that we tried a few things ... a few decks ... like a Binatone system.

S: We were all raving hard. There was Greg who bought the decks with us and there was Toby who had a part share in the decks but we paid him off eventually. Then there was Goldie who was on the scene with us as well and we borrowed the money from him. We were diddling about trying to save this money and Goldie said, "Oh for fuck's sake. I've got a bit of money," and gave it to us. We worked out some agreement to pay him back. So we got the decks. Before, we'd come home and have to drag this huge Amstrad thing into Kemi's room to where Nikki's midisystem was. All we could do was rewind each tune there wasn't even a mixer or anything, just two different systems. And we'd have a rave in the room.

S: We were good at hunting down records. The people at Music Power must have thought we were mental buying all these tunes. We'd just keep playing them at home, till we all dropped off. We'd practice dance moves with Greg. It was getting a bit out of hand, so the decks came at the right time. We'd have this rota of times. We had the decks at our place all the time but Goldie would have a go, then Greg.

Photo by Tristan O'Neill

K&S: We couldn't get a look in sometimes.

S: The first couple of days Goldie was on the decks all the time. Then you'd have a go and he'd be there saying, "Na, na, na, na, na. It's like this." We kept practising, made tapes for a laugh and finally bought a cheap mixer.

K: At that time we were going up to Coventry a lot and Top Buzz was doing it up there. We take our influences from a lot of people. Grooverider and Fabio were the reason we got into it in the first place. Then we started hearing about this DJ called Randall. We found out what station he was on. We'd listen to him, we'd listen to Hype who did this scratching thing, which was different again. And Marvin Connors.

K: Rage was like our club. We'd go to it faithfully. It was like a religion down there. We liked what Groove and Fabio did the best. 'Cos we'd listen to other people but there was something about Grooverider and Fabio – they did this thing the best. We went to other clubs but when you went to Rage, it was more cutting edge and you knew that.

S: Even then Groove and Fabio had the most cutting edge tunes and were prepared to play them. That was a great influence. You'd hear the DJs and pick out what you like. Or you'd work out what they'd do and try to copy that. When we first started we didn't know anything about breakdowns. You'd think, 'I'll just miss that bit.' I can't mix across that 'cos there's no beat, and then, as you get better, you can deal with those bits. You'd find those few chords or a bassline. You'd just find what you like. Although we have one set of tunes, there are things that I'll play and things that Kemi plays. We don't really cross over. There's tunes which float around but it's always worked that if you gave us a twelve inch, I'd play one side and Kemi would play the other.

K: We could only afford one set of records.

S: The more we raved, the more we'd become obsessed with watching the DJs and listening to what the DJ was doing – mixing two tracks together to make another one.

K: Groove and Fabio were the first two DJs we'd heard mixing properly. We worked out that they did this thing 'cos that was one tune and that was a different tune. How were they putting them together? Then someone told us about these decks 'cos I mean what was there before, some guy with a telephone?

S: I can remember this guy in Oxford who mixed on this appalling set-up. He gave me the first mix tape I ever got and I thought how inventive to put these tunes together.

S: Our set as a whole is an endless seam of music that takes you up, down, sideways, levels you out for a bit and takes you up again so that by the end it's firin' and leaving you wanting more. The last track is ultimately the best. Sometimes you have a calm mix that just runs like a chord over a beat. We like to try and mess with a tune making it sound different. You don't even realise that tune is going on and sometimes people don't even realise that you're mixing. When you're mixing you draw out the right tune for the time. You might be on a rolling bassline vibe and then you think "I'm gonna change it now" and go off in another direction. We like to mix. I've always wanted to mix like Randall who is the ultimate mixer for me. Technically, Peshay and Bukem are two of the best mixers. But Randall has this natural ability. He's so quick. A few moves on the decks and then he's standing back having a smoke. He's got an incredible gift and feels the vibes so much. You just feel that energy from him.

K: Mixing has fascinated me from the beginning. It's like constantly remixing. We like to put two things together and they have to work musically. It's all got to work. No clashing chords.

S: In the mix, each tune should be complimented by the other. You are making a different tune 'cos you might completely change the vibe of both tunes or you might make it very simple by doing a simple mix or muck it around completely. Sometimes it's mad what you can get. Because we work a lot with our tunes at home, we learn where the drop is. You can look at the record and see where the drop is. That's all part of it. I'm not a DJ who plays one tune after another with a little mix and a fade. We love the whole part of it.

K: It's like getting involved with that track. You can't just play it, so you mix it and you can manipulate the music to do what you want.

K: We like to reach a crescendo. We hope that people are in the music 'cos we remember what it was like for us as ravers. People like Randall would mix piano breaks and strings and you'd be waiting for the drop and they'd go off at the same time. Madness. So you'd go and try the same thing at home. That would be your influence for that. You pick up lots of different things. We do a rough to the smooth thing. If you want to play soft tunes out, you tend to harden them up with a hard tune. And before they know it, the crowd is raving to a Good Looking tune. We've always said, "Don't underestimate the crowd". Why would they just want to hear one style of music? You think if a tune moves you, then you want to play it.

S: At the Metalheadz Sessions all the other DJs are there. They're big names and have got all the tunes. Sometimes when I get a little excited you'll catch me going to put a record on top of the one already playing. I've been so close to doing that. We do get quite nervous. And when you're there the adrenaline is flowing so much, you're not quite in control of things.

UP-AND-COMINGS

K: We still think of ourselves as up-and-coming DJs. It's only in the last year we've been getting work consistently. Before that you get used to doing the warm-ups. When there is a big crowd there it's really nice. Any excuse for us to DJ.

S: It's our job and we just do it as well as we can. Even if you'd had a row or got a cold, when you get on those decks you have to perform 100% – if not more. We get really pissed off if the decks jumps or if the monitor is in the next room. But it's our job. You've got to see every system as a challenge. Rather than, "Oh there isn't a monitor," or "the monitor is too far over there." You've got to have a go. Any new DJ has got to think that way. When I saw Bailey mixing with the monitor way over where, I thought 'I've got to go for it 'cos there's Bailey there to show me up'. I like that rivalry between DJs.

Despite all the lonely hard work, it's difficult for up-and-comings to break through. Booking agents can play a large part in the process. But only if the DJ is ready.

"It's hard work. When you're starting out, the doors are all closed man. People don't even want to talk to you, let alone give you a break. I get people phoning about mailing lists, they need help with whatever. I'm like "I'm not helping you, no-one helped me. If anything, they turned their noses up." I've really worked hard to prove myself." DJ HYPE

"I took on Andy C as an 'up-and-coming.' With up-and-comings, you try to do as much as you can. Some have residencies from before. Christmas time is a good time for up-and-comings. I'll go through the diary trying to fill gaps for my DJs and if the top boys aren't available, I'll try to push the others. They're all really good DJs, that's the thing. They'll also get a chance on pirate radio as other DJs can't make their appointments and stations stay on air for longer periods of time." CAROLINE, UNIQUE ARTISTS

Sarah Groove Connection confirms that it takes a long time to get to the top. "I worked with Bukem for two years before I could get him any work. We had reports of people sitting down saying he was playing the most boring stuff. Lying down and sleeping while he was mixing. I couldn't get him booked. He'd play for £50 to a £100. He was about to give up and say fuck it – then it all took off. But that was me having to keep on and on saying 'no he wasn't crap – just different.'

It wasn't until we initiated Speed that the whole Bukem thing went off. That's when people realised what his style was. I really got behind him. This was something new. I'm not going to take anyone on that I can't do something with. I've got a new DJ from Coventry on my books, DJ Addiction. He's linked to Carlito, one of the artists on my label. I've started to get him to do warm-ups. He's been on the books for about six months and started to get a bit uptight. He's still a novice. I said, "Listen you can't be acting like this, you can't be despairing. I said it would take a minimum of six months, and you're starting to panic."

I know how difficult it is. People have this false notion about up-and-comings. It's as difficult for me as it is for them. There's no such thing as an up-and-coming just breaking through. I think it takes seven years to get anywhere on the DJ circuit. It's a two-way thing. You've got to be out there. You've got to love it – live and breathe it. You've got to be harassing promoters. I'm offering Addiction for a promotional price, reminding people of his name. It's a little game. People say "I've heard of him" and they forget where they've heard it from – it's actually from me. You start to break them through slowly. I get people to do warm-ups. Now any good warm-up DJ should be able to play for two to three hours in my opinion. The proper Old Skool method. Fabio and Grooverider used to play all night. At Tempo, Fabio and Groove would turn up three hours later than they were supposed to and if the warm-up couldn't cope with it ... There are only a few people who can do that. You've got to be confident enough to keep on going, even if you have to play the same music again. Or a different mix. That's how I know when someone can take the pressure.

You get all these people saying, "God, Grooverider's so famous, can't you do that for me?" I've never known anyone work harder than Grooverider. I've never met anyone more dedicated. Fabio in a different way, but Groove has got out there, done anything and everything. I didn't know it was humanly possible for a human being to work so hard without having a nervous breakdown. He fucking deserves success."

There's been an explosion in the number of DJs. God knows how someone came up with a figure but in '96, there were around 400,000 people in the UK calling themselves a DJ. The Manchester June '97 'DJ Culture' marketing fair for DJs, organised by P&O Events, was absolutely rammed. On the high street, Numark are selling a 'DJ In a Box', including decks, a mixer, headphones and monitor speakers for under £400. Nicky Blackmarket and DJ Wildchild are among those passing on skills to others in workshops in London, Cambridge and Southampton.

But it's still a hard road. Scanning a range of flyers on any Bank Holiday rave day and it's difficult to escape many of the same top twenty names that have been around since back in the day. As an up-and-coming it can be disheartening. If there's no change at the top how can you make it? If there's such a huge pool of fresh talent to choose from, why is there such stagnation amongst DJ ranks?

Eastman explains, "If I'm doing a Jungle Fever, I've always brought in big names 'cos you're risking a lot of money. A couple of times we've brought in people like Hype or Andy C for something a little bit different. That's why promoters keep picking the same DJs. That's the only reason. You need to see Frost, Rider, Brockie, Randall, and Mickey on the flyer. You need to see these names to make people come out of their houses and pay their money.

If you pay ten grand for a venue, plus five grand for flyers, two grand security, x-amount of money, it adds up to thirty grand you're laying out to put on a rave. You've got to get the people coming. By putting maybe like a, Pressure X, a Flirt, who's near the major league, you can get 'em through. All these guys are very good DJs. They play just as good as the Riders and the Randalls. Yet, if I went to hire the Sanctuary, Milton Keynes, and I put on Pugwash, Kane, Flirt, Pressure X, Easy Dee, I might as well throw my money away. It's no disrespect to them DJs. If Kool FM does something in or out of London, people know it's the Kool FM family. And we've got a few big names on the station like Swift, SL, Ital, Brockie, Bryan Gee; we use them and we use all the other crew. Sometimes, people are brought in like young Nikki Slim Ting, who won a competition after sending a tape to the station. But it is stagnant. It's a hard road." Jay World Dance sees high wage demands threatening the old order. "There are some strong ripples in the pond about the fees that some DJs are now commanding. We know that there are some people out there who for various reasons are not getting as much work. Maybe they're not as popular as they used to be but they still want to make as much money as they used to. This means that their prices are going up. They're doing less work, the audience has to pay more to support them which they aren't willing to do, so there's even less work. It's a downward spiral and it's already happening. World Dance and a few other promoters are talking about breaking some new artists into the top flight. We're adamant. We are going to do it. We're sick of some of the Attitudes of some of the artists and management. There are talented people out there who don't get a break. It's our job, as an industry, not just as WD but we have an obligation to some of these kids. They've done their apprenticeship and they need a break."

Kemistry & Storm feel DJs must be responsible for doing much of the work themselves:

K: I don't know if DJs are getting their tapes out. I know in the beginning we sent out so many tapes we nearly broke ourselves and not just once.

S: Yes, we sent them off with our *résumé*, made a nice cover for our tapes. I don't know if many DJs are doing that nowadays.

K: You still have to do that groundwork. And pirate radio is a good way to make your name. I don't see many DJs trying to do that, or even seeing it as important, but it is. It's good grounding. If you haven't got a club to go to, at least every week you've got to go and take your records out like a proper DJ. I mean that's what we used to think, our show was like playing out. Let's go for it, let's really rock it. The audience is out there but you can't see them. I love it. It's just you and the speakers but you can feel something out there.

Clarky: I do warm-ups for Metalheadz and they sort me proper. I've given up doing tapes. I ring people and that but I'm in the position where they ring me. You can't think you're too big to play anywhere. I was playing Blues when I was seventeen. But I've done my years of playing for nothing. It's hard getting the work and a lot of people say you need an agent. Getting the work yourself is the best way to go but it is hard out there.

K: It's difficult to get through. We were lucky, the door was open. At the moment it's very hard.

S: Well I think the doors are open. I think it's time for all the new DJs to come through. Now is the exciting time. We're encouraging all the DJs at Metalheadz to get out there, get tapes together and stop messing about.

Rather than waiting to fill dead men's shoes, you can start your own night as DJs Zoe and Damian Lazarus did with PM Scientists. Based at Smithfield's, Clerkenwell the two play host to their intimate Wednesday nightclub of postmodern music. From there they have played a guest slot on Kool FM's *Super Sunday* and have stepped onto the international circuit. The Brixton-based Livid crew, a posse of 20 DJs and MCs, are climbing the ladder together by hosting several of their own weekly club nights.

RESIDENTS MAKE PRESIDENTS

A DJ really starts to develop when they gain a residency. Aside from having to play out week after week, they can go deep, forge their own style, experiment a bit and build an audience who will get to know them, spreading the word about their name and music. At the Paradise, the crowd watched the DJs with expert attention and rose to the occasion.

"Darren Jay was there, Mickey Finn too, but Kenny Ken was the Guv'nor. Everyone was hanging around for Kenny but it was Randall who was consistent and took the last slot. Everyone was like "Yeah. Yeah. Kenny Ken" 'cos everyone loved Kenny. But really everyone was going, "But you're hanging around for Randall – right." It was all going off. Both of those DJs were pulling everyone in." *KYAN, SURVIVORS*

DJs have their times. You'll hear that so-and-so is mashing-it-up or "my boy's really on it." There are signs like when one arena is fuller than the other and radio shows like Brockie's, where the phones are runnin' red. These are the moments when everything comes together and DJs are hailed, adored, remembered especially by the in-house MCs who never let anyone forget.

B: Back in 1992 - 93 who was the hardcore Junglist DJ?

MC 5ive'0: Rider, Rider. I'm telling you, Rider and DJ blood clat Ron. They brought Jungle to prominence down Linford Studios. All you were missing was your shield and ya blood clat spear.

OTHER PEOPLE'S MUSIC

"The DJs have got mad props off other man's music. The DJs exploit the producers". MC 5IVE'O

"People say they've got big playing other people's music. But DJs can inspire a whole style. It's a two-way thing". SARAH, GROOVE CONNECTION

It is a two-way thing, as many of the performing arts are. A giant section of the Classical music industry depends on musicians and conductors playing and interpreting other people's music just as a playwright needs actors and a crew to give life to the words on stage. Producers need DJs to play their tunes, DJs need producers' music. Rather than exploitation, it's an interactive celebration. Everyone's in it together.

ADVANCING THE MUSIC OR ARTISTIC COMPROMISE?

Is it a DJ's responsibility to advance the music or entertain the crowd? Do you sprinkle the set with records from the direction in which you're trying to take the music? No one wants to have punters just standing and staring unmoved as you rinse out the latest progressive beats. At the same time, ideally, DJs should avoid the situation of late '94 early '95 when, in an average night's raving, punters would often hear a boring and repetitive 'Top Twenty' selection.

It can be a bit of a trap. Is the DJ booked to play their own particular style or should they compromise and draw tunes that really entertain their audience? Especially considering "you're only as good as your last set" in the eyes of the crowd and the promoter. It's a foolhardy or brave person who remains unswervingly loyal to their own personal music policy. Some DJs can go off on one, forgetting their audience, drifting too far into the technical and getting lost up their own Dubs.

As DJ Ron described on Channel 4's *All Junglists*, "You got to keep your eye on the crowd. Somebody told me that one time. I used to do scratching. I'd be scratching and scratching and scratching away. To me I'm doing the best thing on earth. And when I looked up – well, I don't think I ever did look up. Till somebody said to me, "Ron, look at what you're doing." When I did look up, everyone was just staring. No one was dancing. From then it's stuck with me that you've got to look up and play for the people."

Total loyalty to certain music styles won't put food on the table or petrol in the tank. Sometimes however, the public could be more receptive to new sounds. The first few times Shy and Brockie played *Wolf* to the jump-up crews, they didn't even bubble half-heartedly. DJ Ron and Shy FX, among other producers, say that it can take several months for some tunes destined to become floor smashers to break on the dancefloor. Quality Jungle / Drum & Bass can be musically demanding. Poor quality, vacuous, made-for-rave tracks may succeed for a short period. But they do little to push back musical frontiers.

Individual promotions can't be all things to all people. DJs playing the largest raves, may find it difficult to play demanding tunes in the main arena. The crowd may be more accepting of established DJs who risk playing a few very upfront tunes as a part of their set.

It can be a confusing time, not only for up-and-coming DJs trying to find their own artistic voice, but also for seasoned professionals who know the difference between superficial music and tracks produced with real depth. As a professional, Grooverider played pure jump-up tunes to the delight of the massive at Roller Express in 1993 - 94. Instead of arrogantly playing the tunes he wanted to

because he was 'The Great Grooverider', he pleased the crowd and bookings continued to flood into his agency. However, an inner musical dissatisfaction was the downside. Though Rider described the jump-up tunes fun, he found it a difficult period, almost losing his way. It's hard for a DJ to make a career out of buying and playing tunes they don't really believe in. Trying to move with the scene, you can lose inspiration as you lose direction.

Promotions are like brand names and customers buy the product because they know pretty much what they'll be getting. If in the larger events promoters provided another arena where alternative music could be played, it would allow the space for punters and DJs alike to be involved in an adventurous, musical progression which would be difficult to sustain or undesirable in the main arena. Jay World Dance is looking forward to the day when they have five arenas including a space for up-and-coming DJs and Dub Plate specials as well as the main arena. Kool FM at The Powerhouse in '96 ran a Dub Plate arena, featuring Bryan Gee and DJ Ron amongst others, with moderate success.

Smaller clubs and resident DJs have an extremely important role in advancing the music. Clubs like Rage and AWOL built a vibe, progressed the music and developed world class DJs, writing a chapter in JDB history in the process. Smaller clubs and residencies tend to be run more on love of the music rather than for huge economic benefits. Most top DJs advanced through the small club circuit. Radio is also a good forum for promoting a more adventurous music policy.

Repetitive Beats

This has been a problem with big raves for years. One DJ after another turns up, plays their set and splits. The problem is not so much hearing the same tune twice as the 'hour-long climax' syndrome. Each DJ wants to hype up the crowd and be remembered as the one that *rocked da party*. The consequences are that the punter doesn't necessarily go on a musical journey. The audience don't get on that wicked vibe when everyone rides the rhythm on deep, sparse tunes – an experience that is much more heavy and powerful than any short-lived, noisy Rave anthem rush.

"I don't care how many times a tune gets played in a rave if it's tearin' up the dance. A good tune is a good blood clat tune 'n' no-one can diss dat." MC 5IVE'O

Some people do, and a few DJs like Kemistry & Storm are trying to do something about the problem.

S: At [the Notting Hill] Carnival a couple of years ago on the Confusion stand, Nicky Blackmarket asked me which tunes I'd played 'cos he didn't want to repeat them. It's professional so I have to respect him for doing that. People might look at him a bit weird but he's just trying give the crowd value for money by giving them something different. I can't believe DJs who walk in hearing a track and play that track four tunes later when they could be playing something else.

S: They've got loads in their bags ... Don't be shy. Get 'em awt!

"If possible you should turn up an hour before your set but if you're busy that can't be done. At the end of the day it depends on the DJ but if I show up late somewhere, I want to know what's been played over the past hour. I say that if a record has been played in that hour, you've got about an hour's leeway before you can play it again so the punters don't get pissed off. You have to ask the DJ from before 'cos you're not a mind-reader, rather than just play what you want. There's the public out there and they're paying money. That's who you're playing for, them not yourself." *NICKY BLACKMARKET*

Though the funny thing about tunes being repeated through the night is that the same tune might get a better reaction the fourth time it's played at five in the morning, than at 1am.

"I like to play from the heart, that's why I don't like to hear the DJ before me. With the audience, you can't please everybody. There are some people, all they want to do is hear the same music all night. They're up for a good night out. Not everyone's on a musical educational journey, some people are. That's why it's important to get that balance. You want the DJs who're gonna enlighten everyone and you want the DJs who're gonna blatantly rip it up and you want the other DJ who maybe will clear the floor, 'cos it's a new thing. Everyone's got their part to play – each man to his own. I like the balance." *DJ HYPE*

ASK HIM ABOUT THE MONEY

Top Jungle DJs aren't being flown around by helicopter, earning Carl Cox type wages (£12,000 for a four hour set in Ibiza). Though they do make more money per hour than the average high street solicitor. Still, it's a private matter ...

On the road filming DJ Randall May '96
04.11am
Producer: DJs must earn mega bucks.
  Make sure you ask him about money.
B: No man, you ask him, he won't talk about it.

Producer tries to calculate Randall's pay on a 'per slot' basis.
Producer: How many nights a week do you play out?
Randall: I won't tell you how many I play in a week.
  You know I got four tonight, that's all you need to know.

05.08am
Producer: Have you done more than five in one night? Stretching it ... ?
Randall: Forget all these questions about my money.
  We are not here to talk about that. Forget that
  (kisses teeth).

THE HONOUR

The final set of the night is still regarded as the premier slot, especially for a crowd hyping it right through to that blindin' last tune. A DJ stamping the seal of approval on the dance can leave punters screaming for more. At the end of a workout, it's the last DJ that people will often remember. It's an honour, surely? An enthusiastic promoter gave Hype his booking, "Hype man, it's the last set – the Honour set!" Hype replied, not disingenuously "Sometimes I prefer to do without the honour. At least then I could have a bit of a dance."

I'll Always Respect Peshay

Peshay and GQ accepted the booking for a German
Jazz festival, just like any other booking.
It wasn't until they arrived at the venue that
GQ realised the enormity of what they were about
to take on. He peered from backstage at a seated
audience illuminated by those table lights
sedately enjoying the multi-piece Jazz band
playing on stage. After the band reached its
trumpet / double bass crescendo and the applause
subsided, the mini-orchestra of musicians and
their instruments made way for a pair of
Technics decks and a mixer. For one rare
moment in his international career, GQ was
worried. "This was a totally different thing.
What was my man gonna do? The tables and those
musicians man." The kind who'd never accept
electronic instruments on vinyl – these were
'real' musicians.

Everyone looks on. More polite applause and up
steps DJ Peshay. He rolls the disc and a sax
break escapes the speakers. As the jazzy hook
hits, heads start to nod with the rhythm. GQ
picks up the mic, in sixties Ronnie Scotts mode,
he guides the audience on a journey. Gradually,
polite applause gives way to standing, clapping,
dancing and cheering. Peshay the excellent
technical DJ whose records carry no labels had
cracked it. "Boy all those lights, tables,
instruments 'n' shit and he just went up there
man. I'll always respect Peshay."

Behind The Decks

Now this was DJ business.
We didn't meet 'round green baize tables
or in smoky back room Shebeens.
The new generation come with mobile phones
and work at the day job,
living the passion on the other side.
"I'm back in the office on Monday.
Got that twenty quid you owe me?
I'm off to pick up some Plates at Music House.
What time you playing at SW1?
Yo, Kenny about the money."

One Superstar Jungle gathering in North London
on a street with no name.
We'll collect our debts and those Plates.
These are the tunes that are
the gold dust of today.
Killem on the radio, killem at the dance.

Back in the day I went to a rave
and danced the dance
I'm the person who started buying tunes
the maestros Groove & Fabio played.
They inspired me
Now I drive motorways
You fly me to play away
Money comes in
Dub Plates spin out
Envelopes backstage
Mobile phones goin' off
"Yo, I just called to ask you …"
Never a second's peace
Never a quality moment with my girl
With myself?

So I Guess You Could Say
I Had a Good Day …

Kate and I had had a heavy night's drinking
at home in Tottenham but we were determined to
reach Euston Station at noon for the Reclaim the
Streets (RTS) demo.

The organisers probably hadn't reckoned on the
thousands that did show up. A section of the
crowd followed mumbled instructions and coloured
flags down to Brixton on the Victoria Line where
South London was brought to a standstill. As the
police helicopter circled above us, we filled
Euston Road, inadvertently reclaiming one of
London's main traffic arteries. By the time we'd
hit King's Cross, the road became a car park.
Outside the station a line of teenage Tottenham
girls conga-ed through the Rainbow tribe. On the
roof of a bus shelter some guy, or girl, juggled
fire sticks next to a stripped-to-the-waist
skateboarder, who rolled and launched himself
into the air, hitting the ground stylishly –
well, almost. Anyway, the crowd was with him.

Photo by
Brian Sweeney

Peshay

Across the way a bobby radioed, "They've set up a sound system on the balcony of a first floor flat, above the sex shop on York Way … Repeat …" A fire alarm closed King's Cross station to the three block strong throng, so we took to the streets - all of them. Caledonian Road, past Pentonville prison, up and along Holloway Road, past Holloway Women's prison, blocking a major route to and from London's city centre. We used British Gas barriers, public dustbins and street furniture to block the roads. People sit in the sunlight at a main junction, watching jugglers, meeting old friends, chatting street style and festival stylee.

The story was the same all the way up to Seven Sisters Road, where the RTS vanguard had totally blocked the road from the underground station, past Tesco's, all the way up the hill to Tottenham College. At each end of the drag, a single climber, precariously high above the road, hung from a scaffold tripod. Banners strung from lampposts across the four-lane carriageway fluttered against a fresh, clear blue sky. Panning down the top of the hill, a line of police, ironically dressed in fluorescent yellow 'raving jackets' - Tottenham's finest, stood inactive and somewhat bemused. Below to the right, ravers chilled in the municipal ornamental park. I'd always thought it should look that way. Three rigs divided the hill outside Tesco's, with ravers losing it around each of them. Meeting and greeting strangers, friends and friends estranged - the music played on.

Anyway, so I ask the guy on the Chiba City Sound System if I can play - not much good at the hassly DJ thing but - "Local DJ - yeah?! Rude FM - yeah! Well we don't normally let anyone we don't know play on our rig but - yeah man, get your tunes." Two minutes later, I'm leaving RTS (ironically) in the back of a cab, grinning like a Cheshire cat and buzzing like a Happy Hardcore raver.

There's the long wait to get on the decks. Ambient Sounds' cyber-punk, DJ Miss Pink ahead of me in the line-up, pulls out to play a rave at the Rocket. I'm next. It's funny how the training, those radio station hours and friend's parties all come together. The first tune eases the crowd into Drum & Bass after hours of Techno. A calling intro - the vocal sample beckons - "Simon Says" - a white label acquired from God knows where. Camera One - Needle in the groove. Camera Two - Crowd reaction on the B-Line. Camera Three - DJ's happily cautious face.

Tunes come instinctively to hand, the mixes are in, you read the crowd right - the rewinds, shirts off, hands in the air, that fluorescent police line, people banging appreciation on the side of the van's rig and an MC bawls - "Selecta! Selecta! I beg ya please - wheel 'n' come again." You notice it without seeing it all - a curious detachment. Keeping your head when all about you are losing theirs. Being under stress without stressing out. Seeing each system as a challenge. After all those lessons learned, there's the crowd's reward. Their pleasure is your pleasure. Etched onto the mind's videotape. The joy in this space on this road is important. The Rainbow Nation, hands held high, painted faces swirling, trainers and boots stomping in the middle of a five-lane inner city highway. A truly surreal moment out there on Tottenham High Road.

Andy C, the Kemet Crew, Dillinja and Congo Natty's tunes are friends who'll never let you down. Someone else from the crowd grabs the mic and is screaming, "Rewind SelekTa - REEEEWIND! Krust, Krust, DJ Krust come again. He's read the label on the tune and assumed I'm 'DJ Krust'.

But the guy who'd grabbed the mic belongs to a disgruntled local Tottenham crew who want to play their music and play it NOW. They're not interested in the march, or rig owners' permission, and an unknown hand - gold chain around the wrist, plucks the stylus out the groove - mid-mix.

I remember things happening in slow motion. Kate and friends in the near distance, dancing on a raised flower planter. Elphin - my cyber psychic hippy-chick friend swirls around on stilts. The Tottenham crew at my right elbow - hearing them say: "Jus' tek all im rekords." I remember the Chiba City boy's polite pleading dismissed with kissed teeth as a terminal shadow covers the mixer.

I'm a shy bredder but in that street full of people, I remember turning off the music with calculated anger, grabbing the mic and shouting: "Is everybody enjoying the music?" "YESSSSS!!". "Should I come off the decks 'cos there's these other …" "NOOOOOO!!!!!". The crew disappears and there's people saying, "Well done!" Shaking my hand and all these weird, wonderful things - in the middle of Tottenham High Road. I drop *Special Dedication* and get back in the mix as a larger shadow hovers over me. Still half-expecting to be knifed, I look up to see Ben, my largely dreadlocked, Highgate friend, beaming down over me and smiling broadly. For a moment there, it was all going off.

I play on … Tim, Paul and Time, the Chiba City boys, invite me to play the 8 till 9am slot later on at some full-on crusty rave in an abandoned spice mill on Kingsland High Road. I did, with the sun coming up by the canal, ravers on every level and Elphin minus her stilts floating around the countless sound systems. By the end of my set, there were the "We're interested in you playing for our rig", "We're going to Europe, if we could sort you with an air ticket, would you?" questions. All wicked, if it happens, but living in the moment it was '1988 badge smiley face' wicked. Then there was my new slot 10am till 12 on Rude FM and a mad dash across London. Miss Pink calls in from Crouch End saying, "I hope you mashed it up at Seven Sisters." I leave the studio and pass Shy FX on his way home to his mum's house for Sunday lunch. I go home at 3pm to chill for what was meant to be the rest of the weekend, only to hear and rescue a pleading DJ Fuse on Rude FM who's been blown out by the next DJ. Finally get

to relax listening to DJ Indica - he plays some other new style and I end up ringing him for a couple of rewinds. Wish I'd had a tape - listening to his show and the station's new phat Sunday line-up, I feel inadequate - humbled, a change of musical direction may be warranted. The ravers loved my music. But I should have been playing some of Indica's tunes. That's the challenge, what drives us DJs, producers, record shop posse and ravers all forward - the new music.

The march which road-blocked London, from the North to the South, went largely unreported except in the local papers who described the event in sensationalist terms, talking about 'riots' and 'looting'. And no doubt, officials will put the number attending at half whatever it was.

The point of Reclaim the Streets demonstrations? Children are four times more likely to die in road traffic accidents in Britain than in any other European country. We're four times more likely to develop asthma than in the 1960s. Vehicles fitted with 'Bull Bars' can kill at 20 miles per hour. Residents are alienated from the environment outside our front doors because of the motor vehicle - the thing that claims more lives than drugs but is condoned and even promoted on nearly every TV ad break. As an intensive care nurse working in St. Barts hospital back in '89, I looked after a brain-dead baby. A car had mounted the pavement, slamming into his pushchair. Despite his Nigerian parents passionate Christian, mystic chants, the baby died. This happens all too often. As a matter of survival we must Reclaim Our Streets.

The point of DJing - to entertain a crowd wherever and whenever called upon to do so. And when you do - Mi Gosh - There's nothing like it.

So I guess you could say I had a good day.

MCs

"I was playing some rave and there was no MC when I started and it just wasn't happening. Then MC Det came in, grabbed up the mic and that was it. He soon got 'em going." KENNY KEN, SPRING 1995

A disappointed punter stood near the decks on stage at The Island, Ilford during the '95 Congo Natty album launch party. It was a subdued, almost glum affair pervaded by an air of something waiting to happen. DJ after DJ after Dub Plate failed to excite the lethargic crowd. Bored, the punter retreated to build a spliff behind the speakers. By the time he'd sparked up, something in the arena had changed. The ravers were going wild; the Island had been flooded with that familiar electricity. People were screaming, pounding their fists in the air demanding the rewind. Clocking the MC dominating the stage, firin' up the place, the punter nudges DJ Brockie and asks, "Who dat MC?" With earnest countenance and serious voice Brockie replies, "DEMAN". The two stand staring in silent awe at the madness unleashed.

Kool FM's residency, Dublin, winter '97. The MC lays off the mic to let the music breathe. Within minutes the stage is besieged by a gaggle of young lads pleading, "Would ya bring back da fella wit da mic?"

MCs are the visible voices and faces of the Jungle / Drum & Bass scene. They are an embodiment of the multicultural nature of the music. Essentially MCing involves someone speaking and / or singing over the DJ's records. Influenced by Ragga / Reggae sound systems, MC styles cross-linguistic borders touching base with Patois chat, through to Cockney rhyme and Rap. Because of the multicultural nature of Jungle, you'll hear black people sounding like full-on Cockneys and white people chatting fluent Jamaican Patois. MCs fill the gap between DJs, music and the audience. Interacting with the crowd, an accomplished MC turns a flat audience into a good one, a good audience into a hyper one. Spreading their vibe across the arena, these Whirling Dervishes of the microphone can release the energy that is the essence of a proper Jungle / Drum & Bass rinse out.

Oi Oi!

The first time Chalky White took up the microphone at a warehouse rave in the late 80s and chatted to the crowd, the promoters threw him out and tried to ban him from ever attending their do's again. It wasn't that he was offensive or bad, more that people weren't really used to it. Chalky wasn't a professional but he did feel that there was something missing from the rave. Yes you had the DJ, the music, the punters but things seemed a bit muted. He grabbed the mic with the enthusiasm of an inspired amateur and did make a difference to the ravers.

It's doubtful that other MCs found this new niche solely because of Chalky White. These things tend to grow organically and the tunes or the vibe needed a kick. The short stab, cheeky chappie, Cockney − "Let's 'ave ya − Get them 'ands in the air" − chants ruled the raves. And so it continued with MCs like Everson Rat Pack through the Hardcore years of the early 90s. Kool FM's Smurf remembers that the chatting style wasn't part of the Hardcore and Techno scene. On Centreforce, Mikey De Underground dealt with the same Cockney 'Pub MCs' from the Warehouse scene and couldn't really see that style developing much further.

By mid 1991, when they were setting up Kool FM, Eastman told Smurf that he was planning to bring in some chatting MCs from Hackney sound systems. "Err Eastman," says Smurf nervously, "They don't really do that in this music." "Well they do now!" replies Eastman.

More into the Reggae side of the music, Eastman knew all the MCs, or DJs as they were called, from back in the day and combined the two musical styles, Hardcore Breakbeat, embroidered with a fluent lyrical style on the station with Cogee as Kool's first MC. Other MCs who helped forge the way included Master P, Hardcore General, PSG and Top Buzz.

Though Shut Up & Dance used The Ragga Twins on their proto-Jungle releases, proper chatting really came into the scene during the first Jungle raves of '91 and '92 with Telepathy and Roast MCed by Moose and 5ive'O. The Ragga Twins performed at Elevation when it first started at Wonderland on Lea Bridge Road. Navigator arrived during the early stages of Jungle, coming to prominence towards the end of '92.

Many top MCs like MC MC, Stevie Hyper D, Fearless and Shabba also contributed to the early foundation of the Jungle style, with Fearless and Shabba both doing stints on Rush FM. Det became established by early '93, in what Eastman calls the "Year of the MCs." He introduced a style based on Hip Hop's rappers, rather than Ragga / Reggae chat. Skibadee and the rest of the new school like Cleveland Watkiss, MC Conrad, IC3 and Justiyc followed from '94 with their individual fusions of London Jungle patter and Jazz vocals.

One or two MCs on stage were usual but Eastman is also credited with introducing x-amount of MCs to the dance, with Jungle Fever showcasing up to five MCs at once, adding another dimension to the hyper vibe arena. They invented names and catchphrases and spread the language from the streets and dancefloors into the media. As MC 5ive'O says, "We had the names, me and Moose. 'Code Red, APB, Antidote, Junglette – We don't brag, we don't boast – it's strictly the Roast'. We improvised."

CROWD OF PEOPLE, LISTEN!

"The only one who gave us help was God." MC 5IVE'O

Back in '89 MC 5ive'O stepped out from his bedroom, where he practiced MCing over Soul and Reggae tunes with friends, into the Euro Acid of the Crazy Club. "Something just came over me ... I saw MCing as a challenge and I wanted to express what I was feeling. Not just to one person, I wanted *everybody* to know, so when they went home, they had something to think about." From the days at Roast, to the present day stage, 5ive'O is partially motivated by a connection with black history. "It goes back to slavery. We were singing for our freedom." When people outside the scene said that the music was shit, it gave him the drive to prove them wrong.

5ive'O has deep admiration for his fellow senior MCs. He has been behind a campaign to raise their professional profile, ensuring that they are financially rewarded for their talent. And why not? "GQ, Moose, Navigator and The Ragga Twins, they've got skills like a muthafucka."

He feels a strong connection with the streets and has an understanding of the harsher side of everyday life. He'd get on the radio to all the youngsters at Christmas time, telling them not to stress out their parents with Christmas present dissatisfaction. "Some kids don't get nothin' so don't be pressuring your mum and dad. Be grateful for what you're receiving." He knows his words are important. "Why do you think we're so popular? We keep it real. My messages aren't about vanity or glory. They have lyrical content."

5ive'O is always the entertainer. He's often seen on stage with over-sized water pistols, American football gear and that distinctive sharp haircut. "I try to capture the imagination of the listener whether in the rave or on the radio." Still gracing many a Jungle flyer, his thoughts and words continue onwards.

MC GQ

Veteran MC GQ, winner of countless awards, charming heart-throb of the scene and innovator of the rolling *Grrrooove-Rrii-Derr* sound, has long since found an effective lyrical style. At his former residency, AWOL, in front of hundreds in the legendary Paradise club, and thousands on stage at World Dance, he held the floor with strength and grace. Vocally massaging the crowd, his lyrics ride the rhythm with textures of strength and harmony. His physical stage presence is unusual – standing back from, behind or beside the DJ Box.

GQ has always been around music. He and his brothers had their own sound systems. His uncle worked on his own one-man sound system. He'd built the speaker box himself, attaching a pair of wheels to trundle it around from place to place. The same uncle, a school caretaker, used to open the school hall for GQ to practice break dancing. He and classmate MC Det were characters around school who'd use their desks as drums and spool out the "My name is G, in da place to be" type lyrics indigenous to *Wild Style* and the Break Dance film era. Outside school he was eager to flex his voice on sound systems whenever he could.

GQ's name first appears in popular history in '93 with his residency at the Paradise. This was largely because he spent the preceding years working on the underground circuit with Acid House beats in the back room of pubs. He didn't only MC. GQ remembers the days when he DJed before Grooverider at Tottenham's legendary pub warehouse venue on Crowland Road. There was a stint on a pirate station with Matthew B and Frankie Valentine in the 'Summer of Love.' And he hustled illegal venues like the abandoned King's Cross Scala cinema with Tony Trax. When GQ picked up the mic next to Chalky White and Everson Rat Pack, he wanted to take the art of MCing to another level. After the pre-Criminal Justice Act reign of police raids, the Rave scene largely moved inside. AWOL at the Paradise was GQ's first legal residency, guaranteed to take place every week. It was his undisputed home.

"All the ingredients were there. You could go there consistently for three years and it would be tearin' every week. Every week. That club, that vibe was my home base. I'd be locked down … in this 'thing.' There was something special with everybody. The people, DJs – Kenny Ken, Dr S Gachet, Darren Jay, Mickey Finn, Randall – and one MC. That was my home and I could get loose and deal with what I was dealing with."

The hours were long. With the aid of cider, brandy and smokes, he rolled through the early hours to ten or twelve o'clock. He liked to add a different freshness to the sound, preferring to hold back on his golden vocals rather than firin' throughout the night.

On *One in the Jungle*, GQ described one of his happiest moments in the business, "Seeing ten thousand people vibing off the sound of my voice." Backstage between the smiles, he's intense and watchful. Understanding how to exercise the power of his voice, he'll take the punters on a parallel journey. Conscious that he was on a social and musical cutting edge, he raps rhymes about controlling the borderline. He often achieves more by saying less at the right time, in exactly the right place. His head is in the music. GQ asks DJs the names of the records and has become familiar with a range of producers' work. Increasing his record collection, he's itching to get his Technics back from a friend who's had them on a very long loan. MC GQ has started his own record label Emcee Recordings.

MC SKIBADEE

One of the newest frontline MCs, Skibadee has been on Kool FM for three years often working with DJ Wildchild. He has a distinctive clean style and delivery that has endeared him to fans at home and abroad.

"I've always had a love for music. In school I used to play flute and piano. I listened to Hip Hop, Soul, Rare Groove, everything. It's not easy to get into that kind of music over here and be really successful. What I do is like Rap or Ragga. But Jungle is from London so it was the natural way for me to go. It was so easy to be a part of it. I knew people who were doing it just like me.

MC Skibadee
PHOTO BY COURTNEY HAMILTON

When I was listening to Hip Hop and Ragga I always used to listen closely. Hear the rhymes, what they were saying and how they put them together and that gave me an idea of what I could do. Like KRS One, Public Enemy and Capleton on the Ragga side, those guys could rhyme. It's a combination of all of them. But the majority of it is just a London thing. That's where I'm at. A lot of people say, "I thought you was white", 'cos certain things I say is pure London and I want to keep it London.

The first rave I went to was Roast's Valentine's Night '94. It was big. I'd never been to anything like that before. I'd been to Ragga parties but this was just mad – the lights, so many people. I heard the music a couple months before but the Rave scene was something different. I saw these guys on the stage, maybe it was Flinty, Deman, Det and Stevie Hyper. It was just like lightning. I was so happy when I saw those guys, I thought I'd love to be doing that. Me and my mates would sit around, there'd be decks and that and I'd rap to my friends. I could always do that from copying tapes. I've always got my Walkman on. A few months later I was sitting 'round my cousin's house and someone came 'round and said, "You want to come down a pirate radio station?" So we said "Yeah". It was Crystal FM based in Fulham. I went over there and did a set. The manager of the station was really happy. But after a couple of months the station got closed down. They weren't all that good. They were always getting hit. During that period I really worked hard. It wasn't about dollars. It was for me, more than anything. I didn't really have time to watch others. The words just roll out. Now it's not a problem; it's easy for me. I've got to the stage where you can put 10,000 people in front of me and I'll do what I have to do."

His voice is original but Skibadee is concerned about the lack of originality amongst some artists. "People watch the top people and just follow fashion." He'd like to see MCs developing themselves as vocalists and musicians, who are able to work not only in Jungle but other areas of music. But he admits that his popular style has spawned a monster.

CLEVELAND WATKISS

"A lot of people on the scene don't know where I'm coming from. A lot of people say I'm a Drum & Bass MC. I'm a musician, composer, actor. I don't surrender to these terms and genres."

Cleveland Watkiss' journey through the music took him through 70s Jazz, Classical, Indian, Fusion, Electronic, Rock and Pop. Listening to Kool FM was the next stage. "I'd been trying to find my own identity in this collage of sound. I'm not American. I'm from here. My background is the sound systems and I went to the same school as Eastman. Sound systems were what was runnin' for the youth. I've lived in Hackney and I was in search of some indigenous shit representing where I come from and I'm in the thick of the shit. The Blue Note Sessions and my own involvement with them was a written book for me."

He'd done his apprenticeship as a box boy and DJ on the Count Joshua Sound System. Always musically open he checked out the Jazz scene, recreating that 52nd Street vibe in New York, before moving with the Jazz Warriors and Courtney Pine, Steve Williamson, Julien Joseph and another twenty-five performers. His 'raving' was done on the live circuit, in concert halls, festivals and R 'n' B clubs. He's also worked with Stevie Wonder, Sugar Minott and Coldcut. Cleveland's studied the music of old – Duke Ellington, Charlie Parker, Thelonious Monk, Louis Armstrong, Clifford Brown, right forward to modern day composers like Dillinja. "I make it my business to know who the composer is."

"I was originally inspired listening to Kool. They played all kinds of music. My reference is the Ragga side of the scene ... I'm a sponge. I'll plant my ears everywhere. Music is a language. Just because someone calls it a name, doesn't mean I'll close my ears." Performing in the Blue Note, Watkiss has a natural way of interacting with the music and clubbers. Drifting through the crowd with his radio mic, from the back to the front of the club, he wants to hear and feel exactly what the audience experiences. He is constantly conscious of developing links on all levels across music, opening it up.

"I believe in karma. If you believe in what you're doing, that's what carries you through this life. That's why I did Metalheadz each week. They gave me hell if I wanted to take time off. They recognise my link with the music. It was my home as much as Goldie's or anyone else's." Cleveland was introduced to Goldie at Speed by Moving Shadow's Lady Caroline, and later provided the vocals for *Adrift* on the album *Timeless*. A 'drift' is a Jazz term describing a sort of vocal meditation with the vocalist's mind in the realm of time and space.

Before the first Metalheadz night, Goldie adopted a wait-and-see stance when it came to using an MC in the club. Partway through that night he checked Cleveland. "You got your mic?" "Yeah." "Well plug it in man." It stayed plugged in for two and a half years.

From Jazz to Jungle, he's made his mark. Cleveland's less hyper style isn't to everyone's taste. "I don't know if I appeal to everyone but that's not my concern." With the conviction of a mature musician he states of himself and Metalheadz, "We did proper things. It's about a blend of the music – that's the way it should be."

Rhyme Time with Navigator and Deman Rockers & Flinty Badman aka The Ragga Twins
All: An' if a prison you a go
F: Then gwan den serve ya time
D: An' if ya 'fraid a prison
N: Then don't commit crime ... [x2]
D: Wha 'appen Flinty?
F: Wha 'appen Deman?
D: Uh uh – A Rude Bwoy Rocka's me name's a prison.
 Ten years me get an' me a tek it like a man
 an' me na look for sympathy from na one.
 Mi rrrunnn dis place from top to bottom an' de Navigator,
 him a mi right han' man. But Flinty 'ow ya look so
 frighten?
F: Mi not frighten, mi a feel ten-sion.
D: Wha wha wha ...
N: ... Tension, what ya talkin' about?
F: Ya see da bwoy over there 'ow 'ihm a eyeball mi out.
D&N: 'Oo 'ihm?
F: Yes 'ihm.
D&N: Cha don't worry
F: 'Ihm can't tek no eh hm liberties.
F: Hmm. I can do wit a stic-ka Sensi. That would ease mi
 tension immediately.
 ALL JUNGLISTS, CHANNEL 4, 1994

IT'S SHOWTIME

During the dance, a stage featuring the likes of Det, 5ive'O, Skibadee, The Ragga Twins, Navigator and Stevie Hyper is one of the industry's hottest spots. Punters mouth words and vibe off the sounds of those boombastic voices. As the excitement goes into the small hours, the mic is passed from hand to hand. Carried along by the crowd, the atmosphere and their own vocal sparring, it's not unusual to experience a night where the MCs hardly pause for breath. The stomping delivery of MC Det, Stevie Hyper D, Skibadee and Shabba remains a crowd favourite. Pirate radio DJs notice that without MCs on their shows, fewer punters ring in. In the case of Bryan Gee's MC-less show, there are loads of calls asking when the MC will be on. Whilst their contribution to Jungle / Drum & Bass in the raves, on radio and within the scene has been enormous, many people regard these 'Lords of the Dance' with mixed feelings. Some punters and DJs love MCs participation. Others don't. Some revel in the unbroken lyrical, iambic, trochaic and free verse rhythms. Others just aren't in it.

Many people argue over the style, content and presentation of MCs lyrics. DJ Mickey Finn has been quoted describing MCs 'prattling on'. In Summer '95, when *One in the Jungle* producer Ivor Etienne asked the DJs "What makes a good MC?" they invariably answered in the negative. Kenny Ken said, "One that knows when to shut up." Though Kenny does fully acknowledge the need for a good MC in the live context. Comments from the other DJs were similar. "One who doesn't talk over the mix. One who doesn't chat over the space before the drop." To be fair, many senior MCs would define a good MC in the same way. However, at the height of a rave or lost in the beats of a radio station studio, many MCs break all the rules. Check the mix tapes and recordings of those pirate radio shows.

For all the *One in the Jungle* DJs, the choice of MC was a major consideration. In planning the shows, it was important to allow the DJs themselves to choose the MC they most wanted to work with. Roni and Brockie already worked in a team with their MCs Dynamite and Det. It's a tribute to GQ's talent that he was requested by both Goldie and Kenny Ken, DJs from two different areas of Jungle / Drum & Bass.

Rap felt that Moose was experienced enough to allow the music to breathe whilst enhancing the beats. Gerald said the same of Navigator.

It's a question of professional interaction with the music. MC 5ive'O passionately feels that MCs are as important as the music. Jumping Jack Frost and Grooverider are among those who feel the music must come first. Before their booking agency Groove Connection confirms their DJ's place on any promoter's roster, they want to know which MCs will be chatting over their music. If they aren't happy that a particular MC is able to interact with the music in a way that they feel enhances it, the promoter has to come to some other arrangement otherwise their DJs won't be playing.

Rider and Frost aren't alone in feeling passionate about advancing the quality of musical presentation. Grumbles both in and outside the industry persist. The MCs' style and presentation has to match what DJs, as principle musicians in the orchestra, try to achieve for the crowd.

On stage at One Nation, Jungle Fever, Telepathy, Roast, Earth Energy, Det, The Ragga Twins, Navigator, Skibadee, 5ive'O lyric it off and stand — hands poised ready to grab up the mic before the last syllable trails from the next man's lips. Feeding off itself, the non-stop vocal sparring hypes the crowd over every beat of music.

B: It looks like a competition. Is it?

MC 5ive'O: It's not competition. It's just entertainment. Speaking for myself, Navigator, The Ragga Twins and Moose, when we go out there, we're giving you the best of what De Man Dem's got. Just like the Wu-Tang Clan. When Ol' Dirty Bastard bus' a lyric and RZA comes in or Raekwon or Method Man, is that seen as competition? I want to be on point all the time, every time. And when I've done well, I want to improve on that.

B: I was speaking to an MC who said that you're not seeing competition, you're seeing entertainment.

SGC: They've got to be honest. When 5ive'O and those guys started, they were dancing and occasionally saying a few words on the mic. That was when it was at its best. I still love MCs that can do that. They were outdoing each other and that wasn't our scene. That was more what the Ragga scene was about. That's why we got a sudden influx. They could see it was an MC-centred thing. But it got to the point where you couldn't hear what was going on in the background.

Competition or entertainment, young MCs or punters occasionally seize their chance for glory during the rave, trying to grab the mic, giving it their best. Kingsley Roast has often found the chat is nothing but buzz talk for them and their friends. Even more serious contenders can be a problem.

"I get people wanting the mic. I don't have no problem with it apart from giving someone my personal two grand mic. It's my instrument. Would you give someone your sax? If someone wants to flex on the mic, they should respect the evening. I'll take them to the promoter. If he gives them a chance, well go ahead, do your stuff." CLEVELAND WATKISS

Since MCs are out there doing what they feel is their best for the audience, an obvious conflict of interest develops somewhere in the mix. Wise MCs, both senior and up-and-coming, will ask the DJ how they should interact with a particular set. The stage or studio shouldn't be a battlefield of egos. They should work together much like musicians in a band. However, it's not unknown for a DJ to fade down an over-exuberant MC and, if faced with further non-compliance, to pull the mic lead out of the mixer socket. Though some MCs are highly insulted when they hear that particular DJs don't want their vocals over the music, the worst case scenario of DJs disconnecting MCs, has lead some promoters, radio producers and DJs to impose their own solutions on MCs. In effect, dealing with the problem in the prefade, before the audience hear the mix.

On the original series of *One in the Jungle*, there was an in-house decision to ask the MCs to hold back from their usual presentation to allow listeners to hear the music the way the producers and DJs intended. At Kiss 100 FM, there was a feeling that MCs were strictly for the raves. Aside from that, many of the experienced Kiss crew like Kenny Ken and Hype preferred the opportunity to present their own shows. Over on Kool FM, Bryan Gee hosts his own Sunday night show, giving information on each track he plays. In mid '96, when DJ Ron stepped down from the *Supreme Team Show* Friday night slot with himself, DJ SL and MCs 5ive'O, Moose and Strings, his decision was based on several factors. He wanted to escape from the format in which DJs were just seen as tools of the Rave machine, just there to mix.

Stevie Hyper D

He and his brother MC Strings have long entertained dreams of presenting shows with highly developed, less ravey production values, educating the audience about the music and the people behind it. Ron also wanted to give the listeners more information about each tune. Even if a show is pre-planned, it would be difficult for an MC to have the same in-depth knowledge about the records and their origins that DJ / producers share.

The problem lies in the medium in which of the music. Most Jungle / Drum & Bass is heard in a rave, on mix tapes or on pirates. Now it depends on what you see as the role of the radio medium. If you take the liberal BBC intent of old, they believe in broadcasting to educate, inform and entertain. In the relatively informal setting of the pirates, the rave is proficiently transferred to homes and cars via a buzzing studio. MCs inform and entertain. But the shows which educate the audience about the music tend to be hosted by the DJs. Kemistry & Storm in the old days of Defektion FM, without an MC, would do the shouts and give all the track information as it gave them something to say. DJ / producer Aphrodite on his Sunday Pulse FM sessions also gave the audience enough information to be able to go out and buy the tracks featured, where available. He'd also play one of the poorer tracks around, explaining why he thought it was crap.

In being encouraged to present the rave and prioritising 'entertainment' over 'education', the MCs soon become part of the problem. During the first series of One in the Jungle, MCs were encouraged to give out the track information, especially since a potential new market of listeners who weren't used to taking tapes around independent records shops would ring up asking about specific tracks. MCs on formal radio have a difficult job. Actually, they aren't the only ones to blame for not broadcasting the name, producer and label of every track. Sometimes the DJ is left clueless by producers who, for various reasons, have sent them a blank label piece of vinyl. The overwhelmingly prevalent Rave format has led Grooverider to dismiss pirate radio as "joke business."

Rather than dwell on the negative, some have seized the initiative. When Goldie started the Metalheadz Sessions, he wanted a corner – his own environment, where he, his crew, friends and others could enjoy the music in a different way. Though Goldie recognises that MCs are historically part of the scene, he doesn't "want to hear the beats under some Klingon cloaking device." Deman Rockers admitted on

Kool's Open Forum that, "There are a lot of MCs who talk too much." The problem is that much of the music around 1994 - 96 was designed for MCs. Stepping back to view the full circumference of Jungle / Drum & Bass, Metalheadz solved the problem by placing Cleveland Watkiss right in the middle of the mix. As did Bukem riding the rhythms with MC Conrad at Speed and GQ at AWOL.

During the Spring 1997 V Recordings Launch Party at The End, or week-after-week at his Metalheadz residency, or on his Project 23 album, Watkiss' Jazz vocal past has educated him as a musician who can interact with the music without causing disharmony. His type of voice and approach is just one in an array of MCs' styles. Fair enough, it's horses for courses. The V Recordings launch party also featured Bristol's Dynamite MC with his faster rap / chat style. In the rave context with punters benefiting from the MC's vocal lift, Frost was happy to use Dynamite because, "If we need someone to do that style he's the one. He knows every beat of the music. He's even been in the studio when some of the tunes are being made." During Full Cycle's party at The End which was broadcast live as part of Radio One's One in the Jungle, Dynamite was absolutely 'on-point.'

"The criticism of MCs; don't chat too much, don't talk over the mix ... It's all true. The DJ and MC – they're both important. But MCs think they are more important than DJs. They're both important. They're both supposed to interact. When they don't, ain't nothing going on. I'd rather have an hour and a half of silence rather than two minutes of bullshit 'cos space is music as well. People lose that. I'm a musician and I understand how the music functions. When you don't hear me chatting on the mic, there's a serious reason for that." CLEVELAND WATKISS

"The MC was just to compliment the music but due to the way the music went, the MC became more accepted. People like to hear an MC because it added flavour. Then certain things happened with MCs where everyone was just talking over the tunes and not really checking the situation. When I'm working, I like to check it as if I was a punter. What would I like to hear? Would I like to hear a lot of MCing all the time?" MC GQ

He gets so deep listening to the tunes, that despite requests for him to chat over the tune, he'll wait for the technical and artistic mixture to be right.

New Styles

Many see the need for new styles, though it's hotly contested which direction MCing should take or which approach is more popular. During the heat of an MC contest at Kool Skool's under-18 rave in Spring '97, the hyped-up crowd split their screaming votes between the first MC who chewed out lyrics like Uzi shells and the second, who alternated between rapid chat and full-on melodious singing. Only an emergency on-stage conference between a scrum of judges including Eastman, Det, Skibadee, Deman Rocker and Cogee threw the casting vote to MC number one.

Skibadee is Kool FM's fastest chatter on the mic. But this might be a question of using the voice more as 'instrument' rather than as 'messenger'. MC 5ive'O is angered by suggestions that the public can't understand what he says or that his lyrics have no content. "If they don't understand it, fuck off! They don't understand what? Like "Security wanted up front," "Big Up dis DJ," "Selecta Pull Up." Everyone understands dat. So fuck you 'n' all a dem that don't understand." Eastman also feels, "If you listen to some lyrics carefully, they are conscious, like The Ragga Twins. Det gets well deep in his lyrics if you listen properly. A lot of people aren't listening."

Perhaps it's a problem of audience perception. There is a skool of thought which says that MCs should chat less and say more. In contemplative mood after writing his article on Junglists who'd moved from Hip Hop into Jungle / Drum & Bass, *Hip Hop Connection*'s Mike Gazzi imagined two scenarios. On stage with a Rapper and an MC, the MC would probably fare better than the rapper, rocking the party on and on way past the break of dawn. They're more entertainers than PA artists. In the studio, as lyricists, writers, bringers of the message, the rappers have it. And their writing continues to move in new directions.

The standard of poetry or political comment amongst the vast majority of JDB MCs hasn't improved in comparison with the producer's music. You could be in a Reggae dance with an old veteran like the mighty Jah Shaka. People would be nudging themselves and cheering at his tales, as he selects the tunes on his single turntable sound system. Shaka in oral mode would put most Baptist ministers in the shade with his Biblical rendition of the fall of the Walls of Jericho. Similarly, Chuck D's *Black Steel in the Hour of Chaos* powerful oral sculpture amongst other Rap classics like Onyx's *These Evil Streets* or the Fugees '96 Summer sing-along soundtrack *Fugee La* would raise a smile. KRS One is perhaps the best example of an MC who sounds as though he is just talking without the structure of the rhyme bogging him down. He's not confined within a 'glock, cocked, rock, block' poetic structure.

Which Comes First, The Rap or The Music?

In the UK, MCs face a problem. In the US, the music has developed largely as a vehicle for the rhymes. The music wasn't quite secondary but you were most likely to remember Chuck D's name over that of his DJ Terminator X, whose name D constantly raised to the fore. Crowds on the British Dance scene follow the music first, with MCs adding to the spice of the night. British MCs will probably be seen as the poor cousins of American rappers until they can further their art in this quarter.

How much time do they spend writing? Skibadee comes to each new show on Kool FM with fresh lyrics. MC 5ive'O is never far from his *Roget's Thesaurus of English Words and Phrases*. MC GQ, like many, works with a combination of prepared written lyrics and what he calls 'head top' poetry that comes spontaneously to mind as a result of the music and general atmosphere.

"My style is too complex
when I flex it's abstract.
There is no defect in my style of qualities
'cos I produce no substitutes
when I get loose
my intelligent intellect
reflects my skills everyday
My style penetrates
My lyrics elevate etc ..."
MC GQ

MC Det

What Should They Be Saying?

"For me, the first conscious Rap was The Message;
after that it was all over. You had to get out your
dictionaries and encyclopedias checking out the big
words that we didn't understand, like 'Consciousness.'
It works, people actually listen. Kids actually listen."
A GUY CALLED GERALD

"MCs are rubbish. They should be put in a black plastic bag
and driven away in a van. You're all shit. No lyrics and you
don't write. You just shout, "Wheel up" and put your heads
down. It's lazy cause they just turn up and do it ... I've
known Det and GQ from when they were little boys. They
could be rapping about crack, or the number of black males
being expelled from schools or finding a job or going to
school. Conscious lyrics."
SMILEY, SHUT UP & DANCE

Punters can enjoy the rhymes they lay down with their
words although they may not always carry lofty truths. But
there has been some concern about what MCs are actually
communicating. GQ is among those who hears MCs chatting
conscious lyrics but feels their message escapes people
because it's lost in the preponderance of beats.

"It's especially important to have conscious lyrics. Navigator
has always been on a serious conscious tip. When the
Criminal Justice thing was around, we put something on
vinyl. With the way that the government works, artists,
including MCs, should say, "I can't stand this. I've got to
tell people". The way they brought about the CJA was total
Mafia business. People don't really know the details. It's
not public knowledge that you can do time in prison for
attending a rave as far as I know or playing music over a
certain level or that over a certain number of people can't
gather together in one spot. If you don't know this it's
difficult to fight it. The average person into Dance music
probably knows more about what's going on in the US than
they do over here because of what rappers are saying."
A GUY CALLED GERALD

It's like *Rapper's Delight* and we haven't reached *The
Message*. At the end of the day, if the current style of
presentation persists, so will the perception that the
MCs aren't really saying anything. They are in a vulnerable
position.

Perhaps changes shouldn't be forced on the current batch of
MCs who have entertained audiences around the world with
splendid vigour. That does however leave a gap for more

overtly conscious would-be MCs, be they male or female,
to grab the mic. Otherwise, if Afrika Bambaataa's son TC
Izlam is anything to go by, the Americans might steal the
show. Goldie has worked with KRS One and Roni Size has
featured Bahamadia.

MC Det isn't happy about the use of Americans by British
Jungle / Drum & Bass producers. It's down to individual
producers' choice but this often doesn't square with
supporting the whole 'British thing'. He's one MC who has
tried to develop a conscious lyrical style for the stage and
on his album *Out of Det*. He'd like the opportunity to further
his art, particularly after recording the conscious rap of
Freeform Reality. Gradually, evidence of a new skool of
conscious writing is emerging. But GQ, 5ive'O and Skibadee
aren't alone in feeling that a rave stage isn't necessarily
the place for hard conscious lyrics. Skibadee and Det will
present themselves differently on vinyl, where they have
a chance to fulfil their potential rather than be limited to
being rave performers, albeit good ones. Stevie Hyper D
developed a new flex covering all bases with a singing,
chatting, smooth talking, conscious Rap style on his album
The Next Step.

The Way Forward?

*"I'm not in the whole MC thing. I'm doing this
because I've got something to say."* MC HERMIONE

Rude FM Spring '97.
Same station, different location
17.55 Saturday evening,
DJs Agent K and Magistrate call in to say
they'll be late for their show at the top of
the hour. Fugee yells into the phone above the
music. "No, left then right under the bridge
by a rubbish tip. Yeah, yeah, tha … Shit,
battery's gone." He clicks off the mobile and
stomps downstairs with a sleeping bag rolled
up under his arm. It's going to be a another
long weekend.

In the upstairs bedroom with a thick mattress
hastily hoisted over the window overlooking the
rest of the low rise estate, DJ Filthy Rich
bangs out tunes, whilst aspiring vocalist
Hermione, with a hint of vocal nervousness,
chats into the mic. The energy in this studio
capsule is different. The usual frenzy is
replaced with something calmer yet more potent.

Between the calls homing in on a row of back door mobiles perched near the sl1210s, and the brief snatches of static interference spewing out the battered beatbox monitor, she stands flicking through the pages of her A4 note pad. Punctuating the test presses with a beautiful singing style and the "Big Up the Stoke Newington Massive" chat, she chants, "no justice in the system." Obeying all the rules, not chatting through the mix or over the drop, Hermione weaves through themes of social politics and political power. Pacing across the dodgy 70s carpet, she chats on this prime time Saturday evening slot about child abuse, rape and materialism. She gains in confidence as the session goes into overtime. Over the darkness of Doc Scott's *Shadow Boxing*, she sings, "The Rude FM on the 104 point … keeps you alive with the DJ Filthy Rich and the MC Hermione." She chants:

"People in power
the poor they devour
Sitting in Parliament hour after hour
Making up rules, thinking they're right
but they've never been poor
and they've never had to fight
I'd like to put them on the streets
for just one night
No whiskey to drink
no cigars to light
And I'd look them in the eyes the very next day
and see what the hell
the fuckers had to say."

This feels weird. It feels good. Up in this daylight, nighttime, anywhere studio. Across London, Jungle / Drum & Bass is taking another direction.

MC Det sees a way forward through producer / MC collaborations. Ideally he'd like to see more tracks recorded with MCs as vocalists rapping, chatting and singing. With themselves on vinyl, he envisages crowds coming to see MCs perform PAs with DJs backing. After the set the DJ would play for the rest of the night in the usual Rave context. Both he and MC Skibadee have joined forces to extend their talent beyond Jungle / Drum & Bass and produced an album. The Godfather MC Moose has taken a more divergent approach, and turned musician rather than vocalist.

Two tunes, *Heartbeat* and *Forbidden Fruit*, released on DJ Ron's Piccasso label, show the music of a mature performer who's been in the business for a very long time. The tracks are excellent and will surprise many. MC 5ive'O sees his future in television, developing his persona as a performer. Aside from showing off more of his talents, he'd like to counter-act the effects of Tell-I-Vision as a presenter by keeping it real for the audience. A lover of current affairs programs like BBC 2's *Newsnight*, he'd love to interview Prime Minster Tony Blair. "I'd take him 'round the ghetto in a hooded top and show him the real deal."

On the Garage circuit MCs Creed, PSG and DT have established themselves as vocalists with some mainstream chart success. We've also seen a return in 1999 of female vocalists such as Shanie and Kirsty Wilcox. Regardless of how people might cuss MCs, no one can deny their importance and value in making JDB raves the most vibrant, exciting and raw dances around. As that link between the unreachable DJ and the audience, they undoubtedly work. They are part of the cultural hybrid that is Jungle. It should also be remembered that it was MCs who carried Jungle to chart success. The MCs around are undoubtedly talented artists, however there are some who claim they need to work at developing their art further. Move to the next stage.

THE NEXT GENERATION

A year later, same frequency, new name – MC Prime on breakaway station Ruud Awakening slices through my mind with challenging, emotional, conscious lyrics. Themes of loneliness, suicide, the male pain of having no say in abortion decisions … all so real that it brings activity to a stunned halt. UB Nice madly cuts, scratches and rewinds his voice between his real deal words, sounding like the vocal equivalent of Miles Davis. Both Prime and Nice talk, laugh, joke, scream, sing, rap and perform poetry during their road of life sets. Prime and UB Nice and their DJs DM Cut and Rage aren't up-and-comings, they were on the original Weekend Rush, and they are way out there.

Wheel Up Selecta 'n' Come Again!

MEDIA

"They didn't want to touch our music with a fucking barge pole." MC GQ

"The wrong people exposed it to the masses in the first place, a bit like Acid House on the front page of The Sun – partly true but loads of things that were clearly ridiculous. Stereotypes of Jungle being made by crack dealers in Hackney written by journalists who didn't know what they were talking about."
ROB PLAYFORD

It's a sentiment that's repeated time and again by punters and industry professionals alike. It's striking that enough of the population know by now that even the most supposedly credible newspapers and their staff continue to misrepresent facts. Mirroring a loss of confidence in the police, politicians and the church, the Fourth Estate – the press, are regarded with justified suspicion. If they can't get the facts right about civil unrest, wars and corruption how can they be trusted to report our scene truthfully? Especially when they become trapped by their own lust for sensationalism. Watch the ride ...

When Shut Up & Dance released *Green Man* in Jan '92, they were the focus of negative press attention. The record featured dialogue between Smiley and PJ posing as two crack heads. Without the obvious "Don't do crack" message, they adopted a subtle approach portraying the life of a crack head. The hunger for rocks, the necessity of car breaking and stealing car stereos – the misery of this low life but it was too subtle for the press who flagged it as a pro-crack tune.

People's experience of media attention throughout JDB's growth has been largely negative, either because it has ignored, exaggerated or misrepresented the scene, its players, where they were coming from and what they were trying to achieve. "When they did start to write about us they were wrong. It didn't make any difference to us. We just carried on." ROB PLAYFORD

Though the JDB family remain highly suspicious, many have become media savvy and learned to conduct interviews confidently whilst also keeping themselves covered. "When the media did get involved we got misportrayed every time. They were always saying some crap or other like, "Don't the DJs look like muggers?" SARAH, GROOVE CONNECTION

They have had to fight against the distortions caused by journalists, specifically those of the music press. The media was blamed for trumpeting Drum & Bass, whilst stereotyping Jungle. "The bad press has got better since the early days. In '92, Rush and us was getting blamed for supplying half the drugs in London. All those false rumours. I was watching an old video, "Pirate radio supplying cover for drugs parties" – complete nonsense. I think they've come away from that now. People might think, "Oh they're trouble." But there's nothing that bad."
MIKEY, DE UNDERGROUND

But the media aren't entirely to blame. The Jungle community must also take responsibility. When Lucy Pilkington of BBC Pebble Mill set out to make her film, *Jungle Fever*, she was beset by problems in accessing key figures and locations of the scene. One of the foundation meetings was called to decide whether the Jungle family should be involved in the BBC film. "There was a whole discussion whether DJs should take people to Music House because the secret would be out. If we did the BBC documentary, would the scene be strong enough to take everything that would be coming, the taxman, MCPS, the whole thing? Shut Up & Dance had [already] been made a pure example of." DAVE STONE, SOUR

SOUR was on the verge of releasing *Nuttah* and couldn't really afford to miss this opportunity for publicity. Dave Stone felt that if the scene wasn't providing the real characters, then the film would be made anyway, with the wrong focus. Though SOUR's UK Apache did take part in the film, Dave Stone worked to ensure the right image came across, banning a shot showing Apache and General Levy shaking hands in Leicester Square at the time when Levy was under the Jungle *fatwa*.

"At the end of the day it's the media that pigeon-hole everything. It's not about that. Music is all together. It's a vibe not just one or the other, it's everything – the whole spectrum, together, a part of the spectrum." NICKY BLACKMARKET

DISTORTIONS REINFORCING STEREOTYPES

"Rude Girls with extra attitude bring Jungle vibes to the screen," said an *Observer* headline. The accompanying photograph features two black Ragga-Jungle girls. The article describes a TV production to be filmed on Harlesden's Stonebridge estate. The audition called for "Ragga girls, Junglists, rude girls, glamour crews and women with xtra, xtra attitude." (Roger Tredre in *The Observer*, reporting on a Channel 4's proposed production by Julian Henriques.) Though Ragga gyals are a colourful element in Jungle, they are only part of the whole Jungle massive. Tredre's focus promoted a stereotype.

Like many a musical evolution, tracks like Shy FX's *Original Nuttah* and Levy's *Incredible* were part of that growth but it wasn't the whole tree, merely a branch nourished by diverse but traceable roots – supported by a general sub-genre trunk.

When the mainstream press first took notice of the scene, they found a handle that was too easy to grab. The word Jungle became a metaphor feeding a cliché painting a picture. Articles in *The Guardian* and *The Face* complete with photos made you feel that Jungle was solely a black thing. It was as if they didn't want to emphasise the truly multicultural makeup of the scene.

Rewind to late '93. In his shop, Mikey De Underground remembers the term Jungle sneaking into the media with the infusion of Ragga samples into British Breakbeat. Fast forward to June '94, *The Observer Life Magazine*: "If anyone is qualified to report on the Jungle Club scene," says the by-line, "it's former *iD* editor Matthew Collin." Under a picture of two black guys sporting Jungle Fever bomber jackets, the sub-editor's intro reads, "Jungle Fever – Matthew Collin explores Jungle Music, a new controversial and predominantly black phenomenon that is sweeping clubland". The media makes its own images. *New* – well that's if you treat it in isolation and ignore its three year history. *Controversial* – why controversial? The scene didn't have producers sticking two fingers up at the Queen, DJs lobbing TVs out hotel windows or MCs pulling on ski masks in drive-bys across downtown Dalston. Then there's the *predominantly black* tag.

Jungle Fever's Susie G isn't alone in feeling bemused when that cliché gets bandied around. Kool FM's DJ Wildchild recalls, "We were all in it together. We hung out together, moved together, lived together, raved together". Wildchild was almost excluded from the '96 MTV *Turned On Europe* video diary series because, a senior producer felt, they needed a black male DJ – "That's what Jungle was all about" he insisted. I made a stand and the program went ahead with Wildchild.

"The articles in iD, The Observer, The Face – I just thought, well, it's not really like that but that's the edge that the media are going to pick up on first 'cos that's the 'Black Culture' angle. They would never get their heads around the rest of it." DJ ZOE

Most of those deeply involved in the scene could have been caught up in a net of distortion. People like General Levy appeared to believe the image was real. Much of the focus in the mainstream media in 1995 - 96 was on Goldie, almost to the exclusion of the scene's other players. "It's unfair to blame the media focus on Goldie entirely on them. Goldie is a *bona fide* personality. He was the only one on the scene at the time with the character that could front everything. He knows how to get people's attention. He knows how to play the media." MIKEY, DE UNDERGROUND

"In '97 we had a problem with the media 'cos they'd become bored with Drum & Bass. All that media attention wasn't really helpful. A lot of the trendy people have moved on to the next thing. We were pushed into a corner by the media." SARAH, GROOVE CONNECTION

MC GQ is also conscious of the distorting affects of media coverage especially with regard to the Drum & Bass tag: "Drum & Bass has been there since back in the day. The fucking media were talking about it like it was a brand new thing. Randall used to play Drum & Bass at the Paradise. It's not a new thing, like with House and Garage. I used to work with Paul Anderson when JP done Sterns. Now it's Speed Garage — Raggage and all that. It's the media and they don't help."

"The mass media will never take it seriously, 'cos they'll only be in it as long as it's making them money." DJ RAY KEITH, ALL JUNGLISTS, CHANNEL 4, DECEMBER 1994

The scene's scepticism was and is justified.

"That's all folks. Forget Drum & Bass — the truly hip have now moved on."
ANITA CHAUDHURI, SUNDAY TIMES STYLE MAGAZINE, OCTOBER 1997

IMAGES IN RADIO & TELEVISION

DJ Rap on Woman's Hour, Radio Four
Cut to July '95 as Jenni Murray interviews DJ Rap on *Woman's Hour*, one of the oldest radio programs in the world. DJ SS' *Lighter* tune sounds surreal coming from Radio Four as we listen across the road in the Radio One building. Though she tried to prepare well for the interview, the producer's dogged questions were off the mark. "What about the sexist, violent lyrics?" "Well, there aren't any to speak of," I reply. "Even the MCs chat without being sexist or rude bwoy violent." Her calls came over the weekend – "There must be something."

I search through piles of records, hours of music, find one solitary track but point out that Shy FX's and Gunsmoke's track, *Original Gangster* is just one track. On Monday morning I pass the producer the record with very mixed feelings. During the interview as the Beeb waves the sexist, violence flag, Rap burns it up with a blast of lighter fluid. They couldn't see their own stereotype and they were in trouble. The atmosphere in the live studio was frosty as Rap explains; "Shy is an artist who's inspired by his own experiences and those of his friends. They get touched by something and recreate it musically, there's nothing new in that". The

reality of life in North East London may be an uncomfortable truth for the listeners of Middle England. The normally excellent Jenni Murray and the Woman's Hour team didn't know the angles and were more interested in affirmative answers to their own clichéd questions. Rap had rightly been on her guard. The *Woman's Hour* ladies didn't care much for DJ Rap. As she sped off in her BMW convertible towards Oxford Circus with the boom in the back, you can be sure Rap didn't care much for them either.

Just because *Clockwork Orange* is on the shelf, it doesn't make the whole library violent and sexist. It seems there's always problems as the traditional media – the image-makers with their power to misrepresent and caricature, tries to touch the underground. It stems in part from a certain blind professional arrogance.

First Sight, BBC TV South, autumn '94
Before I worked on BBC South's current affairs program *First Sight* they had fallen into the trap of using footage of some youths at a wild Jungle rave to illustrate a point about dysfunctional black males in the education system. However in '96 when *Men Behaving Badly* producers requested a clip from *Radio Renegades* – a film about pirate radio – our editor refused on the grounds that she didn't know in which context the clip would be used. Perhaps my stint in the office had made a difference.

ON THE POSITIVE SIDE ...

There *are* some positive programs made by producers, here and abroad.

Pirates, BBC TV, 1993
This was produced and directed by talented filmmaker Nigel Finch who's worked with the likes of Derek Jarman. He took on the subject of pirate radio featuring Rush FM on Hackney's Nightingale estate and reached some secret corners. Like the best films about the underground, you spend half the time gobsmacked that something so insightful has reached the screens at all.

DJ Rap

All Junglists – A London Some 'Ting Dis, Channel 4, 1994

22.58 Peckham: Roly's yard. MCs chat on the radio about a TV program. He switches on catching the continuity announcer. "And now continuing in the Black Christmas Season …" Roly grabs up the phone.

22.59 Tottenham: Pulling deeply on his spliff, the fastest thing in the attic bedroom is the strobe light on the Technics. Lost in the zone, the bedroom DJ draws another tune from the untidy pile at his feet. The first beat rubs back and forth through the stylus. 'Ring'. His fingers let the vinyl fly. The beat of the bar drops on the one. 'Ring'. Delicate fingers touch the spinning edge. 'Ring'. Teasing the pitch control, yep the beats in the phones are runnin'. 'Ring'. As the crossfader floods the room with the mix, the tunes are clanging. The phone keeps ringing. Concentration gone. Tape ruined. Headphones dashed on the mixer and fist pounds the stop buttons. Whirrrrr … Angry silence. Snatching up the phone. Speaks, "YES." Thinks, 'Roly again.' "Switch on the TV man." "What?!" "Now man, now! It's Kool FM an all De Man Dem." "What ya saying?" Purrrr.

23.02: The box goes on as he seckles into the screen. Kool FM an' all De Man Dem on Channel 4. Rare!

One of the many ravers gracing the dancefloors of 1992 - 93 was Rachel Seely, a film school graduate making her first film. Without a channel on which to show their films, Rachel and producers Shirani Sabratnam and Jo Wiser set out to make All Junglists. Rachel was aware that television has ways of trivialising important subjects by pigeon-holing them in the youth or ethnic minority slot and as they expected their year and a half project, All Junglists was shown late at night as part of Channel 4's Black Christmas season. Stuart Cosgrove's selection of the program was in line with the radical remit of Channel 4's charter. Focusing mainly on the Jungle branch of the industry, All Junglists included memorable footage and hot live action of Det,

Rema Dee, Navigator and The Ragga Twins, the Roast crew promoters, DJs Mickey Finn and Darren Jay, Goldie, Gus, Randall and the Reinforced stable plus assorted ravers. All Junglists also featured a moving interview with Kenny Ken, underscored by music mixed by DJ Ron. Though the film was critically acclaimed, the production crew, lost down some budgetary back alley of minority programming, were left with only enough cash to pay off the cost of the project.

Fereala, Channel 4 pilot, 1996 – Unscreened

One series which never reached the screen in '96, was Goldie's program Fereala. It was described by former Word producer Anne Lavelle as the best pilot she'd ever worked on. Fereala featured life's real deal including secret filming running with a South London pool hustler, a rare interview with Goldie and Sean Stussy at home in Hawaii and a mad studio set up with guests – Grooverider, Fabio, Randall, DJ Rap and Robbie Williams. Channel 4 had a perfect opportunity to broaden the horizons of youth programming. But Fereala wasn't commissioned. They opted for a second series of The Girlie Show and copies of Fereala are still sitting on a shelf.

Club Zone, MTV Europe, '89 onwards

In spite of JDB's suspicion of the media, MTV Europe producer, James Hyman, has been honourably on the case since time.

October '96, Robbie Williams strolls into the glass, chrome and shagpile of MTV Europe. He always seems to be there nowadays. Simone, the unspeakably beautiful pan-European VJ, sits outside in the back of a car, shuffling her notes waiting for James Hyman, long time producer of Club Zone. They'll be late. Always cramming the time envelope with projects in progress, he arrives, they leave. James filling the car with a buzz of confidence. Speeding out of Camden, they cut through the traffic like only TV crews and Jungle DJs can. Heading past a golden Regent's Park, blonde bob dancing in the wind, "Hmmm a Leo …" Simone undresses the boys with her deep astrological insights.

Veering right at the wrong traffic lights, the conversation changes as James pulls a coarse corrective u-turn, discussing the intricacies of the morning's interview. One hundred releases of Reinforced. Simone remembers them from back in the day. Back in the day, when she earned her stripes travelling from Holland to England for long weekends and raving till the cash ran out. *Internal Affairs*, *31 Seconds*, she knew them all. As did James who started working at MTV as an undergraduate, passionately flying the flag for Dance music against the then prevailing Rock bias. He's a self-confessed trainspotter with an awesome collection of magazines and fanzines. Then there's the video library. It's rather extensive.

Well, the thing is, if you happen to be in a job where someone pays you to interview the best emerging artists across the whole Dance spectrum, you can indulge yourself and give those that know a treat. A Guy Called Gerald, Shut Up & Dance, Nicolette, vintage Navigator and The Ragga Twins, all on film in the MTV library. He's captured them all on Beta, Hi 8, Digital and 8mm celluloid. Today he's drawn for a two camera shoot. Video and film — "It's gotta be done."

Parking up early near Dollis Hill tube, he only had a few 'Greats' left to interview. Derrick May, Kraftwerk and, this morning, Goldie, Randall and the boys from Reinforced. It was going to be a good day.

During the interview, Simone talks to Reinforced about the distrust between members of the JDB family and the media prominent in previous years, expressing the hope that all that's finished now. "We're on your side." She also expressed the need for artists to produce more videos. For legal reasons, MTV can only play music if they have it on video. "So more videos please." But Dego explains that unless they can have some George Lucas type production fronting their music, they're not interested.

Radio Wars, BBC South TV, February '96

Cut to March '95 and the making of BBC South's, *First Sight*, *Radio Renegades* — BBC regional current affairs take a positive look at pirate radio. As the researcher who put forward the idea for the program, I can say that it was a very rocky road. *Radio Wars* was the program's working title. The Junglists expected to be stitched up and misrepresented. They almost were.

11.00am, a clear Tuesday morning: A Black MG Turbo with darkened windows clocks a furious 70 mph, speeding out of the *Grange Hill* playground, past *Top of the Pops*, Albert Square and leaves BBC Elstree. Alone and distraught, minutes later I was standing on a hillside overlooking Borehamwood calling Kate on the mobile. "I've left." "What?!" "Left". I needed a spliff badly. "Come again?" "I've left. They've imposed a middle-aged, middle-England Cholmondley Warner-type reporter on my program." Silence followed Kate's desperate "No." I rang off and called a mentor for advice. "A problem hmm?", Roy said in a soothing Welsh accent. "Has anyone important noticed you've left?" "Don't know, don't care." "Of course if you don't go back, you can't change anything." Walking back to the car, scraping the Hertfordshire mud from off my boots, I find a welcome post-rave roach in the ashtray. After a soothing toke, it's time to return to the fight.

During the research phase, just when you relax enough to think maybe you'd over reacted, you hear that Cholmondley Warner intends to call certain Head Teachers, landing everyone in it. Teachers recognise that DJs and MCs are role models and ask them into schools to speak to the kids. It serves a positive purpose. But if a BBC reporter calls up the local Head asking, "Did you know your teachers invite pirates into your schools to speak to the pupils?" it would blow the gaff on a useful community service. Thankfully, the call was prevented. The last battle that remained was persuading the program's editor that DJ Brockie's words didn't actually need subtitling. It wasn't that you couldn't understand Brockie, more a preconception from the project's outset. The editor had been asking, "Are we actually going to understand these people?" The seeds of misunderstanding were there from the beginning.

However, under the mellow but enthusiastic insight of producer David Stevenson, the program was seen in all quarters as a success. It received a big up from the pirates and letters of thanks from the DTI and the Radio Authority. *Radio Renegades* was even used by the management of one pirate station as an instructional video. "Well, it said it all, innit."

People put labels on things, sometimes for their own convenience – journalists, TV and radio producers. To do things properly, get things right you have to work, at least in part, from within the scene. Radio, television, tabloids and Sunday Supplement broadsheets have a way of riding over people lives, like a car-load of joy riders doing handbrake turns in your *cul de sac* with the windows down and the system up, screaming, FUCK OFF YOU WANKERS, out the windows before speeding off to diss the next street. You never know how they'll flex. No wonder people are suspicious. Until each person proves themselves on an individual basis, the image-makers are viewed in the same light as the authorities, with scepticism.

SHOUTING TILL I WAS BLUE IN THE FACE

Zoe Richardson, PM Scientists
Zoe Richardson moved from raver to DJ. Her day job at PR firm Phuture Trax was to inform and persuade journalists to feature the JDB industry.

"I thought I'd have a go at media, and worked in a TV production company that made art programs for Channel 4. The producer was really cool. I remember trying to get her to do a film about Jungle. I did all the research. But she thought it was still too obscure and couldn't see an angle to sell it. So she had me researching some program on Youth Culture, alternative religions, shamanism, trance and Megatripolis. All that mystical 60s bullshit. I realised all the people who controlled the media were in their forties and had done the sixties thing. They could deal with middle class kids in Indian clothes and beads. It made sense to them.

What's really going on and what was really representing the time was Jungle, the real postmodern music. It was all too much and they couldn't get their heads around it. I'd be passionate about it, telling her to wait a year and everyone would be going on about it. When Channel 4 did do a program about Jungle I was really chuffed. The fact that it

wasn't perfect ... well at least it was something. It was predominantly black but the scene was more than black music. You have to think of how it would be sold to Channel 4 as a minority program. You get money to do it if you take that angle, whereas it's as much a white suburban culture as it is a black city culture. But it's less right-on to do a film about a load of white kids in Essex. I've always thought that and it's just a fact of life.

I used to read music magazines and ask why they never mentioned Jungle. I wrote to *Mixmag* in '93. Didn't get it printed or a reply. Someone else did though so I remember thinking that I wasn't alone. My mate Nathan and I knew it was only a matter of time. There was a whole scene out there; the clothes, music, DJs and clubs ... there was a culture. We waited for them to write and it started to happen. But they hadn't actually got it. *Mixmag* really did think it was crap music. I do press promotion with a lot of people who really hated it then.

Phuture Trax was set up by Nikki Trax and promoted different House, Garage and Techno labels. They also worked with early Reinforced, Suburban Base and the first Metalheadz tunes. But trying to get the magazines to write about music they hated was like fighting a losing battle. I've looked back through the press pack for '94 and the only magazine which had something was *iD* on 4 Hero, purely as a result of a PR move by Phuture Trax. The only magazine that gave any real coverage to Jungle was *Generator* who put Goldie on the cover in '94. It was his first cover. I promoted Dillinja and Lemon D but no-one was interested until recently."

Zoe persisted. "There was a Dillinja tune. I knew it was big in the clubs, so I'd tell them that the record was being caned. Tell them to listen to pirate radio next weekend and hear it getting bigged up. I fed them the information so they knew enough to write about it. They didn't want to write about something when they didn't know what they were talking about. It was like a chain reaction." Zoe continues to promote JDB more directly as a DJ and co-founder of club night PM Scientist alongside DJ Damian Lazarus.

Single Minded

Apart from Grooverider, Fabio and Frost, there's been few other people who've been working in Dance music before the mid-80s. Tony Byrne of Single Minded Promotions is one of them. His promotion credits include: A Homeboy, A Hippie & A Funky Dred; Adamski; early work with DJ Hype; the first Top Forty Breakbeat success with *Far Out* on Suburban Base; Baby D; Shy FX; UK Apache; T Power; Nazlyn's *Sweet Love*; Elizabeth Troy; Adam F; Moving Shadow, right through to a semi-management role with Hype and Zinc at True Playaz; as well as the chart topping *V* Classics album. Back in 1990 he took a group of journalists and DJs on a coach trip to Raindance so they could experience some of what the scene was about for themselves first hand.

In essence he's a media-wise operator, who's been a marketing consultant to independent artists and small labels, feeding into the media. During meetings with producers at *Top of the Pops*, Radio One, Kiss 100 FM, MTV Europe and a range of press, Tony's been a lynchpin between the Underground and the Mainstream attracting as much attention for each act as possible, raising the profile of JDB. Tony's a persuasive orator extraordinaire. After the '95 Berlin Love Parade, wearing only the clothes I stood up in, not a *pfennig* or passport in my pocket and just a BBC ID card to my name, I watched him work at close hand – blagging me onto a Lufthansa flight all the way back to London.

Though he's helped JDB from the margins onto 'A' lists at Kiss and Radio One, even up to 1993 - 94, producers found it difficult to accept Breakbeat or Jungle / Drum & Bass as commercially viable music. Part of the process of selling tunes to radio producers involved the use of radio edits. These are three and a half minute snippets of the full tune which combine all the best elements of the track, in a form more digestible to disc jockeys on legal radio. He advises artists and labels, joining them in the studio to produce these edits specifically for radio. The radio edit is now an accepted marketing tool.

Tony Byrne generally represents tracks, artists and labels on the independent scene that need an extra push towards national chart success. Promoting some of the best music, he's able to back JDB with a sense of real commitment. He doesn't guarantee an 'A' play listing for every track he promotes but he has done well to secure a succession of chart hits for artists across the Jungle spectrum.

Hinako Walter, the Japanese Connection

Another of the family who always shows up at x-amount of raves is Japanese born, Crouch End resident, Hinako Walter. She came to London for a holiday in '85, liked it and stayed. After kicking around as a singer in various back room pub bands, she became depressed with the state of the music business. In 1993 - 94, Hinako found Jungle through listening to pirate station Ragga FM. "A Jamaican taught me to be a Junglist." A friend took Hinako to her first raves and suggested that she fill a gap in the market by exporting Jungle to Japan. After a short spell trying to distribute records to the wrong record companies, she linked up with Kamba, the premier Japanese Jungle promoter who first took GQ and Kenny Ken to Tokyo in June '95.

By the end of the year Hinako, alongside Kamba, had written the comprehensive *Junglist Handbook* published by *Remix Magazine* for whom she also writes monthly dispatches. Hinako describes herself as a freelance coordinator and initiator, forging contacts between Japanese journalists and the Jungle industry, helping Japanese musicians find Jungle artists including Dillinja and Peshay to do remixes for the domestic market. She's also touched base with Avex, Polydor, Toshiba and EMI. Hinako's decision to fill this niche was conscious, "What I can do for both countries is make the connection." She's become the UK source for Japanese interested in Jungle.

Though well supplied, the Japanese market is still relatively small. With record companies waiting patiently for the big bonanza, the Rave scene in Japan is growing. Five thousand people partied on the slopes of Mount Fuji at an event called Japan Reggae Splash. Playing a mixture of Techno and Jungle, their '96 New Year's party attracted 20,000 people. Of the Japanese and their newfound love of Rave, Hinako isn't surprised. "Culturally, we love singing and dancing. The tribal thing is very strong."

At home in Crouch End, under the name Treasure House London, Hinako ran a monthly Jungle night called Camouflage in the basement of the local Kings Head pub, with DJs including A Guy Called Gerald, the Trouble on Vinyl crew and Subject 13. She's due to move into production – working effectively, she's making an impression. Even her local paper, *The Hornsey Journal*, has cottoned on to her – "Hinako Spreads Jungle Beat" – granting her a place of honour as a 'Crouch Ender'.

TV TRAILS & ADVERTS

Working in one of Soho's many basement studios, Adam F was surprised to hear some kind of Drum & Bass bouncing off the walls next door. Ad agencies bring in artists to knock out whichever music style the ad firm needs to sell its products. In this case an Australian Rock band was trying to reproduce Jungle. It's standard practice.

The advertising industry feeds on new ideas. Jungle / Drum & Bass is new, cutting edge, driving, young and above all, 'with it.' By Spring '98 it seemed that Drum & Bass was de rigueur for all Sky One's trails. Other companies found that it's also great backing music for car ads, ice cream, deodorant, adding a streetwise credibility to common consumer items. Jungle / Drum & Bass is credible.

Kyan and Ray, aka Survivors

This crew are 'media savvy' and have managed to find a niche for themselves. As advertisers wise-up to the message in the music, Survivors are flooded with commissions from as far afield as Japan and Australia, but they're determined only to make quality music for quality ads.

Kyan and Ray are as passionate about the 30 second stings they create as any of the top name producers are about their 12"s. Living and loving Drum & Bass to the max, if anyone is going to make JDB in the advertising environment, they want it to be them. They're on a mission to keep it real. Ray, a Tottenham boy who plays saxophone and Jimi Hendrix style guitar, did his apprenticeship at raves in fields from Oxford to Bristol. Kyan was nurtured on Hip Hop, Electro and outdoor raves like Castle Morton. Both were visitors to AWOL at Paradise, listening to the beats of Kenny Ken and Randall. Passing through pirate station Touch Down FM with the likes of Mix Master Max, Ryan and Ray desperately wanting to make music, they got on the case.

Driving around town, DJ Bailey played a copy of Ray and Kyan's second track, Lounging, to Grooverider. Rider rewound the tune and contacted Ray on his mobile. "Rider here, it's about that tune." Ray was astounded. He and Kyan cut the Dub Plate and took it with them to the Paradise where Kyan tried to persuade GQ to get one of the DJs to play it. Ray had to split early, leaving Kyan on the stage with the record in his hand, praying someone would play it. Eventually Randall came along and took the Dub Plate saying, "I'll keep the tune — but I might not even

play it". Kyan waited, wound up, till the last record of the set. Randall, with Lounging in the headphones gave the thumbs-up. "When Kenny Ken played the tune in Bristol it got five rewinds." The recognition continues. "Grooverider's let it be known that he'll have any finished tunes of ours of sufficient quality."

As a runner in a TV company, Kyan unsuccessfully tried to persuade them to make a documentary on the Drum & Bass scene. Later employed by a studio, he cornered the bosses and talked to them for over two hours about the music. Maintaining the pressure, he'd slyly leave magazines and flyers around in the office, buying CDs and records for the firm. Finally Survivors made an impression and were commissioned to make music for Kiss 100 FM, Lucozade, trails for Box TV, a backing track for an Eric Cantona documentary and the award-winning Red Stripe ad. Aside from ad companies requesting tapes, their music is circulated amongst the top ten music libraries in the world and they're listed among the best in The British Design & Arts Directory. Kyan smiles, "It's kind of trivial but it shows we're getting our point across." Heavily influenced by Krust, Renegade Hardware, Renegade Soundwave and the classic label, Warp. Survivors make Drum & Bass across the spectrum.

Now highly media literate, Survivors realise that you can't just present an advertising agency with a record or tape, you have to supply them the whole package, otherwise they won't understand how the music could work in context. Survivors refuse to be seduced by the chrome, glass and dollars of the advertising industry. Integrity remains all-important. Survivors refuse to see the artists or music exploited. Whilst working on the Red Stripe ad, Kyan saw a script for another product, which GQ was due to record a voiceover for. Realising GQ was about to be stitched up in a dodgy racist ad, he caught GQ near the studio, warning him that this wasn't a project he should be doing. Checking the script, GQ left the studio in 50 seconds flat with a, "You must be absolutely joking, DEAR."

Chilling upstairs in Survivors' West London studio, we're listening to their tunes and nodding. They haven't made ad music. They've made music for ads.

INTERNATIONAL

Sitting on a long haul flight to Tokyo, GQ asks the Japanese girl sitting next to him, what she's listening to on her Walkman. "Kenny Ken and GQ," she replies. At first she doesn't recognise them. Kenny and G smile and the penny drops. The girl can't believe her luck and accompanies them on tour around Japan.

MC GQ picked up the mic at a rave to dispel any rumours that he'd retired. "If you don't see me around, that's 'cos I'm on a plane to Israel or Germany or wherever, taking Jungle forward, representing abroad."

GQ is one of the number of DJs, MCs and producers who leave Britain almost on a weekly basis to perform at parties abroad. Grooverider and Fabio first went to Japan in 1993. British Jungle / Drum & Bass artists have contributed to the global growth of the music perhaps by initially playing to only fifty people.

A sense of the strength of JDB can be gauged from its growth abroad. Rave organisations, labels and individual artists have been travelling to destinations from Latvia to Auckland, Australia, Canada and Sweden. Switzerland and Japan are now firmly on the map. Rio's '97 Free Jazz Festival featured Neneh Cherry, Jamiroquai and Erykah Badu alongside Metalheadz and Adam F with his band the F Jams. When Adam was announced, he was pleasantly surprised to hear the 5,000 strong crowd shout "Check check check check", the intro to *Circles*, before they'd play a note. As opportunities for DJs to play abroad increase, DJs

like London resident Legacy have built careers mostly playing out of the country. Artists like Rob Playford, Nico, Optical and Ed Rush, known more as producers than DJs, have a healthy flow of foreign bookings. Additionally, for their Y2K celebrations, the Australian Council has sponsored a tour across the continent of British sound system Bedlam, alongside the Mutoid Waste Company.

It's difficult not to notice the huge number of tourists and visitors who now regularly check out raves and record shops during their trips to England, supporting the music once they return home. One of Horace's customers, a DJ from Johannesburg, enthused about the scene there. He and his crew make several record buying trips to London each year. December '97, a friend in Cape Town calls to tell me that my man and the fast growing Johannesburg Jungle scene was featured in a documentary screened at peak time on national Television. V Recordings and GQ have monthly Stateside residencies. MC Moose enthused about the '97 *V Classics* American and Canadian launch tour. He described how it was going off in Washington, Chicago, New York and Toronto. The *Beavis & Butthead* and *Cheers* types that Moose had only seen on TV were raving together with the 'LA niggers' brucking out big time. Even House Icon Todd Terry has been known to play Drum & Bass.

In New York's largest clubs the promoters had never seen anything like it and tried to book the crew then and there for a repeat performance. They're smoking blunts and listening to Roast mix tapes on street corners in LA and NYC. One of the Afrika Bambaattaa's Zulu Nation said of Jungle, "We've got to embrace this shit". He described how at first they didn't like it, but one guy had a tape, then another. Tapes were passed around. Before he knew it, he was playing a tape 'round his girlfriend's apartment and they ended up making love. "Yeah, we've got to embrace this shit."

It might be difficult to appreciate the impact of a few mix tapes sent overseas. But people record and mail mix tapes around the world with a lot of commitment. Some tapes have been rebroadcast on local radio stations. In this Internet age, Jumping Jack Frost and Bryan Gee are among the JDB artists taking part in Internet shows, again making use of new technology to increase the reach of the music. As Hype said, "You see that Space Station [Mir] that's been goin' 'round up there, I'm sure they want to book me". Well even if that's a slight exaggeration, the astronauts can always log on.

THE LOVE PARADE BERLIN SUMMER '97 METALHEADZ / HARD:EDGED SESSION: AN EMAIL FROM MY MATE DANIEL

"The Love Parade's been getting bigger every year since it first took place back in 1989. It started off with 150 people dancing down Kurfürstendamm following a small lorry with a sound system on the back. Lorries became trucks – 250 Watts became 20,000. It's become the bloody biggest party this planet has ever seen, with one million people from all over the place going crazy and dancing towards the Brandenburg Gate at Berlin's centre – total chaos. Though recently the Parade has changed to another Oktoberfest. Hardly anybody who went to the early parades goes there nowadays – except for the parties before and after. Devoted Ravers arrive about a week early to get into the mood for The Big One. They start partying on Wednesday, through Thursday and Friday, the Parade on Saturday with countless events all over the city on until Monday afternoon. I met people the following Wednesday who still hadn't stopped partying.

There is a special mood in the air. In 1993 - 94 a new style of music could be heard at some of those parties, on some of those trucks in the Parade: Jungle / Drum & Bass. 1997 was to be special. 1996 - 97 had been Berlin's year of Drum & Bass with a number of big events taking place – Kemistry & Storm played there, but all resident DJs were from Berlin. Those events had a name: Hard:edged. And they were! Old warehouses, empty factories. Vicious lighting – and people going mad on the dancefloor until daylight. The city had caught the beat.

Love Parade '97, Saturday night: The Big One. Hard:edged have invited the Metalheadz. Doc Scott, Goldie and Grooverider. We decide to start early and get there by eleven o'clock. The air is still warm from the day's heat. While we are waiting beside the canal for the show to begin the blue in the sky vanishes, leaving the stars behind in the dark. People pass by, all dressed up. There are three big parties in this road. "Excuse me, do you now which party this is?" I tell him. "Ah, right." He goes, "How are we going to get to Tresor from here?" My French isn't good enough to sort out the next one.

The queue gets longer at the entrance – I hear people speak in Spanish, English, and German. Some stepping to the beat from inside. Two bottles of champagne are shared out among us to ease the suspense. By the time we reach the front my feet have started moving of their own accord. Beat's calling. The bouncers search the guy in front of me, I'm next. We go into a wide yard. Gravel on the ground, some trees and a couple of bars, an empty factory to the left, perfect chill-out area.

The crowd moves in. The venue: one wide room — looks like the mixture of a railway station from 1984 and a 19th century French market hall. Twenty by fifty meters, bare iron pillars holding up the roof six meters high. Above the bar at the back is a square of TV sets suspended from the ceiling. At the top end is the stage. DJ Xplore is spinning the tunes.

I stand watching the screens beside the stage. Mad animations and visual effects, simultaneously shown on the TV sets above the bar. Blue, green and purple, like the light on the dancefloor. Warm up. A girl in blue combat trousers, bra and fur waistcoat passes me by — fire red hair — vanishes among the jumpin' ones. Yes, I like it!! Meanwhile the crowd's flow has carried me along, past a pile of speakers, a real tower five meters high, two meters wide. There is one in each corner of the arena. I can feel the bassline in my stomach — and my body follows.

An hour later, maybe ten minutes, I can't tell. Finally my legs have reached the bar. As I turn around to look at the stage DJ Bass Dee comes on and whips up the crowd. He's probably the best in Berlin. The hall is packed, and there are still people milling in. I manage to be heard by one of the ladies behind the bar. With a smile she passes me the drink. I feel like easing off a little and head for the yard. Well, stumble, get pushed about and finally reach the doors. Outside, all over the place people rolling spliffs. There you go, this is what I love this city for. I stroll around for a while. Junglists from all over Europe have come together it seems — to have a party. Somehow I get talking to a guy from London — pirate radios, parties, the Blue Note, DJ's. When I turn around to go back inside I feel up-to-date again. A group of people is pushing past me. I've seen those faces before — The Metalheadz have landed. Walking on the moon.

I've reached the arena again — the MASSIVE of my dreams. Some bloke's jumping topless, ladies virtually same. Rastafarian, Grunge, Hippy or just happy Raver. I can't tell where the dancefloor begins — right behind the entrance, I suppose. Bass Dee's still on the decks, the crowd is screaming. MC Flux turns the heat up step-by-step … give me a rewind, I beg in mind, give it to us. But no remorse, no prisoners taken, he keeps on pushing. Denying the whistles' calls. Sweat is streaming. I'm soaked — everybody

is, and this is just the beginning. Two guys in baggy trousers have a dancing competition, shouting and going crazy like in an MTV trailer. Drum & Bass — dancing like there's no yesterday and no tomorrow. Bass Dee gives us a rewind — now I know the real meaning of 'raving mad'. This is hard-edged music. I need a break yet my feet won't stop. When Doc Scott is announced, whistles pierce my eardrums. They die away under the beat's pressure, starting anew.

I leave the steppers behind in search of a drink. As I enter the yard I walk past a couple snogging in a corner. Well, it almost looks like they are having sex … who cares? I get into one of the queues in front of the first bar I get to. A friend of mine who set up the sound system comes up to me. "We need help to get some stuff in", he says and drags me off towards the entrance. 'The stuff' means eight engine-driven speakers. The sound they produce is so low the cones have to be driven by little electric engines instead of magnets. I remember a story about Michael Jackson getting sued for using them at a concert. People got internal injuries from those deadly deep subs. We half shove, pull, carry them inside and place them on two sides of the arena. They are plugged in when Goldie takes over the decks. He knows how to do a show. The arena is packed and he pushes the crowd, building up the pressure until each tune is greeted with blowing whistles. 'Bass' has a new meaning. Those speakers grab you right in your guts, shake you and don't let go. Dance or be sick!

The arena goes mad, *Share the Fall* and the hall explodes. The air is filled screams and shouts. This is WICKED. We are taken away in a wave by the oncoming beat — the crowd can't get any higher. I'm drenched to the skin and my body no longer obeys my commands. Merciless. I have to keep on dancing. This is bliss. Limitless freedom. Being just here, just now. I've taken off my shirt, wearing a fur waistcoat instead.

One of the dancers next to me is dressed the same way. Grin. He laughs and tells his girlfriend. We dance at each other, doing our own show. Jump up — the arena looks like a Jacuzzi. Heads bobbing up and down, arms raised into the air. Tunes all melting into one. Goldie leaves the stage and gets down on the dancefloor. While Grooverider takes control he goes wild in the crowd and the massive follows.

I've lost track of time. Behind the stage the world is getting brighter again. The windows in the roof haven't been covered, sun bursts through the shadows. All of a sudden everybody is bathed in the warm yellow light of the early dawn. I've never seen such a beautiful crowd. Smiling happy people everywhere I look. Some of them dancing in trance — far away in another dimension. The guy in the fur waistcoat is back again. His bald head covered with a thin layer of sweat, a split goatee on his chin. Smiling he passes me a spliff. Easy. I dance towards one of those speaker towers. There's more room there, and the best sound — the loudest, too. Go wild as long as it lasts.

Nine o' clock in the morning. The Metalheadz have left, the music has stopped. I walk down to the canal, just a couple of metres away, enjoying the warmth of the early sun. Floating on the water is a wooden platform with sofas and benches. Beside it is a bar where I grab some coffee and sit down. Sunglasses are a vital necessity. There's mellow music from a stereo in the bar. I relax, watching the Ravers coming from the party. Chilling, chatting, smoking. After a while, some friends of mine come in. I lost them hours ago. We sit in the sun, feet in the water, sipping our coffee. This is the real deal. The guy in the fur waistcoat walks past with his girlfriend. They get a drink and join us. Skin up, have a smoke. Reminiscing the golden moments of last night. "Are you going to see Kemistry & Storm at the old Yaam this afternoon?" somebody asks. "Yes, I'm sure I will."

ANOTHER EMAIL FROM DANIEL BERLIN APRIL '99

Last Friday I went to the WTF Yard-opening party — they have a wicked backyard there. The building is five floors high, and the yard is a stretched Octagon, symmetrical with brilliant acoustics. They've installed a proper lighting rig with spotlights and disco mirror-ball right high above the floor — and behind the decks a four-by-four metre photograph of DJ Kemistry.

When the crowd was really movin' — the MCs calmed it all down: the music stopped, the lights went dim, and they called for the lighters in memory of the DJ Queen, who actually was a WTF resident. The crowd went quiet, lighters came up, and stayed in the air for three blinding tunes. Nobody danced during these. And after we all had a big party, in memory of DJ Kemistry — RIP.

Man, I can't believe she is not gonna play anymore. All the people I spoke to felt the same. They can't believe it. A good friend of mine told me that when she heard about the accident she cried for more than an hour …

And me? I sat there, wondering, remembering the night Goldie played in this theatre with Kemistry & Storm playing in the lounge. Those nights at the Blue Note when I couldn't keep my feet still 'cos Kemistry rolled out the basslines. Dancing till I felt I couldn't move a finger. Man, to me she was the Jungle Queen. I'll never forget those nights. I won't forget her, many people won't. She's left her footprints in the dust of time.

YESTERDAY, TODAY & TOMORROW

"UK Dance is the next advancement of British Rock."
DAVID BOWIE

Enter the future. It seems an odd route of progression. All this electronic music is now being performed live. Far from destroying the live music scene, JDB is now feeding back into it. Previously, British bands would play music you could dance to, now from the stage, they're playing Dance music ... Is this the next advancement of British Rock?

A BAND

It had almost been ten years since I went to see a band at the back of a pub. But 'Minx', live Drum & Bass was a good excuse. Back in time, forwards into the future. On one side of the stage, the longhaired guitarist pumps out riffs altered by an array of effect pedals. On the other side a keyboardist drove both drum and bass. The combination was knitted together by the vocalist's beautiful, spiritual, almost Celtic, strains. The music lifted the gloom of a thousand back room pub gigs. As Annie Nightingale strode through the bar past DJ Wildchild, you knew that British music would never be the same again.

PROJECT 23

Project 23 has been in the air for centuries. In 1993 - 94, Cleveland Watkiss and Marque Gilmore, aka Inna Most, met in a New York bar. As Cleveland walked through the joint, he caught the beats of a drummer playing passionately over the only Jungle record the DJ had. Watkiss was stunned by the madness of the combination. Linking up with Inna Most, Cleveland suggested that if he really was into Drum & Bass, he should come to England. Inna Most packed his drum kit, left New York for Hackney and formed the nucleus of Project 23 with Cleveland.

The number 23 is significant, powerful and associated with the universe and the millennium. It is part of Watkiss' conscious energy. He was 23 when he left his nine-to-five to make music. On the *Project 23* album, the lyrics of track *23*, tell the whole story of a journey through JDB.

Back in '95 Project 23 was one of the first groups to take Drum & Bass onto a conventional stage when they performed at the South Bank's Purcell Rooms with saxophonist Steve Williamson, Talvin Singh on tablas, Inna Most on drums and DJ La Rouge on Technics 1210s. It was early days for this type of venture. So much so that the nervous promoter asked the audience not to harangue him if they didn't like the new sounds. He needn't have worried.

APOLLO 440

Sitting in a friend's flat in Muswell Hill thinking about Goldie, Roni, Gerald, Nicky and all De Man Dem, their words echo in my head, "this music of the 90s is the music of the future". Sharing a spliff it sounds almost like clichéd slogans. Then Justin extracts a CD from the monstrous pile and turns up Apollo 440's *Ain't Talking About Dub*. It was a Rock stomp enthused with Drum & Bass — complete in itself. Jungle / Drum & Bass had percolated down, grown up through the masses. The slogans fell apart to reveal a truth. Their sound was a proppa and powerful adjunct in the tree of musical evolution. They ain't rampin'.

ADAM F

The crowd trailed off with the last of Galliano's notes, leaving the pitted, muddy quagmire that marked the front of Glastonbury's Jazz Stage. In the time it took to get a beer, a sizeable audience had seeped from all walks of England into the space before the stage. The great fluorescent Raver alongside the greater bearded Hippy. The inner city lives eye-up the slick University Chick, with her nervous, fresh-faced, *Swallows & Amazons* kid sister in tow. Under a dark grey sky with feet sucked into glutinous mud, they danced to the effervescent champagne notes of *Circles* and the dark steeliness of *Metropolis* produced by the synthesisers, drums and brass instruments of the F Jams. With passion the crowd screamed, "ADAM!"

RONI SIZE / REPRAZENT

At Finsbury Park's '97 Essential Weekender, Reprazent didn't just get by. They mashed the place up.
[see *A Festival in Haringey?*, p.176]

DJ BOWIE?

A tent at the '97 Phoenix Festival, David Bowie plays some Drum & Bass — as a DJ, on Technics 1210s. Perhaps in the future there'll be a time when divisions between the people involved in the Jungle scene will fade. What's good now is that people are distancing themselves from the disagreements of 1995 - 96.

A BIRTHDAY PARTY

Away from the arguments that threatened to disrupt the JDB scene, Cleveland Watkiss invited some friends to his birthday party. He asked a few of them to bring some records — in case they fancied a spin. Downstairs in the smoke laden Blue Note, MC Cleveland Watkiss DJed next to Marque Gilmore's drum kit that had been set up on stage. The sound system, always too powerful for the basement club, was perfect. Proper, serious business. It was an evening where anything could happen musically. Brockie & Det flexin' in black leather coats were alongside Swift and Footloose, who showed up to give Eastman support as he played a remarkable set. Twenty years in the business, his music mirrored the sign above the Jungle Fever shop, playing 'all kinds of Drum & Bass'. Inna Most was on the drums, with both Goldie and Talvin Singh at the decks improvising off his beat — there was a whiff of the spirit of the old Bass Clef. Call it a birthday party, a Jazz DJ impro night, you were back in the days when Miles Davis, Dizzy Gillespie and a host of stars crowded along NYC's 52nd street. You could look forward to the days when Talvin Singh would be dropping *Flight IC408* at World Dance (and deservedly winning the 1999 Mercury Award). It was good to see people from so many different camps. Goldie, Talvin, Eastman, Grooverider and their crews. Outside the glare of the media, this special event was about music and friends.

A FESTIVAL IN HARINGEY?

A festival in Haringey? Check the information centre. Yep, the yellow, smog-impregnated, fluorescent poster on an illegal fly-posting site by McJobs, Bruce Grove, displayed all the right ingredients. Call Caroline Unique on her mobile – "Essential, that's really the only thing in London this weekend." Announce it on my Rude FM show in that studio squat.

Like any good event, the vibe starts several streets away. Security turn away car-driving blaggers from Finsbury Park's rear hill side entrance. Ravers Sally and Maddie wait anxiously for Goldie to turn up with Sally's birthday tickets. Randall draws up in his white BM. I dash across and shout above the beats, "Off already?" "Yeah. Gotta play some festival in Germany. Lufthansa won't change the tickets, so I did the warm-up. Kemi 'n' Storm are playin' my slot." "Is Goldie coming?" "Sure man. He's playin' – Alright B. Laaytahh."

Reassure the ladies and skirt the metal fence enclosing the mishmash of sounds in the park. It wasn't my imagination; I'm walking faster as I hear Drum & Bass echoing off the trees. Goldie's Merc rolls past with Attitude, followed by a Mad Max pick-up full of ravers. Sun blazes down festival stylee on the orderly, disorderly, colourful crew in front of the gate. Plans made days ago come together. My mates from Brighton mill around sorting out tickets. Craig and A Guy called Gerald give up on their friends and head for the entrance. The Essential staff doesn't know the score and fail to recognise a stylishly cropped yellow-haired GQ, who waits around, anxious about getting in without a pass. Swift

bowls out and manoeuvres G quickly through the crowd. I'm stalling, still meeting friends from one of Positive Sound System's raves on a Brighton beach. Courteously rude to the growing posse, I slip off and collect a press pass. I'm on a mission to get my head inside some JDB speakers.

"Access All Areas" suggests the colour of the pass. The guest area is full of people – music journalists and general hangers-on. Why do people stay *here*? It's dead. Walk by security besieged by blaggers and onto the festival's main drag to be greeted by a collection of sounds, ethnic food smells and head stall nick-nacks. The park has become a comfortably-full small town. I inch 'round clutches of punters seated in the sunshine, drinking, puffing and enjoying Haringey council's unlikely gift. I'm on a mission. "Met-ul-eds?" The crusty biker gives vague arm waving directions. "… Ah man, yull 'earrit."

The Metalheadz tent looms large and Eskimo Noise's powerful electronic sound system causes no distress in this built-up area. Inside, the backpackers, new and old style ravers, bob to Doc Scott's grooves. Weaving through to the front barrier despite my "I want it to be madness" anticipation, I can't find the bubbling crew. Scott releases the next tune and it feels like I'm the only one in the place, jumping up and bawlin' for the rewind. Still, they're grooving – clearly into it.

Step 'round security and join the backstage crew. Gus and his ever-present Sony camcorder rests up in the sun by some garden furniture. "Gus, about the Metalheadz logo …" At festivals, unlike clubs, you actually get a chance to communicate with relative clarity. GQ and his lady Bianca stand near the tent entrance. My eyes readjust to the shade inside. On stage, a six-year-old girl dances to Scotty's tunes. Cleveland's ready to flex. The crowd is dancing and it's alright. But there's something missing. The music is the usual. But there's something missing. The stage isn't lined with a gathering of De Man Dem. The people are having a good time but this vibe is different. Perhaps it's the size of the huge tent. Maybe this is what it's like when we move into the mainstream. It's success of a sort and I dance trying to get into the new deal. MC Moose arrives from nowhere. He scopes the scene. "It's not like the old days Moose." "How ya mean? Look at me." His black Nike sports vest is soaked. "You wanna go over the World Dance tent." "I didn't know World Dance were here." "B, It's rrrrunnin'."

Back in the sunlight, I'm on another mission and run straight into my Brighton Posse. It's always a mistake to think you can go from A to B at a festival. We sit, chat, drink, smoke, meet more people, lose others, enjoying a quality moment in the heat of the rays. The festival vibe builds. And the music's calling. A tall guy with one of those tall floppy jester hats strides alongside his Asian girlfriend in a tiger skin cat suit. Beneath a tree, a model-like Japanese girl swigs Woodpecker cider from a plastic bottle, while a bloke staggers by to join the row of geezers slashing on the perimeter fence.

The World Dance tent stands at the rear of the site. People dotted here and there dance to the shock waves radiating from within. An orderly queue of ravers tries to squeeze into one entrance, others leave 'round the side, steam rising off weary, drenched bodies. Around the back, it's a Jungle / Drum & Bass 'Who's Who'.

Roni Size heads into a portacabin changing room, with his name like 'Star' taped to the door as Ellis Dee's music vibrates over Daz World Dance, Tracy Ton Promotions, DJ Rap, Hype, Krust, Swift, SS and Kenny Ken. Meeting and greeting, everyone pausing for brief and deep conversations as they're pulled by the flow in different directions. I stand chatting to Mickey Finn wearing those mirrored Oakleys. Turns out someone might ghost write his life story. "Well, 'sgot every fing innit? Sex, Drugs … Drum & Bass." Our conversation is punctuated by involuntary rubber-necking with both of us mouthing, "The Wimmin", with anguish as yet another Goddess drifts by. Inside the tent, Ellis Dee gives way to Hype but stays dancing by the side of the decks. Heading for the speakers I pass Daz leaving the stage. "It's always the same," he says with exasperation. "Why do they always want more, more lights, more volume and more bass?" It's the promoter's lot.

Inside the tent I'm greeted by the essential tableau, a clutch of De Man Dem bogle and nod inside the heatwave. Horns, whistles and screams pulse from x-amount of people rocking, from the front, to the sides, to the back, to the front, the full circumference. The Jungle Fever regular, 'Russian' armed with sunglasses, horn and kerchief, leans against the barrier. Pounding beside him, a stereotypical 'Asian shopkeeper' gentleman, arms held high, shoots a lighter flame in the air. This crowd's only interested in rollin' from peak to peak and the pressure threatens to rip the canvas roof apart. Time to join the heart of the dance.

Follow a leopard skin head and little bobbing rucksack directly to the front amongst designer fabric and sweaty flesh, end up next to Elphin, a friend and free spirit of previous festivals and raves. To my left, a cyber punk, with serious platforms and pink-black plaited hair, stomps like a proppa raver. I used to see her midweek in the City of London and she was always the brightest thing on the street.

"You got any Rizla?" someone screams. On my right, a yout in an orange jeans jacket stands building a spliff in his bredren's out-stretched hand. An island of calm in the sea of manic movers. He shouts above the sound, "What you doin' with that tape?" "I'm writing a book." "Thought so. Needs to be done. It better be good."

Roadies, long haired, dreadlocks and shaggy t-shirts, dart between MCs, monitors, cables and scaffolding poles, setting up for Reprazent's live performance. Roni's on stage with his camcorder. This time, no one wants to miss out on the proppa memorable sights. He stops filming to help the roadies connect the last of the cables to synths, mics, keyboards and a Technics 1210.

DJ Hype scratches up beats and blends in *New Forms* as DJ / producer Roni Size heads off to return as a musician with his band Reprazent. Dressed in hooded army waterproofs, Krust, Die, Suv and Roni arrive in an onslaught of smoke, strobe lights and air raid sirens. The Bristol massive is up in the place. Somewhere in the storm, Dynamite MC steps forward dominating the stage like the meaning of his name. They didn't just get by. They mashed-up the place.

Stretched between piles of Syquest discs, computer monitors and keyboards, Roni looks much more like Rick Wakeman than the product of any DJ culture. Except this isn't the old days. The crowd doesn't stand, stare and adore. Reprazent play Dance music for the dancing audience and when band gives way to DJ, it's all just another part of the show. DJ Rap bangs out the beats, bobbing to and fro – the way she does. MCs Moose, Normski and Fearless chat to a crowd partying, as ever, like it's their last. Scarcely does Rap get through a mix and the crowd is jumpin,' bawlin,' screamin' for the rewind. Mi Gosh are they 'avin' it.

Kenny Ken follows Rap and the energy amongst the ravers rises again. Backstage DJ Ron, his brother Lenny and his bredren finally arrive as the sun goes down. 5ive'O struts through security onto the stage, muttering "Pass, rass clat security pass," grabbing up the mic, indignant that anyone should "prevent me from entertaining my public." DJ Bailey slopes past with a box of Dub Plates. "Rider's on at Metalheadz." The biggest decision of the day. "Shit, Rider or Kenny Ken?" It's truly painful. Draw for Rider. Leave World Dance catching sight of 5ive'O, mic in hand, flanked by a couple of oversized, dancing fairies with wings.

Take turns to carry Bailey's Plates and chat about all the gutting things I've missed; Fabio, Andy C, Adam F, the whole Anokha tent with Talvin Singh. Too many things to think of. "Damn these Plates are heavy." Trip over people chilling in the darkness and run into a publisher in mellow mood clutching a beer. "About that deadline …"

The Metalheadz vibe has shifted up several degrees. Centre stage, I catch sight of the great Grooverider dominating the decks, spotlight shining off his bare, black, domed head, shoulders and arms. The atmosphere is boosted when Goldie bounces across the stage and slams his hand down on the deck, demanding the rewind from Rider. Suddenly, I'm standing next to Kate. We'd lost each other within five minutes of arriving at the festival. A chance to dance but all too soon the crowd are screaming for, "One more tune." Seconds later, we're running like nuttahs for Kenny's last tune at the World Dance tent – missed it. Run back to Metalheadz and join the football crowd chorus – "One More. One More. One More. One More …" On the stage, Rider stands back, hands on hips and waits. I'm asking the original Pied Piper, "One more tune please, Groove, just one more tune." "Well it ain't up to me." He shrugs, resigned in the glare of the house lights and turns to attend the avalanche of orange Dub Plate flowing sleeves around his feet.

I'm analysing the vibe between the two tents and wonder if it's fair to differentiate between sorbet and ice cream. Meet Goldie outside in the fuzz of a site light. "It was alright Goldie, just …" He's ahead of me. "I told Daz. Sort it out. Have everyone in one big tent." He was right. An end to the divisions. It's time to go forwards.

Roni Size

A NEW DAWN

Running up to Christmas 1999 I split with Kate my girlfriend of over ten years, I was pursuing one of the Jungle Dons through the courts for non payment of salary, the bank was threatening to repossess my home and I'd just been diagnosed with Multiple Sclerosis. The Millenium was going to be interesting.

Y2K was nothing more than 'why worry?' Just like London's New Years 'River of Fire' – why bother to show up? But *All Crew Muss Big Up* had done better than I could hope or dream. There'd been a fair few good reviews. All copies sold out making it cultingly impossible to find. I'd even heard that mates had nicked the book from their mates. In spite of all the positive feedback about *All Crew* reaching me, I found myself withdrawing from the scene. Not going out much, buying tunes or even listening to pirates. I had taken DJ Ron to court for non-payment of salary. The judge found 'the Don' guilty but he skipped the country. I never saw a penny of the thousands of pounds awarded and suffered in debt for years. I needed a break from it all. That's part of the reason why I returned to my day job as an ICU (intensive care unit) nurse. But everywhere I went I'd be hearing voices. Not schizophrenic voices, just talk of Jungle Drum & Bass. I guess producers are always hearing music in their heads. I always wrote sentences in mine. I just wished I could go out without storing a blow-by-blow account of everything in my head. And fuck I just wanted to be a punter again.

But I had to understand that I was a London boy who'd always read the city through music. That's the way I'm wired. Driving to work at 7am through empty back streets from Tottenham to central London, I'd see buildings automatically thinking, 'I went to a warehouse rave there, that's where Kool FM had their first studio, Kemi and Storm lived in that flat there or Essential held a wicked festival in that park there and from King's Cross to Tottenham we reclaimed all of the streets.' Sunday morning I'd see people on a balcony with music blaring, basking in fluffy early light. Or I'd get off the tube as clumps of monging ravers from Fabric and Turnmills, eyes like saucers, floated onto the train at Farringdon as I left for St. Bartholomew's ICU. I'd remember the previous Friday night's buzz at Kings Cross Station and the intersection of tribes, glad rags and record boxes criss crossing away on London's Underground. But I took a different escalator, concentrating on different things.

I love people and had learned the skills to take care of the critically ill. I'd been out of nursing for five years. If I didn't sign up again soon I'd loose my registration and have to re-train. I'd worked at Bart's Hospital on and off since 1988. I knew the hospital, unit and staff and it was great to be back. Strange but in one way, the energy of a mad ICU rinses you out like a proppa Jungle rave. Both are hi-octane.

Kate and I had been together since Sussex 1989. She was 18 straight from school. I was a 28 straight from ICU. We were great together for many years, but Kate needed her own space, left and found her own place across the tracks in leafy Highgate. We stayed fleetingly in touch but sometimes things were raw and painful. It was the first time that I'd suffered a broken heart. They don't tell you this in school but a broken heart really hurts. I was so worried about mine that I asked one of the girls at work to record an ECG of my heart just to be sure I wasn't having a heart attack. But the doc confirmed that mine was just an ordinary pain — normal heartache. Kate wasn't to know that within months of her leaving I'd be diagnosed with Multiple Sclerosis. Nor if I'm honest should that have been the reason for her to stay. She had her shit to deal with, as did I.

Multiple Sclerosis (MS) is an incurable degenerative disease of the nervous system. Around 80,000 people in the UK have it. And probably more than a few more thousand people are suffering from it and don't know or won't admit there's a shadow of a problem in their bodies. Chances are that most of you know or has heard of someone who suffers from it. MS typically strikes people in their thirties and forties. The MS Society UK once ran stylish posters of beautiful nude models in shades of grey and white. The figures lay crumbled on the ground; their spines had been torn like paper from their backs. I'll always remember those posters. Back in nursing school hearing about all the different diseases you could contract at any moment; our tutor explained that people of predominantly European descent were prone to suffer MS. So I crossed that one off my list. Little did I know that although our parents from overseas where MS is not prevalent were unlikely to contract it, their children born in the UK were showing up with the disease in full flow. Now MS is thought to be caused by a combination of genetic and environmental factors.

Our nerves run like fine wires from the brain through the spinal column down to our fingertips and toes. Nerves are covered with a fatty coating called a Myelin sheath, not unlike plastic insulation on electric wires. In MS the myelin sheath is damaged, making it difficult for messages from the brain to reach parts of the body they're seeking. Symptoms include: mild pins and needles in your hands, fatigue, blindness and an eventual inability to walk. Foul Play's Steve Bradshaw died of complications from MS. There's a few classifications of MS ranging from slight to severe. Mine's called Relapsing Remitting MS, which means it comes and goes. It's about halfway on the scale. I've occasionally had to use a wheelchair or one of those electric scooters. Multiple Sclerosis is what they call an autoimmune disease. The theory is that your own immune system turns against itself. White blood cells that normally protect the body by attacking invaders like bacteria fight their own body, munching away at those Myelin sheaths. The result is that impulses pass with difficulty from the brain via nerves to wherever they're needed.

MS is different in each person. When I have an attack or relapse I feel horribly fatigued. My fingers and palms tingle with numbness. My legs go limp; feel heavy, uncoordinated and incapable of walking any great distance. Then there's the bladder thing. Imagine you suddenly have to go. Try running through a crowded bar on dodgy legs with a bursting bladder. I soon learned not to have a pint in the West End and tube it home to North London. By the time I'd reached Seven Sisters I'd be grabbing my crotch like Eminem and doing a very strange walk to the nearest darkened corner to pee in. People would be walking by kissing their teeth. I did care but the relief — Oh my ...

Out bowling one night with workmates I told Gamal about my MS thing. He thought for a moment, took a big sip of his pint and said, "That's shit." We both creased up laughing. It was the perfect reply. If I dwell on it — yes it's crap not being able to walk for miles, dance well or skate wicked like I once could. But you can sit there and wallow in it or stand up and go forwards. I chose the latter.

Jungle Drum & Bass Samples

Though I was going through my own wilderness years, I did have occasional forays right into the groove. Here are samples of Jungle, Drum & Bass.

Every so often Shy FX's name comes up on my mobile. "Shy man, what's happening?" "You alright B? How's your health? Good. Can you and Jane come down the studio? I need you to do another special." "No worries Shy." "And I need to get it done as soon as – you know how it is." "What's new?" A few years ago Shy FX started making exclusive intro dub plates for his gigs announcing his arrival. The basic scenario was that you'd hear the theme from *Sky News* followed by an anchorwoman (my mate Jane) announcing that Shy FX is arriving at such and such a venue. We switch to the reporter (me) live at the scene. With the crowd goin' mental, in my best sports commentator losin' it voice I describe the arrival of SHY FX – by helicopter. It was always a giggle. T Power was often there. He and Shy would mix it down and Shy would cut a dub for the venues he's about to play. It's strange to think that our voices have been heard in raves across the globe. Then one day listening to ads on Origin FM I heard one for Telepathy. I rang Jane straight away. "Jane mate we've been sampled." We both shouted, "Yes!"

In September 2000 I was over in Sydney visiting Red Anna and George, friends from my MTV days, and catch the Olympic Games. I'd brought some tunes along just in case there was a chance to play out anywhere. After a few days I'm on this Reclaim the Streets march that brings traffic to a halt outside Sydney Town Hall. I'm kneeling in the back of a van playing D&B to an assorted mix of crusties, Olympic athletes, tourists and shoppers dancing in the streets. The sound

system and decks are wired and running. Everything is covered with red dust. Turns out the van's owners have just returned from the desert where they've been demonstrating against Uranium mining or some such. The vans' electrics came from solar panels on the roof and recycled chip oil served as fuel.

Anna & George introduced me to D&B artists Sub Bass Snarl who invited me play on their 2SER FM radio show and DJ in their pub / club on the last night of the Games. An enthusiastic studenty crowd danced away as a TV high in a corner broadcast the closing ceremony. After the gig a group of us left for a roof top view of the fireworks over Sydney Harbour. One of the crew worked in a tall office block a few streets away. Wind blown we watched fireworks explode, the rings on the bridge go down and what looked like a jet fighter igniting a whole lot of fuel blazed the sky. Now that's what I call a river of fire. Well – a sky of fire.

Around spring 2003 Shy FX and Tania UMC sort a late guest list – plus one. I hadn't been out for ages but fancied a night in Fabric. It might have been True Playaz, I can't quite remember. I do remember that my mate Kirsten and I wandered off the street right into the middle of the main arena. It felt like we were standing in the centre of a racetrack. Everyone was goin' absolutely Radio Rental. In the fortress of the DJ box I could see Hype scratching the arse out the decks. We shuffled away and found a dark corner to recover in.

I occasionally checked Mass to hear Dillinja and Lemon D's awesome Valve sound system. This was soon after the policy of targeting dealers rather than punters effectively liberalised the enforcement of drug laws in Lambeth. There was a more anarchic edge outside Brixton tube station than usual. On Coldharbour Lane stood a gauntlet of dealers offering, "coke, whizz, weed and Eees."

Inside Mass, once a church, everything swayed and swirled like a messy Saturday night at Glastonbury. Mass has a long wide spiral staircase leading up to dance floors, chill spaces. I'm not tripping but the place feels tripped out. Step 'round a girl on the steps, her arms around her friend's neck as she retches again. Onwards and upwards, the music grows louder. Leaving my stuff in the cloakroom I catch sight of ladeez posing in the mirror, fixing hair and makeup. As a final touch they stuff in earplugs and trot back to the main arena.

The circular atrium spirals down to the main floor. People on the tier above mosh before two large speaker stacks. Rear centre, base of the room stand more speakers, decks and DJ in the amplified heart of Valve's sound system. Totally addicted to bass we dance in militant sound. When my feet failed me I sat on a large speaker near the decks, head nodding, body rocking at the epicentre. LK plays and I'm feeling the music and atmosphere thinking, 'There's nowhere else I'd rather be.' I became an occasional regular and went along a few times with top raving mate Lou.

I started listening to pirates again. I'd tune into Origin FM's Overdose Sessions with DJ Overdose playing wicked music and giving good track information. When I couldn't afford to go out or was too ill, his show was something to look forward to.

The occasional DJ gig came along. London's Champion Sounds crew invited me to play slots in various West End bar venues they'd secured. One place wouldn't have us back. The manager expected a nice Housey crowd with girlie girls, not ladeez with attitude, MCs chatting, people banging walls for rewinds and screaming up the place. Another bar didn't ask us back after we rinsed their speakers. Every now and again I'd play clubs in Berlin and Frankfurt.

By late 2002 all this occasional DJing meant passing by Black Market Records – the way you do. Not that you're going to buy anything … no. Miss Pink works there after the sad demise of Ambient Soho. Now I had a bubbling Nicky Blackmarket and an enthusiastic Miss Pink persuading me to buy more tunes than I ever wanted to. Then says Nicky, and he's been saying it since the last copy of the book was sold, "You've got to get that book of yours out again. I've 'ad people in the shop askin' for it."

True I'd been receiving letters, emails and orders for All Crew even though it had been pronounced sold out by me and the powers that be. So I wrote a proposal to one of JDB's great and good asking them if they'd like to co-publish All Crew Remixed. 'Got to take action now' I thought. Yep has to be done. Wrote the proposal and let it sit on the PC.

A year later I'm in Black Market and Nicky's still going, "You've got to get that book of yours out again. Why don't you get someone to get behind it? Geddit back out there." I'm back home checking my emails. One's from a college student bowled over that she's finally tracked me down. She's dismayed by my reply. "I'm really sorry it's sold out. Yep every last copy gone." She's not happy. Needs it for her dissertation, etc. This was getting out of hand. 'OK which file did I store that proposal in?'

I noticed that whenever All Crew was advertised in Knowledge magazine there was a marked increase in sales. They'd just hosted the Knowledge D&B Awards in November 2003. We were both impartial observers of the scene. They dealt in words, as did I. Maybe I should send them this proposal? I knew it made sense. A few weeks later Rachel and Colin from Knowledge invited me for a chat. After the meeting All Crews was rolling.

BACK ON THE ROAD – BASS CAMP HERBAL

Spring 2004 I'm home sprawled on the sofa recovering from a 12 hour shift but feel restless, edgy. It's Sunday night and somewhere across London there's a guest list with my name on it. "Katie (after a three year break we're back together again), you know what? I'm goin' clubbing." "What!!"

Change out of uniform into glad rags and cruise into town. I switch through pirates, Origin, Rude and Kool, landing on Ruud Awakening. DJ Quest takes me through Tottenham, Stamford Hill, Stokey then Dalston. Some things don't change. Day or night Dalston's always buzzing. At 11.30pm a row of tail lights head into town. Smartly coiffured crowds perambulate by club Pier One along this high street. A sample on Quest's tune sings, 'Just be good to me.' Exactly what you need for a clubbing night.

Some things do change, like the London skyline. Driving towards Shoreditch The Gherkin pokes into a grey blue sky. 30 St. Mary Axe is both its name and address. It's visible from many areas across the capital. With drums and driving bass, MC flowing, I'm shifting through gears and rolling into Shoreditch, the latest part of London to be colonised and revitalised by Club Culture. A row of riot police with smiley faces is sprayed on a railway bridge over the road. Large clumps of clubbers line up, huddle or hustle 'round narrow designer doorways along the road. Blokes unpack silver flight cases from a double parked van carrying them past a wall where someone's painted, 'War is just so last century.' I park up and rock up to the front of the guest list queue. A girl from halfway down the punters' line asks the bouncer, "'Ow long do ya think it's gonna take for us lot there to get in?" She points dizzily. "At least an hour love. It's one out, one in. And no one's leaving darl." He turns looking down at me: "Right. Whose list a' you on?"

Sunday night at Herbal is Grooverider's night Grace. Inside the entrance Miss Pink's at the till greeting faces familiar and unfamiliar. Shy and T Power walk out from the main room. "Ah Shy man when you on?" "I've just come off." "Shit. I've been stalling too long." Miss Pink hands me an all areas laminate and I follow Shy and T up to the VIP lounge. The scaffolding stairs bustle with people chatting in Spanish, clutching water bottles and frosted WKD. Next floor up Hip Hop plays to bar side bubblers. I get talking to a guy on the Polish D&B scene. Then meet Carl from *DJ Magazine*. He's recently become a father and we chat about baby things as people sluice around us. I lose T and Shy then remember Ray Keith's downstairs on the decks.

The main room is L shaped and smoky. Brooding-firin' speakers bare down on floor bound dancers. MC's lyric on his lips. Red lights, thick gold chain on wrist reflect in black vinyl as Ray rewinds the track. The crowd have been cookin' for hours in a space of house party dimensions. We're hearing driller killer b-lines. Frost and DJ Die are here. I meet another friend Emma and there's much shouting mouth to ear. She's openly skinning up. I'm feeling nervous. "Don't they mind puffing in here?" Smiling, shouting back, "Well, it is called Herbal innit." We both crease up laughing. Jill Scott in the mix sings, "Your style, your smile, your familiarity." There are 70's afros and African tie-dye tops in this tight post-industrial space. Just how we like it. We're brocking out a stones' throw away from the old Blue Note and it's great to be back.

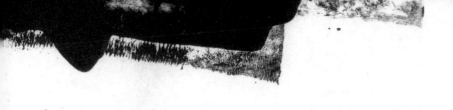

THIS IS OUR MUSIC

"Jungle is the Culture. Drum & Bass is the music."
MC 5IVE'0

"We were just making two beats in Huddersfield, now this thing's gone global." L DOUBLE

"I love Drum & Bass more than I love Mother Russia herself." ALEX, ST. PETERSBURG

"The Internet has opened it up for everybody, especially the whole instant messenger thing. Being able to send your latest track to someone on the other side of the world in 15 minutes is a really handy thing to be able to do. Matty's always on the computer chatting to someone involved in the industry."
KILLJOY – CONCORD DAWN

The constituency of Jungle Drum & Bass has grown way beyond the hoods of North and East London. Grown beyond Leicester, Bristol and the rest of the UK. Beyond Canada, the USA, Brazil and Australasia. Tom at Red Eye Records calculated that 60% of their record sales originate outside the UK. Rachel and Colin at *Knowledge* confirm that North America is responsible for a third of their magazine's sales. GQ is among many UK D&B artists who regularly play parties in Canada and America. Vegas of Bad Company commented, "If you look at a map of America we've played all the cities from the east coast to the west." Ben XO, moderator on website Dogs On Acid, is aware that the split of people logging on is one third UK, one third US and one

third the rest of the world. Years back I mentioned Latvia when speaking to MC Skibadee. "Latvia," he ponders a moment. "Yeah Latvia. Been there." The five Olympic rings represent continents of the World. Drum & Bass has them all covered. The most exciting thing is that these far flung destinations have spawned their own scenes, entertained by local talent, not solely by artists from the UK. Tania UMC who sends artists all over the globe has a pretty good view of Drum & Bass' growth. "There are little pockets in South America. I know there have been parties in Venezuela but I think they are concentrating more on home grown talent. Marky has done immense good for Brazil. It is a good approach to promote your own artists. America has done that really well. There are a lot of good DJs in America now. I remember them calling Formation to get on the mailing list when I started. Now they are America's top DJs. It's good to see that and it can only promote something good in the Drum & Bass scene."

Clayton TOV agrees: "What I like about it now is that it's universal, before it was a London thing. It's surpassed that by miles. It's a worldwide thing. It was bound to catch on because it's music that everyone can relate to. The amount of DJs that go around the world flying the flag – it's good. It's a unique scene."

In 1999 reporters would ask me, "Who do you think the next big thing in Jungle Drum & Bass will be?" "Haven't got a clue," I'd reply. I knew people would be developing their art in various corners, away from the media glare. I'm happy it works that way. I would never have predicted Tali, Concord Dawn, Pendulum, Marky & XRS, Hive, Dieselboy, Ryan Ruckus, TeeBee, Fanu, D.Kay, but they're all making strong contributions to Drum & Bass. It's become their music. They've earned the right to say, "This is *our* music."

Andy C has been DJing in Eastern Europe for a couple years: "It's mad. It's getting bigger and bigger. I played in Estonia and there were 2,000 people. I have heard that St. Petersburg has had over 10,000 people. Romania, Slovenia, Budapest ... it's fantastic. They have got great producers as well. It's really, really kicking off." Andy feels that they're going through a period of discovery. Finding that simple pleasure in hitting the weekend and letting your hair down: "It's fantastic. I love going to Eastern Europe."

It was going off in Innovation at Club Colossus in Spain, June 2004. I said to SS, "This is the best since Bagley's '94." "Yeah it's alright. Not as mad as in Russia." "What?!" It was almost impossible to believe. "Russia?" This wasn't a case of, 'you should 'ave seen the one that got away.' SS spools through pictures on his mobile. "Oh mi word." It looked bigger than a World Dance party back in the day. Vegas and Maldini said the same. They're losing it in former Eastern Europe and all the way past Russia. That's the new Frontier.

Tania UMC has adapted not only to changes within JDB but also with global politics and economics: "In terms of big promotions the States has slowed a little. There still are parties there but promoters aren't prepared to pay extreme fees for flights and visas. With what happened on 9 / 11 it's too risky to just go with a record bag and think that you can get in. If you get turfed out you're not getting back in for five to ten years. It's really important that people get the right paperwork before they go. Russia is doing immensely well at the minute and so are other Eastern European countries like Poland, the Czech Republic, Estonia ... it's firing."

One problem is that the economy in these countries is relatively weak compared to our own. Importing UK artists might cost the promoter a month's wages. Tania feels that things are improving, even though some places only deal in cash: "Quite a few countries joined the European Union (EU) recently, that will probably make a difference to them, strengthen their economies and hopefully they will be able to do better things. We have seen big improvements in Russia but it's hard currency only – American dollars." One thing that aids promoters is sponsorship by commercial companies like Red Bull, Grolsch and Nike: "It's a lot easier for European promoters to get sponsorship than it is for us in the UK. A lot of the promoters in Germany have huge sponsors. Those former Communist countries want a piece of the action."

"We Ain't Come Here to Fuck About"
MC GROOVERIDER, GLASTONBURY 2004.

How many of you love JDB to the max but find that few of your friends do? I like that about our music. We are the die-hards. Like those who stuck it out through Glastonbury's mud years. Respect to those still around when the going gets grimy. High Contrast from South Wales was introduced to Jungle by friends who then moved on musically: "I didn't know anyone else into Drum & Bass at all so I ostracised myself from a lot of my friends who were all skaters or came from a Punk kind of background. They saw me as the enemy. I pissed off a few friends who were fed up with me only wanting Jungle in the car to and from college. People thought I'd lost the plot and had become really closed minded about music. I'd be talking about it non-stop. The irony is that now you see them coming to the nights and really getting into it."

Why is Everybody Always Picking on Me?

Your Jungle audience still takes their raving very seriously. It's said that the Drum & Bass crowds saved the festivals. Our tents are always the maddest. Dancing with 15,000 people at Fabio & Groove's Glastonbury session felt very serious — especially with Rider giving it loads on the mic. Us headz can be fiercely protective of our scene. Both Fab and Groove complained on radio about the Godskitchen Global Gathering bash in August 2004. Seems Environmental Health Officers made promoters turn down our music, reckoning that it was too loud. But music from the House tents was clearly audible. Same again at the Shoreditch Festival in September 2004. You could clearly hear a Reggae sound system around the corner but we hard to turn ours down. Fabio & Grooverider were right to ask, "Why is it always Drum & Bass that gets singled out?"

"When you go to major festivals it seems that Drum & Bass tents get dealt with a lot more harshly than others for some reason. I don't know if that's true or not but it seems like that. X amount of people have paid their money to be entertained just like everybody else but the D&B arena isn't the most fantastic. They spend less money on it, spend less on the sound system and they have more restrictions than anybody else. I don't know why that is. It's like a conspiracy. But hey, what do I know?" *GROOVERIDER*

There was a time when uninformed media types and Joe Public criticised or misunderstood Jungle Drum & Bass. At first I was angry. Out of that anger came *All Crew*. It was a book for OUR people. And it was my way of saying to closed minded outsiders, "Fuck Off and leave us alone to do OUR thing." I'm happy that the negative media hype has moved on and the scene has matured. Tania says, "We are in a better place now than we were ten years ago." I was speaking to L Double at 1Xtra asking, "Did you think that our music would have grown as much as it has?" He answers with genuine surprise. "We were just making two beats in Huddersfield now this thing's gone global."

The Thing with The Heart

I was trying to understand why so many people across the Globe have taken to Drum & Bass wracking my brain with this theory and that. "What is it about our music?" Chatting to Vegas and Maldini from Bad Company their answer was simple: "What happened when you first heard it?" Failing to find the words I end up gesticulating, placing my hand on my heart. "Exactly." For some people it's like a lightning bolt that hits them straight in the chest. And for many of us, there ain't no goin' back. You still appreciate other sorts of music but you know when you've found your musical home. It's a love thing. I like the stories you hear about people toughing it out in the name of Drum & Bass. A DJ at 1Xtra sent out a shout in response to an email: "A big shout out to everyone in Baltimore who braved the rain for the Drum & Bass festival. Unfortunately the MCs nearly got electrocuted, but in Drum & Bass you expect things like that." The title of one old skool tune makes me laugh, *Jungle Owes Me Money*. How many people do you know in this scene who've given so much for so long but would never be financially reimbursed for their contribution? Yet they still carry on giving just a little bit more. Wouldn't it be wonderful if everyone could get rich through their involvement in Jungle. And people do need to be paid. But for a lot of us — It is a Love Thing.

Worries

Unprofessionalism could affect the scene adversely. L Double commented that, in his dealings with people from other music genres, Drum & Bass artists are known to be the most difficult to work with. I know from years of personal experience that dealings with our scene are — shall we say — challenging. Some artists and 'their people' miss appointments, keep their mobiles off, don't return calls emails or fail to follow mutually agreed plans. They can go 'missing' for days or be spectacularly late. It's difficult to promote the scene in all the depth it deserves. Laurence at Electric PR represents a ton of artists, including Marky and XRS, also has her own experiences: "If you think Jamaican timekeeping is bad Brazilian is even worse." Photographers from *DJ* magazine waited two hours for Marky and XRS to arrive. The pair were due to grace its cover. Golden sunlight faded behind clouds. When they did arrive, the light was awful and they almost lost their opportunity to front the magazine. In their defence Laurence commented, "They're just laid back. Just very laid back."

It would be grossly unfair to tarnish the whole scene with this negative reputation. I've also dealt with many on the scene like Hospital Records and the 1Xtra crew who are bang on it. Tania UMC is one person who's happy that the business side of the scene is less 'street' than it once was: "I'm glad it's a bit more professional. Everyone has got very business-like."

This is *our* Language

There was a time when Good meant Good but somehow that wasn't good enough. Along came Bad and Wicked which meant better than Good. Years down the line those terms are inadequate to describe the best tunes or vibes – especially in Jungle Drum & Bass. Things went from Terrible, to Horrible, to Nasty, to Sick, to Absolutely Disgusting. Worry not. It's All Good. Rider uses "Disgusting" as a jingle on radio – as in, "Grooverider, stop that right there sir. That tune is Absolutely Disgusting." It's the highest accolade for music of excellence. Say it with a frown and a disbelieving shake of the head for emphasis, and when we go out we love to get grimy. Though I have to say the phrase, 'It was off the hook' for another blindin' night is rinsed. After Innovation's Spanish *soirée*, Skibadee commented, "It was off the chisel man." At least that's what I think he said. Don't know if it'll catch on but we need more superlatives to push the boundaries of language like producers do with music and technology. As long as you're feelin' it. Splendid. Oh and err a Big tune really is a BIG CHOON.

The Word on The Net is Dogs On Acid

"You never used to hear people on the streets chatting about websites, now you do."
XO, MODERATOR DOGS ON ACID

For many of us the Internet has become invaluable. You can use it for shopping, research, find up to the minute information, communication, entertainment – and on and on. The Net is such a vast resource. Chatting to XO we both wondered, where does one start? Let's start with nuclear war.

The American Department of Defence needed computers that could communicate with each other even in the event of nuclear war: "The Net started off as a research project known by the acronym DARPA. They invented the protocol by which computers communicate in such a way that information can be routed around the network without needing individual links between every computer. If one of the facilities got taken out, the others would still be able to communicate. I think it started in the late 70s with three or four universities and the DARPA research facility all cross-linked across America. It got to the point where more and more universities were joining up: government departments, corporations, telecom companies and they linked up with the UK network; then you had the big transatlantic thing. Every time you access a website the computer that actually serves out the web pages is in a facility somewhere. Your request is probably going through five or ten other computers to get to its destination. And it's sending the information back that way as well. That can be through any number of companies cos they all have agreements to carry each others traffic." Back in the early to mid 80s a number of groups had what we now understand as broadband access: universities and large companies where it was common to have fast unrestricted Internet access. The Americans have free local calls, which is an enormous advantage. They can dial up the Internet on a local number and sit there all day, never having to worry about the phone bill. This makes a huge difference in how you can access the Net.

In the days when using a browser was slow many people used email, chat rooms and Usenet Bulletin boards. Usenet was a massive news system in which people would post replies to threads. These threads would branch off into more threads covering thousands of topics. There's always someone out there who shares your interests. It doesn't matter who or where you were. There'd be people bored at work, stuck in doors with limited mobility and those hanging out at home smoking weed all day – everyone could communicate. The Internet constituency wasn't as wide as it is nowadays but nevertheless it provided a great democratising opportunity in which anyone with access could take part. The Net was much slower than it is today.

Google didn't exist but there was also less to find. Searching for Jungle yielded little save hits related to botany: "Internet chat rooms, Internet news rooms and the whole forum thing are an extension of that. Chat rooms allow communication in real time. They're like big party lines. Everyone can make their voice heard. Many came into Jungle because they heard others talking about it on the Net. So their first experience of Drum & Bass came via websites." Some people only listen to it on the Net. But that's an improvement on sending mixtapes to friends abroad. Ben XO is one of the moderators running Dogs On Acid's technical side on a daily basis.

As a teenager Ben listened to pirate radio and tinkered with computers. He first gained Internet access in '96 through his mum's firm and started looking for Jungle: "The thing I came across first was a web page run by some Dutch guy that had a whole load of tunes which he'd written in a Jungle style. There was another guys' site where he would hold competitions like seeing who could write the best tunes using certain samples." The first dub plate page on the Net was run by a Canadian guy ripping audio from wherever he could. XO ran his own site. He'd record Kiss FM's Wednesday night shows on his PC, select clips of new tunes and post them on his website's Dub Plate page. When Kiss FM pulled Andy C from his Wednesday night slot XO posted a petition on his site explaining to fellow Junglists that if Kiss continued with Andy C, he could continue supplying them with dubs via his web page. Dan received around a hundred supportive mails, though not from Kiss.

The Drum & Bass Arena site arrived around 1996. It would be updated every week but it was far more basic than it is today. When XO visited chat rooms in 1997 he found nobody had heard of the DJs famous to him. A few DJs from the UK were mentioned but not as many as there were US DJs. Those logged on Stateside raved on about Dieselboy and Dara from New York City: "You get an appreciation of different Jungle backgrounds. North America has its own DJ circuit with DJs that most people here would never have head of. Yet they're playing out every week – not just every week but three times a week. You get people jet setting around North America the same way you get DJs here who jet set around Europe." Drum & Bass has spread globally with the growth of popular Internet access. In Hungary – SKC and Chris SU; Australia – Pendulum; New Zealand – Concord Dawn, Tali and Bulletproof; USA – Gridlok and Hive; Canada – John Rolodex. Fracture and Neptune gained quite a cult following by taking Jungle back to its roots with their complex breaks. Breaks, Edits, Choppage, Drum Funk – whatever you want to call it has a big following on the Internet but not necessarily in the clubs: "A high proportion of people on message boards prefer to listen to Drum & Bass at home. On the other side there are people who feel that Drum & Bass is only about going out."

Ben XO started posting on Dogs On Acid six months after it went online. He'd been in contact with Brian Peace, hired by Fresh as Dogs' first Webmaster. The Webmasters deal with technical problems as they arise. He was the voice to the public when things didn't function. Brian had been running his own dub plate site similar to XO's. Ben made Brian's acquaintance over the Net. When Brian stepped down from his position as moderator he recommended XO for the post.

THE COMPANY

Bad Company UK wanted to explore the potential of the Internet. Dan Fresh had always been interested in utilising message boards as a medium for carrying up-to-the-minute news and dynamic information, posting regularly on breakbeatscience.com. Computer literate since childhood, Dan taught himself to program Java and HTML. He created the Bad Company message board himself, as they couldn't afford a programmer: "In 2000 I tried to get together an MP3 site with Prototype (Grooverider), Ram (Andy C), Virus (Ed Rush & Optical), DSCI4 (Trace), Matrix and BC. This fell through because everybody was too disorganised at the time."

Bad Company's message board soon grew in popularity. Fresh decided to use this opportunity to construct a new kind of site based around the board. But this would have its own identity moving away from Bad Company themselves, providing a neutral Jungle Drum & Bass platform: "I thought that giving it its own name would help so I came up with 'Dogs On Acid' which I figured would stick in peoples heads."

After Brian Peace stepped down as webmaster Ben XO assumed his technical and moderating responsibilities. XO had many ideas that could promote Dogs' full potential. Fresh invited him to utilise his BSC in Computer Studies and extensive D&B knowledge. Running the site proved to be very expensive so Dan Fresh approached potential backers: "I went to Adam F, Grooverider and Sasha from Cobles who used to own Lucky Spin. I thought this would also help dispel people's fears that the site was based around my own self promotion." Dan continued to involve as many people as possible, which broadened the site's scope. Dogs On Acid now operates in close in partnerships with Beatport.com, Chemical Records and Tarzan.co.uk. They're open to any partnerships which could help present the type of content that people would like to see on this dedicated Drum & Bass site. DOA needed a new logo, so in true style they launched an online competition. It was possible to observe the development of the logos as designers posted their graphics on-line; asking people what they thought. Crossfire, a producer from Belgium, won.

DOA is the busiest Dance Music forum on the Net. It's had over two and a half million hits since going live in summer 2002 and claims over 25,000 registered users. Drum & Bass fans and stars alike visit it. The forums are place to chat with other Junglists. Artists can read what's being written about them. Ravers can bitch about artists or argue with each other. DOA's home page is easy to navigate. The site sports several features including: The Dog House is where people can chat live to artists online. The Board is the general chat forum, The Grid is an area in which producers exchange technical tips, while The Booth hosts a mix forum. Dogs On Acid features many sub directories holding vast amounts of information, records and merchandise. Bailey has used it to check where he's supposed to be playing. Dogs On Acid is basically a one-stop Jungle Drum & Bass shop.

"Dogs On Acid and Drum & Bass Arena are the best ones. Everyone seems to go on there. Dogs On Acid more for the producers cos you see the names come up. I find that D&B Arena is too young. Dogs On Acid is a little bit more mature." DJ E, RUDE FM

Because both Drum & Bass Arena and Dogs On Acid cover the Jungle scene there's bound to be some similarities in their content. But the main thing that took off on Dogs was The Board — the forum. Fans across the globe converse sometimes using a mixture of English and their native tongue. Information posted by fans is often interesting largely because of the gossip they contain. Producers might have a small feature on the news pages. A large number of DJs and producers have posted over the years. Doc Scott held one brilliant thread in which he posted, "Ask me some Q's, anything, music, politics, movies, it's late and it's hot!!" Other brand name artists have taken their time to answer people's questions on Chat Live. The encounters have been both informative and entertaining.

Brian Peace: Post here to chat to Grooverider ...
    Remember KEEP IT CLEAN.
Grooverider: Is this fucking thing working or what?

Pigz: Did the Fugees or anyone ever contact you
    about *Fugees Or Not*?
Hype Next question ...

The talk keeps flowing, "When's that tune coming out?" "I really rate this." "When are you playing?" "Were you at Telepathy last night?" People discuss politics, post jokes, animated pictures and even ask which mobile phone they should buy. It's fairly common to log on post rave before you crash out and write about the night you've just left. And before the party? XO explains 'Roll Call' threads: "Someone posts up, "Who's coming down to Ram at The End tonight?" I think people do it to see how popular it might be before they go. If you get 20 or 30 people saying, "Wouldn't miss it!" you know it's probably going to be a good night. Sometimes you get, "Who's coming down The End tonight?" and read, "You must be joking. We're all going to Traffic!!" All the big cities in the States have their own Drum & Bass message boards. All the Junglists end up meeting each other. They probably live quite far apart but they'll travel for two or three hours in the car to go to a night because they don't get the big DJs so often. Same thing in Europe."

Miss Pink has visited Dogs On Acid often over the years: "The forums can be really bitchy. I'm a lurker. I very rarely post anything. A lot of the DJs obviously have a look. Not from an ego perspective but to see what people are saying or what people are looking for. Quite often if someone slags something off, the DJ will reply. They get a response asking, "Why did he say that?" or "What did you mean by that?" which is amazing. It's so interesting to read. Sometimes I go on at the beginning of the week and someone has posted up that week's releases. What's coming into the shop Friday before even I know."

The two computers that house Dogs On Acid are located on an anonymous shelf in America. DOA also has an office in Hertfordshire north of London. They gain revenue from niche advertising and merchandise sales. When you buy records online through Dogs, you're linked to Chemical Records. XO is one of twelve moderators including two Mikes from the States and Australia respectively. Jho coordinates the editorial and feature content as well as moderating the site. Although he's Press Officer for Adam F and Fresh' label Breakbeat Kaos his role as a moderator is impartial. All the other members of Bad Company (D-Bridge, Maldini and Vegas) also moderate Dogs On Acid. Moderators' tasks include dealing with complaints and inappropriate postings like pornography or copyrighted material. They can't read every post before it goes online so moderators tend to rely on complaints bringing problems to their attention. XO is available 24 / 7 to solve technical problems that might occur.

Dan still works on the site. Sometimes it's making calls or just posting messages but he finds it difficult to be involved in the site as much as he once was. It's a question of neutrality: "It's very difficult now to be neutral on that site; I don't want people to associate it too much with Breakbeat Kaos but obviously us both being part owners doesn't help. I try to let it run its course to an extent." Dogs On Acid employs people who are neutral in both their music tastes and opinions because Dan's position is decidedly tricky. He was grilled recently for deleting a post on behalf of one of the scene's big names: "Dan, it really doesn't set a good example when you censor peoples opinions mate!" He knows: "It's like walking a tightrope. Trying to contribute, allow freedom of speech and yet avoid posts on the site winding up the big guns. But we do our best."

Dogs On Acid remains an excellent, entertaining and educative information centre for all Jungle Drum & Bass headz. And every now and again there's a little bit of controversy. Big Up.

Despite all the moaning about *our* music, we've built a scene to be proud of. It's something to be celebrated, not constantly denigrated. This is going out to all members of the Jungle, Drum & Bass family. Especially the massive.

The Scene — Big up the Family,
you know who I mean.
When we all come together we all get lean.
Kemistry's still here
And we all miss Stevie Hyper.
If you're part of that scene
show love and burn lighter.
Dynamite MC, The Scene

DANCE TO THE BEAT
OF A DIFFERENT DRUM

"I think it's healthy because no matter what Jungle Drum & Bass you like – whether it be Liquid, Jump-up or Dark – there's good music on each side. Everyone's making good music. Musically I think it's the best it's ever been." CLAYTON, TOV

FROM HOSPITAL TO HARDWARE

The musical range which is Jungle Drum & Bass has expanded. We've always had genres within the spectrum: Intelligent, through to Jump-up, Dark and Hardstep. Now Intelligent has become Liquid, Jump-up is still jumpin' and Dark has become positively demonic. We've had the Bouncy, New School, Clownstep and Soulful. You can divide them into subsections but they cross over. People are taking influences from so many different sources. Record shops once placed labels of certain styles together but that makes less sense than it once did. Over recent years we've witnessed far greater cross-pollination of styles than we've previously experienced. Producers from a wider range of musical bases have added to the mix. They've even been brave enough to include instruments like the electric guitar previously considered as Dance Music's greatest enemy. It's refreshing and daring, like the raw Punk energy of Lemon D's *Generation X*. When I first heard it I swear I could see former Sex Pistol Johnny Rotten in spiked dog collar spitting the lyrics "... And then I'll crush you." It's amazing that Lemon D performed that wicked vocal himself.

Labels like Hospital and Good Looking have tougher beats than the Ambient / Intelligent coffee table music of old. High Contrast has no problem taking to the decks and spinning his own tunes between Mickey Finn and Andy C. The whole spectrum couldn't be tougher. If it was melodic or jazzy it had to remain in the easy listening corner of Drum & Bass. The tracks of Marcus Intalex, D.Kay, Calibre, Carlito, Addiction, Klute and Hospital Records are melodic

but their beats are hard enough to play in any set. Dylan is spearheading the Heavy Metal battalion, even remixing Metallica tracks. Night Breed's *Pack Of Wolves* attained Radio 1 playlist stature and was respected by Rock enthusiasts as a credible track.

There are several international producers whose influences stem from Trance, Hard Rock or Heavy Metal. Pendulum's *Another Planet* reached the Top 40 in the UK. Doc Scott released their first tune *Vault* on his label 31 Records in 2003. *Vault*, one of the year's anthems, was sent to Scotty from Australia via AOL's Instant Messenger system (AIM). Concord Dawn are already household names in New Zealand because of their Pop music success, but they also make hardcore, Punk Rock Drum & Bass. Concord Dawn released *Don't Tell Me*, an excellent got-to-have-it track which I hassled Black Market for until it was released.

"There are a large number of people – mostly Americans who are into Jungle because it has the same raw energy as Punk Rock and Heavy Metal. And they've made the switch. They're the people who like the real Dark stuff. You forget all the people that don't appreciate the Jump-up vibe at all. It means nothing to them. You get these personality clashes on the forums between the people who like Jump-up but don't like the stuff that is too Dark and Hard. The people who like Jump-up are often kids from the UK. The people who like the Dark stuff are often kids from the US. They don't appreciate that they have different backgrounds." XO, DOA

When DJing on Internet radio XO reads messages from friends in Florida saying, "I don't want to hear any of this Hospital shit. Play some Tech Itch." He feels that there are a lot of amateur American DJs who want him to play more Renegade Hardware. XO prefers to play the whole spectrum from Hospital via True Playaz to Renegade Hardware: "I can't stand it when people stick to one sub-element of Drum & Bass when you can play the whole thing."

Carnival after-party, Plastic People 2004: Randall, Cleveland, Frost, Flight hang out amongst the nicely vibing crowd. Zinc drops *LK*, Stamina sings the lyric live and it's all screams and hands in the air. Zinc pulls back the track and Marky bounds irrepressibly across the floor tapping Dillinja rhythmically on his shoulder asking, "When we gonna do the vrooom vrooooom – Dillinja *LK* remix?" "Let's do it man. Let's do it."

It's not a question of just remixing and repackaging old tunes. It's more like, "You know that tune back then which was wicked? Well technology and experience have made it bloody blindin." At one time you might have called our music 'Intelligent' but this time around it's Liquid and its IQ has gone way up and although you can listen to it at home, its place is not on the coffee table. When pop group Girls Aloud's *Sound of the Underground* graced the charts it made me smile. Yes, it was Drum & Bass but it wasn't our sound of the underground. DJ Ron explains, "I don't think Andy C or Grooverider are going to be tearing out Girls Aloud down The End." People complain about the state of our music. Calibre on Fabio's show was moved to ask, "Who are these people?" Who indeed? The thing is another big, big tune always comes along. By mid August 2004 we had *Golden Girl* by MC Conrad and Makoto. It's the essence of soulful Drum & Bass. Rider admitted on radio that it had moved him literally to tears. I won't forget the first time he dropped it down at Grace – spiritual – insanely spiritual.

WHO RUN TINGS?

New or younger people are drawn into the scene with roots born of Techno and Trance's faster beats. They may have contributed to a feedback loop that has accelerated our music. Somewhere between the crowds, DJs and producers a force has driven D&B's beats per minute ever faster. Instead of rolling along between 160 - 170bpm. Some tunes are now racing at 178, threatening to exceed 180 sound barrier. Both Storm and Andy C feel that the BPM's have evolved with the music. It's not everyone's taste. So just like the mid-90s when JDB's movers and shakers held the Foundation meetings to define musical directions, 40 headz met in summer 2004 and called for order. The word on the streets was that this meeting was supposed to be a secret – wasn't it? Whether it was or it wasn't the rumour mill ground on all channels.

Land Line:
You hear about the meeting?
What meeting?
The other day with 40 DJs 'n' producers.

E-Mail:
Know anything about the meeting?
No, it's a secret.
That's all you've heard?

AIM:
The meeting with the 40?
Word is if you weren't there and you don't know then you ain't gonna know?

WWW:
... Moderators pulled posts about the meeting off the Dogs on Acid forum.
Serious? Heavy.

Text:
M8 eard woz bout da BPMs
U nt ther. fought u woz 1 a da 40
Not me m8 – wernt invtd.

Radio 1:
Fabio said something about BPMs on his show.
Can't just have met cos of the BPMs. I know dem mans.

In Da Club:
I 'eard scene's supposed ta be in a mess.
It's like that Foundation thing back in the day.

Mobile:
... Wot meeting? I'm on 'oliday ... in Bali.
Sorry. Don't you hate it when that happens ([:-{

Days after The Meeting I was chatting to L Double at 1Xtra. He gave me an exclusive and I didn't know it: "I know for a fact that artists are talking about that. Brand name artists. Maybe a lot of the youngsters who've been in D&B five years or since they were 16, that's all they've known since they became musically aware. We're from fuckin' Kurtis Blow, Rare Grooves, so we're like, "The thing's too fast." We have to dictate sometimes. Yeah it's about the kids. It is. But sometimes youth is wasted on the young. And you've got to fuckin' show 'em a thing or two. Maybe doing a few tracks and slowing it down across the board would work. You do it, I do it, he does it, they do it, we all do it."

A few weeks after The Meeting DJ Flight opened the issue for discussion during her 1Xtra show: "A lot of you may know already that there was a meeting of some D&B headz." The Future Sound of Cambridge were guests on her show. Logistics had attended the meeting and was willing to talk about it. Most people there were producers. They'd gathered to talk about whether or not the music was getting too fast. They were trying to stop Drum & Bass turning into Gabba: "Initially it was supposed to be more to do with the music. It ended up being a free-for-all discussion about the state of the scene as it is. We talked about bringing back some flavours into the mix, distribution, labels, everything was discussed. It was mainly about the music, trying new things. Every producer has their own style. It was an attempt at making things more interesting for each other. Hopefully the outcome will be more exciting collaborations, remixes, that kind of thing. It was really positive to have a load of people from the scene."

That sounds very positive. Artists proactively caring about our music. Not willing to let it fragment and slip away into something unrecognisable. Before news of The Meeting had spread Fabio alluded to the BPM topic. He mentioned the vibe during the last night of The Sanctuary expressing the view that if the kids wanted the music to be faster then the DJs and producers should please the crowd. I was shocked. Fabio and crew, I've sought out your music because you are innovators. I leave my yard to go out and be tested by your new sounds. I understand that there is a symbiosis between producers, DJs and audience and I'm there to follow the leaders. I go along with L Double. Many of us old uns have been around good music since the year dot. Some of us have been DJing for 20 years, knowing and appreciating quality music. There are X amount of people in the scene – artists and punters who've earned informal degrees in Jungle, Drum & Bass. Call me arrogant but I'm not taking the lead from people who've just finished their GCSEs. I'll get off my soapbox but regular posters on the 1Xtra message board – D&B graduates DJ Bailey, Dave Darkside and Flowjoe seem to agree.

"I'm not saying that I think it's better slower because I like all kinds of flavours within the D&B sound but when it was a bit slower (say about 160 BPMs) it was easier for producers to make more intricate patterns in a tune whereas now it's mainly about the two-step sound of D&B. Is this because of the speed of D&B or are producers just getting lazy?" *DJ BAILEY*

"Funny you should you say that, we were chatting about this the other day ... the two-step thing drove up the speed, and the sound never really recovered from the '97-'99 years as far as BPM goes. The production is wicked and better than ever in my opinion, but it's just that wee bit too fast for a fat, lazy, lolling, skank – which was part of the joy of Jungle for me ... the ability to shift up and down pace from an arms-flailing brock-out, picking out the individual snares on the "majors" to a cool rubber-spined bassline skank. Now you tend to see less interesting dancing, for starters ... I'd love the speed to come down a wee bit, maybe not as much as 160, but somewhere in between what we have now and what we had then, so we can keep the odd nice crisp spanky two-step in a set and still enjoy more fully the trippy, mentalism and energy of the breaks! I always felt Jungle the most when it had that Roots / Reggae bass and pace with the drums straining to yank it along at a faster speed than it actually was." *DAVE DARKSIDE*

"Yep Dave. Maybe not 160, that might be too slow, a compromise perhaps chaps? You're right, the dancing is less entertaining. It was nice when a track like *The Helicopter Tune* came in and the crowd were bending down low, jumpin' and spreadin' out and brocking wild, he he. Surely that's the point of D&B being so good? The movement and lovely rhythms to shuffle to ... Some sets nowadays force you to have 35 Red Bulls before you can even adjust to 'the ride'." *FLOWJOE*

Jungle Drum & Bass has always been what L Double describes as, "umbrella music." We've always had flavours. It's wicked that the Dub vibe is running at the moment. I hope it won't be rinsed till it's rinsed out. It's also good that artists acknowledge our music is in danger of slipping away. That would have been tragic. I feel blessed that Jungle Drum & Bass has been in my life because I love dancing to the beat of a different drum. But please, just not too fast.

"It's not about beats per minute is it? It's about good tunes and bad tunes. Nobody's stopping anybody from making slower tunes – whether they're shit or not. If the tune is good people are gonna play it. Do you think anybody's sitting around thinking, 'Oh this is 170bpm?' Jeeeez. Who does that? Nobody! The beats per minutes talk is fraud." *GROOVERIDER*

PRODUCERS

"When Drum & Bass was on the front cover of Muzik or The Face, everyone was into it. But as soon as it wasn't fashionable they all went away. The only people they still know are Goldie, Bukem, Andy C and Hype. People don't know who Bad Company are. They don't know Calibre, High Contrast, Marcus Intalex or any of the names that have come through."
ROHAN, BASSBIN

LETS GET DOWN TO BIZNESS

The production of Jungle Drum & Bass has improved immeasurably in recent years. Headz now experience laminated walls of sound the likes of which legendary 60s producer Phil Spector could never have imagined. Today's D&B enthusiasts feel the keen skills of producers like Hype, Andy C, T Power & Shy FX and Roni Size amongst many who embody decades of production experience. Then there are relative newcomers from Bad Company and John B through Calibre, High Contrast, Marky & XRS to Concord Dawn and Pendulum who've taken Jungle, kicked it around in their studios in a multitude of new directions. JDB's own weapon of mass creation veteran Andy C confessed, "The standard of production is so high currently – with so many wicked producers blowing your mind every few weeks. The mix-downs, the level of detail and the sounds – it's awesome. So you've got to be on point." Grooverider concurs: "There are people making shit all over the world now. Because of the way music is and the way access is nowadays people can send tunes to you no problem. Everybody's up on their technology and they're doing their thing so there shouldn't be any reason why people outside the UK shouldn't be able to make this music and make it well."

I was chatting to American producer / DJ Origin who affirmed, "Drum & Bass producers push technology far harder than in any other genre." Technically they're unparalleled. L Double of Flex Records agrees: "I still don't think you can beat the technicality of the Breakbeat and production that we do. I've been shouting that for 15 years. That's what drew me in. I was into production and the production quality was at the highest in Jungle Techno. Man was coming from House and Hip Hop with old unsynched drum machines and fuckery. I was like, "Wicked. Authentic sounds 'n' all that …" But as far as trickery and bussin' tings up; Jungle Techno was miles ahead … Miles ahead."

BCUK

I've turned off the North Circular Road driving into Golders Greens' deep suburbia. The street is lined with posh motors, manicured lawns and houses costing the Earth. It's the kind of place where behind net curtains middle class residents keep themselves to themselves. Safe to say there's no vibe on these streets. So it's a strange place to go looking for Bad Company, the biggest noise in Drum & Bass since the close of the 20th Century. We're underground in Golders Green. Vegas waits on the driveway. We ran into each other a week ago on the Croydon train. Since then Bad Company UK have played St. Petersburg in Russia and rinsed it.

Fresh is out of town so we link up via email. Maldini's in the lounge. We'd like to sit, chat and puff in the garden but don't want weed smoke billowing over the fence disturbing the neighbours. So it's back into the lounge. The studio's front of house nudging into the bay windows. 1210s, mixer and speaker monitors occupy one wall. A mixing desk and an Apple Mac monitor lines the other.

Bad Company's gang of four consists of D-Bridge, Maldini, Vegas and Fresh. MC Moose introduced Fresh to Vegas who'd been promoting parties in Japan. Moose knew they'd hit it off. He was right, they became great friends. D-Bridge and Maldini were at Renegade Hardware under the name Future Forces before joining forces with Fresh and Vegas. *The Code* and *Sub Phonics* were their last tunes for Renegade Hardware but the first for the quartet. In Summer '98, Michael – Vegas, Dan – Fresh, Jason – Maldini and Darren – D-Bridge became Bad Company UK.

They left Renegade Hardware for the usual reasons artists leave labels. BC UK gained freedom but found themselves without a studio or money to buy one. This initial hardship bound them together. They borrowed money and set up a studio in Dan's parents' house in Maidenhead, west of London. Vegas recalls the all night sessions, smoking loads of cigarettes and eating awful food: "We were having a laugh making tracks. We all kind of just banded together. We'd already worked in a studio and the sound was starting to happen. It was different to what we were doing individually. It was a new kind of sound with lots of different points of view; with the result that if four people are happy, it's probably good."

True enough. Their first tune *The Nine* shot to the top of Radio 1's Drum & Bass chart and stayed there for three weeks. It recently received over 130,000 votes on Drum & Bass Arena's website confirming it as fans' top D&B tune of all time. *The Nine* is still being re-pressed. *Inside the Machine*, their first album, won Best Album at *Knowledge* magazine's Drum & Bass Awards in 2001. BC UK have had a string of plaudits for a record bag full of tunes, including remixes of *Mo Fire* and *Barcelona* which reached Number 21 and Number 14 in the UK national charts respectively.

Dan explains that they all had different musical influences: "I grew up around music. When I was eight my school did a musical IQ test. They sent a letter to my parents telling them I'd had the highest results in the test ever since it started! I used to be into Classical Music and had a mad interest in computers. When I first heard Hardcore I was hooked. My other influences before included The Cure, The Pixies, The Stone Roses and Jean Michelle Jarre ... I was the Indie kid out of us." Fresh was also the computer bod. He's been getting to grips with software for as long as he can remember. Vegas and Maldini have also been around computers since the black & white days of that game Pong. They've all added talented ingredients to the Bad Company mix. Maldini describes their first studio: "That was a mad one. We were running an Atari ST and an Emu with shitty speakers and a really noisy desk. We got the Mackies with the first money we made but that was quite far in. *Nitrous*, off the *Inside the Machine* album, was done using an Atari ST." He laughs remembering their software: "It was Cubase Version nil, it was so slow. The thing took about half an hour to load up and crashed all the time."

Poor studio equipment wasn't a barrier. The essence of their music shone through. Fresh explains what BC UK wanted to achieve: "We wanted to get back the raw energy from the Hardcore days and add a bit of a metal influence. At the time the music was very empty. Although that emptiness made it special in a different way. Tunes like *Ghost Faced Killa* and *Metropolis* sent me nuts. But when we did *The Code / The Nine* we realised there was a road we could explore with more hardcore energetic tunes." They seriously upgraded their software along the way using Logic, Innuendo, Cubase and Reason to make tunes including *Nightmare On Elm Street* and *Temple of Doom*. The music that bound them together had its conception in the boys' vibing off each other. Vegas and Maldini explain their production process: "You hear different things and sometimes you pick up on something and make a Drum & Bass version of it. Or it's organic in the studio. It can be

Bad Company

Formation

another type of music that you're listening to and pick up on. It depends. When you work with different people you can hear something that they are playing which they might not be able to hear. From that you can build something around it. You might get a vibe a off a certain sequence that someone is playing or *vice versa* and it builds that way. It's like that game you play at school where you draw a head, fold the paper and somebody else draws a body. One thing leads to another. It depends. You can get a vibe off a break that can make the riff. You can hear something that might dictate the b-line. It depends what you're listening to." Vegas adds: "When you grow up with music you can hear what's wrong. You know how things should sound naturally unless you're tone-deaf, which means you really shouldn't be doing music. It's a natural thing which people normally understand."

Unlike the Pop worlds' producers, BC are not interested in bashing out formulaic ditties. Their ethic is, 'That's done. What's next?' Neither Maldini nor Vegas would find anything worse: "If you do the same thing all the time it'll kill you. A lot of producers we were witnessing would catch a little vibe and make 10 or 15 of those. We'd be onto the next lot of samples and next bass ... Otherwise it's not progression." "It just pushes everything backwards. What's the fucking point in sitting down and writing *The Nine* another 10 or 30 times? What's the fucking point? *The Nine* is *The Nine*. It's been done." Fresh concurs, "Drum & Bass is all about progression."

Understandably there have been differences along the way. The four artists still produce tunes as Bad Company UK but they're also pursing other projects. Fresh flies between the England and the States working with Adam F: "For some reason the others weren't happy in the studio with me, probably cos I'm a stubborn motherf**ker and don't listen 90% of the time!! We were writing tunes together less and less, because I'd been engineering for them for so long. They had a steep learning curve to get up to speed. So there was a while where they were neither involved in much of the stuff I was doing, and at the same time didn't finish anything themselves. That's obviously all changed now." Vegas agrees, "Everyone was Bad Company altogether and now we are doing our own tunes for different people, remixes and all that and doing Bad Company. We're putting together an EP which will have tracks from all of us." Maldini and Vegas have started a label called Defiance signing talent from New Zealand called The Upbeats.

D-Bridge is making the music he always wanted to make describing it as, "Beautifully aggressive." He's also been involved in collaborations with Concord Dawn, Fierce and Commix. The Bad Company relationship is, admits Fresh, going through changes. But they haven't split or have they? "I am very happy that they are finding themselves musically, as I am. It's a shame it took such a blow to make that happen." What advice would Vegas and Maldini give new producers? "Believe. Just get yourself some sort of studio equipment. Get in there now and start learning. Start ringing people up. Start hassling labels for tracks. Get about. Get out of your house. Be active."

FORMATION

"I've been representing from day one. It's been a long time and I am happy to be here still. It's about maintaining, trying to keep up standards, trying to do our best." DJ SS

There must be a thing in Drum & Bass that makes you cram 24 hours with far too many tasks. So I'm dashing hot and sweaty to catch the 11.55 from St Pancreas station. Signs point around King's Cross' extensive building site. In the future the new Eurostar terminus will be here. The station is further away and in the opposite direction from where I need to be. 11.52 — time is ticking. Running, trotting, stepping, treading, tripping over my feet, stumble 'round another corner and … fuck. They've built a whole new station. "Leicester? You want platform 12 mate."

London is such a huge glob that you think anywhere outside it as the end of the Universe. So I've unpacked my laptop and started tucking into all the goodies I panic bought for the long journey to the Midlands. I'm nicely settled then hear "Next stop — Leicester." 'Leicester! Leicester is in the Midlands. Shit I thought that was bloody miles away.' Stuff laptop and sandwiches away. Fall out the train as they're

blowing the 'all aboard' whistle. Hit the
platform as the guard runs up and scowls at me
for leaving the door open holding up the train.
I follow a cabby's directions to Charles Street
home of record shop 5HQ and the offices of
Formation Records — one of the oldest and most
prolific labels in Jungle Drum & Bass.

Leicester town centre is similar to many
identikit high streets across the land and
suffers the same monotony that's infected the
UK's towns. I cross the road and enter 5HQ's
long tunnel entrance. The shop is spacious.
A booth for Internet access and DJ lessons is at
the rear of the store. Upstairs is the Formation
office and Cara: "Tania's just dashed of to meet
you at the station." "Really! They wouldn't do
that in London."

I'm here visiting Tania of booking agents
Underground Music Collective (UMC) and Leroy –
Scratching Stein aka DJ SS, head of Formation
Records. Both are stalwarts of the Jungle Drum
& Bass scene. Formation has already celebrated
its 100th release. We retire to a wine bar on
Charles Street. DJ SS is one person who's been
around for so long, it's difficult to know where
to begin. We could start with *Lighter* or *Black*
but that would be about 12 years too late. I've
brought a record with me. There are no details
on the label save the red, white and blue of
the Union Jack. "Is this one of yours?" I ask.
He doesn't know. Could be. Might be. Probably
was. "Thanks man. Whenever I play this tune out,
it mashes the place."

HIS HANDS ON DECKS, OUR HANDS IN THE AIR

SS has loved records since childhood, catching the funky
vibes from a stack of 7-inch singles in his mum's house.
In the early 80s Leroy enjoyed Electro and came into music
as a breakdancer. He was so good that he was featured on
BBC TV's *Pebble Mill at One*. As Electro departed SS found
the only way to hear the music was to play it himself. He
bought some awful belt driven turntables and practiced
cuttin' and scratchin' every day after school, with his mum
shouting, "Turn that down!" But she could see the boy was
hooked and encouraged him. SS has been a DJ since before
a time most people knew what a DJ was. At 15 Leroy found
himself DJing on the Midlands circuit and gaining his first
residency. He played all things Hip Hop, Rare and funky to a
packed Sunday nightclub that had previously been dead. The
club's promoter never knew his DJ was too young to enter
the club. By '88 SS was playing Acid House in the fields.

SS produced his first tune, an Electro influenced House track,
in '88 with a friend's help but it wasn't until he had an
experience with a band that he found a new direction:
"I was in a P-Funk group as a scratch DJ. It was a 20 piece
band or something ridiculous. They had singers, horns and
I'd be scratching. We used to do Limelight and Brixton
Fridge. I remember going to rehearsals one time. I'm
looking for the band and this guy presses a button on the
computer and I hear all this music. I'm saying, "Where's
the band?" And he's saying, "Nah, forget that band
business. That business is over." It was all in the computer.
I thought, 'You know what? That is me.' 18 months later
I got an Atari."

Most producers talk about getting the vibe right when
they're in the studio. Same with SS. He loves his grooves.
Like many producers home and abroad he'll go hunting in
record shops for elusive breaks and doesn't have a problem
with buying compilation CDs of old classics from HMV or
Woolworths who've now become purveyors of all your Funk
and Rare Groove needs. You can never have too many
breaks. I'll lay my cards on the table and say without
reservation that I hated Whitney Houston's *I Will Always
Love You*. Hated it. Whenever that track was on I'd be
leaping for the off switch. Comediennes French & Saunders
did a hilarious piss take that had me in stitches. Then along
comes DJ SS who produces *Black* that has me, and everyone
else, leaping in the air, screaming for rewinds. Raving to
Whitney Houston? He also had us losin' it to the refrain
from *Love Story*. SS, what's going on?

"To tell you the truth that tune was a VIP for Grooverider. I whacked it together in a few hours. He started playing it and everyone jumped on it. The other side was the main track. It was called *Lighter* but it didn't have the piano. It's *Love Story*. Rider played VIP Roast or somewhere like that and everybody was on it. I played the original out last week at an Old Skool party and the place went mad. Listening to it brought back memories but the mixdown on it is terrible." SS vibed off Whitney's voice: "That vocal really touched me. So I went down HMV, ripped it off the CD and put it straight in the tune." Leroy went back to his roots sampling Rare Groove and R'n'B vocals: "That is what we are missing in the tunes, quality vocals not just sampled off every acapella compilation that everybody has rinsed. I wanted to do something different with the R'n'B thing. I wanted to make something that people could relate to."

Over the years Formation has become a huge stable for new producers who SS has taken under his wing: Twisted Individual, Zen, John B, Generation Dub to name a few. Formation produced the *World of Drum & Bass* album, touring it around the globe. Many producers have progressed to making albums. SS took his time to release his own album *The S Files*. He's used original vocals on many tracks and feels that the present musical environment is better for its release than in the Techno influenced times of a few years ago.

SS remains an excellent DJ, smooth and comfortable at Grace. Diamonds around Rolex, spinning black vinyl with no labels. The dub plate's sample sings, "Keep on moving – don't stop." SS faultlessly mixes through his head, hands and record bag for the dancing crowd in clouds of smoke and rays of coloured lights. The scene's faces move through the crowd. MC System hands me a flyer for Traffic – Beats in the Fast Lane this Friday night. Rider waits his turn to spin. The floor once sparse is pumping with forms and energy – keep on moving SS.

I'M IN THE STUDIO

There was a time when I would have been writing this on a typewriter. Remember those? Now thanks to IBM, I talk – it types. From this keyboard I can research so much more than I could with a Travelcard and a phone. There was also a time when you'd have to physically visit a studio and pay an extortionate amount of money per hour to make music. When powerful technology arrives it's human to exploit it. Technological freedom enabled people to turn their bedrooms into studios. We've gone beyond that. "I'm in the studio," now means that your head is in the studio and the studio is on your laptop. That's freedom. Since artists log untold hours on plane journeys they can continue making tunes whilst travelling. L Double was very early on the case carrying his studio around. Before L moved to London he made it his business to understand his laptop and relevant software. Cubase, Logic, Reason, Ableton Live, he's used them all: "They call me 'The Mac helpline'. Everyone calls my phone, from Rider to Ron, Kenny to Mickey – the fuckin' lot of them ring my phone when it comes to Apple cos I've been on it since 1995."

The technological and Internet revolution has made relatively easy to use software readily available enfranchising interested parties across the globe. Dogs On Acid moderator XO has a good perspective of Drum & Bass across the Net: "These days you can write a good tune on your computer with just software from the Internet. That really started to happen when Cubase and things like that became big. Now you've got artists from Russia writing stuff using software that they can't afford but they've got anyway. They've broken out of the whole downward cycle of post Communist Russia and made a name for themselves."

THE PROCESS OF PRODUCING

I first met T Power in '95 when SOUR took Jungle to Berlin's Love Parade, and I've met Shy many times over the years. I really wanted to watch them make tunes in the studio. I only needed to ask. You know it's for the book and everything. I just had to choose the right moment. We're in Swerve at the bar. Fabio's on the decks. I pluck up the courage: "Mind if I hang around when you and Shy are making a tune?" He's really polite but I clocked a hint of an expression which said, 'No way man. That shit's private.'

Producers can be very funny about having outsiders watching their creative process. There's some dictum in physics that says that you change the nature of an experiment even by observing it. Or is it just a case of keeping secret ways of working secret? Bad Company's Maldini has his own opinion: "It used to be a thing that people didn't like other people in their studio because they would discover all your secrets. Now there's so much software and everyone is running the same thing. Whether it's cracked or they bought it, it's all the same thing."

DJ Flight set The Future Sound of Cambridge the task of making a tune during her two-hour show. They rose to the challenge admirably, but we couldn't see how they went about it. So I drove to Milton Keynes to check DJ Flapjack and Cool Hand Flex and their label Default Recordings. It's open house when they're in the studio. Mind you, Flex made tunes in the back of De Underground with loads of people around banging on the walls. I'd heard it was like making a tune in a rave. So I'm 'round Flapjack's yard, we're chilling, chatting, drinking X amount of red wine. Every now and again Flappers disappears upstairs to his studio. The studio thing. The private thing. Don't want to transgress. After a couple of hours and another bottle of wine, "Oi Adam, mind if I have a look at what you're doin'?" "No worries." Flapjack's hand operates the mouse deftly, teasing, twisting, nudging samples and beats, then pushing them back into the sampler. Save – play with volume and tone, coarse tune – semitones back into the Cubase. The studio is in a smallish room. There's Yamaha NS-10m studio monitors, an E 5000 Ultra sampler, a Behringer DDX 3215 automated mixing console and Cubase SX software is running on a severely upgraded PC and not much else. "That's all you need," agrees Rohan of Bassbin Recordings. "We've got the basics: a sampler, computer and mixing desk. You don't really need much else." The software revolution now means you can scrap most of the hardware and make tunes using one computer. Rohan mentioned Breakage makes tunes this way.

Shy FX and T Power have moved away from most of their old skool studio hardware, opting for a Mac G5 running Logic Audio 6; rounded off with two sleek Dynaudio BM6A monitors. Their studio, neater than Shy's old bedroom was (he asked me to mention that) has a fair few bits of kit they don't use and should flog at a car boot sale or donate to a local school. Unused are Prophecy and Trinity keyboards. Unemployed is the Virus. Unplugged are the Focuswrite compressors. Although T Power loves their sound he has much more control using the computer. They're now using plug-ins. And their chosen software – Shy? "We use Recycle quite a lot. We kept the old Mac G4 for that before the new version came out. When I think about the amount of time I used to spend cutting beats manually in the sampler, I'd never go back to that. I prefer Recycle to Phatmatik software as it's just a lot easier to use and does what I want much quicker." T Power has affection for soft-synths: "I really like the Absynth plug-in, but it's a bit fiddly for some people. It's great if you want to make complex sounds and have control over the oscillators, LFOs and envelopes. But sometimes you just want to knock up a cheap and cheerful sound. The EX1 is great for that. You can twiddle a few knobs and you've got what resembles a bass sound really quickly."

You've made the tune but constructive criticism is essential. Before relocating from Newcastle to Leicester Adam and Jake of Generation Dub sent tracks to SS for a second opinion: "You've put your all into a tune. As soon as you put it in the mailbox your thinking, 'I hope he likes it.' Sometimes you'd have to wait for ages and you would be calling every other day. And they'd be times when SS says, "It's not quite there yet." Then we'd have to go back to the drawing board. That could be quite hard." But they wouldn't have it any other way. Their first track, *Ghostbusters* topped Radio 1's Drum & Bass chart. After six months at Formation Generation Dub released the dancefloor anthem *Body Snatchers. Snatchers* and *Freak Show* were the only two tracks from the same artists included on Fabio & Grooverider's *Drum & Bass Revolution* CD for *Mixmag*. And I couldn't help noticing that *Margarita* by DJ SS was their first tune. No surprises there.

GOING TO HOSPITAL

"We don't like to be pigeon-holed as a Liquid or Jazz label cos we're not. We are happy releasing a Dillinja remix alongside a very soulful piece from Danny Byrd. It's not about what sub-genre it is. It's about: Is it a good tune? Do we like it? Will our people like it? Will people trust us enough to buy it and then like it?"
TONY COLMAN

It started in '87 with an Acid Jazz band called Izit and their first tune – a hit called *Stories*. Tony Colman formed Izit, one of the first Acid Jazz revival bands bracketed with Push, The Brand New Heavies and Incognito: "It was more about live performance than records. We were doing it the old skool way – learning your trade, your craft." Tony released *Stories* through Pig & Trumpet, a label he ran with the co-producer of *Stories*, Andrew Missingam. They pressed 500 7" singles cheaply with financial contributions from the band. Izit recorded a 12" version in Tony's bathroom at home in Tottenham: "Well, half the band was in the bathroom. The other half were in the lounge." *Stories* did rather better than they expected: "It was mad. There were white vans pulling up outside my house and geezers with loads of money saying, "Give me a thousand copies." It was really lucky start and addicted me to this trade."

But Tony knew something more musically exciting than *Stories* was happening along the street: "My mates in Tottenham were making Hardcore. I started hearing Breakbeat at 130 - 140 BPM and thinking, 'That's what I want to be doing NOW.' I was in Japan on the road with Izit looking over my shoulder thinking, 'I'm missing out.' Pig & Trumpet could have invested in Trip Hop but that became more about stroking goatees: "It was really dull. We weren't prepared to go that way." Tony was very excited by Jungle Drum & Bass so closed Pig & Trumpet. The turning point for Tony was a long Izit tour that ended in Australia: "I was burnt out so I took myself to the Philippines with a load of CDs one of which was Goldie's album *Timeless*. It's still the greatest Drum & Bass artist album to this day. That showed me what was possible. I thought, 'That's my destiny.' That was it – decision taken."

Tony and Chris founded Hospital Records releasing their first tune *Harp of Gold* in spring '96. Both were heavily into Lounge Music but wanted to articulate a coalition between Lounge and Jungle with Hip-Hop attitude. They wouldn't be producing coffee table Drum & Bass. Hospital was born into the middle of D&B's Intelligent phase. Around that time Fabio and Bukem had fallen out. There was also a co-incidental split in Drum & Bass with Dark on one side, Good Looking on the other and little in between: "People didn't know how to pigeonhole us. In Black Market we'd be racked up next to Good Looking. I've got a lot of respect for that label but I didn't want people to see us as being like that. We felt we were an entirely different kettle of fish." Hospital Records have more affinity with Roni Size and Alex Reece. They've worked in their own bubble, avoiding scene politics.

Tony and Chris didn't find running Hospital records easy: "We were ready to give up after our sixth release and start making House." They released a last make-or-break tune, *Songs in the Key of Knife*. Chris remembers with some relief: "That turned a corner so we ditched the House label and worked 24 / 7 on Hospital. After … *Knife* and the first London Elektricity album *Pull the Plug* Fabio was on the phone saying how much he was into the stuff we were doing and started playing loads of tracks off the album. A lot of people came on board after that. With him and Groove having their radio show which is entirely international you just get that exposure instantly."

Hospital have signed many artists since then including Cyantific, Phuturistix, Logistics and Nu:tone. They also signed High Contrast who Chris and Tony recognised as a big talent: "His hair has come a long way since his first album. It's the size of a dub plate now."

Hospital recently bought a former day-care centre from Age Concern moving premises to South London. The budget conscious label crew saved money by using their DIY skills. Investing in property was a big step but they're happy that their music has made it possible. The music and the bank. Tony points around the studio, "You see that electric piano? The bank owns that now. See my trainers – the bank owns my trainers. But it feels really good taking us on to a new level, and the staff work really hard. Everyone's locked down on their area; whether it be distribution, merchandising, website – we're all continuing trying to get better." They stage a monthly Hospitality night in Cardiff and have released a DVD covering London Elektricity's live performances with all the visual extras. I have to say, this crew are really on it. They've moved, renovated their new headquarters in double quick time and have still been able to release High Contrast's album *High Society*.

THE SHINING HIGH CONTRAST

Lincoln, aka High Contrast, was always creative. As a child he'd make models, draw comic strips and write short stories. Taking steps into the world of filmmaking was the next level. Although he played piano and keyboards, Lincoln wasn't interested in the type of music dictated by the lessons. Surprisingly he didn't listen to music for pleasure until he was 17. He was interested in film soundtracks but had no appreciation of music in general. High Contrast doesn't know where he comes from musically, he's just driven by creativity: "The medium is irrelevant. It's just me making things. At the moment it's music. I love Jungle and it is part of me. But I can switch to film and jump back and forth. Jungle is the perfect medium for me because I'm a perfectionist and a control freak. I can make it on my own, in my own time. The nature of sampling as well – I don't have to rely on people to play instruments. I can stand back, pick and choose things that I like and piece them together. I can take things from any time and place and construct it all at home in Wales."

Lincoln was spurred on to make tunes by a free Cubase demo, which came with a magazine under the banner 'You can even make your own Jungle tunes.' So off he went undeterred by not having any understanding of how Jungle was structured. That free copy of Cubase only had two tracks. So he could only use one track for the drums and the other for one set of samples. If he wanted to add other samples something else would have to go. Lincoln also listened to his tunes through poor quality speakers, and as he'd never been clubbing he didn't know about the bass in Jungle: "I'd hear *Timeless* but never hear the sub bass. When I actually heard it on a big system it was a revelation for me. I had been making tunes for six months without a b-line." Building tunes for a year without a bassline allowed him to concentrate more on the musical side of his tracks: "What drew me in was the nature of sampling, beats and speeding up breaks. It was more the sampling angle than the sonic angle. The first thing I sampled was my mum's Motown CD compilation. I rinsed it."

Lincoln broadened his horizons by leaving his hometown, heading off to Film School in Cardiff. It was a good move as he met a multitude of people from different backgrounds. It's also where he first heard Jungle: "When I use the term Jungle I get this blast of imagery – it's very hard to articulate but it's the essence of vibe. I just picture a dark club, the atmosphere, the music and something quite beautiful and special held within it. The word Jungle is infused with magical properties. When I'm making a tune I'm trying to capture that moment on the dancefloor with my friends with a tune like *Brand New Funk* coming on and looking over at them and saying, "Yes. This is a wicked moment." I'm trying to capture moments like that." Lincoln visited Bristol checking out parties and record shops in search of music.

High
Contrast

PHOTO BY CLEVELAND AARON

High Contrast started by trying to make Dark tunes like Bad Company's. He was also inspired by the '96 - '97 Jump-up years, which may surprise many people. Lincoln was influenced by Nicky Blackmarket's mixtapes as much as he was by Bukem's sets: "I love the energy of Blackmarket and the depth of Bukem. I was trying to bring those two together." His producer / DJ name High Contrast reflects the Bukem / Nicky Blackmarket range of music he likes to create and play. He found his own musical voice using film soundtracks infused with 60s and 70s Jazz, Soul and Funk. The blokes in his local record shop couldn't understand why this Jungle producer was buying Sal Soul records. He loves the strings: "I was trying to make tunes to play which I couldn't buy."

High Contrast first made tunes at 180 beats per minute because he wanted to be able to spin them whilst DJing. The DJ booth where he played had no CD player and a MiniDisc without a pitch control. He gave copies of some of his tracks to Digital who advised him to slow his music down: "It sounds like Happy Hardcore." Lincoln also gave tunes to Nicky Blackmarket, Sappo and Krust and he's pleased that they seem to have forgotten all about them.

Lincoln worked as the Drum & Bass specialist in Cardiff record shop Catapult giving him a valuable musical education. Like many people he saw House music as the enemy, but listening to it in the shop Lincoln heard sounds that he wanted to infuse into his own music. He started producing tunes in a major key making them sound more uplifting — which wasn't to everybody's taste but Hospital Records would feel differently. High Contrast met London Elektricity in 2000 when they came to gig in Cardiff. He sent them some tracks including *Suddenly* which he'd slowed down from its initial 180 BPM. Hospital Records snapped up *Suddenly* for their compilation *Plastic Surgery II and* invited him to sign an album deal. His music hit the scene at a time when people wanted to hear something different, something more musical. High Contrast now stands alongside Calibre and Marcus Intalex as a brilliant producer.

He doesn't really like the name Drum & Bass, finding it restrictive: "Since it has become Drum & Bass that is what the music has become. What I find most interesting is all the other elements aside from the drums and bass." Unlike other producers, Lincoln doesn't start with the b-line or drums when he's constructing a tune. He'll start by using a musical hook and try to find drum and basslines to fit. He has the knack of finding interesting samples. Listening to tracks he first made, Lincoln can hear that the essence of his ideas was there even though his technical ability was lacking: "I never thought that this thing would become a career. Instead of watching films all the time I was on a computer every day. I managed to fob my way through university Film School and got a 2:1 out of it. I signed with Hospital just as I was finishing the course." His first album *True Colours* garnered plaudits from all-comers. When Fabio played *Return Of Forever* at Glastonbury 2003 I swear my vision went widescreen catching ravers tramping through trees and wood smoke. For his second album, *High Society*, Lincoln's literally moved from the basement to the rooftops where he's triumphed once again. It's fitting that the cover of *High Society* was shot on Herbal's roof. He's sitting there with *savoir-faire* — only John B rivals his wonderful big hair. After our interview High Contrast rolls a sneak preview of the promo video he's made for *Racing Green*. It's a brilliantly crafted tribute to Stanley Kubrick's classic film *The Shining*. I reckon the University of Cardiff should give High Contrast a Doctorate in music. He's already earned it.

CLAYTON — TROUBLE ON VINYL

After his Acid House days Clayton wanted to release records. In '92 he and partner Mark took a series of courses in sound engineering and music business management. By '93 they'd made their first tune, Reinforced were their inspiration: "I looked at what they had done and thought, 'They're young, black, from the inner-city. Why can't we do what they've done?'" In true style they borrowed money, clubbed together and bought some studio equipment: "Our studio was in a friend's front room but there were too many restrictions. He went to work at nine so we had to be there at nine, out by five. You couldn't make no noise because of the neighbours. That went on it for about eight months but we released four tunes."

You might not have liked their music but you would have remembered their bright fluorescent artwork. They left their mate's front room and set up store in a former antiques shop: "In '93 we started Trouble On Vinyl, in'94 we started Renegade Recordings and in'95 we started Hardware. Trouble On Vinyl is your straight-up party tunes. Back then it was more their Hip-Hop / Rap influenced. Jump-up as they say today. Renegade Recordings is the Liquid Funk. Hardware is of your more futuristic dark side. We were the first label to have three different sorts of imprints to cater for different sides of the scene. We started getting recognition about '96. It was a long slog. For Trouble On Vinyl it was our seventh or eighth release that got us known. For Hardware it was our fourth tune and Renegade Recordings it was probably our fifth or sixth tune. We've been in it for a long time and there are not many labels that have been around as long as us. Each of our three labels are up to about release number 55. On Hardware and TOV we've done five albums each and on Renegade we're on our third album. We've released a lot of tunes and I think that's why we get so much recognition. We picked up Best Label at the *Knowledge* Awards in 2003. We are one of the few labels that are very consistent."

TOV are starting a new project, a DVD magazine: "Its called *Code Of The Streets* and it's going to have interviews and features with everyone in Drum & Bass – artists, producers, MCs. It's basically a magazine but more visually stimulating. You can only get so much from an interview; with this you hear it literally from the horse's mouth. Plus I think that DVDs are the way forward. People want to see stuff instead of just reading about it. When Drum & Bass is long gone, when they're talking about the pioneers, I hope they'll mention us."

THE RIGHT CALIBRE

Unfortunately there isn't space enough to honour the vast variety of producers past and present. If I did this book would be larger than a telephone directory. But there was one person who I couldn't miss out.

"You ask a lot of artists. I think he's probably the most important artist in the last few years. I think this guy is the most important artist of the lot. He's not going to admit it but this guy is as close to genius as you can get in production of Drum & Bass." FABIO

Calibre. Where do I begin with Calibre? His music underscores so much of my life. It's funny because the first time we met I didn't have a clue who he was. Embarrassing I know, but there you go. Lars and Pamela, owners of Berlin's Icon club, invited me to play. This DJ on before me strayed 15 minutes into my hour. I was nervous – agitated, just wanting to get my set over with. Consequently, I wasn't really listening to the music. God if I had known then what I now know I would have said, "Keep playing mate. Have my hour. Watch mi tunes. I'll be up front dancing."

Fabio and Flight champion him but it's not like they've had to force his sound upon us. He guested on Fabio's show in September 2004. During each track I was thinking, 'Yep. I'll have that one and that one and oooh – especially that one.' Belfast resident Dominic encapsulates a Reggae passion. On a recent visit to London he took a spiritual journey catching Reggae Don Mikey Dread on a Notting Hill Carnival sound system.

Calibre's tunes masterfully hug your body with cool Jamaican riddims. Pretenders try to copy his style. They usually fail to understand the source from whence the samples came, producing lacklustre imitations. He's deep, real deep. Even though you recognise his sound, he's definitely not in the same old same old groove. That's a mad level to achieve. And when Rider drops a Calibre tune down a side street at the Shoreditch Festival, the groove armada groove that special moment. One tragedy is that Dominic has stacks and stacks of unreleased material. Please don't go to your grave as Miles Davis did with a mountain of unreleased material stashed away. We need your music.

Choppage, Edits, Drum Funk —
Whatever You Want to Call it ...

It's cards on the table time again. The fact is I can't do edits. Something odd happens in my head. I tried listening to Paradox on L Double's show. I didn't last ten minutes and I tried really hard. Music has a powerful effect on me. And broken beats leave me somewhat discombobulated and my brain needs re-booting. I'm not dissing the sub-genre. I appreciate the amount of time and expertise that underlie the fundamental Art of Choppage. Many people love these tunes but I guess they're not part of my Journey through Jungle Drum & Bass Culture. Bailey plays them because they're challenging. But respect goes out to Chris Inperspective, Paradox, Breakage, Fracture & Neptune, *et al.* "Sorry Bailey." "For what?" "You'll see ..."

Music House Not Cuttin' it?

"You'd leave Holloway Road and walk straight into this old Jamaican shack." PAM, MILTON KEYNES

Time is more precious than ever. And people expect more for their money. I loved Music House but I never had to queue there all day waiting to cut a tune — DJ SS did. "The thing with Music House is that they got a bit sloppy. That was their mistake. You would go there, into those small rooms, a bit shabby, no comforts. You think they would fix up the place, bring in a little entertainment, cos they were making change. Man's travelled from Scotland. Foreign man used to come to Music House. I've seen man from America, Finland, Germany at Music House all in a big queue. Don't get me wrong cos I love them mans to death. But you would be there all day then have to drive home late when I could be making a tune or playing with my kids. Them days of just sitting about are done."

In so many other areas of the scene people have grown up, fixed up and become more professional. Now the top places for cutting plates are Heathmans, Transition and our old friends Metropolis. DJ SS is one top producer amongst others who've taken their custom elsewhere: "Heathmans are killing it. You can email them a tune — don't even have to leave your home. Blam! They cut it and send it back to your yard next day. You're not wasting no time."

Vegas misses the old days: "You used to go down there and see a lot of DJs and producers. There would be a little buzz. When the tune is cutting and all of the proper heads are there and they all suddenly react to a tune, it can make a tune that day — while it's being cut." That community has gone. Nowadays producers don't meet as they once did. The communication network is AIM. There are other instant messaging software programs to choose from but AIM is the industry's choice. People speak in real time with each other. Producers send their tunes through AIM. Convenient, yes, but exclusive dub plate bizniz it ain't. There's some disquiet about DJs having tunes they shouldn't have but do. Though that's nothing new.

"I remember going to Music House — people used to thief your DATs and cut stuff they weren't supposed to. It was messy but fun. It was an open house for DJs. You'd be smoking and chilling — having a joke and gossiping. Nothing's changed, except now it's all done on AIM. AIM is the new Music House." FABIO

POINT OF SALE

I'm in Black Market Records on a dull, rainy Tuesday afternoon ostensibly to collect a bunch of flyers and catch up with Nicky and Miss Pink. I'm definitely not buying any tunes. Absolutely not. End of month poverty 'n' all that. Warm funky House sounds pulse through the ground floor. Keisha is sorting tickets and stacking merchandise at the rear of the shop. Downstairs is my Drum & Bass home from home. Do all of us love a basement venue or is it just me?

Black Market was re-designed in 2001. Its nicely frosted glass and designer black interior is the model of a DJ friendly shop. The counter is inset with rows of amps, headphones and Technics decks. By each turntable there's a pocket to stash the tunes plucked from racks on the walls and a kaleidoscope of labels and stables cover those walls. Around the corner there are a few mix CDs – Black Market specials. Between shuffling staff, tunes, his mobile and a well-thumbed diary, Nicky beams the best smile in Drum & Bass. Miss Pink is the first woman to sell JDB at Black Market. She offers advice to customers, dishes out discs to punters buying JDB and Garage and still finds time to play tunes through the JBL speakers.

January through February can be a little slow for new releases. Then comes the flood. Ram, Breakbeat Kaos, Dread, Beta, Valve, Ebony, Formation, Virus, Prototype, V Recordings, Full Cycle, Congo Natty … and on and on. A Russian female punter expertly beckons a list of tunes from the racks. The geezer next to me plays a tune. I hear it buzz in his headphones.

I suddenly come over all desperate and tap his arm: "Oi mate, what's that tune?" I'd been in the shop weeks before trying to sing the chorus of Concord Dawn's *Don't Tell Me* to laughs from staff and punters. But I had to have that tune. Just the one. "And errr, that Tali tune *Blazin'*, the Shy FX & T Power remix." Love that Reggae rhythm. Clarky hands me the tunes. "Do you take plastic?"

That's the trouble with record addiction. You start off buying the odd 12" and before you know it you're on to EPs, LPs and double disc CD mix compilations. After breaking the promise I made to myself I know I'll feel guilty when I hit the streets with the merchandise stashed in a clear plastic bag. Leaving Black Market I'm halted at the door as the rainstorm becomes a hailstorm. Shit, I never know what the weather's playing at nowadays. I'm always getting my clothes wrong. A geezer, head down, hood up bowls in and we almost crash into each other. He looks up: "EZ B." "Randall." We greet in a confusion of hugs and handshakes. Fluently punching his number into my Nokia he says, "Call me," before disappearing into the shop. Walking back through Soho in the rain with my tunes I was feeling that going to Black Market was always an event. It's difficult to remember a time before Black Market existed. Shame if it all became a virtual reality.

Desperately Seeking Promos

Black Market sells more white labels than finished copies. And that's no indicator of the amount to order – so called pre-sales. If shops over order, they're stuck with the stock. For some customers, especially the youths, getting hold of promos is essential. It's far cooler to be seen playing white labels than records with finished artwork. This demand has led to problems on the supply side. Although DJ Bailey listed new releases during *The Shipping News* slot on his 1Xtra show, he acknowledged that a fair few people already know which new releases are due out each week. He now plays three tunes from the list. Record shops receive a limited number of promos. Although Black Market suggests that you can buy anything in the shop online, Miss Pink knows that's not the case:

"Within half an hour of us putting a new hot promo on the site we will have sold five times as many copies as we have physically in the shop. Then we don't have any copies to give to customers because they have all sold online. There was a lot of bitching about us. We'd put stuff up but disguise the name and put it in as something stupid. But people would notice and think that if it's got a stupid name it must be hot stuff. Someone inevitably will get Black Market's distribution schedule and post on the net what's due in the shop that week. We'd get people phoning up and asking, "Have you had the promos from SRD?" And if I said, "Yes" they'd be going, "Why isn't it on the site?" It's a no-win situation.

"It's ridiculous. There was one day when me and Nicky were literally hiding under the counter. It's embarrassing. We'd had some stuff in. Nicky was going, "How can I stand up and say, "You can have one of these, but you can't." It's like that. This week has been very bad because Shy FX & T Power's track *Number One* has been a big, big tune. The tunes arrive in the shop that morning. Clive who used to work in the shop rang up asking for a copy. The guys from Social Security on Hospital rang. Certain people had phoned already and said, "Can you put one aside for me?" We've got ten copies. Ash had already been in. Then Clarky phones up, he needed a copy. There are about 10 - 15 people who come in every week and spend a good deal of money so we need to sort them. A lot of people who are doing radio need them because they're playing during the week."

It's also out of the producers' hands. Most big tunes are supplied by distributors who could press more white label copies for retail. But it's difficult to predict how many to manufacture against finished discs on the record's actual release. Punters might already own the white label. Nicky hassled the distributors, "Look we supported you all this time, you have to sort us out." And distributors now provide Black Market with far more copies.

Demand for promos ahead of finished copies in Drum & Bass is so much greater than in other genres. House fans will wait for finished copies. To a certain extent it's down to teenage desire. They'll snap up any white label. Miss Pink knows only too well: "They are really into the white label thing. Doesn't matter what the music is like. It's the belief that if you are playing something on white label it's going to be good. It's ridiculous. Tomorrow I guarantee we're going to get 15 - 20 kids coming to buy records and all they want to know, "Is it a promo?" You could say to them, "Have you got everything on the wall? Have you listened to everything? Do you know all this stuff?" But they are not interested."

Always There?

It's a difficult time for independent record shops. Many D&B stores have closed failing to live long or prosper. London is one of the most expensive cities in the world to live and work in. Overheads are high and it's difficult for businesses to survive. There are a fair few customers buying tunes to play as DJs or aspiring DJs. If you feel that because of the scene's stagnation you're not going to get a chance to play and build a career then what's the point of buying tunes? And then there's the competition. Wednesday afternoon in June and Black Market seems ever quieter. Perhaps it's just a phase but Miss Pink's noticed that Saturdays aren't what they used to be. The massive from in and out of town no longer congregate in D&B's holiest of the holy as they once did.

Page three of *Knowledge* provides some answers. It's obscene. Bare, bold, sassy, indecently stripped down for all to see, an ad for HMV. '3 for £10 − Buy any three classic Renegade Hardware singles on 12" for £10 or £3.99 each. Buy now: www.hmv.co.uk'. I'd long since forgotten when you could buy a 12" for under a fiver. When prices crept over that nice round £5 mark, it was only by a few pence but you'd start feeling it. Black Market try to keep prices down but one of the shop's owners feels, "If you're a DJ and you need that record, you'll pay for it." It's an economic truth that the bigger you are, the more financial clout you have. Independent shops can't offer the same deals as majors who benefit hugely from sale or return (SOR) deals. Nor can independent shops hold huge amounts of stock for customers to eventually purchase. I must confess that after Ray said, "Sorry man we ain't got none left − but we can order it for you ..." I went to HMV on Oxford Street and bought the tune there. It felt sacrilegious, like dissing The Church.

His Master's Voice − HMV Oxford Street is the oldest record shop in the World. There was a time when you'd have to book an appointment before arriving to listen to your record in a private booth. Nowadays some people shamelessly do their listening in Black Market and their purchasing in HMV. HMV state that they're "Maintaining a commitment to vinyl." Many people can't make the trip into central London and have been forced to be more pragmatic.

"I buy my tunes on the Internet. All my little local record shops are shutting down. When you live on the outskirts of London going into town is a bit of a trek. I have to travel an hour and a half before I can get to a fuckin' record shop. I miss going to the record shops and hanging out." DJ E, RUDE FM

But what about the record shops? What about The Church?" Clayton from Trouble On Vinyl sighs with some regret: "The record shops make the most mark-up out of everyone. I've not exactly got a violin out for them. They have got to keep up with the times too. If you don't embrace technology you'll get left behind. You'll be like a dinosaur."

SURFING

Know how it is, you're home alone surfing the Net finding your fingers walking over your keys' desire. No one will know. I know it's naughty but ... 'Go' Red Eye, Ipswich. OK I'm gonna buy tunes online but please conceal my purchases in a brown envelope. In some ways I admit being conservative with a small c. Perhaps I don't like change. I value loyalty but have come to understand in business terms that's not always the most economical way to go. I've been at the 'World's Local Bank' for 15 years. They give a fair service; occasionally sort out more cash if I need it. But I haven't checked for deals elsewhere. Nowadays loads of people are on the '0% interest on all current account balance transfers' thing and any deal that benefits their pocket. It's all about better deals and more choice. With a full time job and being a father, not unlike many others, DJ E can't spend a Saturday travelling to central London for tunes. I have mobility problems. It's getting to be a long walk from Oxford Circus to Black Market and it's difficult finding the time. But I'll emphasise that as long as the shop is there I'll pay Nicky *et al* an occasional visit.

CHANGES

We generally have more choice. I'd love to support independent stores like Black Market forever but my resources are limited. I felt bad about buying tunes in HMV as I didn't feel my cash was staying within the scene. Tunes from Juno, Red Eye, Drum & Bass Arena and Chemical, purveyors of music to the JDB masses, that's a different matter. So I logged on. I timed how long it would take to buy a record and I clicked the 'Buy' icon in less time than it would have taken to reach the underground station. I soon forgot the stopwatch consumed by listening to the huge variety of tunes Red Eye had on their site. Navigating their pages and finding music was child's play. Everything was so frighteningly easy.

NOW HOW DID THEY DO THAT?

Chemical Records are one of the largest Internet record shops and are based in Cheltenham and Bristol. They supply over ten different genres of music as well as the usual Dance Music accessories. Their online store is easy to navigate and you're able to preview most of tunes you'd like to buy. Good businesses develop in stages. Back in '97 Tom's record shop Red Eye in Ipswich started selling tunes by mail order. They went on-line in '99 with the aide of a friend talented in web design. Red Eye received a stack of orders overnight. Tom saw the potential and they grew nicely filling a niche. Red Eye the shop is still on the high street. Staff use the normal postal system to dispatch packages. Red Eye has customers from all over the world. My order arrives by the next morning.

"60% of our customers come from outside the UK with Europe, USA, Canada and Australasia being the strongest. The rest are in the UK. Being a comparatively big business to a normal bricks and mortar we have the opportunity to keep everything that is available in stock. People use us and other similar stores to pick up bits and bobs they can't get elsewhere, even if they don't do much shopping online." TOM, RED EYE

B: Sorry to ask but how do you feel about the probable demise of shops like Black Market and other independent record shops?
T: Guilty, but what can I do about it? If you ask around the distributors I have gone to great lengths to stop online stores having exclusives etc. I want there to be a level playing field.
B: Are you having an affect on the distributors? A few like Vinyl and Alphamagic have closed down.
T: Not apart from being their best payers / customers, no. The reason they go down is bad management and bad payers.

It's sad to hear businesses have gone to the wall. 'Bad management and bad payers,' I agree with Tom. My dealings with Alphamagic were particularly tortuous. Dylan received copies of *All Crew* for sale through the company. After he left I found it nearly impossible to reach a responsible party by phone. They took months to pay up – if at all. I visited them and found a lazy office with some guys perusing Internet porn. When I eventually managed to speak to the company boss about missing stock, it'd be correct to say that he behaved like a cunt. What goes around comes around.

NO POINT OF SALE?

There's a bewildering array of formats and equipment through which to access music. AM, FM, Cable, Vinyl, cassette, PC, CD, DAT, MiniDisc, MP3, DVD, DAB, mobile phones, iPod – have I missed anything? Thanks to Dance Music Culture, vinyl should be around for a time to come. Cassettes? If you're anything like me you'll probably have bags of them stashed around the house. Remember tapes twisting into knots and snapping? And it would take an eternity to find the track you wanted let alone do a rewind. The Digital revolution changed all that giving us comparatively instant access. As it was in the past so it is now, companies also give us tools to speedily reproduce copies. Loads of copies. As access to the Internet via broadband increased, global music sales fell for the fourth successive year. The International Federation of the Phonographic Industry (IFPI), a music trade group representing firms including: Warner Music, Sony BMG, EMI and Universal reported that the market had declined by 7.6% ($17.5bn), an acceleration of the 7.2% fall in 2002. Aside from copying CDs, file sharing and piracy were also blamed for causing the biggest fall in sales since the launch of the Compact Disc in the 80s. But there's an overwhelming belief that the music business has only itself to blame. It was slow to move in this Internet age and was left playing catch-up. That's if they can ever catch the electronically literate younger generations with little money and a taste for free music. I contacted Ms. Louise Finkle Head of Music at a North London school and spoke to some of her 13 - 15 year old students.

Back to school and lunch time. It's sunny outside in the playground. A steadily growing group of well-behaved kids in school uniform fill the classroom. There's a drum kit centre floor and posters citing a list of past and present good tunes is blu-tacked to the door. Decorum flies out the window when I set down a carrier bag full of fizzy drinks. It's everyone for themselves as all the cans disappear in seconds.

B: What kind of music are you all into?
Emma: R'n'B, Hip Hop, Bashment, Garage and Soul.
B: Are you working or getting an allowance from your parents? I just wanted to ask cos the more money you have, the more access to music you'll have. What access do you have to money?
All: An allowance …

B: How much are we talking about on average?

All: About a tenner a week.

B: £10 a week doesn't pay for a CD album.

All: Naaaa ...

B: So if you want to get hold of music and you don't wanna or can't go down HMV or anywhere, how do you get hold of tunes?

Ben & Matt: Kazaa

Emma: You download them.

A whispering voice: Yeah but it's illegal innit.

B: How do you feel about the artists not being paid?

Ben: Tell them to sell 'em cheaper.

B: So do you feel CDs are over priced?

All: Yeah.

Ben: Someone told me it costs 5p to make a CD and they're selling them for £13.

B: Would you visit sites that sell music for a pound?

All: Uh-a. No. Naaa. (Lots of head shaking – faces saying it ain't gonna happen.)

Emma: If you know you don't have to pay for it then you don't think about it.

B: So there's no going back on that one?

All: No (More heads shaking.)

B: What about ringtones?

Matt: We used to but that's old.

Emma: You'd be like "Oh, send that to me, send that to me."

B: How did you get hold of them?

Ben: Internet but someone knows someone who knows someone.

Emma and all: That knows someone that knows someone ...

Matt: Or you compose it.

B: So again you're not paying for it?

All: Naaaaaa

No surprises there then and more power to 'em. Peer-to-peer filesharing software sites like Kazaa make it possible to watch MTV Base then download a track in minutes. The IFPI lost its case against Kazaa in the Dutch Supreme court, the highest European court to have tackled this issue. Their judgement means that companies who provided peer-sharing software can't be made responsible for what customers do with their product. Firms who produce video recorders can't be made responsible for pirate copies. With 17.5 million users Kazaa is the largest filesharing network.

Millions of tunes are exchanged every day. As a consequence, EMI were forced to axe 1,500 jobs last spring. A report commissioned by the British Phonographic Industry revealed that over seven million people in Britain have downloaded music illegally. The research demonstrated a direct correlation between illegal downloading and falling record sales. Figures in 2002 revealed that individuals downloading music spent 31% less on albums and 59% less on singles.

The BPI admits they've underestimated the size of the problem and would launch legal procedures against suspected lawbreakers – even if they were teenagers. BPI chair Peter Jamieson said, "There is no clearer evidence of the damage that illegal downloading is doing to British Music and the British Music industry. Illegal file-sharing is causing real financial damage to artists, songwriters, record companies, publishers, retailers and everyone involved in the business." They'd prefer customers to visit legal sites and pay £1 per tune downloaded. To drive the point home last March the IFPI launched 247 legal cases against alleged culprits in Canada, Germany, Italy and Denmark. Not to be outdone, The Recording Industry Association of America filled 1,997 lawsuits in September 2003.

In an attempt to re-capture the market the BPI are launching an official download chart. Radio station GWR introduced a service in which you can legally download tunes. Hear It Buy It Burn It allows you to do just that and has been used by thousands of listeners each week. With the advent of gadgets like the iPod, artists and radio stations are in competition for your listening time. They'll have to evolve or become maybe not extinct but irrelevant to would be listeners. Clayton at TOV has an eye on the future: "The internet is costing us record sales. People can go to illegal sites and download our music without paying for it. It pisses you off but it's just part and parcel of the business. We've set up an online shop, which has been really successful. We've cut out the distributor and record shops."

Keeping ahead of the law will always provide sport. The technological genie is well and truly out of the bottle.

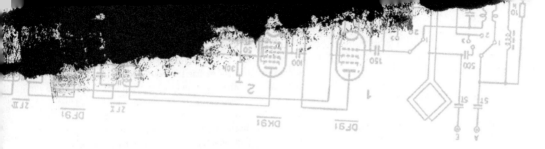

WIRELESS

"I have to take my hat off to the BBC. They have done a great job as far as Drum & Bass is concerned with Fabio & Grooverider's Show, 1Xtra, even their mainstream shows. Mary Anne Hobbs, Jo Whiley and Annie Nightingale all play Drum & Bass. Even Sarah Cox plays it. It's great." TANIA UMC

Fabio & Grooverider continue to fly the Drum & Bass flag high on Radio 1. Both their shows are extremely entertaining and educational with a host of interviews. They'll cover everything from the latest quality producer to the scandal of Stamp Duty when you're buying and selling a house. You find yourself thinking, 'I never knew that.' Groove arrives announcing, "This is Rider Radio!" threatening to, "Shut the place down." When he loves a tune – he loves it. The interplay between him and producer Mike over *Odyssey* was hilarious. DJs desperate for the track called Rider. And Groove sang an on-air reply, "Don't-ring my-phone" to the tune of *Odyssey*.

"We're going into our sixth year now. I use it as a gateway like the Internet where people can upload their shit. It's a means to talk to everybody who's listening to this music and wants to know more. I try to explain what the music actually is about. At the end of they day it's about what gets on the dance floor, but it's not always like that. There are certain tunes that are not meant for the dance floor cos we have that side of our music as well. You get to express that side of music as well." *GROOVERIDER*

I've few criticisms of the BBC regarding Fabio & Grooverider on Radio 1, but Drum & Bass has done its time on the graveyard shift. They should have an evening show.

BBC 1XTRA – IT'S A STREET MUSIC TING Y'ALL

"I listen to 1Xtra – that's where I make my music for. The one thing that Drum & Bass never had before is a home, but we have now." RONI SIZE

It's not often that technologies arrive to provide us with a plethora of new radio and television stations. Back in '95 / '96 Beeb technicians kept going on about bandwidth, broadband and the huge possibilities it would provide. It wasn't until mates bought computers, had their homes wired, started downloading music and listening to new stations that I began to understand. I signed up after hearing satellite and cable also gave access. Catching Bailey's Sunday show I knew I'd been missing out. 1Xtra had a whole different feel. When some people called it, 'Pirate for Grown-ups' they weren't being derogatory. The station represents an impressive number of black music genres including D&B, Garage, Hip Hop, Dancehall, R'n'B, Soulful House, Soca … All transmitted digitally across the globe. I've spoken to people in Russia and Australia who regularly log-on to 1Xtra and Radio 1 shows. 1Xtra carries the BBC's stamp of approval without the corporation's stuffiness. Kiss FM is down to Hype and Adam F who play alternately on Saturday nights, but 1Xtra are taking things forward. This crew had to be checked out.

Ray Paul, recruited from BBC London, now Executive Producer of Specialist Shows & Live Music at 1Xtra, explained how the BBC decided that it would venture into digital radio and create stations such as 1Xtra to satisfy different niche markets: "A team of specialists was drawn together to form 1Xtra. All had worked in black music for a number of years in different roles around the country. The core team spent 18 months building 1Xtra." When recruiting staff they scoured the country's universities and clubs for

L Double

prospective employees. Applicants didn't necessarily see themselves as BBC people but they all loved black music and radio: "We looked at the best talent around. It took a long time to set up what we wanted, what the BBC wanted and, more importantly, what the audience wanted." L Double remembers the early days: "They didn't even have a name for it when Willber Willberforce [Programmes Editor] called me. First it was gonna be Urban, then it was going to be Station X and then it was 1Xtra. It was just a concept."

L was cautious because of his previous radio experiences where he found that despite good ratings, Drum & Bass was accorded less importance than other music genres. However Double knew that Willber had lobbied hard to get things together so he went along with it. Willber approached Lee asking what kind of show he'd like to have and listened. Double rolled out his ideas and the man from the BBC said, "Yes." A team of people brainstormed for months creating the right format. Marching through to their second year, L Double's Tuesday slot *Connexions* is the station's flagship Drum & Bass show. 1Xtra's definitive chart is determined by listeners' purchases in shops around the UK. Broadcast teams update the playlist. Another popular feature is *The Cutting Room*. Aspiring producers are asked to send in their demos to the station. The best three of the week are posted online and listeners vote for their favourite track. The winning tune is played in full on L Double's show. The audience picks the best from the Top 20 at the end of the year. Several winners have gone on to release their professionally mastered tracks, achieving success on the Drum & Bass scene.

Ray isn't fond of the 'pirate station for grown ups' tag. 1Xtra has the edge pirates have but its production values are far higher: "The ethos of what we do probably stems from pirate radio purely because of the music we cover. But in terms of production we've got the BBC hallmark." From Ray's experience the poor presentation of black music in the past has worked against it: "Speaking personally as someone who's worked in radio for 15 years, I think one of the problems which has let black music down is the presentation of it. We try to not let standards slip. All of us have worked on non-black music radio. I know how it is to produce a Rock show. I strive for that standard on my shows. I don't accept the argument, "Oh it's a Rap show and that's par for the course." We should have the same exacting standards.

"In no order our five main genres are Hip Hop, R'n'B, Drum & Bass, UK Garage and Dancehall. D&B has three hours on a Tuesday with L, two hours with Flight on Wednesday, two hours with Bailey on Sunday, in addition Sappo and Friction present a four hour mix show on Thursdays. All of those shows are non-playlisted and cover the whole spectrum of Drum & Bass. On top of that we also have D&B throughout the day. Like any other station it's how it fits with the rest of the station. If something is a little bit too spiky it may stand out like a sore thumb and you'll do it a disservice."

The atmosphere at 1Xtra is relaxed and unstuffy. Staff and managers stop to chat in corridors about certain tracks. DJs pass by just to hang out because it's a good place to be. In fact it's hard to tell staff and DJs apart. They have the same enthusiasm for music and a genuine passion and love. 1Xtra DJs and production staff aren't afraid to break the mould. One night I logged onto Bailey's show and thought I'd found the wrong station. A '94 / '95 back-to-back four hour session with Bailey, the Heartless Crew, Shabba D and Navigator bust through the PC. Proppa.

BAILEY – HE'S ABSOLUTELY GOOD YA KNOW

Yalding House, Great Portland Street, Sunday June 13th. A visitor's badge is pinned to my t-shirt. I'm back at the BBC. Radio 1 is in the basement. 1Xtra is on the third floor; its logos wrapped around the windows. The coloured ring around BT's tower glows above the rooftops. Bailey and I are doing the interview in a quiet blue room. 22.50 Dave King the producer of the D&B shows pops his head around the door: "Five minutes Bailey." 1Xtra is run from one floor and broadcast from one studio. Beyond the glass the Heartless Crew play their last tune as Bailey slides in. Dave explains, "We're hot-desking so if you wait till the Heartless Crew come out …" Although the show is broadcast throughout the floor we're blasted by live sounds as one of the boys emerges from the studio. Scant minutes before eleven we bundle in quietly. It's moderately plush and air-conditioned. Walls lined with perforated metal sheets swallow sound.

The medium-sized square room is divided by a curving desk behind which sits the broadcast assistant Uche Uchendu. He's gifted with an encyclopaedic knowledge of JDB and is training to be a producer, driving the show as Dave is at present. During the shows Uche posts track details online and handles listeners texts and emails. Dave sits turning on a chair behind the desk surrounded by studio hardware. Behind him Bailey rolls his first tunes. Jingles and effects embroider the music. Phat microphones branded with 1Xtra's logos hang in vibration free elastic cradles in front of all our faces. He gesticulates as his mic is open to the digital world, "It's Bailey LIVE …" – His voice is too loud. In microseconds Dave shoots arms out like an octopus reducing the volume. "It's Bailey live on 1Xtra. Sunday eleven 'til one, rolling out Drum & Bass stylee." Very tidy.

Studio etiquette dictates radio silence when the mic is open. Otherwise listeners might hear an unprofessional rabble in the background. To catch Bailey over the music we have to wear headphones. "Yeah man. Summer flavour you know what I mean? It's comin' nice and easy." A beautiful track called *Incanto* by Visionary flows underneath with a Brazilian flavour. "Now I played a few tracks last week on a Dubwise tip and let me tell you something, there's a lot of Dubwise around at the moment. Expect a delivery real soon. That seems to be the vibe of the producers at the moment. And you're gonna hear it here first."

Bailey breaks the show down informing listeners of regular features like *The Shipping News* and *The Predictor Track*. He singles out a track that should do really well and asks listeners, "Do you think this track will be big? Text me on 88111." I didn't expect Bailey to be DJing facing a wall. It reminded me of doing shows on

pirates with the decks resting on a draining board. But similarities to pirate radio end there. This crew are as professional as professional can be. There are three Technics decks and a couple of Pioneer CD players. Consoles around Dave are crammed with old skool equipment – carts, MiniDisc and CD players, all soon to be replaced by a fully digital studio.

Behind the tracks Dave, Uche and Bailey fine-tune the show. They ensure that all sound levels are correct, checking tunes in pre-fade, that all relevant information is broadcast and ward off any deafening silences caused by stuttering CDs. Bailey warns us that he'll be rolling into a dark mix. The webcam shows the studio and the backs of our heads. "Right going live," Bailey warns before he fades up the mic. We hear "This is a world exclusive," saluting a Concord Dawn track before Bailey slips into the 30 minute mix with Dillinja's *Precious*. A few people from the office dance outside the large studio window.

Bailey started listening to Hip Hop and Electro in the early 80s when still in school. He'd watch Westwood on TV back in the days of *Ensign Radio* and record any program showing DJs scratching. But like many people the only access he had to equipment was his mum's hi-fi. He bought cheap decks but knew a friend with Technics: "I used to go round his house and wake him out of bed every morning. He used to sleep in this bedsit and would go back to bed and I'd be mixing on these decks." The same guy owned a small sound system, which Bailey would help set up and play on: "Boogie Bunch and Rampage sound systems were all over the place. I wanted to break through but if you weren't in a crew it was hard work. I was on my own. I don't have no Hip Hop crew." Luckily Bailey's resourceful contact also set up a pirate radio station, which Bailey broadcast from. He also introduced Bailey to House music in '88, which he loved, but it was '91 before he went to a club.

Bailey

One contact led to another and Bailey met MC Flux on the station. At the time Flux was MCing for Grooverider and Bailey started going on the road with the pair. They hit Moving Shadow's night Voodoo Magic where Flux introduced Bailey to Kemistry & Storm, mentioning that he DJed on a pirate station: "I was playing and they called saying, "Nice set." I was like, "What? Kemistry & Storm are listening to me on some no-name pirate station?!" I was excited. They called me in the week saying, "We're starting up this thing called Metalheadz," asking if I wanted to be involved." Bailey became one of the residents at the Blue Note alongside the Loxy, Ink, Clarky and Marly Marl on rotation once a month. Staying on top of his game, in the second year of the new millennium Bailey got a call from the BBC. This time around he knew this could mean big tings:

"There was a period where I came into the Radio 1 studios downstairs and did a lot of pilots. I didn't know what was going on at first. They invited me in to do some pilots and see what I was like. As far as I knew they had a lot of other people coming in. I was thinking that sooner or later it might be a case of, "Sorry but you're not good enough." But I just kept coming in and coming in and one day they just said, "Yeah, we want you as part of the team." Nothing could have made me happier than that."

It's been a great show and Bailey plays the last few tracks and Choppage beats flood the studio. I remember that I haven't told Bailey about the Choppage thing and me. I'm typing away on the laptop trying not to listen but Bailey draws me in mentioning All Crew — referring to it as The Bible of D&B. A cloud of writer's block descends around me and my brain is lacerated by shards of broken beats. Suddenly Bailey, live on air, online, across the globe is asking what I think of the track. I manage a very weak, "Errr well — I errr … well … I'm not really feeling it Bailey." I wish I had a picture of both our faces.

FLIGHT'S NEXT CHAPTER

Frankfurt's DJ Simon tells me to look out for this DJ called Flight. A few years later I'm sitting in the 1Xtra office as Dave and Flight run through the final details of her Wednesday night Next Chapter show. The two hours from ten 'til twelve are printed on A4 paper and depicted in the form of a pie chart; 60 minutes equals 360 degrees. They did that back in my days at One in the Jungle. Saves everyone trying to keep everything their head. Flight's been away for a couple of weeks and there are loads of items to cram into two hours.

Her first tune is a jazzy number followed by Calibre's Can't Stop the Fire. "I'm going in," Flight warns. It's headphones on and our silence. She announces the Breaking New Talent slot, then deftly mixes from vinyl to CD. Uche steps out to collect tonight's special guest from reception. We're into the monthly Guest Mix. Flight chooses the best set sent in by listeners. This month it's by DJ Psylence. It's not an exaggeration to describe Flight's rise in D&B as meteoric. She's had skill and luck along the way as many people do. However not many people end up with residencies at Metalheadz and Swerve and a prime show on 1Xtra — even though she initially refused to use the mic.

Flight was introduced to 1Xtra through Rachel, one of the station's original producers. Like many of us she hadn't been paying too much attention to all the chat about digital radio but was invited into the studio to record a series of demos. There was one persistent problem. Her music was great but just like on the pirate shows Flight refused to approach the microphone: "I never used to go on the mic. There was two hours of music and that was it. We used to get calls and texts for shouts and I wouldn't do them. I did not want to get on the mic." 1Xtra approached its launch: "I had to come in a month before the August 2002 launch. Rachel called and asked, "Can you come in and do a show next week?" "What?" I was so sick. It was horrible.

My hands were shaking and I had to have a little miniature Jack Daniels to get through it." Flight hails Rebecca as she walks through the office: "Remember how nervous I was?" Rebecca was the broadcast assistant for Flight's early shows. Flight covered other 1Xtra Drum & Bass shows, later hosting the first *Final Chapter* program after the station's launch. Rebecca reminisces: "The minute you got that first text message and realised that there was someone listening, I remember you being quite excited." They both laugh. Flight learned to use the mic eventually, realising that people actually liked hearing her. She has a very natural way of speaking on radio.

Shouts come in from Margate, Stoke, bigging up all people who went to Innovation in Spain. Uche returns with Breakage, Flight's special guest. She's thrilled to have him back in the UK after being away in Sydney and Adelaide. He's been chilling, playing Breaks and picking up an Australian twang. Flight had started producing tunes with Breakage and she's lined up an exclusive. So exclusive that Breakage hasn't got a copy himself. Flight has had many guests on her show and some of the interviews have been very controversial. It's refreshing to hear people in the scene speaking their mind rather than saying, "It's all good." The *Next Chapter* is always entertaining.

As it's my book I can get to write what I like – almost. Friends have said, "Oh you've written too much about 1Xtra." Like I'm doing them a promo, but you have to remember there was a time when we could only hear quality music on pirate radio. I come from the days when you'd have to string a wire from your beatbox to a curtain rail. The Beeb gives you Drum & Bass on tap – with some limitations. Their Internet Radio Player interface is awful. It's clunky, crashes and you can't rewind tunes. Even my mate Ben in Brisbane complains. So Fix Up.

PIRATE RADIO –
KEEPING THE HOME FIRES BURNING

"How would people know about raves? It's fundamental and we'll always use them. You've got to support the pirates. The risks they take just to be on air. Pirates are important and I don't think they get enough respect. Yes you have got Radio 1 and that's massive, but pirates support the local. They support the underground. A lot of the stars in the game today wouldn't be around if it wasn't for pirates."
BRET, TELEPATHY

THE ORIGINAL RUDE FM

Sunday 3am, Rude FM's in party mode. DJs Psylence, Effect, Haze, Jess and Lady Flava spin one tune each back-to-back. They're boisterous. One of the crew's on the mic, "We've all got work in the morning, but we don't care. We're 'ardcore. Right Fugee?" Cheers go up in the studio.

Researching the book takes me to some very unlikely places. Today I'm in court. I have a noon appointment with DJ E of Rude FM – the original Rude. There was an acrimonious spilt between the station's founders which has left the people involved with little to say to each other. Ruud Awakening is now managed by Syrus and showcases a wide range of music including Drum & Bass. DJ E has been on Rude for ten years straight. That probably places him in the top five of London's longest serving pirate radio DJs. We sit in a pub garden. He buys me a drink and we start talking. And the court business? He works there.

Rude broadcasts seven days a week 4pm to 9am. "Drum & Bass – that's what it's all about. I live it. It's like a religion. We've been doing our own thing like any pirate station. We make sure the rig goes up. We make sure that Ofcom, the new DTI people, are not about and all the rest of it. Make sure that you have got somewhere to broadcast from, all the usual pirate shit man. Nothing really changes. We are trying to get better. I think we're established now. Ofcom are proper on it but they can't get to us because we've got Fugee."

They seek him here, they seek him there, but they can't find Fugee anywhere. Fugee is one of London's longest serving pirate radio technicians, being in the game for almost 14 years. Ofcom know Fugee's name but they can never find him: "That's why we are always on and booming. He's always one step ahead of them. I've been on the station for over ten years. I love it. We've lost a couple of studios. That will be for legal reasons, because we had a couple of squats. But we have got proper places now, paying rent and everything. Squatting is difficult nowadays but we know people like councillors and shit. We get stuff sorted. As long as Fugee wants to come on we'll be on. He's up on the roof every other night. At the end of the day his first love is Rude FM." No disrespect to Fugee's girlfriend DJ Lady Flava. "We're still getting all the shouts and we have our regular listeners. We get shouts from outside London as well as Aylesbury, Southend, Ashford. We've got a big transmitter now." "Why still risk pirate radio when you could broadcast on the Net now?" "Cos not everyone has got a computer. Fair enough, with the Internet, Ofcom don't come after you. I prefer just switching on the radio and listening to a pirate." Astonishingly after 12 years on air Rude FM remains unnominated by Accelerated Cultures Awards.

ORIGIN FM

A sunny Friday afternoon. Mister T and EZM are 'round my back garden chatting about Origin FM. We've lost track of time and EZM realises he's late for his show. In a flash we're dodging traffic in the Beema. Along the way he's handling calls and pointing out illegal aerials on tower blocks: "You got single stacks and double stacks. See that one there? That goes straight up with the one bar that goes across? That's a single stack." "And what's the difference?" "Double stack handles more power." "God they're so obvious now you point them out. Surprised Ofcom don't pull it down." "Thing is they can't get the rig. It's pushed down somewhere tight with a car jack. Or we D lock it and they can't get to it. Rigs come with holes so you can put a D lock through 'em." All very clever. Then he mentions the tree: "Had a rig up in a tree once. It was there for ages. They never found it." "How d'ya get power to it?" "From a lamp post." "That's some old skool warehouse kinda business."

Fifteen minutes late we're driving quickly down London's side streets. EZM's uneasy. He's due to put the station on air for the weekend. Turning up the volume on the system tuned to Origin it's quiet: "If people switch on and hear that (silence) we'll lose listeners." We park up and head for the spot. It always makes me smile when a studio is located so cheekily. Bet the neighbours haven't got a clue. EZM's straight inside running Origin's station identity jingle. We're in a medium sized, two room set up. All the windows are shaded and the equipment's in one room. This gaff is tidy. It has a working loo, even the washing up in the kitchen has been done. EZM's on the mic welcoming London, opening with High Contrast and Calibre.

The decks, mixer and CD player are resting on a board perched on upturned filing cabinets. All output is channelled through a transmitter in a metal box sitting behind the Technics 1200. The rectangular room's slightly smaller than the 1Xtra studio. There's a poster on the wall announcing a forthcoming station meeting, neat diagrams showing DJs the correct mixer settings and one asking DJs and MCs to plug the events stuck on the boards behind the decks. Under a pair of small, wall mounted JBLs there are colourful posters and flyers advertising One Nation's Carnival After Party. On an adjacent wall there's a large map of London covered with a forest of coloured pins. Security is so low-key that you forget that you're in one of London's secret locations.

EZM's scratch mixing 5ive-O's intro to *Warning* using a Pioneer CD player: "This one's forthcoming on the *Dubplate Killaz* album. I tell ya, it's goin' to be large." The mobile buzzes with texts: "Hold tight Dean. Shout out to Paul in Dagenham. And out to the blingers on 658." When M plays *Dready* I have to ask for a rewind: "Goin' out to the Zy:on inside the ride." EZM gets a call from Vegas, the next DJ up. He'll be late: "Going out to Vegas. Get your skates on. All I've had to eat today is two Weetabix at breakfast and I'm hungry."

Vegas bowls in with apologies and records. He and EZM chat about a problem with the stylus. EZM repairs it with selloptape as the ad tape rolls by. After Vegas has rolled we're on the road travelling home in the back of the Beema. Vegas on the stereo spinnin' Brazilian flavours.

Tony, aka Mister T, formerly of Rude FM, founded Origin FM. He approached EZM for finances and general support. Tony was happy to leave Rude after being stuck on the graveyard slot for two years. He and EZM drew in a group of people who would fund the station. They included one of Desire's backers. Tony and EZM would be performing most of the hands-on activities. Tony had gained previous technical and logistical experience from being on Passion FM and Rude's management. EZM learned the ropes from Mister T: "How to set the aerials up, jack a rig – all the normal stuff to get things up and running." It was a time of great change and they felt mystically bound setting Origin up by the last day of the century. All of the station's newly ordered equipment arrived on New Year's Eve. They went live at 8pm, December 31st, 1999. EZM remembers, "At that point we didn't even have the name for the station. We were just writing these names down on the wall and Rick picked it from *Valley of the Shadows* by Origin Unknown. It connected with all of us."

Origin first broadcast from Mister T's block of flats, with the studio in his own yard, a very risky strategy. "It was a direct link. Blatant. We run it for two weeks." They broadcast on different frequencies until one became available. EZM remembers, "We had a few dramas with some stations which we had to sort out. Not through violence ..." "Well," interjects Mister T, "there was some violence. But we had righteousness on our side. We played the game completely and utterly right. We sat back and saw that a frequency wasn't being used for two months. Made a move on the third month. That's when there were a lot of other people, about three stations clashing and we had to confront each station. Some amicably, others it was done in a bit of an off-key nature – know what I mean?" But then there was that time when ten big guys arrived looking for the Origin crew. Mister T waffled his way out and EZM ... "I owned up man. I like to talk things through. I told them who was backing us and they sort of backed off. They didn't come back on after that."

I had always assumed that it was the rig doctors who allocated frequencies on the FM dial. They might advise you that someone is already using the spot otherwise you tell them and they build 'em. It's like, 'Pick a number, any number.' The Origin boys weren't really that bothered where they landed on the dial. But T does feel that the station benefits from being in the middle of the FM band. He also feels it's a plus point nestling near Capital Radio on 95.8FM, one of London's biggest commercial stations: "People are always going to be scanning through and will be stopping off on us."

Origin's founder members go way back to the raves in the fields. T remembers raving at Fantastic Ibiza in Lambeth '89. The venue consisted of two tunnels with 2000AD in one, Ibiza in the other: "It was an every Saturday event for two years from when we started in April '89. The vibe of Origin is to do with the fact that we are promoting the origin of warehouse raves from when it was all one." EZM describes Origin's musical concept: "We've always played Drum & Bass, Old Skool, Jungle. That's what we had in our collections. That's where our roots were and that's what we had to play." T adds: "We wanted to cater for the full curriculum; from where it come from, its original roots, House, which is the godfather of it all. Drum & Bass being a branch now. We wanted to hear the history from the beginning. We wanted to reflect all of that." "We wanted to play music how we've seen it grow," EZM confirms.

It costs around £2500 to broadcast illegally. That will pay rent for the studio, the rig, and the aerials. T explains that they have had their share of busts: "You've got to have a few rigs. When we started out Ofcom were in full force. And we were losing one rig a week at £250 a time." On these occasions EZM gets out the collection plate, this time buying in bulk: "We'd club together and buy ten rigs which was two and a half grand." That was too steep for their financial backers who pulled out scared off by spiralling costs. Mister T and EZM financially supported the station themselves. They've had rig raids, but no studio raids (touch wood). T thinks he understands why: "Origin hasn't had a studio raid and other stations on half as long have had three or four. The bottom line is that at these other stations you had people talking about drugs, the gangster vibe and all that kind of stuff. It's totally the opposite of what the meaning of a radio station is and that's to play music people wanna hear."

After Origin's launch, they'd recruited enough DJs to cover the peak broadcast times, however playing four or five hours sets wasn't uncommon. It's only now that the pair thinks of losing all those valuable tunes in a studio raid. Thankfully that didn't happen and they moved out of Mister T's flat broadcasting only at evenings and weekends to being on air 24 / 7. It's great switching off *The Today Program* and listening to Drum & Bass early midweek mornings on the way to work. There was a time when only the Reggae stations were so blatant. On one occasion Origin managed to stay on air for a year by using that rig hidden up a tree. EZM smiles: "But they found another rig we hid in a tree. So that's not the answer anymore." Origin uses RDS, which allows text to scroll along your radio's digital read-out.

They aren't *blasé*. M tells me about Ofcom who replaced the DTI. "They are bang on it. We've had to resort to coming on in the evenings and weekends now. They've beaten us back." T's pessimistic about the long-term future of pirate radio asking, "How long can you or any station last?" But the reality is Kool and Rude have been broadcasting for over 12 years.

Simon Bates, Ofcom's Communications Manager, confirms that Ofcom is responsible for enforcing the Wireless Telegraphy Act, under which illegal broadcasting is an offence. The Radio Investigation service is now called Field Operations and is still headed by our old friend Barry (cake tin) Maxwell. The Communications Act 2003 made unlicensed broadcasting an offence arrestable by police. More people are now being apprehended and prosecutions are expected to continue to rise. Simon Bates confirms that the number of stations is falling and expected to fall for the third year running. There have been a total of 228 successful prosecutions since December 1999.

Despite the risks Origin wouldn't be an Internet station. Mister T feels that he doesn't just want to appeal to people with computers: "It's obviously access to the World Wide Web but it doesn't have the power of the FM dial. The realness is all there. With a FM station people in London can relate to it and where it all started. You can be in your car and not at home with the computer. Driving around in your car is one of the main ways of people like to listen to music."

Origin management receive phone calls every day from people wanting to join the station. But the schedule is packed. Even the graveyard slots are full. The government is still trying to shut them down. What irony that, from Peel to Bailey, the BBC has a 40 year history of recruiting former pirate radio DJs. After all, they still have the skillz and the tunes.

ORIGINAL PIRATE MATERIAL

"That's what it was about for me – the excitement. I'd be listening at home tuning the radio thinking, 'That's us'. Between the BBC's Alistair Cook and Letter from America and Baker's Dozen there was us, Radio Haringey – The voice of the borough. That's what it was all about." 'TOM', FORMER PIRATE TECHNICIAN

Pirate radio technicians seldom talk about their work, but 'Tom' is prepared to shed light on the technicalities behind Haringey Radio's set up in the early 80s. John became involved in pirate radio because he was very interested in technology and loved radio. In 1981 Citizen's Band radio or CB radio gained some popularity. It enabled people to send messages to each other via radio: "All of a sudden there was a legal facility to talk to other people. That naturally progressed. When I was 13 I started building transmitters to broadcast 27 megahertz on CB radio over a long distance, expanding to VHF radio. Dick, a mate who'd been DJing in North London pubs, suggested we start a station. Simple as that. We soon discovered by digging around a little bit that there were local businesses hooked into the whole idea of pirate radio. A company in Finchley sorted us out with an aerial and told us to get in touch with a person called Harry in South London. He would help with rig design. The moment you showed an interest you got drawn into this whole thing called 'Pirate Radio'. It was the excitement of it all, building something with a few transistors, a car battery, soldering iron, buying cables, making our own aerials, setting it all up, getting it to work then listening to it at home.

"We'd set up on a tower block in Edmonton in the dead of night using a 20 foot scaffold pole as an aerial. A relative of mine had these keys — fire brigade keys. They were called FB2s, FB4s. They allowed you to get access to the top of a tower block. It was all about getting hold of fire brigade keys. There were also council keys. I had 'em all. We went up and set up all this stuff. You were ever so exposed up there. We were sweating thinking, 'What if the caretaker comes or the police?' We were looking for electric supplies, 13 amp fuses, and adapters for the lighting sockets, for a place to put the rig. There'd be dead pigeons everywhere. The wind's blowing, you're slipping around — all of a sudden there'd be a bird fluttering. It was comical." They'd switch on for four or five hours and sit in their car at the bottom of the flats to see if officials might arrive and confiscate their equipment which happened on one occasion. The shows were pre-recorded and broadcast on tape. Listeners would have to write in with their requests. When they broadcast live they used a telephone box down the road as the studio number:

"Anybody in pirate radio in the 80s knew the name Eric Gotts. They would feel the hairs on the back of their necks stand up at that name. He was commonly known as Eric. It was all very gentlemanly — dreadfully so. It was only if you were causing a lot of interference or broadcasting stuff that wasn't satisfactory that they would get involved."

Tom was very worried about being caught. Both he and Dick came from very respectable families. Tom's father was a Home Office civil servant working in the government department responsible for tracking pirates. He turned a blind eye when Radio Haringey was broadcast from his son's bedroom. British Telecom, who were responsible for monitoring radio interference from pirate radio stations, also employed Tom: "It's not something you would broadcast as it were. It was clandestine — very clandestine. When we turned our transmitter on we knew were doing wrong. In '88 / '89 the government invited a large number of pirates to a meeting in this church hall they hired in Luton. Everyone was really nervous and crept in giving false names. We were kids and all the big boys were there. Eric was there. The meeting was chaired by one of the people who used to trace pirates. They gave assurances before anybody spoke explaining the purpose of the meeting was to try and regulate pirates in a way that quality was maintained. And make sure we understood the rules and regulations and gave advice on technology. They asked

everybody to talk about their station and what they aimed for. The government thought well — Pirate Radio — we're on the outside — Let's try and embrace it all and get into it." "The Conservative Government???" "Yeah, well, the idea wasn't to get information and close people down. It was to try and keep in control and understand a little bit. We tried to create a community station well before community licenses. We did local charts from Music Power Records, and read out the local papers. It was just a laugh."

Nowadays technical details are blatantly available on the Internet at www.y2kpirates.co.uk

RADIO INTERNET

The Internet has provided us with a mind-boggling range of Drum & Bass radio stations. Stations worth checking include Pyrotechnicradio.com, Bassdrive.com, dnbradio.com, barebass.com, drumandbassworldwide.com, koollive.co.uk, kunninmindz.com, lifefm.co.uk and planetdnb.com. Many traditional pirate stations including Kool, Rude and Origin also broadcast over the Net as well as on FM. FM's days are numbered as it will be switched off in the near future and the Internet / DAB will be the only way to go. Most criticisms regarding Internet stations focus around its inaccessibility. You must be near a computer before you can log on. Though as mobile technology improves more people will log onto radio sites.

DJ Flapjack drove to Rude FM in London from Milton Keynes for several years; now he doesn't have to leave the house. He pops upstairs, logs on and DJs to the world from his bedroom studio. In turn we can hear DJs from all over the world playing on the same station. Shouts come through on a monitor rather by mobile, though locations are global. Some veterans like Rude's DJ E feel that broadcasting illegally adds an extra edge. He reckons that turning up at a legal station with a record bag isn't the way to go. When guests first visit a pirate station they love all the cloak and dagger business connected with unlicensed broadcasting. But Internet radio is the future.

INNA DE DANCE

"I think that Drum & Bass is so fucking healthy right now. It's grown up. It's the strongest genre of Dance Music. It's got the fiercest, most loyal followers. It's tight. It's close knit. And they support each other. You only have to look at the amount of raves and parties that are on. It's not the same in Techno, Trance or House. It's madness now." LONDON ELEKTRICITY

"I think the London scene is rinsed. The club scene in general is rinsed. You can hear the same DJs three-times in a week, which is ridiculous. I don't think it's good for the scene at all. We need to start cutting back just a little and concentrate on quality." DJ SS

Clubland has always been in a state of flux. We've witnessed a shift away from corporate superclubs like The Ministry of Sound. World Dance style mega raves are not as profitable as they once were, but many large promotions are still here. Slammin' Vinyl and Helter Skelter have been around for ten years. Helter Skelter became Accelerated Culture and now hold their parties in Birmingham. Some venues have closed down. The end of a 15 year era was heralded by the news that The Sanctuary was to be demolished making way for MK Dons' new football stadium. Club UN is now a block of flats. Other large promotions such as Promised Land, United Dance, Hardcore Heaven are still in business. Desire, Breakin' Science and Best of British promotions have re-surfaced. One Nation is under new management but you might see Terry Turbo on TV. He's taken up acting. One Nation's new promoters remain true to the spirit of a One Nation party. Telepathy is still with us and, like many other promotions, they're trying something new, promoting Basstronica. Shabba and Skibba front MC Convention. My old favourite Jungle Fever is thumping. Eastman and the lads still give out flyers themselves. And I hope we haven't seen the last of World Dance.

Many artists and audiences expressed a preference for smaller, more intimate nights. D&B has been represented to the max in Fabric, and in London's new clubland based in and around Shoreditch. There's Cargo, Herbal, 333 and Plastic People to name a few. The area feels safer and more relaxed than the West End ever did. Though up West, Movement and The End are very much taking care of business. There are so many different nights taking place weekly, bi-weekly and monthly in London and across the UK that it would take several pages to list them all. And it'd probably be quite boring, but I must mention Swerve, Traffic and all the different crews who hold their dances at Herbal — especially Rider's Sunday night Grace and that after hours lock-in. You're literally spoilt for choice. You could go out on Wednesday night and rock home on Monday morning.

Some people feel our scene is passing through difficult times and DJ SS feels that, "The club scene in general is rinsed." I have to say that the vast majority of nights / events I've attended have been top notch. They're generally full of people and have a great vibe. Edinburgh's DJ Kid said the same. His Manga and Jungle Magic nights have run for almost nine years: "Scotland is the strongest it's ever been Drum & Bass-wise. The amount of nights going on are unbelievable. It's not just Manga. There are five or six other nights as well. It's the healthiest it's ever been." Before 1988 I knew what it was like to check boring clubs. And our scene's clubs are not boring. Fabric hosts their weekly Friday night sessions. Their Junglist tribe aren't saying, "Same old same old." Of course clubs can vary from week to week but it's generally very good. Faster is a new Saturday night blast in Islington. If there wasn't demand for these parties they wouldn't be promoted. The only thing that's rinsed is me and punters after another blinder.

One Night in Heaven

Just off central London's Strand fashionable punters buzz by a swath of bright red and white posters advertising DJ Ron's No Frills night at Hackney Central. On this north bank of the Thames the streets are lined with gleaming bodywork. Cars are jam parked anywhere there aren't forbidding double yellow lines. Clubber's silhouettes in cars are talking. Others walking with a mission chat into electric blue squares of floating mobile screens. On this mild May night guest list and punters queue to pass under the arch of airport style metal detectors. Eastman appears in the club's doorway walking under the sign 'Heaven'. We haven't spoken in years. There had been some misunderstanding way back when. Catching each other's eyes Eastman walks over to the barrier, both of us offering a warm handshake. There's a little time to chat before Smurf and his crew arrive. Smurf – Kool FM's original technician left the station six years ago to make music of his own: "It's not Drum & Bass, it's Breaks." "Smurf man, it's all good."

Scanning the queue there's a very ethnically mixed group. Eastman calls me over. I don't know if he knew about my MS but he opens the barriers to let me through. He doesn't know or care that Tania UMC has already put me on the guest list: he gives me a free ticket anyway. A security man approaches to search me but Eastman waves him away. Leaving us space to talk, telling tales in minutes of the years of life that we've both lived through. I need to apologise to him: "Listen Eastman about that …" "Forget it on both sides. We're both bigger men than that." Sealed with a heartfelt handshake: "Alright Brian, straight down there on the right." Descending the stairs towards the drums and the bass I can honestly say that I'd missed the Kool FM Family more than I ever wanted to admit.

Beats 'pon beats boom from both arenas. Heat meets Fever in the foyer of the club that once held Rage. Energy and people flow around the stairs. Muffled beats and MC shouts are punctuated by opening and closing doors. A swirl of gold chains, cans of Red Stripe and nu skool hooded tops walk, dancing through. Kool FM raves always come from the heart of the Jungle. There's something extra in a races-mixing mixed race mass of people. Piling into the Fever arena we're subjected to sustained controlled explosions. When people ask, "Where's Jungle gone? What happened to Jungle?" I'll tell them, "It's here man. Jungle is here." And this is Jungle Fever.

The DJ box sticks out into the crowd like a truncated pier. People flow around and behind, dancing wicked all along the grey metallic bar. DJ Ital pumps out storm force rhythms. The power's same as it ever was. *Take A Ride With Me …*

I'm sitting near the DJ box on a church pew. There are four of them along each side of the tunnel affording loads of seating near the heart of the party. The dancefloor is an eruption of arms, legs, elbows; bouncing bodies, banging heads – ultraviolet on white t-shirts. *By the Power of Ra.* Incredible youthful energy radiates. I catch a fellow clubber's eye and we look at each other, smiling, knowing and feeling this quality moment. This is mad. It's making me remember why I came into this music in the first place. This is Jungle – Drum & Bass.

Ital, head bobbing, Sennheiser wearing, spliff smoking, piles on beats upon nastier beatz. Souls on the floor vibrate through their dancing. Ridiculous intensity vibes through this blue and purple half pipe tunnel. A girl in red micro shorts moves through the crowd as another, legs sky high, glides by. Leather jackets, jeans, t-shirts pass by. Not a soul stands still. Back in the day Jazzy B shouted, "If you're not dancing Fuck Off!" He'd be speechless here. Smurf picks his way through a crowd losin' it to *Odyssey* all as one heaving bobbing organism. Relentless seismic waves of rhythm, buffet the muscle bound, stripped to the waist, sweat streaked, corn-row heads. Power pile driving on the floor, around the DJ box. Moisture shines on pierced navels and over tattoos in the smalls of girls' backs.

Shy and Eastman are by the door as I'm leaving. A long walk later I fall into the car. After a few turns I'm totally lost down a warren of No Through roads. I should know this area of town but I'm dizzy and confused, then figure out what's going on. It was the Fever. You can't walk into that kind of energy and walk out again unscathed. It had turned my senses upside down. I pulled in, got out the car and breathed fresh air. Needing to get my head back together, "I've just been in this thing man."

PUNTERS AGAINST SANITISED RAVES

Niki Dimensions has mixed feelings about the scene's sanitised edge. People have said the same of Glastonbury, scrubbed clean of its Scallies and anything-can-happen soul. Bret Telepathy commented, "You have that edge to it – an edge of realness. A lot of people like that. I liked that. I'm not gonna lie to you." "Are you glad that you don't have to break into warehouses anymore?" "In one sense you do miss it. It added to the 'oomph' of it all. I was younger then and more up for it, but I would still like to go for one of their field licenses if I thought the market was there. It's too corporate now. The realness is from the original heads and you can't take that away from them. Heads like: Paul Ibiza, Jarvis, Tony Holston, Dave Roberts, Genesis, Finbar, Tarquin – crazy people but they knew what promoting was about."

MIRIAM FROM TOTTENHAM, D&B CONVERT – FORMER ROCK FAN

"The bouncers are a lot nicer at Jungle raves. The Rock club ones are probably people who couldn't get in the police or were school bullies. D&B bouncers are more laid back. They don't rough you up when they search you, but they are really thorough. At Rock clubs they're really violent."

Miriam finds people inside Rock venues can be quite intimidating and look down on you if you're not wearing the right gear: "If you're a Goth in the Rock room they look at you weird. It's all about how you look. The fashion people stand there posing proppa hard. It becomes a fashion show. In Drum & Bass clubs you get a whole range of people. And the Goths are there as well. You get the skater kids, the Townies, Garage people and such a wide spread of ages. I was at The End and there was this guy who looked over 40 and he's raving topless. The older people are having as much fun as the younger ones. People go up to them and say, "Top mate. Hope I'm doing that when I'm your age." You don't get anyone judging you or people watching you dancing and thinking you're an idiot.

"Staff at The End look after you if they know you're on drugs. At one club my friend was having a bad time, the bouncers just kicked him out in the street. At The End they are concerned. They take care of you. If you want to take drugs you've got to feel comfortable. If anything happens you want to feel safe. In Hip Hop clubs if you dance with some guys their girlfriends get really pissed off. They stop dancing and they're looking at you, talking about you. I was really feeling uncomfortable. So I went into the Drum & Bass room a couple of feet away and everyone is having a good time. When I go out with my boyfriend we get there and it's like, "See you at the end of the night." I sometimes see him from a balcony raving with some girls and don't actually care. You get a lot of possessiveness and jealousy in Garage raves. Definitely. You don't get that in Drum & Bass nights at all. You can dance away or act like an idiot and you don't feel self conscious cos no one's judging you. And if they are no one actually does anything."

AND THIS ONE'S FOR THE LADIES ...
Now it's often been said that the harder sounding Drum & Bass drove the ladies away but: "I like it really hard" – Laura from Croydon; "Definitely liked it harder" – Sue, Haringey Council; "I love it when it gets really grimy" – Miriam from Tottenham. So I wouldn't dare generalise.

SORRY WHO'S LIST ARE YOU ON?
AHHH, ... LAURENCE'S ...

1995, Metalheadz, Blue Note. One step down
from the DJ box. There's a tall woman, dark
hair, head down, dancing by herself completely
absorbed in the beats. She's been turning up
for about six months. Arrives at nine, leaves
at closing time - clothes drenched from all the
dancing. Doesn't speak to anyone. No one speaks
to her. That's fine. She's only interested
in the music and she takes her music very
seriously.

Grace, Herbal 2004. She's there amongst the
crowd one Sunday. Most top artists now know her.
And most of us in the club have reasons to thank
her. Laurence and her company Electric PR have
been hugely responsible for giving exposure to
major Drum & Bass producers in the mainstream
media. Her efforts and energy have helped keep
the scene alive, publicise artists, their music
and draw new people into Jungle Drum & Bass.

*"The last night of Metalheadz at the Blue Note I was
reminiscing about my time there. The first nights when
I went straight downstairs and danced my thing:
to when it was kind of champagne at the bar and
hugging everybody."*
LAURENCE, ELECTRIC PR

Public Relations is her thing. The roll call of
artists and labels who Laurence has represented
is truly prodigious: Andy C, Bryan Gee, Bad
Company, Peshay, Photek, Fabio, Marcus Intalex,
Marky, Paradox, J Majik, Jonny L, Matrix, Full
Cycle, Moving Shadow, Ebony, True Playaz,
V Recordings, Virus, Valve, Reinforced.

Laurence's office lies off a leafy road in
Kentish Town. She is intense; juggling calls
on the landline, mobile and cordless phone.
Her fingers jab through emails, AIM flashes on
screen. I don't know how someone can have all
those conversations at once. She reminds me of
an air traffic controller. The office walls are
lined with posters. Shelves are full of box
files, crammed with press cuttings. Her window
over-looks a small courtyard covered with
greenery and ironworks. We leave the office and
intrusive phones to have lunch and a chat.

"So what's a French woman doing in London promoting
Drum & Bass artists?" "I have been living in London for
over 15 years. I'm very passionate about music. It's always
something I've taken very seriously. I got into PR well
before I got involved with the Drum & Bass scene. My first
job was at Creation Records. Primal Scream had just
released their breakthrough album, *Screamadelica*, in 1990.
Creation boss Alan McGee really needed to have a
connection with his artists. All the people signed to Creation
had very strange personalities. I always joke and say that
being with people like Bobby Gillespie from Primal Scream
or Kevin Shields from My Bloody Valentine gave me all the
weapons necessary deal with Drum & Bass artists."

"Passionate about music", Laurence became interested in
Acid House, leaving Creation when the company's musical
focus didn't correspond with her own. She went freelance,
setting up her own company, Electric PR. Ninja Tune were
amongst her early clients. Laurence raised their profile in
the media before moving in the direction of Jungle: "It
started to be quite fashionable and I started trying to find
out more. I'd tried going to Black Market but found it very
intimidating so I went to Virgin Megastore and bought a
compilation album. It had fantastic tunes like *Burial* and
It's A Jazz Thing. I started listening to all these things and
thought 'Yeah I really like that.'"

Laurence knew Jungle parties were taking place but friends wouldn't go with her. She started listening to pirate radio: "Every time you slightly moved the radio you'd get another station, but what bothered me was that they were not giving me any information about the music and that is what I wanted." A friend of Laurence's also in PR had started working with Bukem, which led her to club Speed. That's where she started meeting faces like Mark and Clayton from Trouble On Vinyl: "I met Phil from Vinyl Distribution and said, "Look I really want do something. I am in PR and I like Drum & Bass." And he actually got Dr S Gachet in touch with me. So I did a bit of work with Gachet. That was probably '95 or '96."

Laurence can't represent music if she's not into its culture. Metalheadz at The Blue Note was where she'd go deeper: "I started going religiously every Sunday night on my own – which was okay for me. For about six months I didn't know anybody there and nobody knew me. I would be one step down from where the DJ was, on the dancefloor. I'd arrive at nine, leave at midnight completely soaked with sweat and not talking to anyone." Laurence really started rolling forward in Drum & Bass public relations when a contact, Simon Goffe at Heavyweight Management, hooked her up with Bristol duo Flynn & Flora. They gelled well and Laurence managed to place articles about their album *Native Drums* in a spread of publications including *NME, Melody Maker, The Face, iD* and *Select*.

In Spring '97 Bryan Gee was about to release V Recordings' first album, *V Classics*. Simon suggested to Bryan that Laurence handle the PR. Bryan confessed that he didn't like Laurence when he first met her but gave her the job anyway: "That was my big break. The press started with a Jumping Jack Frost interview in *Muzik* magazine, but things didn't run smoothly. Frost wanted to see the article before it went to press. That's not uncommon in Drum & Bass. In Rock / Pop you'd have to have the clout of Oasis to command that sort of influence." *Muzik* sent over the article and Frost came back too late to make all but a few changes. And Frost wanted changes: "I went to the V office with new copies of the magazine and showed them to Bryan and Frost." Frost dashes through the pages checking the article and, "He threw the magazine and had a real strop at me. And I said, "You know what? I'm not going to take this shit

from you. You were already very lucky to have a look at the article and change things. You got back to me too late and I still managed to get some of the changes. Oasis are not treated as well as you are so don't give me any shit." Frost gave me really nasty looks for a couple of weeks and after we made peace I thought, 'I am not going to get intimidated. I have done my job. I've actually gone out of my way to help him.' So Bryan and Frost became my best ambassadors."

Although some Drum & Bass artists like to pretend that they're not interested in who gets what magazine coverage, they were phoning each other asking, "How did you get in there?" They all started beating a path to her door. Things got scary. Especially after Main Source folded: "I remember getting calls from Hype and Ram in the same day and I thought, 'Oh my God. I can't do this. This is obscene. I can't do this.' And then I thought, 'You know what? I'm gonna give it a shot.' Over five years later and Laurence is keeping the scene alive, pushing the media to cover artists' music, which feeds back into the scene. Since we met in spring, Laurence has filled my record bag with, Tali – *Lyric on my Lip*, Dynamite MC – *The World of Dynamite*, Marky & XRS – *In Rotation*, Roni Size – *Return To V*, Remarc – *Unreleased Dubs* and Andy C's *Nightlife 2*. To be honest I don't think I had that much respect for PR people until I met Laurence. She supports great artists who make excellent music. Laurence is one of the scene's strong characters – even if she prefers to remain behind the scenes. It allows her to get on with what she has to get on with. If she didn't believe in the music she promoted, rest assured she'd be off.

FABRICLIVE

One of my favourite London clubs has to be Fabric. They've just celebrated their fifth Birthday. Fabric isn't one of those corporate superclubs. It was conceived by Keith Reilly and designed to put clubbers first. It's a clubbers club. The 1,600 capacity is divided between three arenas and they can host live bands in all three. Fabric's re-connected with the old warehouse spirit. You can wander around and discover new areas, lose your mates, end up chatting to others, sip cocktails at the bar or get down and grimy in the arenas. Fabric is wheelchair accessible and even has a lift. There's an abundance of chill-out seating and slouching mini-beds, gently fed by music piped through from one of the arenas. Staff are chosen for their knowledge of and enthusiasm for Dance Music. They must also fit into the team. Security is tight but polite. Paramedics are on stand-by ready to deal with casualties – from the man with the nasty stiletto injury on his toe to those who choose to push their own body's boundaries.

The cracking sound system is dedicated to electronic music and has been upgraded four times since 1999. And sound engineers tweak the systems during the night to optimise their quality. The set-up is also designed not to damage your ears, but if you are determined to stick your head in a speaker all night, Fabric does stock earplugs.

They've always had a commitment to Drum & Bass - even when the media had stopped writing about our music. Fabric hosts a Drum & Bass session every Friday. You'll get a grown up senior crowd dancing steadfastly to big brutal bass. "Is it like this every week?" "Yeah mate - Every week." True Playaz hold their nights there and Andy C is a resident. Three times a year the whole club is dedicated to D&B.

My favourite space is room three upstairs under the arches. Andy C, who's being playing the club since it opened, didn't know there was a room three - neither did I. When I did discover it I won't forget a mad session watching Mampi Swift double drop his way through an entire set. The space in front of the DJ box turned into a proppa mosh pit - wonderfully rowdy.

"It was wicked last night. First time I've been to Fabric. I was hanging over the side of the DJ box, my face was in Andy C's face when he was mixing - Probably pissed him off. Had my head in a speaker for about three hours - ears still ringing. Knocked some Yardy's drink outta his hand but he didn't mind. Left about six. We were all so grimy, grimy on the bus with people going to work, setting a bad example to schoolkids. Brilliant 21st birthday."
MIRIAM FROM TOTTENHAM

WE'RE ALL GOING ON A DRUM & BASS HOLIDAY: INNOVATION 2004

"This is the best fuckin' rave of the year. Who says this is the best fuckin' rave? Say yeah!!"
MC SHABBA ON STAGE AT INNOVATION

Hotel Guitart, 25 degree heat. England thrash Switzerland 3-0. There's a hilarious bonding session over the balconies. Lads 'n' lasses share smoke-ables, music blares from beatboxes: a positive paella of sounds. Supper's included but many are too excited to eat. *En route* to Colossus other club greeters fail to entice us. Beaten by bright yellow Innovation wristbands. No contest. Nights of pounding Jungle await the faithful from Holland, Germany, Spain, Scotland, Wales and England.

Reach queue. Geezer tells a war story: "Couldn't believe it. Got nicked. Tell ya I was fuckin' screwin'. On me fuckin' birthday a-n-all." The guy's from London, arrested at Barcelona airport. Turns out the plane is at 30,000 feet. Some bloke reaches up, swipes thousands of Euros off the duty free trolley. "… Gives us all a wedge … Don't even know 'im. An' I've got an once of weed down me drawers." Plane lands. Police board. Handcuffs. Carted off. Searched. Hours later they're back on the street off to the rave with the money and the skunk shouting, "Nice one bruva!"

The queue in classic post-match, pre-rave mood chant Hin-ga-lund under Innovation's banner. IC3 waits for a pass. "Aren't you supposed to say, "Don't you know who I am?"" He laughs. That's not his way. Andy C's looking for dinner. "Which one do you want? McDonald is that way and Burger King is that way." Riddla walks alongside: "Last night was fuckin' Men-tal. We're talkin' Bagleys '94 / 95 bizniz."

Inside the club's courtyard folks sit 'round tables under sun shades. Colossus's smooth steel, marble floors; crazy legs tap dance on podiums. Shabba chats. Frenzic's broadcasting to the world live on 1Xtra. The station's logos festoon the club. *Return of Forever* mixes in. It's fiercely hot in a room behind the decks.

No one's dancing. One man's seated. The room's a cupboard. A BBC technician, who looks like a bank manager, monitors and tweaks our output. An unsung hero. "Nice one mate. Like Jungle then?" "I prefer a bit of R'n'B and Bashment myself." Other side of the wall, women wiggle 'n' wind. Lights play over Kat, Rachel, Pam, Flapjack, Lucy - original Ipswich crew. Lucy jigs atop a column whirling green fluorescent rods.

"Love's a message that I bring to you.
There's no reason to be mean and cruel.
Spread Love all over land,
Every woman girl and boy and man,
We can walk together hand in hand
This part of the masterplan."

In the courtyard it's …

"Alright? Ow ya doin' bruv?"
"Alright. Alright. Laters."
Ciggies in hands.
Feet in trainers marching.
Chatting rave chat.
"What's yer name?
Where you from?
'n'
What you on?"
"Got any pills?"
"Naw - Thirty five each 'ere."
"Our's woz twenny."
"'Erd some geezer paid 'undred Euros for five."
"Sick innit? … Errr 'ow much is 'undred Euros?"
"I dunno. Back 'ome it's free fer a tenna."
"Wouldn't buy Charlie here. It's-a-rip off."
"Listen to this. Right.
Last night there's a bunch a people
only got a-couple-pills between 'em."
"Naaa!"
"Chopped 'em up 'n' snorted 'em."
"Innit."

Three big blondes, white hats, red shirts, mini-skirts, big white furry boots stride through Brockie, Navigator, Hype, Andy C, T Power and Shy. All the names you wanna see on a flyer. "I say, "Re-load." You say, "Re-load." "Re." " "Load." "Re" "Load." *Odyssey* - Mental - "Selecta. One time. Selecta - Beg ya pleeze. Rewind - *Odyssey*." "Innovation – In Da Sunshine - Woiiiiiii!!!!" "What do we smoke? We Smoke Weed." *Arsonist*. Sound system's suffering. Bare chests. Tattoos from shoulder to wrist. "*We're in heaven - Trust me.*" Slow strobes. Fast action. *Pack Of Wolves* howls. Stage-side the track's MC, Raven, all passion and dreads, shouts his lyrics perfectly. Compulsive rhythm and beats, the JDB machine is cranked fully firing the funky James Brown scream in yer chest … Get the picture? "We all went on a Drum & Bass holiday."

THE BEST SPEAKERS I EVER HEARD

"And he did this track with this geezer goin' 'It Ain't Too Loud.' You people ain't 'eard proper bass. I like to feel the bass in my chest. To me it's the right level."

We're sitting sipping beers in a café floating on the river. Catching up in East Berlin's warm spring sunshine. I'm telling my mate Daniel about Dillinja, Lemon D, *Killa Hertz* and the whole Valve sound system thing: "It's official man - 'The loudest sound system on the planet,'" I say with vicarious pride. *The Guinness Book of Records* have been down, measured the levels 'n' everything." "Well that's not what counts," says Dan pulling on a spliff staring across the water. "*Wie meinst du das … What d'ya mean?*" There's a discussion, another beer, then we're suddenly jumping on trains and trams heading across town. "*Wo gehen wir hin … Where are we goin'?*" "To see Willi. Willi and Fanni."

Lemon D
& Dillinja

Snigger, "What?" Snigger. "Very funny." "Sorry."
"It's their real names." "*Really*?" "Yes, *Really*.
Anyway they're in love and build speakers
together. Willi's been designing and making them
for about twenty years. He used to work in a
company with some other guys and customers paid
top dollars for their wares. Now it's just the
two of them. Fanni's the apprentice. And they
make the best speakers I've ever heard."

Daniel hits the buzzer and we slope up to the
third floor apartment. The amiable couple,
shoulder length dreads flowing, warmly meet and
greet us. Above our heads is their bed on a
wooden platform, beautifully, skilfully crafted.
We sit beneath it facing six narrow rectangular
white speakers across the width of the room and
talk technical: "Cos in London there are guys
called Dillinja and Lemon D who've built a 96K
rig … " "Well, loudness isn't really the thing.
We go for quality." I'm shown designs on squared
paper and colour brochures of finished works.
Back in the early 90s Willi started a firm with
a friend building top-notch speakers that sold
for €60,000 a pair. They only sold a couple of
pairs a year but they always sold. He bailed out
when it all became too much of a business. "Who
were your customers?" "Mostly really rich people
… the odd Sheik, a guy who owned an airport and
a complete sound freak who sold everything to
buy his babies. When I went to his flat to
deliver the boxes he only had a mattress,
records and an amplifier."

Willi gets deep in sound, describing pressures,
waveforms, Hertz and why those deadly deep subs
don't work if the room's too small. The long low
frequency waves don't have enough space to flex,
before they start bouncing back off the walls,
colliding with each other and sounding messy.
Willi points to a coaxial speaker cone sitting
in the top of each tower. Basically you have two
concentric circles. The wider circular membrane
plays the mid frequencies, the innermost disc
plays the high frequencies and both pulse
together along the same axis producing a more
natural sound. A cross section of the tower
reveals a snaking horn running the length of the
speaker box. The horn's narrow at the top, wider
at the bottom. The mouth of the horn takes up
two thirds of its height and opens at the back.
As the speaker cone moves in and out, pressure
builds up behind it, pulsing sound under
pressure down the horn shaped passage that opens
behind the rear of the tower. The crucial shape
of the horn is calculated using formulae and
software to increase the depth and power of the
bass exponentially. The wall behind the speaker
is used to amplify and resonate the bass. There
are no dials or switches. The loudness is
altered by moving the speaker nearer to or
further away from the wall behind it. "And the
amp? How powerful is the amp?" "It's that NAD
in the middle. 25 watts per channel. You don't
really need much more." "Mate you'd have trouble
reading from a light bulb that's only 25 watts."

"Please sit here. Trust your ears." The
listening chair in the middle of the floor is
about six feet in front of the speakers. Willi
selects a CD from the pile on the floor. DJ SS'
Black floods lovingly across the room. The raw
imperfection of its early production clear for
us to hear, but there was a different level to

the track that I'd never experienced before. He moves on to A Guy Called Gerald and the music becomes properly three-dimensional. I was sitting in the music. Then he plays Bob Marley's *Redemption Song*. Daniel and three dread heads sit silently nodding as Bob stands playing his guitar in the room. The sound is alive and dynamic. Even with the volume turned up we could easily hear each other speaking. "I don't know how to explain it," says Willi. "You can really *feel it*. All of the music." The clarity was breathtaking. When we hear a Jazz CD, *Super Bass 2*, featuring three live double bassists you can see or feel where on the stage each of the musicians is playing. Then Fanni reminds me that this particular pair of speakers at €800 are practically the bottom of their range.

Willi's mad about sound, acoustics, music production and reckons Pink Floyd's *Dark Side of the Moon* was one of the best albums ever recorded. He'll tell you why the systems in certain clubs sound awful. He gets deep about speaker cones, and sketches the design of a speaker in which the audience is surrounded by the bassbin: "It would be wicked. I once installed it in my car - a Merc. Seriously. But every now and again everyone should try to go out to live concerts, hear real instruments." Willi loves music, all kinds of music. Before we leave he starts reminiscing about when Jungle first landed in Mannheim: "The first time I heard the music it went straight to my heart. Mickey Finn played back-to-back with DJ Hype. It was wicked. You could see the rivalry. Anyway why did Jungle stop? What happened? I really loved that sound."

Back on the streets I had to admit that those were the best speakers I'd ever heard. Daniel talks to Fanni about owning a pair one day. I'll put in an order myself. I love going to Valve but I must admit that having to stuff earplugs in your ears did distance you from the music. By the end of most nights I've pulled the protection out wanting, needing, to feel the beats and damning the consequences. Not exactly safe sound. After meeting this couple and their speakers I'm left thinking that it might be too loud after all.

TOO LOUD?

Some clubs and promotions now supply earplugs. It's advisable to wear them. In spite of sound systems being adjusted to prevent ears ringing, a few people have commented that they've experienced tinnitus, a sign of temporary or permanent ear damage. After visiting one London club Laura from Croydon became worried when her ears were still ringing over twelve hours after leaving a party. I was concerned enough to speak to a specialist ear doctor. Dr Tony Sirimanna is a Consultant Audiological Physician based at Great Ormond Street Hospital: "Tinnitus may be temporary, especially at the beginning. If exposed to harmful levels of noise for a sufficient period of time your ears will ring and you may also have some hearing loss initially but may become permanent depending on the period of exposure and the frequency. Once established it may not go away." I know Fresh could have benefited from this information. Unfortunately this colossus of producers suffers from tinnitus.

GROOVERIDER'S LOCK IN

Bass Camp Herbal. Park in the usual spot, waved through by the bouncers, laminate from Miss Pink and head inside for an unusual night. Open the door and it's mad, intense. Andy C's double dropping on the decks. Herbal's massive are on the stomp. I'm deck-side and 5ive'O, mic in hand, says, "Big up the Brian from Zy:on inside." Reaching behind Andy our fists greet. I'm installed sitting around the corner as the action unfolds. It's a mixed crew of Shoreditch, Tottenham and industry. To my right Rider's unwinding the twisted cable of his headphones. Music from open-mouthed foghorn speakers reverberates through us. Black dreads, white dreads, multicultural dreads fly, the air smelling sweet with weed. In the *melee* two girls snogg. A flickering orange lighter flame illuminates the face of an unimaginably fit tanned blonde. She's wearing black knee-length boots, a short low cut midriff exposing black leather dress and is dirty dancing with a tall mixed race guy; his long dreads whiplashing in the beats. This is the groove corner.

Lights on. End of night. Stop to speak to Miss Pink who's packing up the door, handing back the last few coats. Polite bouncers sweep out stragglers. Across the street the Kool FM posse stand 'round chatting. They've been handing out flyers for a forthcoming event. Andy C steps into a very sexy Mercedes 500L and heads up Shoreditch High Street.

Back inside I run into Rachel from *Knowledge* and friends Ryan and Sarah. We traipse up to Grooverider's after party. The room's illuminated by light from fluorescent square tables. There are several leather sofas, a long bar and decks. Rachel is like, "I've been coming here for months and didn't know this place existed." "I did but didn't know that there was an after party 'til Rider and Fabio mentioned it on the radio."

The DJ flows through a mixture of Soul, Rare Groove, Hard House and Drum & Bass. Rider, 5ive-O and Frost mingle. In comes *Twilight's Last Gleaming*. We're lost in chat. Rachel is asking how much I intended to cover the American Drum & Bass scene. Then I found myself speaking to Ryan about the health of the American scene. High sales of vinyl are an indication of the number of DJs now playing Drum & Bass. Hive with his tune *Bring It On* signals the forefront of the new wave.

The night passes quickly. Dawn. Time to leave. Rumours circulate about people having sex in the toilets. Everyone's looking well and truly mashed. It's been a good night. I've met lots of interesting people but at the end of the day, no matter who is throwing it, the after party is, after all, just a party. Definitely fun but the main event is the main event. No matter how star-struck I get nothing replaces the dance.

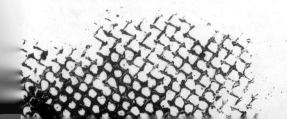

WAR STORIES

Trouble like back in the day hardly ever happens. Most events are paragons of politeness with people saying, "Sorry" and "After you." There's a post on Dogs On Acid. A guy at Herbal had his spliff accidentally knocked away by a member of staff. Quick to apologise the employee is down on the floor searching for my man's spliff. Even security teams seem more chilled out. It's good that Jungle Drum & Bass parties have matured.

The few violent incidents I've witnessed have been minor. One was an embarrasing Brits abroad occasion in Spain during Innovation. Within hours of the first tunes rolling our hotel manager was threatening to kick us out; and we'd come to the attention of the town's police and mayor. The mood was set after England's win against Switzerland. You had the best and worst of British exports: Drum & Bass with football hooliganism. Most trouble affected only one hotel and was caused by the usual small minority of late night / early morning revellers yelling pissed up repetitive chants, "Hin Ga Lund, Hin Ga Lund." Chairs were thrown in the swimming pool. Some fuckers were shouting "Sieg Heil" down the corridors. Except the idiots couldn't pronounce it properly. My most scary violent moment was at Rollercoaster in Brixton when I got punched in a fracas that seemed to end as quickly as it started. The guy who delivered the blow apologised wholeheartedly. I wasn't his target.

The outer environment of Jungle parties has largely been cleaned up, but there are concerns about how we're treating our inner environment – our own bodies. The violence we inflict on ourselves with drugs is worrying. We're familiar with most of the issues around tobacco and alcohol consumption so, let's do drugs. I've seen a fair few things whilst working in festival medical tents that have definitely ruined my buzz ...

F*M*S

One of the best things about nursing, apart from it being a rewarding occupation, is that you can work almost anywhere in the world. And joining the right organisation can get you into festivals free. If you do a bit of work that is. I grew up watching that TV medical series *M*A*S*H* set during the Korean War. It focused on the antics of medics and crew stationed in a mobile army surgical hospital. Nursing in a festival isn't the same as being at war but we have our share of casualties. My first outing at the Eclipse Festival was a one-off but I later enlisted with the best firm in the business, Festival Medical Services, in May 2001. FMS cover many events including Homelands, Reading and Glastonbury. It's nearly always a giggle. Our mobile hospital is stationed in large marquees and staffed with a posse of nurses, midwives, doctors, dentists, psychiatrists, mental health nurses, physiotherapists, podiatrists and paramedics. Though we come from all over the country, we all gel together as a team. With waiting times in minutes rather than hours FMS performs better than many Accident & Emergency departments outside Festival Land.

Customers arrive with anything from sunburn, hayfever and sprained ankles to pregnant women about to give birth and adverse reactions to substances. The average festival population are a pretty select group as a fair percentage arrive with the aim of getting well 'n' truly fucked. Clients – post cocktail of drugs spin in and spin out. It's okay to tell us what you or a friend have taken. We won't tell the police. We want to get you fixed as quickly and safely as possible. So it really is good to talk. Most punters are treated on site, others are sent straight to hospital. For many it's not a problem; at least not in the short term. For others it all goes a bit wrong.

INCOMING

Festivals in England and rain often come together. The Eclipse Festival in Plymouth 1999 was no exception. It had been wet for days. One afternoon paramedics inside our medical tent were trying to stop a rivulet flowing through the treatment area. Two strapping lads approach me, slightly spaced. To look at them you wouldn't think there's a thing wrong. "And the problem is?" They point to their boots. "Mind taking them off please?" They unlace their boots in unison squeezing out feet encased in muddy, slimy socks. "And the socks please." Both unpeel their socks displaying the soles of their feet. "Hmmm. Excuse me a moment. I'll be right back." They shrug. "Andy, I think you should see this." "Hello, I'm Dr Whitely. Might I …?" They stick out four feet. "Thank you. I'll be right back." I'm whispering, "Andy, where are you going?" "To get my digital camera. That's classic World War One Trench Foot. Gotta have that for the archives."

A couple of years later I'm on duty during Homelands. It's Saturday afternoon and an ambulance crew radios in. They're not sure what's wrong with their patient. They arrive trying to hold on to a guy who's swirling around shouting nonsense. His arms are doing the helicopter. He hits the floor then tries to stand, knocking into everyone and everything. He's a danger to others as well as himself. Half an hour later, six of us are holding him down. The psychiatrist and medics decide that some sedation might be in order. So he's jabbed in the bum with a syringe of Haliperidol. A while later we're still holding him down so he gets another jab and finally settles. After several hours spent lying on a mattress in a quiet corner he eventually comes to. My man stands up straight, adjusts his attire and leaves the medical tent refusing to discuss the matter.

In summer 2002 I was on duty at Glastonbury. It's Friday night and I'm in the Pennard Medical Centre opposite The Other stage. Rosy, a gorgeous Welsh doctor, and I send a girl to hospital. The poor thing's managed to drink some of her Amyl Nitrate. Nitrates drop your blood pressure horribly. The ambulance drives off, blue lights reflecting on faces and tents. The radio crackles with a shout about a guy's who's collapsed near The Glade only a few minutes away. We arrive running. He's one the ground, semi-conscious and fitting. His girlfriend explains, "… Did a trip 'bout an hour ago. We've done 'em before and this ain't 'appened." We make him safe and wait for an ambulance all bathed in music and lasers blasting through the fields. Fireworks explode overhead. I was interested (just on a professional level) asking Rosie, "I didn't know you could fit doing LSD." "Oh yes," says she. There's an embarrassed moment then we both chime, "Errr, so the research journals say …"

Homelands 2004. A woman in her mid twenties lies on a trolley not making much sense. We garner a few details. "Jane can you tell us what you've taken?" Her head and eyes roll. The corners of her mouth are sticky with goo. Her body's arching with mini convulsions. Between gurning and gritted teeth she says "Mick-sees" "Sorry?" asks posh Dr. Moystin. "Mit seees." Doc looks confused and needs a translator. "I think she's trying to say Mitsubishis – they're a kind of Ecstasy." "Oh I see. Thank you." She scribbles notes. "And how many have you taken?" Jane's eyes roll between her mumbles. She's still for a moment then says, "42." Doc looks aghast. "You've taken 42!?" "It's the answer. The Answer." The number 42 rings a bell. Doc going into meltdown looks at me: "42?" Jane writhes and gurns a little more. "Jane," I ask, "is that The Answer … The ultimate answer to Everything? Life, the Universe and Everything." Jane contorts, nodding her gurning head. Doc looks very confused. "I think she means, '42 – The answer to Life, the Universe and Everything.' It's a *Hitcherhiker's Guide to the Galaxy* thing. I don't think she's actually taken 42 Es."

A few weeks later it's Friday night / Saturday morning at Glastonbury. Kate, Curly Sue and I have left Fabio & Grooverider's Radio One stage fully rinsed out. We're chatting about the music and 15,000 people going for it on the flagship Drum & Bass slot – 'What a ting.' We're doing the slow walk back to the tent. Thoughts, lost

in music, strange sights filter through.
Ahead of us there's a full panic goin' on. A jeep, lights flashing, bounds down a track towards us. Security men are running, shouting, dragging people lying on grass out of its way. Headlights shine on a crew of medics in fluorescent jackets. They're performing cardiac massage on a pale young man. I recognise some of them from my shift. I don't really remember thinking about going to help, just found myself there alongside the medic, paramedics and some guy from the SAS. Neil Clinnings, aged 24 from Lancashire, was later pronounced dead. Festival magazine *Select* described his death as 'drugs related.'

We'd been busy in the medical tent earlier that evening. A few people rocked up having mixed their regular prescription drugs with party pills and powder. All washed down with copious amounts of alcohol. One woman, "Retch ... Gulp ... Oh I'm so sorry," threw up over my jeans. "No it's okay really. Don't worry" I'm mopping up the mess thinking, 'Hmmm Eau d'Cider.' A few people were given a quiet place to lie down in, watched over by mental health staff. Others were sent to hospital. Don't know if it's because I'm growing older but I began to feel a little disturbed by it all. I'm glad that FMS are there for them. I understand hedonism but off its head seems to be off its head, face and tits. I don't know what to think anymore. What's going on? I'm calling for the Big Gun.

IF YOU DON'T WANT TO KNOW THE SCORE, LOOK AWAY NOW

His name's not on any flyers but he's proud to have been in the Rave Scene from before the beginning. Meet DJ Henry – The dapper Don. Sorry that's Dr. John Henry. His name might be familiar from the Leah Betts case in '95. She died at home during her 18th birthday party after taking an E. Back then Dr. Henry was a consultant at Guy's Hospital, London in a department called the Poisons Unit. Medics would call for advice about poisonings and chemical incidences of all kinds. He's been on TV numerous times and was one of the few experts not to be taken in by Ali G. He's since moved to St. Mary's Hospital, Paddington and has become a Professor. Es, cocaine and other illegal recreational drugs are his speciality.

I arrive at the Accident & Emergency reception for the interview. Professor Henry comes to meet me himself. He's a very likeable person. His office is neatly crammed with files, books and journals. The keyboard sits neatly under a monitor displaying a humungous number of emails. John

talks about his subject with the same enthusiasm as anyone else in the scene. Like our artists his mobile rings. There are comings and goings through his door. Though we're in a hospital and he's the Professor we are talking about the scene – and he starts by mentioning a new release. "I am just reviewing an article by an American guy about new drugs – 'Ecstasy a new drug'. Oh come on," he sighs, eyes rolling skywards, dropping the article flaccidly on the desk. He's disappointed that the writer hadn't found anything fresh for him to analyse.

Back in the day Prof. Henry became alerted to problems associated with 3,4-methlyenedioxymetamphetamine: MDMA aka ecstasy. In 1992 he published a paper describing six or seven serious illnesses connected with E in the highly respected medical journal *The Lancet*: "Seven overheating deaths, five road accidents and six cases of liver damage in the UK. There was nothing like that in the States. There they had one or two cases of adverse reactions to MDMA. Our paper set the standard. It became clear that things did happen with this drug. The other point I was able to make was that most of the complications were related to the circumstances. That was a key thing and lots of people couldn't understand that. 'How could you die after taking one tablet?' It is very complicated.

"We wrote another paper in 1993 about two people who had a low sodium problem. They got very spacey and ill. Then I went to Leah Betts' inquest in 1995. In '98 we published a small paper showing how levels of your anti-diuretic hormones go up with ecstasy. It happened in all eight people we gave the drug to." "You performed human clinical trials?" "Oh yes." "So we're not talking about rats' brains." "We gave a small dose to eight people. That was really interesting. It said that anyone who took ecstasy is at risk if they drink too much water. It became clear that if you drink too much water it stays on board. Most people if they drink too much water they have a few trips down the corridor and they get rid of it. But with ecstasy it just stops the kidneys responding. The brain tells the kidneys what to do. Kidneys can't think on their own. The sensor is in the hypothalamus and the pituitary gland is what sends the message to the kidneys. It's a lovely feedback mechanism. If you drink a glass of water your blood will become just that little bit more dilute. And the brain will say 'You've got to pass out some dilute urine.' It's beautiful. But with ecstasy you completely muck it up. The kidneys will not to respond no matter how much water you drink. If you're dancing and sweating and you replace the fluid there's no problem. But if you're not dancing the fluid just builds up inside you. The blood becomes dilute and your brain swells up because it is surrounded by dilute fluid – like a currant swelling up in water. You have to wait until the ecstasy has gone before you start peeing again. Sorry that's a bit medical and technical but I hope it will be of use.

"One more thing is worth thinking about. A certain number of people die every year and a large number of people take the drug. At the moment the figures are that between half a million and two million tablets come into Britain every week. That's serious numbers. That means a large number of people are taking it. There's clear evidence now that your memory ability goes down when you do take this drug. You don't become a zombie, but it just takes the edge off certain brain abilities related to your memory. You may find that people weren't able to do the things that they were to the same degree. If that's happening among millions of young people then it's serious. One death attracts a lot of attention, even nowadays because they're not hardened drug addicts. They're usually young people out to have a good time and everything goes wrong. It's a tragic story."

"Do you think there's greater understanding in the medical profession and society about what Ecstasy is about?" "There's more understanding but there is not much knowledge about the fact that it affects your memory. People are very aware that if you do things wrong as far as exercise and fluid are concerned you'll have a problem. But they don't realise that you're affecting your mental ability – in a small way. I must emphasise that you are not going to give yourself Alzheimer's. You don't become a zombie. But you are taking the edge off your brain ability." "I've heard that that a rising number of people are mixing drugs heavily." "That's increasingly so. They don't think twice before mixing drugs even if they don't know what is going to happen." "I've also heard that the incidence of cocaine use and cardiac arrhythmias (heart beat irregularities) is also on the increase." "Cocaine used to be a rich person's drug. People in the street didn't use it. It's really interesting actually." He takes a piece of paper and draws graphs. "You have the 60s, 70s, 80s, 90s, 00s." Then you had Es. Late 80s it comes into being. Whether it is still taking off or levelling out I don't know but a large number of people use it. In '96 Coke-e-dokes started to take off.

"One problem is that journalists are almost always trying to invent new trends. Once I got known for Ecstasy they'd come along and say, "What about this?" "What about that?" They want it to happen to get a new story and a new angle." With the click of a mouse he surfs through files for figures. "Now this is the interesting one. 139 cocaine related

deaths in 2002. With ecstasy it tends to go up and down but now it's near enough 60 deaths a year."

He surfs through stats about other class A's, emailing me his PowerPoint lectures as we sit. The main things are alcohol, ecstasy, cocaine and maybe a bit of Ketamine. And GHB. There's a sort of party pack. They might start off with a bit of alcohol, then they might have an E, a bit of speed. Everyone has their preferred pharmacology." John's been around the clubs but catches most on TV. He does a brilliant impression of a gurning raver:

"The main thing with cocaine is that we get a lot of chest pain turning up in our emergency department. 10% of people who come into this hospital with chest pain have taken cocaine. Blood vessels everywhere tighten up and your blood pressure goes very high which puts you at risk of stroke. Your heart is working harder but because your arteries are constricted you get chest pain. A small number have heart attacks." He goes on to describe the thickening of your arteries. We chat about physiology and how a bad reaction to E can send your temperature rising, liver and kidneys failing, brain damaged by a stroke, bleeding to death through wounds you never knew you had, with blood that won't clot: "On the whole this acute episode doesn't happen to the vast majority. More than 99% of the time they don't kill and but in less than 1% of cases they do."

I ask him about drugs and Rave folklore. 99% of the time Es are not spiked with heroin. Though there was a time when you might have had a bit of LSD and a bit of an amphetamine mixed in but that was small time business trying to cash in on the big-time business: "The business of contaminants doesn't mean very much." And the Prof. describes tales that Es aren't as good as they used to be as, "Cobblers. There's a lot of shine about it." I'm surprised when he confirms that ecstasy is the only real dance drug. He's disturbed by my tales of people necking five or six Es in a session: "There was one time when I was at a teenage plus party. A single parent mum knew drugs were going to be taken so she made all the teenagers have a good meal first, dealt with the dealer herself and stayed up all night to make sure the children were OK." "That's a good mum." "What general advice would you give?" "You can enjoy yourself without taking anything. People have lost the ability to just enjoy themselves. They feel they have to pump it up in some way. And that's a pity."

Well there it is. Just Say Know. It's OK you can look now.

GROOVE RIDIN'

"I still feel that pressure, 'Okay. These people are paying for me and I'm supposed to make them dance. That's what it's all about — you are supposed to be bringing the party. You are the new entertainment. Before you had a band, now you have a DJ." STORM

"DJing is about making people and yourself feel happy. I love music. To see a whole crowd in front of you loving the same thing you're loving; that's the best thing that I could probably wish for." DJ CRISSY CRIS

THE BEST THING EVER ! – JAMES, AGED 10

East Grinstead, January 2004. Lou, Max and Natalie hold a housewarming party. It's a quiet, laid back affair. I'm playing Rare Grooves and Disco sounds. Meet James: He's 10 years old and his eyes are glued to the decks. I know that gaze and instinctively pass him the headphones. I get him to stand behind the decks explaining, "That's the tune they're hearing now. What we have to do is keep those people dancing and make those people over there dance even more, but we have to do it before this track ends." James concentrates lip bitingly hard, the way kids do. There's a spread of CDs: "Pick a tune." He draws Michael Jackson's *Billy Jean*. "That should do it. Pop it in the player. Good. Found the track …? Hear it?" He nods. "OK, when I say, move this fader across to the left … Slide all the way. Now watch this." People pile onto the kitchen dancefloor and those already dancing give it more 'oomph'. James' eyes are sparkling, he beams broadly. Pulling off the cans saying, "That's The Best Thing Ever!"

DJ INTERNATIONAL

The Olympic Games, Athens 2004. Thousands of athletes and officials march into the opening ceremony viewed by billions around the planet. And the backing track is supplied by – a DJ. The Games' organisers included a DJ in one of the World's most prestigious events in recognition of their contribution to youth culture. DJ Tiesto should go in the *Guinness Book of Records* for having played to the largest audience in human history. DJ Culture is now so ubiquitous that it's difficult to imagine a time before DJs were taken so seriously.

ANDY C – THE DJ'S DJ

"When I first started out I'd be shaking and my hand would be shaking trying to get the needle on a record, but now it's more about anticipation and excitement. That's what kind of buzz you get." ANDY C

We take DJs seriously but also expect more. We want faultless mixing. We want more plates per hour and we want as many double impact double drops as possible. Andy C's a master on the decks. How many times have the public voted him Best DJ? He's also the DJ's DJ. Storm came to Swerve after her set at Herbal. Andy had tried to persuade her to play after him. Storm was like, "Fuck off, I'm not playing after you!" She spent Andy's set looking at his hands with other DJs around the box in a ringside scrum doing the same. I've watched him on a few occasions. It takes a few sessions before you can really appreciate how he does what he does. At Grace he's intensity itself and flyin' funky – Too Dam Funky. Andy's very quick in the mix, having two tunes running for most of the time. And mi God does he rinse the guts out of the Allen & Heath mixer. His fingers blur over the dials, busy as bees on speed. He explains what he's up to: "That's all just EQing on the mixer. Sometimes when you're mixing two records together you need to EQ out frequencies on some records and hopefully make them sound like they are meant to be one tune. It's the same sort of principle as when you work in the studio. You have to maybe EQ out a bit of bass, mid or take the tops down a little bit and *vice-versa* just to the balance it out." Feet don't dare fail me now, Mr. C is in the building.

MELTDOWN AT THE END

I come home from work and crash on the sofa in front of the box with Kate and red wine. I get up to change out of my uniform and make ready for the night. Kate gives her warmest, 'Stay here with me' pout. And I'm like, "But Kate it's the Ram Records party at The End and Andy C's doing at two hour set."

Ram's logo is projected on a concrete car park opposite the entrance. Below the street, metal stairs lead to an open door pulsing waves of energy with Dynamite MC bawling, "Let's GO." Rays of coloured lights scan over untold people dancing in a smoky haze. They're vibing at the bar, on the stairs over looking the main floor, beneath the arches of two tunnels. Above our heads screens dense with pixels show a DJ's hands on decks, whilst a digital man runs through it all. The DJ box floats like the prow of a boat plunging forwards and ever into the storming sea. The artists on board are in the heart of the action. Huge speaker stacks tall and dark stand all points: north, south, east and west. Sound quality is excellent and it ain't too loud. A track's breakdown leaves people gently swaying, silently moving. They explode when drums and b-line boom. There's

militant energy in the air tonight. People are here to do some serious business. Dynamite sings old skool Jungle lyrics. Ed Rush or Optical dashes down the next big tune and the massive push it deeper. It's like the crowd and DJs are goading each other. Like they're all shouting, "Bring It On." Across the floor people's body language speaks with poses and gestures – speeds intensity, that's Jungle semaphore. You're seeing freedom of expression. If you could bottle this energy there wouldn't be wars over oil.

It's about this moment, place, vibe. West Central Street, underground London central. 70s fashions are still in – again. Long crocheted skirts here or impressive lamb chop sideburns there. His and hers Afro hair and unisex trainers. A *Pack of Wolves* snarls from all sides, ripping up the floor with sharp electric claws. You know we'll demand a rewind. The tune is runnin'. I could even see it going down at Castle Donnington. "Put your hands together for ED Rrrussssh & OptiCalllll." Moose looking peaceful and dapper drifts by the DJ box.

It's amazing that you can leave Jonathan Ross on TV at home, hit town and land up in a mad atmosphere like this. There are familiar faces and you're here with people who've followed the call. A geezer's just come up to me, smiling and sticking out his fist in greeting, shouting, "It's a brilliant night innit?" I nod, "Yeah it's a great night." And he's off dancing again. Another guy sits down next to me. Turns out he works here at The End. "What's it like working here?" "Fuckin' wicked." "And the sound system's good." "Yeah it's the best in the world." Turns out that he'd been at Homelands last weekend and didn't rate the atmosphere. "Everyone's been saying that it weren't that great really. You got a lighter?" he asks before heading off for Andy C.

Ram Records

Around the box there are concentric rings of
geezers. A few ladies but loads of geezers and
the energy's pumped up. Dynamite's bubblin' and
GQ steps past Red One to the floor. People are
on it, shouting, smiling. It's well after 1am
and Andy C's late for his own party. *Odyssey*'s
chords insinuate themselves into the mix. Havoc
follows the drop. Purple, blue and ultraviolet
lights scan mayhem. The b-line bores deep like a
pump action drilling through hard core. How do
you follow *Odyssey*? *Bring It On*.

Moving Fusion go into overtime and overdrive.
Andy C's over half an hour late, elbow and arm
space is at a premium on the rail around the
box. Dynamite passes the baton to GQ as Roni
Size' *Strictly Social* flows between them. Beats
drop relentlessly. Moving Fusion are killin' it,
but in the breakdown you can hear funky music
from the floor next door. I feel like getting a
bouncer to make 'em turn it down.

With a "Mr C is in the building!" Andy C finally
arrives delving through tunes. He's waiting to
go on, bouncing up and down. Andy's unwinding
his headphones and stepping up to the decks. I
swear there's a ringside crush. People jostle
for position, craning their necks to catch sight
of his hands. His first beats come in and it
gets grimy. Lungs screaming hoarse, eyes closed,
fists pounding, "ReeeWiinnd." By track three
Andy's bouncing up and down so much that I'm
scared he's gonna knock himself out on the
equipment above the decks. Spinnin' tunes he's
dancing like a mad 'un. GQ standing next to IC3
shouts out, "Watch the ride."

Barbed b-lines lash the club. It's hyper hyper
and there's a positive stomp goin' on. Time and
minds are lost in complex mixes. A guy let's out
a proppa James Brown scream and I'm reminded of
graffiti sprayed on the side of a Glastonbury
tent, 'I feel better than James Brown.' The
dark, brooding chords of the *Shadow Boxing*
remix floods the floor underscored by *Odyssey*,
the tune that every DJ plays. Tired legs push
me to the sidelines. I could hug The End for
having sofas on the dancefloor. I'm deeply
plugged in like everyone else. "Red One wanted
up front." Swirling purple, red, blue lights
diffuse smoke pushing us out of space and time.
We know we've reached that level. Andy chops
tunes making musical phrases into looped
sentences. This isn't just underground, it's
bloody subterranean. "Got a light?" "Yeah hold
on." I'm fishing through my pockets in a daze.
I was so deep in this whole thing that I'd zoned
out. "No sorry can't find it." "No worries bruv.
It's a blinda innit?" I smile agreement slipping
back and away into intensity, wallowing in rich
energy. You're seeing the rawness of Life
itself, sitting in a pool of joy.

It was a while before I noticed I was crying.
I'd been overcome by the emotion of it all.
I remember my shift at the hospital. We started
at 7.45am. The first baby died by nine. My own
patient was having fits frying her brain and
doctors had told another's mother that nothing
more could be done to save her daughter. I'd
watched that mother sit by her baby's bed
playing with her every day for months. You could
see that even though she spent most of her short
life on the end of a ventilator, mum still
brought happiness into her world. I guess that
day I'd seen the essence of two things: Death
& Life — a heady, heavy experience.

I stayed until the end of the set. In the loos some guys discuss the merits of Andy C. Walking back to the car I knew I'd been right to have this night. Acknowledge Death and celebrate Life. Sitting in the car writing notes helps me step down from the intensity of Ram's rave. The sunroof is open to a peaceful powder blue sky. I'm into the second sheet of A4 when, "Oi, you must 'ave seen 'em. You woz 'ere when we passed 'ere last time." There's a guy banging on the passenger window. Another bloke's shouting down through the sunroof. "You woz 'ere." "Sorry. I really don't know what you're talking about." "He's lying. 'Ow can ee not 'ave seen 'em?" Turns out their car has been burgled. "Look mate I've been sitting here writing this" I wave some pages. "Sorry I didn't see a thing." A third guy bowls up going, "Ee must be one of 'em. Get im'owt. Search 'is fuckin' car." They're rattling the doors trying to get into the boot. I'm like, "What the fuck …?" Hit the central locking, spark the engine and get right out of there thinking, 'Life. Sometimes it's all just a bit too much.'

The Double Impact Double Drop Thing

Perhaps DJs and punters are now talking more about double drop mixing but it's been around as long as Jungle Drum & Bass. L Double explains what it's about: "My personal interpretation of it is when you've got a tune and there might be a low part in the middle or breakdown of that tune. You know in 32 bars or whatever it's coming back in. So you take a different tune. This tune might have a longer intro than 32 bars but you mix it from wherever you need making both tunes drop together – at the same time." It's a whole other level. Andy C clarifies: "You get a feel for the records. I just started doing it to get to a bigger impact. It's interesting when you get two tunes smashing into each other and the madness they can create through the sound system. You know your tunes. You can look at the grooves and see how long the intro is going to be on one tune. Sometimes they happen completely off the cuff."

There are some DJs whose whole set is constructed around double drops. Andy C, Mampi Swift and Friction come to mind. I watched Swift at Fabric double drop through his whole set. One time he rolled through 62 bars of an intro and dropped bang on the beats. And on more than one occasion he rewound entire mixes. Madness. It's one particular style. Origin's EZM feels it's a basic skill that all DJs should have: "They should know how to do it. A lot of DJs don't study the tunes. DJs that study their music and tunes they are playing have done their homework. They know where the tune drops, how it drops, and how long it takes to drop. They give ravers the best of their ability." Mister T practises the art but understands it's not always appropriate: "If you've got someone flowing a whole set of double drops you can't get no better than that. But sometimes that's not what people want. Sometimes they want a continuous flow of flavours." If you get your timing wrong you'll create a complete mess. And not all tunes are constructed to be double dropped. I love Randall and Fresh's style of long, deep rolling mixes creating paragraphs of third tunes. But many DJs like to keep it clean cut. They'll slam a tune on a bridge or on a drop keeping vibes hyper. The hyper DJing style isn't to everyone's taste. No sooner are you dancing to one tune than it's covered by the next tune coming in. Flowjoe posting on the 1Xtra Message Board in July 2004 isn't into it: "What's the rush? You only need to mix tracks at lightning speed if you select a crap one in the first place and the crowd get bored of it within four bars. Why go to all the trouble of killing yourself and making the art of DJing into the art of being a robot."

Surely Flowjoe's exaggerating? Well, maybe not. I've loaded Andy C's *Nightlife 2* into the laptop. The tracks are excellent, the mixing is faultless and the musical interpretation is quality, but we hear 29 tracks in 66 minutes. The longest track, Photek's remix of *Ready She Ready*, plays for 3 minutes 45 seconds. The shortest, Baron's *A Modern Way* runs for just 56 seconds. The Producer disc two is far more laid back containing 14 tracks. Andy feels he's trying to make the most out of his slot: "I go up there and try to have as much fun as the people on the dancefloor. I enjoy it so much. I don't think you get long enough to play so I'm always squeezing in as many records as I can. I'm just out there having a good time."

John B

John B is another DJ / producer who takes having fun very seriously: "I think I try stuff others might not have the guts to stand up and do, and I try to push the sound in directions that haven't been exploited yet — sometimes it works, and sometimes it doesn't, but at least I try. I wouldn't be happy if I just sat on my arse and produced / DJed the same disposable, meaningless, play-it-safe stuff that seems to be popular. I'd rather try to push things a bit and challenge listeners / clubbers. As far as the image goes, again, I just want to be different, I don't want to be another dude posing moodily with a thugged-out expression. It's just not me. I admire the way people like Bowie, Madonna and Marilyn Manson control their image and change it as their musical styles develop. In this day and age you can't just stand there looking bored and smoking while you DJ. You have to be a performer, have a bit of character and more interaction with the crowd. And besides, it's fun to get more dressed up and try to learn how to put on eye make-up when you're drunk. Or persuade hot American girls to do it for you."

Old Skool

DJs have given workshops to interested parties for some time. I was invited to teach a class at my local comprehensive school by the music teacher Ms. Louise Finkle. The youths at White Hart Lane school had a bit of a hard reputation. I wasn't sure what to expect when I pulled into the staff car park. Teenagers in uniform approach. I'm thinking, 'What now?' But they say, "Please sir, can we carry the decks?" The first time you stand in front of a whole class is nerve-wracking. I'm in luck they've turned up for this extra session in their lunch break. I wouldn't want to be taking their double maths class. They're attentive as we roll through theory into practice. I've produced handouts asking, 'What are the main elements of a sound system?' And another with pictures of equipment which they have to 'join up in the right order'. The boys were quick to get on the decks. I had to make an extra effort to get the girls involved. The session went well and I was invited back. Thank Christ I didn't know an Ofsted School Inspector was in the room at the time, but Ms. Finkle and I passed.

Nu Skool

I'm chatting to my mate Curly Sue about DJing, and she chimes, "I know someone who's doing a DJ Course at college." "You're joking — this lady I have to speak to." Kerry is 23 and is studying a full time course at South Bank College, Folkstone. If successful Kerry will gain a certificate in DJ skills. She's brought her file along. MCFE Intermediate Candidate in Music Technology (DJ Skills). It's a well-structured package that includes Understanding Music Production as well as DJing. There's all the academic lingo — aims, objectives, course overviews, assignments. Kerry's file is full of hand written notes: "We're learning all about the theory side of DJing. For our assignments we have to create a 30 minute CD. We choose five to seven tunes and beat match them. Plus we have to do a three minute track using Reason. I'll be doing my track in Drum & Bass. You have to say how you want it to sound, when you want it to drop." There's even a section on Health & Safety. It covers everything like anatomy and function of the inner ear and how to avoid tinnitus, as well as knowing where the fire escapes are in the venue: "This section includes: Structure of Music — beats, bars and phrases, tips for mixing, how to beat match, how to count the BPMs. There's another section on how to get access to music on the Internet. This is about copyright, and this is about getting sued." And on and on.

The course is very comprehensive and I have to say it gives a brilliant holistic grounding in DJing. Us old uns had to get by in a very *ad hoc* manner. We muddled through over the years but there's some essential information we could have benefited from.

Take Flight

Natalie was born and bred in South London. "All the greats come from South London," she says with a smile. Flight went to her first illegal event in Croydon when she was 15. Hooked, she kept partying reaching many of the capital's brand name parties – Orange, Innovation, PM Scientists and, of course, Metalheadz Sunday Sessions at the Blue Note. Natalie started buying tunes, learning to mix about seven months later. Flight knew the Special Branch crew who had been putting on nights for years. They played some Jungle. Flight loved London but departed for studies in Wales. She didn't finish college but did learn to mix on a friend's decks. Natalie visited the Special Branch boys on returning to London: "They had been making mixtapes. A couple of the guys left the decks to mess around on the PlayStation. I got on the decks and they pretended not to be listening. When I started mixing they were like, "Stop the game. Bloody hell, when did you learn to mix?" I carried on from there. That was the beginning of '97."

Kemistry & Storm inspired her most in those early days. Flight checked an Innovation club night: "Rap was playing second last. By this time I was standing watching the decks all the time, not even dancing or anything. I remember seeing these people walk up thinking they were just Rap's mates. And then they go on the decks. Stevie Hyper D was like, "Yeah Kemistry & Storm." I didn't know what they looked like before that. I saw Kemi start playing. She had brown skin and dreadlocks and I had never seen anything like that in Drum & Bass. There are hardly any women as it is but to see a black or mixed-race woman doing her thing. They fuckin' blew me away. They were playing such different tunes from everybody else. I remember watching and thinking, 'Bloody hell.' The crowd was going off and it was wicked. A guy that used to come out with us saw me watching them and said, "That'll be you in five years time." And I was like, "Ah shut up." But they had such a deep impact on me that I did want to become more involved in music."

Flight became involved finding work in Trix Trax Records and Phuture Trax PR. Both jobs meant free tunes and contacts. After only six months mixing experience Flight landed a slot on pirate station Pressure FM with MC Stamina. She also became friendly with Kemi and Storm: "I started giving them tapes. I gave them my first ever mixtape." "No." I was horrified. You might give your first mixtape to a close friend, a sibling or chuck it in the bin, but never to a pair of top DJs, but Flight's a different thing: "I've still got a copy of that tape at home and it's alright. The mixing's tight for a first tape." She wasn't being flash: "I just wanted feedback and didn't know who else to give it to. I idolised them so much I thought that I'd give it to them to see what they thought." Kemi & Storm liked the tape encouraging her to continue. After a succession of tapes they asked for one more. Turns out they'd mentioned Flight to Goldie; saying it was time another girl was brought in. "I was like, "No fuckin' way!" I just didn't feel that I had enough tunes. I think I'd cut a few plates at that point, but they really wanted me to do it."

Sarah and Jo in the Groove Connection office also liked the tape and passed it on to Goldie who may never have listened to it. This was around that time that Kemistry died. Metalheadz stopped. Everything stopped. When Headz began again Flight figured her tape had been forgotten: "I was leaving the club and Goldie said, "I heard you want to rinse out in my club." I waited until I got around the corner then started jumping up and down on the spot." Later she sat down and thought about it: "Fuckin' hell, I can't play for Headz. I haven't got enough tunes. I'm not good enough. Everybody else is up there, I'm down here." But friends were encouraging. Flight's first Headz session at Dingwalls in mid-summer was one of the first occasions Storm had played since Kemi died: "It was a very emotional, strange vibe but it was wicked. There were loads of people out. I was really nervous but it went well." Metalheadz recruited her as one of the new breed with a residence on rotation. Six months later Fabio also recruited Flight for Swerve.

Flight

Photo by Cleveland Aaron

The CD Thing

"I believe a performing artist as a DJ has to perform on the wheels of steel. Simple as that." DJ SS

The CD thing is one of the most political issues in Drum & Bass. You have DJs like SS who might only use them to test a new tune. John B and Concord Dawn play them all the time. Bailey, Flight and L Double stand 50 / 50 on the matter. To sum up points on each side: Negative – people won't visit record shops to buy a CD single. CDs make music available digitally, which could increase piracy. That would be another blow for record shops and producers. CDs don't sound as good as vinyl and the audience can tell the difference. How can DJs pretend to be supporting the industry if people see them using CDs? It sets a bad example. DJs who are earning enough should spend some of that money on dubplates not CDs. It suggests a sloppy attitude on behalf of the DJ who hasn't bothered. It takes longer to cue up CDs, they stick and jump so you'll lose the vibe. And finally Bailey? "The main thing for me is it doesn't look good. If you're playing CDs and nothing's moving it doesn't look good."

On the positive side, CDs are far cheaper than the £60 it costs to cut a dub plate. Music becomes more accessible as it's easy to make copies. The crowd don't actually feel the difference. They're lighter to carry around than a box full of dubs and vinyl. Plus you can squeeze loads of tracks on one CD. Records get scratched and jump. If they're lost or stolen they're replaceable. It doesn't matter how it looks. It's all about the music.

John B sees the positive side: "My issue is more dub plates versus CDs anyway. If I wasn't doing this professionally and didn't have access to non-pressed stuff then of course vinyl would suffice. It's more fun to play anyway, but at my level, unless I want to piss away 10k a year on plates and associated excess baggage costs on tour, then CDs are the only logical choice for me."

DJ SS is steadfastly against DJs using CDs for most of their sets and doesn't support it: "Not at all. It's fine if you've got a tune and want to test it, that's all right. But with the money that we earn to go out with a CD case, I think it's a piss-take. DJing is an art form and they are making it too

easy. The punters are not going to come into a record shop to buy one track on a CD. They won't do that. And once it's on the Internet they can download it for free. You are not going to go to Black Market to buy a Pendulum track on CD. Forget that. You will travel from the other side of London to get it on vinyl but not on CD. That piece of vinyl is a collector's item. Vinyl has been there from day one. We grew up on it. This is how we built our business. Our scene was built on dub plate culture, the Reggae thing. The whole soundclash thing is built on vinyl. When I come to your show, open my bag and you see 80% plates man's thinking, 'Rare. This guy is serious.' Now if you open that CD thing up." SS pulls a disdainful face, shaking his head: "I'm telling you Influx and me played in New Orleans. That party was jammed. He played CDs warming up for me. Next thing you know the CD is jumping. People are shaking their heads, and he couldn't get the vibe. That's what happens. You speak to promoters who pay the artist to fly over and a man comes and plays CDs. They feel raped. The next point is that the vibe when you're playing CDs is not running. I don't care what they say. As a promoter I'm not booking anyone for no CD set. Hell no. I would feel raped. Make the effort like the rest of us do."

"I've invested in the scene for a long time and that means buying dub plates. Any international DJ that's making money should make sacrifices. First it's money for vinyl. If there's anything left, forget clothes, shoes, make-up – it's dub plates first." DJ STORM

Autumn 2004, Manchester. I'm playing a wedding. First one CD player goes down; then the next one. It's all gone quiet and everyone is looking at me. I'm fiddling with phono leads, looking for loose connections and a woman shouts, "Done this before? You wanna get some lessons mate." Luckily I've brought along one deck – just in case. Grace at Herbal, September 2004. Fresh has just come off the decks. The crowd's been jumpin' and Grooverider puts a CD in the right hand player. Nothing happens. He ejects it and pushes it into the left player. There's silence. He jabs at it a few times before it works. It's not often that Rider doesn't come out blazing.

"Vinyl will always be here. Vinyl is our bread and butter. 75% of our annual income is from vinyl. We'll never discard vinyl but you've got to sell music in other forms whether it be CDs, MP3s or whatever."
CLAYTON, TOV

A Wheelie Thing

To outsiders a DJ carrying a DJ box looks cool
and glamorous but they're heavy, and awkward.
Angela, a brassy twentysomething year old,
strides into Kate's Osteopathy clinic. She's
a 'hair's pressed back into a pony tail, big
hoop earrings, baseball cap on side-ways, all
the make-up' North London kinda G'yal. Angela
has a pain in her upper right arm. "Hobbies?"
asks Kate diagnosing. "I play a lot of tennis.
And I'm a DJ." "Hmm," says Kate. "Record box
too heavy? Have you thought of getting a wheelie
thing?" "A Wheelie Thing! I'd be laughed outta
my club." She tuts. The session is over and
she's been advised to ask her mates to carry her
tunes in future. Kate has one last question:
"Do you play vinyl or CDs?" "Vinyl. It's all
about the vinyl man." By the way Angela,
Great Grooverider has got a wheelie thing.
It's built into his record bag, and mighty
fine it looks too.

Mastering

One of the problems with CDs is that they aren't mastered
which is one reason that CDs burnt straight from software
don't sound as good when compared to vinyl. Mastering is
the final stage of the recording process during which the
music is finessed. Stuart Hawkes at Metropolis has had
years of experience and you can hear the difference.
Technological innovation marches on. Bailey watched a
DVD in which Jamaican Reggae artists were using CDRs
and even FinalScratch.

This might seem a bizarre connection but the events of
9 / 11 have also affected the CD thing. Before I could always
blag my tunes into the aircraft's passenger cabin. You can
still get away with it if you put your tunes in a small
enough record bag. Otherwise it's into the hold with your
tunes. Then what happens? They can go missing as
happened this summer to both Nicky Blackmarket and DJ
Storm. Nicky, who never used CDs in his set before, is now
thinking of taking them on trips abroad.

The Last Straw or The FinalScratch

The last straw for committed vinyl DJs is technology like
FinalScratch. It's one of several systems designed for artists
to DJ digitally. They range from the software based Traktor
DJ Studio which you can play from just your laptop, to
FinalScratch which combines hardware with software so the
DJ still maintains that traditional tactile interface, you can
use decks. Now the thing is they incorporate features like
looping, sampling, turntable break effect and the ultimate
sacrilege — auto-beat mixing. Companies manufacturing this
technology are well aware of DJ politics. They're listening
and are trying to tackle problems with each new version.
"FinalScratch is in an elite class of its own. It is one of
technology's most innovative — state of the art — piece of
equipment, that has taken DJing to the next level." So says
House icon Kevin Saunderson. Their website also informs us
that Judge Jules and LTJ Bukem are also proud owners.

I'm instinctively against digital DJing probably because my
parents bought me a plastic turntable when I was three.
It had plastic records, a stylus and I could rewind my
nursery rhymes. My two and a half year old godson Jake
owns Tomi decks. One turntable makes cutting 'n' scratching
sounds; the other squeaks electronic effects. He also has a
light blue Black Market t-shirt sporting the words, 'Future
DJ' across his chest. The thing is, if Drum & Bass stretches
technology, a new breed will come along, rinse out
FinalScratch and drive crowds mental. My friend George
who's DJed off a laptop maintains it's still as hectic and
exciting as using CDs. You still have pick tunes, cue them
and keep people dancing.

I'm chatting to Boomer, the first DJ in Russia to have
introduced Jungle to the country in 1994. He started off as
a Hip Hop DJ and has all the skillz. He's judged DMC
championships, loves vinyl and can definitely perform on the
wheels of steel. Boomer's on stage as the DJ before plays
his last few tunes. I'm a bit surprised that after pulling out
tunes from his bag, Boomer unloads FinalScratch. Now we
all know what we think about that kind of thing.

So Boomer boots up his sleek silver laptop placing it next to the decks. He rests the circular FinalScratch module by their side and links the laptop to FS with a USB cable, adding about five phono cables to the decks and CD players. The computer crashes three times before the FinalScratch software looks stable. A-Sides arrived to play 1Xtra's mix show only to find that his FinalScratch had broken down. He apologised to listeners whilst the studio crew hurriedly burnt CDs from his laptop. A reviewer on Stanton's FinalScratch web site acknowledged that setting up the system can be fiddly. The DJ plays a couple more tunes while Boomer sorts himself out. My real DJ prejudices were being justified. This seemed to take ages. FinalScratch boots up. The screen's split with columns of tunes. A soundwave like in Cubase runs above each column. Boomer then puts a FinalScratch 'record' on each turntable. They resemble normal vinyl but are encoded. As he cues the tune the waveform moves back and forth. The stylus on the record is exactly mirrored by a cursor line cutting through the soundwave vertically above the tune's cursor. When he rolls his first tune, he's physically rolling the decks. Boomer's actively mixing. He's not on automatic pilot.

He selects a Fresh tune from the computer. Producers send him music via AIM direct to St Petersburg. I'm peering fascinated at the list of tracks and artists. Boomer, "Oops. Sorry mate," trips over me trying to select a next tune from his laptop. I'm sat at the side of the stage watching people losing it in the usual way. This guy next to me is loving the music. I ask, "What about that FinalScratch thing?" "What does it matter? Do you think they care?" He points at the crowds. I feel I've asked a stupid question. "Just look at them," he emphasises. Up on the decks Boomer's scratching, dropping tracks playing music he loves to a crowd who love dancing. FinalScratch has won a score of awards. At the risk of having my headphones broken over SS's knee and being drummed — without bass — out the DJ community, I have to stay I was impressed. Very impressed. ("Was that OK mate? Just put the cash in this brown envelope. Tens 'n' twenties. Safe.)

The Girl with The Frilly Collar

"Many people have issues around confidence. Me? No, never." DJ Zy:on

In 1989 at Sussex Uni there was a campus club called The Crypt. Various union affiliated groups or blaggers like me and mate DJ Damien would hold rocking nights down there. One time I was just passing and looked in. The Women's Group were holding a party. A few people jigged about on the dance floor as a DJ meekly placed each record on the turntable. She sported a pudding basin hair cut and wore one of those Laura Ashley blouses dappled with little flowers. A frilly collar encircled her neck. I was scoffing thinking, 'Not exactly Oakendfold swaggering on the decks is it?' She seemed the very metaphor of a wilting lack of confidence. And didn't project any self-belief. Her sister was probably called The Fear. I never liked to admit that I could be affected by either of them. But over the years they'd both appear by my side — especially when I had something challenging to do, like go on the decks. One time I had The Fear really bad.

Touch down Frankfurt, October 2001. DJ Simon and club Space Place's promoters had flown me, DJ Zy:on, over to headline a Friday night session. Writer on the decks sort of thing. I'd played abroad before but this was the first all expenses paid, headlining deal. I can't say what it was like when other DJs played their first club abroad. Back home though I was really excited about it, but did the usual London thing and played it really cool. Casually let it drop that I'm DJing in Frankfurt that weekend. Nonchalantly carry my record box through the departure lounge and feel buzzed on the flight. I'm collected at the airport by Simon, Frankfurt's premier Drum & Bass DJ who carries my tunes to the car. I'm driven around town and it all feels exotic. Simon hands me a flyer. Zy:on's at the top. We visit Pro Vinyl record shop — which is a café, sofas, spliffs and tunes kind of place. And it's all gooood.

So, back in the car, Simon's proud of having invited a succession of artists to play in Space Place: "Last month we had Peshay here and the time before that it was Storm. She's been here a few times and rinsed it. And Bryan Gee … Flight …" I must admit that I didn't hear much more of what Simon said over the next few hours. I started thinking, 'Storm, Bryan, Peshay! As in 'I'll always respect Peshay'. Fuck. What the fuck am I doin' here? This is way outta my league'. My stomach became a mass of wriggling maggots. My head spun. And that girl with the frilly collar took her place on the back seat of the car. Right alongside Sister Fear. I'm not a celebrity. Get me out of here.

"… And DJ so 'n' so is coming out after you. Should be a wicked few months." "Yeah man. Simon, can we go back to the place? I need some kip." I'm lying on the bed trying not to feel sick. We drive to the venue and there are people queuing outside the warehouse. I think of Lambs and Slaughter. Simon's carrying my tunes into the club and there's people saying, "Zy:on" and "Guck mal jetzt kommt der DJ" (Look here comes the DJ). I take refuge in the Hip Hop room at the back of the club chatting to punters, more as a distraction than anything else. Hoping not to hear beats. I try to bolster myself with, 'Don't worry Zy:on they're just local boys. You're from London. You'll blow 'em away' bravado." It doesn't work. Chopper D was on the decks. Solid set, good tunes, faultless mixing. Simon's next – same again wicked set, wicked tunes, excellent mixing.

Half an hour before my set I thought I'd better sit behind the decks and sort out my records. The girl with the frilly collar and The Fear came along. I'm trying not to see how many people are crowded on the dancefloor. It was goin' off. I hope no one notices my hands shaking. Me and my posse behind the decks, Ms. Frilly collar with lambs. Last tune is running. Simon explains the mixer but all the dials and faders are blurred. The MC's on the mic, "Space Place give it up for DJ Simonnnn!." Shouts, screams, applause. Cue the first tune. The Terror starts to laugh in my headphones. I'm running on default drive. "Now all the way from London Town, All Massive, All Crew, give it up

for the DJ ZiiiiiiYONnn." I let the first tune roll, put the next tune on the deck and started to mix it in. Except I couldn't hear a thing. Panic had messed up my ears, the beats became muddled. I was thinking 'You can't clang out the first mix. Just get through the first mix.' There are people looking at my hands just like people look at other DJs hands. I put my head down staring at the mixer. Somewhere in the fog I had DJ Storm in my head saying, "Deep breaths. Focus. Settle. Breathe. Focus. You've done this so many times before." I counted the tune in and let it roll, slid the cross fader and slip into the zone. It might have been on the third tune that I noticed Simon nudging my arm and the MC shouting "Zy:on, rewind Zy:on." There are shouts and hands held high across the warehouse. Back at Frankfurt airport, staring at planes arriving and departing. I'm feelin' Saturday night's lesson. Believe in yourself. Put the work in. Don't underestimate yourself. And lay off the skunk before you play.

NERVES OF STEEL

Brazilian DJ Marky plays back-to-back with Zinc at Homelands Summer 2004. Actually they had a pair of decks each. That was a-whole-other-story. Thing is it was really late. I was tired, cold and had another few hours in the medical tent to fulfil my free ticket obligation. I drifted backstage of the Movement tent in my break. I couldn't quite see Zinc as he was further away. But Zinc and Marky were flinging tunes to each other through the mixer hyping the packed audience. I've never seen anything like Marky in Drum & Bass. He's got his right leg up next to the decks. His body's rocking, bouncing on his left leg, as his right arm flings his hand caning the crossfader. Marky's face – mouth open, twists in pleasurable animation. He's DMC on D&B and I can't believe the music we're hearing.

So What Does it Take?

"How do you get to play for Telepathy? We get thousands and thousands of tapes and CDs. As time has gone by I'm looking for a DJ that is unique. He takes risks − not trying to copy what the established boys are doing cos there's no sense in that. So when I'm given a CD I go with my own instincts. If I put the CD on and I begin to get that feeling that alerts me to them, I start to look at them deeper. And I'll say, "Send me another one." If I feel that second one does that as well, they'll go down in the book. I've got loads of guys who potentially I feel they're good. I'll be honest with you, if their mixing is what I call 'bake beans,' they'd probably wouldn't get a look-in. Alright, the mix might not be 100%, but if the tunes are good and the way they're putting their set together, I'd probably give them an early slot. Because I know doing a CD in laboratory conditions and playing in the real world is two different things. So I'll give them an early slot just to see how they handle all of that and how they still sound. And I'll just keep booking them for them to learn. Cos I've learnt through years of experience − from all of them − you craft your game. You've got the raw talent. You're not going to be brilliant from the beginning and you learn by doing events, events, events." *BRET, TELEPATHY*

Originality is The Key

Flight invites DJs to submit a mix that she'll play during her *Next Chapter* show. The problem was that she tended to receive mixes that were either hard and dark or soft and smooth, polarised at the extremes of the D&B spectrum. Few DJs were being adventurous enough to play the cross section of styles being made by producers. Flight wasn't being negative. It was strong of her to express that, if we were only going to hear the same old obvious mixes that section of the show would be curtailed. And good on her.

We're back to Fruit Salad again. Fabio praised good Drum & Bass DJs who have come from a long musical heritage, and have the ability to play different styles of music. Though some people were a little surprised that Fabio asked Ray Keith to play Swerve: "When I booked Ray a few people were like, "Oh Ray's playing is he?" "Yeah, damn straight he's playing." We're all DJs and DJs that have been around for a long time, we can switch and change our style. Ray is one of the originals. We started off playing House Music in '88. He's more than capable of changing his style. Don't underestimate any Drum & Bass DJ. Ray is proof of the pudding. He came down and played an absolutely exceptional set."

Representing

Working in the D&B scene I'm given a pile of paper and music. I can honestly say there are not enough minutes in a human day to give it all serious consideration. But sometimes a package arrives at the right time and place. First thing one morning the postman knocks with an envelope from Scotland. Inside there's flyers, biog, discog, professionally presented picture CDs − all the bizniz. Spookily Kid texted me just after I opened the package. As I look through all the gear, I'm taken back to Kemi & Storm's flat. They're explaining the importance of doing tapes, a *résumé* − all the bizniz when you're posting out your DJ demo. And Kid's done all that. What's more, the first CD I randomly pick off the pile, *Summertime Selection* gets the rewind after a minute. It's not style over substance or label spin. It did exactly what it said on the tin. Maybe there are people out there whose DJ demos are triple pack DVDs, but with me just randomly picking this out of the pile, Kid's reached me ... Sorry, just one last rewind ...

Life After Kemi

"Kemi died in '99 and a lot of people lost their faith in me – for whatever reason. I got straight back on the decks. I didn't want to be in this life without her, but the music was the one important thing for me. We learnt that together. I thought that Kemi would be pretty pissed off with me if I just gave it up. There are still days when I don't want to be here without her. The pain never, ever goes. All you do is cope with it better." *DJ Storm*

John Peel

26th October, 14.41. E-mail Rachel and Colin at Knowledge and Indy at BBC. Can't believe I'm writing this: 'It's just came over the news, John Peel suffered a heart attack and died on holiday with his wife in Peru. He was one of a kind. He'll be missed.'

John Peel meant so much to so many people. He lived for music and radio, serving his time as a pirate radio DJ before signing up to the BBC. John championed underground music for near on 40 years, helping promote countless artists and musical sub-genres. He contributed much to Jungle Drum & Bass playing a fair few quality tracks himself way before *One in the Jungle* – and giving Fabio, Grooverider and Bailey space on his show. Passionate about music, he has DJed on the circuit and played Fabriclive Sessions. A couple of weeks ago, Grooverider commented about a recent Radio 1 DJ dinner. Judge Jules, Trevor Nelson and John Peel. Paying respect, even Rider was star-struck.

John was the first person I interviewed back in '87. We sat on a wall outside Radio 1. He wasn't this 'Big DJ' type. He was warm and human. We met occasionally over the years. He was always a humorous, down to earth, wise, comforting voice. John was an immense national / international treasure. Like with Stevie and Kemi we can't believe he's gone. Rest in Peace and Beats John Peel.

Stevie

1999. A frail old lady is helped on stage to accept a special *Knowledge* award for her son Stevie Hyper D. Gingerly holding the microphone she says, "Junglists are you ready?" – and brings the house down.

Generation Next

Jungle has been around long enough for artists' children to become artists themselves. Live'0, son of 5ive-0, has taken up DJing. Logan D, Mickey Finn's son, has become a DJ. And Tracey Ton Promotions and partner Kenny Ken also have a DJ son – Crissy Cris. He was on the decks by the age of six. Kenny gave him his first mixing lessons at ten years old: "Every time I had a chance to go on the decks I practised for ages and ages." Crissy was persuaded to send a tape into Kool FM. He and Logan D played back to back on their Under 18 special guest show. Eastman received many requests from listeners asking to hear the duo again: "I was 11 or 12 when I first went on. Logan was about 16. We were both proper young. After a while we got our own Sunday afternoon slot. I've been on Kool for about seven years now." One of Crissy's crowning moments was winning a DJ competition. He was 12. The other contestants were in their mid-twenties: "All the older DJs, were going, "Oh my God. I got beaten by a twelve year old.""

He first DJed at The End and a party in Germany when he was 13. By 14 he'd played in Canada. The foreign bookings still flow in. Like his father Crissy has turned his hand to producing. He's happy making Garage and Hip Hop as well as Drum & Bass. He sold almost all 500 copies of his first tune and continues to produce, working with Skibadee. He's now producing an album: "My plan is to make it really big and be the best DJ."

Clayton and Mark at TOV are also investing in the future: "We do workshops for kids too. Kids that have been in trouble. I get them to do something constructive. I especially want to put something back in the community. I remember when I was trying to break through and I couldn't even get a job as a tea boy in a studio. We had to start a label and learn from our mistakes. From being in that position I could see that the kids need someone to point them in the right direction."

LYRICS ON OUR LIPS

During my Drum & Bass wilderness years I got right back into vocals. I listened to Missy Elliot, Angie Stone, Jill Scott, Alicia Keys, Ms Dynamite, Bowie and a whole case full of CDs. There was Eminem, the quintessential American, followed by The Streets, a right eloquent British geezer. *Weak Become Heroes* is a classic Generation Rave choooon. I'm too embarrassed to say how many times I rewound that one. When I drifted back into Jungle a chorus of voices uttered new styles. Voices that propelled D&B tunes into the charts. Kele Le Roc on Shy FX & T Power's *Shake Ur Body*, Stamina on *Barcelona. LK* was played in the depths of a Valve night. The room filled with the sunshine of Stamina's voice enfolding acoustic guitar strings. *Mo'Fire* featuring Navigator's astoundingly powerful voice burst through the radio when I was least expecting it. I thought, 'What da fuck?' Followed quickly by, 'I want that tune – now – and don't tell me it's not in yet.'

Many of the old Dons – GQ, 5ive-0, Navigator, Det, Shabba, Skibba, Cleveland Watkiss, Dynamite MC, Fats, IC3 and Fearless are still holding the mic. The Ragga Twins have staged a welcome return. Stamina emerged taking *LK* and Jungle into the charts. Globalised Drum & Bass brought us Tali and *Lyric On My Lip*. It was a long time before her album left my CD player. Shabba and Tali represent the two extremes of the JDB MC spectrum. Their upbringings and geographical locations are literally a world apart, but both convey messages in their performances. There's Shabba's skilful double speak and Tali's versatile song and chat. Shabba and Tali: it's all about Fruit Salad.

MC SHABBA

"Sometimes I go places and white kids are amazed. One time in Croydon the dance is full of Yardies playing Sizzla and Capleton. I was thinking, 'Boy, it's gonna have to be a bit deep to play Jungle in here', but we fucked up the whole place. People were screaming, knocking the bar goin' "Rewind! Rewind! Pull-up!" All grabbing my hand. And I was like, "Raaaa." "

MC Shabba started MCing when he was 13. Unbeknown to his parents he gave up school for 18 months opting for a life of hustling and petty crime on Hackney's streets: "I had to go out and do certain things. Most of my friends went to jail. I never went to jail. I was either going to go down that road or this road. At 15 I was like, "I can't move with these boys even though they're my friends and I grew up 'round them. They're bad company." When Shabba left his old life behind, he was able to concentrate on pirate radio. He started running errands for Weekend Rush's studio crew. Shabba first spoke on the mic giving out shouts. He soon became the station's night duty manager: "The only thing that kept me off the road was music. Instead of me going out trying to thief a car system, why not be in the studio doing something positive?" He was inspired by Bounty Killer, Beenie Man and Punk groups because of their energy and how they performed on stage. "The Bashment man was always entertaining and that's what I'm dealing with. A lot goes into the performance, what you put on the stage, not just what you say. If there's some way you can get the crowd going with movement that inspires me."

Shabba

Shabba first made inroads into performing on stage between '92-'93 at club Busby's for a promotion called Outrage. After a little over a year he was performing with Mickey Finn and Jumping Jack Frost gaining his big breakthrough with Telepathy at The Wax Club: "You could catch me there every Friday night. Ten years down the line I'm still there. I'm travelling the world, I'm making records, I've got my label, my website. I never thought it would get like that."

Shabba's journey thus far isn't untypical for a top MC. Though he lived near Clapton, Hackney (an area they now call 'The Murder Mile') his family wasn't poor. Shabba's father was The Sex Pistols' Tour Manager. Along the way, Shabba, born in '77 – The Year of Punk – met Johnny Rotten and later groups like Guns N Roses: "It was wicked. I loved their energy." He used that energy on pirates like Kick, then Kool FM and on stage from bookings which came through Kool's agency. Everything went well until 1997, the year of the producer / DJ backlash against MCs whose bookings fell. Shabba weathered the storm. Things began to pick up for Shabba by '98, especially foreign bookings.

HE'S BIG IN JAPAN

At the age of 15 Shabba had recorded a track with his father's friend. Five years later the tune reached Number One in Japan. He was invited to the States to record an album: "I put the lyric down, people loved the tune and wanted to see who'd done it." So Shabba spent six months touring America, Japan and South Korea performing to crowds as large as 10,000. The five million dollar tour was paid for by Sony. The gigs were expensive because, "They used to smash things up all the time cos it was a Punk band. Hundreds of thousands of dollars worth equipment got smashed up. It was a crazy tour." Shabba also gained experience from rappers Cypress Hill and Lil Kim who joined the tour at various points: "I was 21 touring with 35-40 year old men. They had all been through it and were multi-millionaires as well. I've got videos of concerts and shit. It would blow man away if they watched it. I was trying to do something different. I didn't know where it was going to lead. It was a boost for me." He remained busy on the international circuit during his time in Japan, returning to host his tenth anniversary party held in 2000 by Telepathy.

Shabba wanted to spend his energy on other projects like his record label Highly Blessed, but there were too many demands on his time. He progressed slowly but surely, releasing his first track Listen to the Mic Man in 2002 on his label. There was one problem: "I had all these kids out there going to buy my tunes and none of the DJs were playing my tunes in the rave. That told me something. You don't need these mans cos at the end of the day you've got your fan base. People wanna buy something with me on it."

MCs are back in favour and Shabba has been busier than ever. He and Skibba have taken to the stage many times in the ever-popular MC Convention parties. They held the sixth Convention party with a 'payback' rave in October 2004. The line-up included: S & S, Fearless, IC3, J Swif, Biggie, Mad P and Yardie: "It's definitely MC time. From last year it's been hectic out there. We've created a market. You've just got to feed that market." Aside from headlining the bigger raves you may find Shabba in some small club deep in the countryside. You might think these are only bread and butter bookings but Shabba loves the intimate vibe of the smaller parties. He also has a masterplan: "A lot of promoters ain't got the money to book a load of DJs and MCs. I've capitalised on the littler things. So when I do the bigger things people know my lyrics.

"I get ideas and work off that. Before I never used to write. I used to try something and if it worked, it worked. Now I'm writing it and making it work. I'll think of things that will lead to somewhere else and I'll just write that situation. Sitting down writing to a beat is very boring. If you've got an idea going write that idea." Shabba's been writing for his performances and his album. Keeping it real, he's gone deep, deep enough to cover local and global politics: "My lyrics are about what's goin' on now. I got a tune out called The Streets." He raps, "There's bare arms house on the street, living in the ghetto things ain't sweet." He's also troubled about our post 9 / 11 world: "There's madness out there and things going on with the war and terrorists. I ain't going to be able to change the world, you ain't gonna be able to change the world but I can entice the people to hear my point of view on the thing. Do it in an exciting and educational way where I'm taking the piss out the government. At the end of the day they take the piss out of us. I'm just trying to tell people, "Look. This is a joke."" From his history, fanbase, lyrics, album, website, contribution and commitment to international Jungle Drum & Bass – Shabba has got it goin' on.

This Girl's Aloud – Tali

"One night, I was having a brilliant time and this DJ called Silencer, I don't where he is now, but he changed my life." TALI

Homelands 2004, I'm sipping beer, listening to beats behind the Movement tent. MC Moose and London Elektricity slope by. I recognise a woman from last year. Her face shines with charisma as she runs around energetically arranging last minute guest passes for friends waiting in a car outside the festival. Later that day we're coincidentally deck-side. I knew I'd regret not asking her name. "Tali," she smiles as we rest on scaffolding. Fabio is on the decks. The tent is filled with thousands of ravers losin' their all. Over the next few months I'd experience Tali's powerful, versatile stage performance and rinse her first album, *Lyric On My Lip*.

Natali Scott, now more familiar as Tali, hails from a small town in New Zealand's North Island. She grew up in a lush paradise where you can surf in the morning and ski in the evening. Tali played piano, wrote poetic rhymes and attended drama school developing her nascent skills. She walked into Rave Culture whilst at university in New Zealand's capital Wellington where she took a performing arts course: "To start off with I was going to all genre raves – Techno, House – everything. But there was always a bit of Drum & Bass at the end. One night I was having a brilliant time and this DJ called Silencer, I don't where he is now, but he changed my life. He dropped the Krust remix of *Maintain*. From then on I was absolutely hooked. As Drum & Bass became more and more popular in New Zealand, people started to put on pure D&B raves and I became a total Drum & Bass addict."

On a Mission From God

Tali entered a televised, nationwide talent completion. She instinctively avoided performing dodgy cover versions, opting to use original material: "The judges thought I stood out because I wasn't doing the cheesy stuff. I didn't know if I wanted to be an actress or a singer. I'd studied both at university. And as cheesy as it sounds, I actually got down on my knees and had a little prayer. I was like, "God, if I do well at this talent contest I'll take it as a sign that I'm supposed to be a singer. If I don't, an actress." It's our gain Tali was on a mission from God: "I came third in the grand final. So I took that as a sign." It was at this point that Tali's MC career began to escalate.

She joined the Scientific Crew presenting a local radio show alongside former boyfriend, DJ Mosus. They also ran a production company and were the first people to book Bailey, Shy FX and Bryan Gee. This connection bolstered her skills. When Bailey's MC couldn't attend, Tali stepped in – even though it was only the fourth occasion she had MCed on stage. Truly smitten by MCing and Drum & Bass, Tali decided to take a gap year and move to Melbourne, Australia. One of those classic, 'right place at the right time' moments happened. Roni Size and the Full Cycle crew were in town for Australia's Big Day Out festival. Tali treated Mr. Size to a spontaneous lyrical display. Dynamite sat on the bench while MC Tali took the stage for Roni's set.

With Blighty calling, Tali packed her bags and flew north: "When I first got to England, I was living in London, teaching, cos I'm a trained primary school teacher, but that kind of dried up. Then I got the call from Roni to come to Bristol to make music. He knew that was my dream, I told him when I'd met him in Melbourne. He said, "Stay focussed and make it happen." I'd be going down to Bristol all the time. Every time I went I never wanted to leave. He actually gave me some pocket money to live on, because he didn't want me teaching or waitressing. "I want you to concentrate on the music, because I've got big plans for you." That big plan was to join Full Cycle and make an album."

MC Tali

Tali had something new to offer the Art of MCing. Not only could she chat lyrics, Tali could sing. That skill would place her alongside Conrad, Fats, Stamina and Cleveland Watkiss who also sing and rhyme: "It's really hard for me to be on the mic and not bust into a rhyme, cos I've been into rapping since I was about ten. Most people back home couldn't understand why a white girl from 'down country' would want to MC!"

Tali has also been inspired by people who are both vocalists and producers like Missy Elliot and she'd like to produce herself: "I'm looking to buy my own studio. I make music by relying on other people. Sometimes I can be sat at home thinking, 'Fuck, I need to be in the studio' but the guys aren't there. That can be frustrating. I want to be able to sit in my studio and make beats, play at my keyboard and write a tune, so when I go to Roni or whoever I can say, "This is what I've done so far." I want to be able to meet them half way." Tali's independent skills have brought her this far. We'll be hearing a lot more of her in the future.

Tali has also been inspired by people who are both vocalists and producers like Missy Elliot and she'd like to produce herself: "I'm looking to buy my own studio. I make music by relying on other people. Sometimes I can be sat at home thinking, 'Fuck, I need to be in the studio' but the guys aren't there. That can be frustrating. I want to be able to sit in my studio and make beats, play at my keyboard and write a tune, so when I go to Roni or whoever I can say, "This is what I've done so far." Hopefully they can progress naturally from what I've given them. I want to be able to meet them half way." Tali's independent skills have brought her this far. We'll be hearing a lot more of her in the future.

BUBBLING OR BABBLING?

The same pros and cons arguments circulate. You can understand them. You can't understand them. DJ E explains Rude FM's MC policy: "We don't have MCs." I have a story from a guy who loves MCs and one from a girl who locked herself into the loo at a rave, clamping her hands over her ears screaming, "Shut up!!!" There are fans who will skillfully recite lyrical phrases. Equally there are detractors who can do that, "Manmana ne na na nah na nah" imitation of the double talk style. I'm having a *deja vu* moment, but I have a feeling that we've been here before. I won't rehash all the old arguments, just deal with the central issue of intelligibility. Their stage / vocal performance is so evident in a dance, surely we should be able to understand what the are saying. Back to the North London school.

B: There's a lot of that fast chatting style around what do you think?
Ben, Emma, Matt: You have to listen.
Ben: Old people complain it's just noise but we're young and we understand.
Emma: You've got to actually listen. If you get the rhythm then you know what they're saying.

Miriam from Tottenham: "Skibadee and Shabba are wicked. I hate MCs that don't actually say anything. My cousin is a Garage MC. He says the same thing over and over. A lot of it isn't even words, he just goes, "Bla ba ba de la ba," when he runs out of rhymes. Skibadee and Shabba say something and sound really good." And there's Laura from Croydon, a dyed in the wool Jungle raver. Laura loves her MCs, is the proud owner of some 30 odd tape-packs and says, "Unless you rewind them a few times you can't understand what they're saying. How can you understand them if you're off your face in some rave?" MC System, Traffic resident, concentrates on good quality hosting: "I came into Drum & Bass because I like the music. A lot of MCs aren't listening to the tunes and chat over breakdowns, vocals, drops and the mixes."

Disgusted of Tottenham

The DJ / MC stage can work well when one artist frames the other and they're not involved in a power struggle. The following examples worked against the sprit of our music.

An Origin DJ is playing the last tune. It's a summery Brazilian influenced number. Enter the MC. "Yo bruv, yo bruv - what is this? Stop this tune? Stop it. Stop it." DJ twists the stop dial. "Listen bruv, what's this?" The tune's whirling to a halt and DJ spins it back. "Hold on. Stop. Stop. Stop. Stop. Right. This one says … Let go of the tune bruv. Now this one says, 'Urban Star - Crystal & Mek D&B Remix. *You Are My Star Ship* vocal mix.' The MC laughs contemptuously. "It's not coming back on bruv. That's why I told you to stop it. You know what? I've never 'eard of 'em. No disrespect but Crystal & Mek [makes disparaging noises]. DJ mutters something in the background. "I don't care if Bailey plays it. Bailey's a good friend of mine. He bangs out some beats but that's not one of 'em." I'm staring at the radio hardly able to believe my ears. The MC continues to belly laugh pitifully, verbally humiliating the DJ till the ads roll at the end of the show.

I'm at Grace resting on a pillar near the decks. What happened next was a dis-grace. Mr. MC chats fast over tunes that don't need it. He stops to build a spliff. Up steps my girl. She speaks to Mr. MC who passes her the mic. She has a wonderful voice and a great singing style that contrasts well with the music. After a couple of minutes Mr. MC takes back the mic and stuffs it in his pocket. Not to be put off, my girl politely keeps on asking to continue. MC shakes his head and continues building. Along comes MC Brand Name. He's hanging and not even due to perform. Mr. MC whips out the mic passing it to MC Brand Name. I'm thinking, 'Oh well, fair enough, it is MC Brand Name.' Then MC Brand Name howls down the mic like a dog. No lyrics, just howls. My girl doesn't get a look in. Not good chaps. Not good. It's supposed to be about the music, not gender wars. Fix up.

One Love

The whole Art of MCing will continue progressing and our music will benefit holistically. Dynamite brought us a graceful gift with *The Scene* from his album *The World Of Dynamite*. MCs Det, Skibba, Shabba, Cleveland Watkiss, Dynamite MC, 5ive'0, Stamina, the Ragga Twins, GQ & Fats voiced the brilliant *One Love* produced by DJ Ron & Patife. It's a timely pro-peace tune, but Gentlemen next time, please don't leave out the ladeez. Time for me to pass the mic. Navi - you're on.

THE EVOLUTION OF THE MC

BY NAVIGATOR

What is the definition and function of an MC? Master of Ceremonies, Mic Chanter, Toaster, Rapper, Lyricist, Poet, Presenter, Host or maybe even a Conductor are all names that could be used in conjunction with the term. There are many ways to deliver lyrics, interact with the crowd and a DJ, project or record your voice. In Jungle / Drum & Bass the two main applications of MC's skills are linking the DJ, music and audience together and lyrically performing over tracks being played. As an MC myself, I have experienced the overwhelming feeling a vocalists gets when everything gels together perfectly in the studio or an electric crowd response is obtained. The adrenaline rush is incredible. For me there is no higher feeling and I have been addicted to it for over 25 years. Contrary to popular belief, it didn't all start with Hip Hop.The evolution of the MC began as more of an impromptu live performance and lifestyle rather than the vocal art it has become accepted as today. It undoubtedly has a firm foundation in Roots Reggae and Hip Hop Culture and has now gained a wealth of international respect.

It all really began with Reggae music, which is a direct descendant of the Ska, Rocksteady, Bluebeat era of the late 1950s early 60s. Singers of that time would ad-lib or improvise over spaces in the track, much in the same way as MCs do today before and in between their rhymes. Early pioneers include Prince Buster, Desmond Decker, Scottie and Toots & the Maytals. When Reggae came to the forefront the lyrical toasting aspect came into play, the original Jamaican dancehall DJ / MC used to play or select records and also hosted, chatted or toasted on the microphone. The vocal version of the track would be played first, name checking the singer or the studio it was recorded in, then the flipside (or part two) was played, otherwise known as the version, dub or instrumental. The DJ / MC would then perform freestyle lyrics or rhymes over it. Hence the term "Ride 'pon the rhythm, ride 'pon the version" or "Sit down 'pon top of the rhythm, sit down 'pon top of the version. The classic Jamaican film *The Harder They Come* starring living legend Jimmy Cliff, includes several scenes that portray how it was done. U-Roy was the first Jamaican MC to record vocals and have chart success as a toaster. King Stitt, Lord Comic, Dennis Alcapone and many others were doing the same thing. U-Roy had three hits in the late 60s, *Wear You To The Ball*, *Wake The Town* and *Rule The Nation* in the Top Ten for several consecutive weeks. He gained credibility and recognition as an artist, catapulting him into the history books as the Godfather. This paved the way for a new wave of toasters to be accepted into the Reggae music industry as recording artists.

Sir Coxsone Dodd – Studio 1, Duke Reid – Treasure Isle, Bunny 'Striker' Lee, Joe Gibbs, King Tubby's and Prince Jammy's, were some of the most famous producers and studios with whom artists wanted to record. These studios produced the hottest rhythm tracks of the late 60s / early 70s. A turning point came when studios started recording singer / toaster combination versions of those classic tunes, normally using the song's chorus as a hook and then having the toaster perform the verses. After a while it became apparent that the toasters were gaining popularity in their own right. The studios built very powerful sound systems that they would play parties with. This was an ideal way of promoting the records, the artists and the studio name. A difference was now marked between the selector and the toaster. The selector played the tunes and dub plates of new tracks. Dub plates are one off pressings that might never be released. The most popular toasters would frequently attend these parties performing their hits. Sound systems were a breeding ground for the upcoming new generation of toasters who were being inspired by established stars. Pirate radio stations and rave parties could be viewed as the modern day equivalent of the opportunities that the original sound systems provided.

In the mid-late 70s Reggae changed to a more Roots and Culture Dub style as opposed to the more Country & Western or Motown Soul influenced era that had preceded it. The Rastafarian movement emerged and had a huge influence on the sound and the lyrics of the music being recorded. Reggae Dancehall had developed its own identity and its message was of a more conscious nature, promoting freedom from mental slavery, denouncing 'Babylon' as the political system that was brainwashing the people.

Producers were recording tracks and voicing them themselves, which led to many becoming producer / artists. It was a trend that caught on very quickly and kick started a lot of careers, for instance, Lee 'Scratch' Perry, Jah Shaka and Prince Fari. The music became very raw and sparse, vocals were used as an intro and then delayed to lead into the rough basslines and equalised drums, snares and beats, which is why it earned the tag Dub or Dubwise. But there were still vocal versions of all the tracks. Linton Kwesi Johnson, a Jamaican Dub-poet, also had considerable success. His style of delivery is spoken word as opposed to melodic and is comparable to today's chart topper The Streets. The lyrical content of Linton's recordings were stories of real life experiences and racial discriminations that West Indians and their offspring often encountered from British nationals and authorities whilst living in England during the 60s and 70s.

When Sound Systems played at parties, the vocal side of the tune was used as an introduction to the instrumental. This left of space for the toaster to improvise or freestyle, pushing him to the forefront as a presenter and lyricist. Everything runs in cycles and in the late 70s / early 80s Reggae Dancehall became firmly established. Sound systems emerged having a strong presence worldwide. The migration of West Indians, especially Jamaicans, to Europe and America spread the message far and wide. Many people aspired to be a selector or DJ, much the same as the youths in the UK are aspiring to be producer / DJs or MCs nowadays.

The classic Reggae film / documentary set in Jamaica called Rockers is another example of how it was, it stars a whole host of singers, DJs, MCs, musicians and other people that were at the forefront of the industry. For an insight into how the sound system circuit ran in the UK in the mid 70s to early 80s, check out the film Babylon which starred Brinsley Ford of Aswad. Babylon is typical of how the UK youths of that time got their inspirations to make it out of the ghetto struggle and achieve success in music.

Catchphrases that toasters were known for gained them fame and popularity. For example, General Echo who performed on a sound called Stereophonic the Bionic, would sing, "People are you ready, BO! Oh lord, to come do the stereophonic rock steady, BO! Oh Lord." With no disrespect intended to late, great Jungle MC Stevie Hyper D, but "Junglists are you ready, BO! Oh lord have mercy" was his interpretation of General Echo's lyrics. Even the word 'Jungle' was derived from samples of famous Reggae Dancehall MCs who made references to Jungle and Junglists. In Kingston, Jamaica there is a notorious ghetto area much like a UK housing estate or the New York City projects. It's called Tivoli Gardens, it is like a concrete jungle, hence the name 'Jungle' and people who live there are referred to as 'Junglists.'

The 80s were the decade of the new school. The lifestyle referred to as Hip Hop Culture started to make its mark internationally. Young African American, Hispanic and White communities initially inspired it, but the influx of Jamaican sound boys into New York City was also a major influence. Breakdancing, Graffiti Writers, Street Apparel, DJing & MCing all became synonymous with the term Hip Hop. The DJs played all styles of music including: Reggae, Calypso, Motown and Soul. The drum patterns behind Hip Hop are broken beats otherwise know as breakbeats, as exemplified by living legend James Brown's Funky Drummer. Kool Herc, the founding father of Hip Hop DJing, used two decks to mix and scratch records together at block parties, which led to the rise in popularity of people like Grand Master Flash, Afrika Bambaataa and others. In 1979 Sugar Hill Gang reused the backing track from Le Chic's Good Times and had the first massive worldwide hit with Rappers Delight. The media tried to dismiss it as a short-lived fad, but the music captured the hearts and minds of the youth and gave them a way to escape the oppression of the system. It was seen as a way to express their pain, disillusionment and struggles, and became a source of hope and encouragement to help elevate self-esteem. The menial positions usually on offer to people from an underprivileged background and the need to have the formal qualifications for a better job were superseded by the opportunity that Hip Hop gave these aspiring artists.

LL Cool J, KRS1, Public Enemy, Run DMC, and NWA became spokesmen and leaders for the movement. They helped start record labels like Def Jam, selling the music on the streets because the majors had no idea how to promote this genre of Street Culture. Little did the majors know that

MC Navigator

PHOTO BY COURTNEY HAMILTON

Hip Hop would go on to become the multi-million selling phenomenon it is today. More recently new school rappers like Jay Z, 50 Cent and Eminem have risen to prominence. Later that decade saw the birth of modern Dance Music through the inception of House music. At the same time the birth of digital and computerised influenced production made programming beats not just something musicians could do. Doors opened to a whole new dimension in making music in home studios and truly revolutionised the meaning of the term 'recording studio'.

In 1985-86 Reggae Dancehall went digital. The first digital hit was called *Under Mi Sleng Teng* sung by Wayne Smith, the story is that he was switching off a Casio synthesiser and it made a sound that caught his ear, he recorded the sound, played a bassline with it and the rest is history. It started the Digital Dancehall era, which was capitalised to great effect by the likes of King Jammy's. He also had a sound system and an army of singers and MCs who all went onto become stars in their own right. One very successful act was Chaka Demus & Pliers who had a string of hits like *Murder She Wrote* and *Tease Me*. The Dancehall scene went through a change during this period; sound systems like Stonelove started gaining popularity, the selectors became more vocal again and started to clash with each other, seeing who had the best dub plates and the slickest tongue. The DJs or Toasters became stage show artists, performing their songs with a live backing band. They would also clash with each other lyrically; in both cases whoever got the biggest response from the crowd would win.

In the mid / late 80s came the rise of Techno from Belgium and Acid House in the UK; both are direct descendants of House music. Reggae Dancehall, Hip Hop, Breakbeat and House were also bombarding Britain. Up-and-coming producers were fusing them together, which created a hybrid sound that gave the UK an identity of its own. MCs were always a part of it, becoming steadily more and more popular. By the beginning of the 90s the Rave Scene embraced Hardcore and subsequently Jungle exploded with a ferocity that would be felt worldwide. The vast majority of established UK MCs of that period like Rebel MC, General Levy, Top Cat, Rodney P and Roots Manuva graduated from Reggae Dancehall or Hip Hop Sound Systems. The natural progression of the music gave UK MCs access to large fan bases and they continued to command respect at home and internationally as their careers progressed.

UK MCs reinvented and launched themselves in a variety of ways; some were hosts like Moose and Creed. Others were more lyrical like myself. The UK Rave scene paved the way for a new wave of record labels, pirate radio stations and illegal parties. The classic Jungle documentary *A London Something Dis* is a good reference guide to understand what that period of time was like for the array of people involved. Further development in the mid 90s saw the emergence of UK Garage making another huge impact, in much the same way as Jungle did. Jungle evolved into what we now know as Drum & Bass; pushing MCs like Skibadee, Shabba, Foxy and Eksman to the forefront. The creative cycle has bred new sub genres of MCs, flows and styles. UK Garage has now evolved into Dubstep, Sub-low or Grime. MCs like Dizzee Rascal, Wiley and Shystie are heralded as the sound and expression of the future. Even the way in which words and street slang in lyrics have mutated over the years has almost created a new language. Innovative music and vocal expressions reminds us that we have to remember where we came from, to know where we are and where we are going in the future. Who knows what will be the latest thing in 2010?

REMEMBER HISTORY REPEATS ITSELF

Right now, as you read this, history is being created by doing what we love and believe in. We are subconsciously and subliminally inspiring a whole new generation of aspiring MCs to develop in a time dimension that we might not be alive to witness. All MCs have influenced the future in our own unique and progressive way. Music has always been a vehicle for expression of creativity; vocalists whether they are MCs or singers possess a gift. It is a blessing that commands a high level of respect from listeners who appreciate its value.

Projection of your voice is a combination of vibration and frequency, with thought and lyrics added to the equation, its power penetrates and leaves an impression on the listener. The intensity of your frequency and the rate you vibrate determines the level of the impression you will make when you embark upon your individual expressive journey.

SPREADING LOVE: DRUM & BASS LIVE

LONDON ELEKTRICITY

There have been other live D&B bands, Reprazent, EZ Rollers and Kosheen with their award winning anthem *Hide U.* Kosheen were with us until they moved to rockier climes. *Knowledge* magazine recently featured ten live D&B bands including: Keiretsu, Obedientbone, Step13 and Deadsilence. London Elektricity live at The Forum and Homelands 2004 was a whole different business. Live Drum & Bass, with towering vocals, a rapper, keyboards, samples played live, a double bass player and two drummers getting wicked.

Tony Colman started as a musician before he turned to DJing and producing. Tony learnt to play guitar joking that it might get him a girlfriend: "Actually it worked – I met my wife on a plane to Japan." He's been in several bands over the years. His initial musical influences came from Led Zeppelin, Uriah Heap, Thin Lizzy and Black Sabbath. He joined a Punk band whilst still at school but also absorbed Kraftwerk, Philip Glass, Steve Reiche, John Cage, Varese – very minimal, clean composers as well as XTC and experimental New Wave. He also loved Grandmaster Flash's tune *The Message*: "That changed things for me in a massive way but the first Dance record that really touched me was when I was in a disco, I was 16 and got off with this really fit girl. We were dancing to Chic's *Le Freak*. I had hated any music that was funky – couldn't stand it. Suddenly I was an avid collector of James Brown and P-Funk."

SPREADING LOVE

"We fly. We fucking fly. What that means in musical terms is that we never even think about what we're doing. None of us think about it. Because we are riding high and shining. It's brilliant to be in a band like this. Each person is at the top of their respective area of music. I feel so lucky to have these people in my band. It's absolutely amazing." TONY COLMAN

Fabio & Grooverider hosted John Peel's show for a month in 2003. John always featured live sessions. So the guys gave Tony a call: "You can't turn down an opportunity like that. They knew we had never done it but said, "Can you put it together?"" So London Elektricity's first gig was live and nationwide: "I got everyone that I'd been working with in the studio or wanted to work with and ended up with Chris the Jungle Drummer, Andy Waterworth on bass, Landslide and me on samples and vocals. Liane Carroll sang lead vocals alongside Robert Owens with Stamina and it worked." Although listening to it now, Tony admits, "It was so loose. We all do other things. Liane Carroll has got a big career as a Jazz vocalist. She's one of the leading jazz vocalists in this country. I have worked with a lot of vocalists but I have never worked with anyone who comes so close."

London
Elektricity

Let the Drummer Get Wicked

"For me it was all about being properly live, warts and all. The important element is that the beats are live. And for that you have got to have an amazing drummer." Tony Colman

Nicky Blackmarket always asked Tony when he'd be putting a band together. The problem was Tony didn't have a drummer, and not just any drummer: "I need someone who lives it, breathes it, is a Junglist and plays the drums." "You should try the Jungle Drummer. I've been doing DJ sets with him. He's a nutter." Tony gave Chris a call and their first meeting was unforgettable: "For two hours all he did was slag off all the other drummers who play Jungle. He completely destroyed them but did it in a really humorous way; including imitating how they play." Tony signed him up recognising that there was an edge to Chris' playing: "He was quite loose but he really had the anger. He was fucking angry. And his sound was wicked. Absolutely wicked." Tony gave him some advice about tightening up his performance. He returned a few months later – bang on it and has been working with Tony ever since: "He's one of a kind. Other drummers before him have never really captured the spirit of a pure Breakbeat like Chris." The Jungle Drummer works with many cutting edge artists like the Scratch Perverts, A Guy Called Gerald, the Mixologists and has played on *Top Of The Pops* for *Shake UR Body*. Chris hosted Dekefex in Brixton and features on Killa Kela's new album. He and L Double have been on the road together playing gigs on 1Xtra, Glastonbury, Germany, Austria and Portugal. He grew up drumming to DJs: "Most of my drumming is based around DJ sets. I've really studied people mixing. If a DJ scratches I can put that into a drum context in my head. I'm looking to remix Drum & Bass with live drums." Chris is spearheading the way for a new generation of Jungle Drummers, but feels he's only just starting. This Jungle Drummer must be seen to be believed. When you do see him you won't believe your eyes – so trust your ears.

It's All the Way Live

When London Elektricity take to the stage they are not performing to a backing track. Nor are they synchronised to any form of click track or tempo track or sequencer or DAT or tape or computer: "We play in our own time. We can speed up or slow down whenever we want." That's far more exciting than watching a band performing with a computer. Tony finds that tedious: "I would prefer to hear a really good DJ than a band who've got playback running." Tony and Landslide play samples live on stage, and to those that think that means it's not live because they're using samples Tony says, "You try it." He and Landslide spend weeks in preparation, chopping and time-stretching their samples: "Arranging samples for playing live is an artform in itself. It can look easy when we're doing it but making it look easy is the hard bit." They take their slices of samples and map them out on their keyboards, playing them in time with the drummer and bass: "We have found a way to play samples live and turn them into new instruments." They prefer to use an Akai s6000 to store their edits rather than a computer, which are notorious for crashing. Playing live has had a real effect on the new album Tony's working on pushing him a lot harder as producer and composer: "When I am in studio, I'm also on stage." And when they're on stage they're fabulous.

Photo by
Cleveland Aaron

IT'S ALL GONE PETE TONG

It was 1996 or maybe '97
I remember saying to friends back then.
"I'm a bit anxious. The world seems too stable."
But a few years into the millennium
there's havoc on Earth –
mayhem like beheadings.

I watched documentaries on TV.
Most of it was bad – sad news to me.

The Palestinians & Israelis
still fight each other
circling around
like a ship without a rudder.

Sharon's solution divides
Palestinian communities.
With a new great wall sli
cing through houses and villages.

Newspaper editors wouldn't print
John Pilger's stories
'bout atrocities in the 60s committed
by American soldiers.
He wrote of troopers cutting off Vietnamese ears
keeping them in wallets to show to mates.

Abu Ghraib Jail – disgusting
Pilger says that's nothing new,
such things are an American Army custom.

First Chomsky, now Michael Moore
both dedicated to revealing the score.
They've been explaining for years
why Planet Earth's in a mess
and about the might of America's Military
Industrial complex.

The Commander in Chief
spouts Freedom & Democracy.
Protest groups sing, "Hail to the Thief –
we're wise to your skulduggery."

Whatever conspiracy theories
'bout the Towers attack
Bush & Co. still links the towers
with Al Qaeda and Iraq.
Blair ran 'round the word
believing that claptrap.
Grudging apology won't bring people back.

War kills civilians.
They call it, 'Collateral Damage.'
Neither UK or US officials
calculate what figure that is.

Our PM ignored one million in London marching
insisting they'd find
"Weapons of Mass Destruction."
Said, "He was right.
We were wrong."
Look now.
It's all gone Pete Tong.

Horrors Russian soldiers visited upon Chechens
are tenfold doubled
when Chechens murder children.
Sat sobbing watching Breaking News
about Beslan and "Terrorists in a school."
Chechens want Home Rule.
Doesn't justify methods so cruel.

Remember the nursery rhyme you learnt
way back when,
'bout all the King's horses
and all the King's men?
Now the world's Humpty Dumpty
our leaders nursery rhyme Kings.
No surprise last year's big hit
asked where the love is?

No solutions
for a planet sinking low.
Buddhist pray for peace
chanting Nam-Myoho-Renge-Kyo.

Было время,
когда все говорили:
"Поехали в Россию !"

I first visited Russia in 1980 when it was part of the Soviet Union. East and West were involved in Cold War. We lived under threat of nuclear annihilation. They called it Mutually Assured Destruction – and it was MAD. I landed in Moscow to catch my first Olympics. The colourful Games contrasted starkly with a soul-less USSR. The streets were lined with massive concrete Eastern Bloc architecture. Cars and people felt grey. Few were allowed to own private vehicles of any hew. The West's bright reds, yellows and silvers smacked of Capitalism's Evil. Long snaking bread queues fed into shops with little on the shelves. Tourists sold Levis on the black market to dodgy geezers down dodgier back streets. Big Brother watched. The masses had no Freedom. Take the Blue Pill – live the system.

Nearly 25 years on top DJs, who ignite madness on dance floors across the globe, are saying "Reach Russia." Whilst respecting the Western scene, in chorus they say, "If you wanna see where it's going off the most, get yourself over to Eastern Europe. Reach Russia." June 2004: cut to Innovation, Spain. Dinner with Riddla, Andy C and IC3. "It's not surprising really, Andy explains. "They've got freedom, economy's picking up – discovered raving – drugs. It's like '88 for 'em. And they love Jungle. Love It."

October 2004, St Petersburg (SP). Russia's 'Grooverider' DJ Boomer and Artist Manager Nastya collect me from the airport. Rolling into town I'm catching the sights. Nastya does her tour guide bit intermittently translating Boomer's commentary, supplementing her own: "When you were here before there was no electronic music?" "Nah." "Then Communism. No money. No cars. No decks." "No Nastya. No decks." I scan a massive Soviet era building. Out front stands a mammoth statue of Lenin full of revolutionary zeal – windswept coat flaps behind. His commanding arm rouses the masses across the road into … McDonalds. Streets vibrate with advertisings bright colours. Mercs, BMWs, Volkswagens and Ladas cut each other up, narrowly missing trams and packed buses. It's everyone for themselves, 'til everyone's stuck in a traffic jam. A man, small rucksack perched mid back, roller blades between cars. Boomer and Nastya's mobiles buzz. "Where you want eat?" asks Boomer, "Chinese, Russian, international, Japanese?" We wind up in DJ SS' favourite restaurant: "They make best steak here."

It's cosy. Classical reproduction paintings hang the walls. A young waiter dressed in a hassock places menus on our table. "Spaceba." Nastya and Boomer double take: "You speak Russian?!" "Only four words – *Da, Nyet, Spaseebo* and *Dasvee Daneeya* – Yes, no, thank-you and goodbye. Everyone is saying "Russia has the best parties."" Both laugh with satisfaction. Nastya remembers SS' party: "The World of Drum & Bass was best." "How long has Drum & Bass been in Russia?" Their Russian conversation is speckled with "Jungle. Sound System. Promoters. DJs. Drum & Bass."

Jungle landed in St. Petersburg in 1994. Boomer's credited with being the originator: "It started my flat. Sorry English is arrrgh …" At the end of the 80s electronic music went unheard. With the average salary being $20 per month, people concentrated more on surviving and less on dancing. But UK Jungle tapes percolated and circulated. In '94 there were only seven Technics decks in the city. Boomer owned two of them. He'd drive several hundred kilometres to buy vinyl in his nearest D&B record shop – in Finland: "I didn't think they'd have Jungle in Finland." "And why not?" "Permission to leave Russia difficult. Finland is easiest way," Nastya adds.

Over years of tapes Boomer felt House, UK Hardcore, finally finding Jungle: "This my sound. It FUCKING GREAT!" I'm laughing seeing him do 'the thing with the heart.' Nastya's curious: "Thing with heart?" I explain. "Ah yes. No words. Goes STRAIGHT IN." Boomer liked the Hardcore sound describing it as, "Sunshine Music. But Jungle sound is more bass. MY SOUND."

Boomer imported Technics from The United Arab Emirates. He started learning to mix in '92 by watching Hip Hop DJs on videos he also imported: "Hip Hop DJs here very strong. Killa Kela came and very impressed." Boomer excelled becoming a jury member for Russia's DMC. He's survived on a huge collection of Electro and old skool Hip Hop tapes: "Old Skool?" "Da! Afrika Bambaattaa, Grand Master Flash, Whoudini – Old Skool." Boomer moved from the Russian sticks to St Petersburg playing Hip Hop and House. But it was difficult to break other styles.

A *nouveau* tycoon invested in Port FM a legal radio station in '98 - '99. He hired Boomer to direct music policy: "It like 1Xtra." Port became an important resource for new headz broadcasting to St Petersburg's five million residents. Boomer and friends founded Russia's first D&B club. After that success they opened a record shop devoted to Drum & Bass. Inspired DJs flowed in. In 1999 Boomer *et al* staged a legal tour covering many cities. He's troubled the decks in the extreme north. The temperature outside read minus 50. Inside they raved. Nastya describes one of their first illegal open air parties: "Decks. Speakers in forest. Big crowd. Mushrooms all about. Music. It was crazy." St Petersburg and Moscow have a strong D&B following. Boomer flies around Russia and Eastern Europe playing out every weekend. His diary is full for the next six months. He's even been invited to Mumbai (Bombay) to rinse D&B there.

SP's D&B massive tend to be 17-19 years old preferring harder styles. Old 'uns check House clubs feeling uncomfortable around so many teenagers. Promoters find foreign artists very expensive because they must pay for visas, flights, hotels, promotion, etc. Punters pay an average of $3 on the door. So promoters from other cities unite to book UK artists, touring them around, helping balance the books. Boomer credits promoters who've staged parties in far flung places; boosting Jungle ever more over-ground: "Drum & Bass live in heart and club. If no club, no Drum & Bass. Because Club is Church." "And," laughs Nastya, "God is DJ."

Moscow is Russia's financial and political centre but St Petersburg is its cultural home; like Washington and New York. Electronic music spread from St Petersburg to Moscow. Most Russian DJs are from St Petersburg. DJ Groove also from SP is now based in Moscow where he and friend Dan promote D&B. They also remix pop tunes. Boomer makes music. Though he's still learning he has made music for ads.

The restaurant fills with diners. A lady in evening gown takes to a mini stage, microphone in hand, singing Russian ballads. We leave for a tour of city sights. Night lights illuminate beautiful classical architecture. Nastya's and Boomer's mobiles buzz. People call asking, "Where's the party? What time are you on? … The after party?" All the usual business.

We rock up walking into a courtyard beyond a courtyard. A small entrance leads into club Port: four stories high, capacity 5,000 - 6,000. Vaudeville architecture nestles against concrete and metal work in a post-industrial menagerie of spaces and dance floors. Cash rolls into its numerous bars. We walk over glass set into the floor. The ground is sixty feet below. Boomer heads for the decks setting up his Finalscratch. The Hardcore DJ steps down and Boomer scratches into *Colossus*. The crowd bounce as one shouting, "Oi. Oi. Oi. Oi," football stylee. Front of stage Jungle's physical iconography is in full effect. Lasers slice smoke. People on podiums resound to pumping sounds. *American Girls* dance through the speakers; crowd mouths, "I like American girls …" We could be at Freshers week in England. They're indistinguishable from other D&B masses. Hands and cheers fly high along with whistles and foot stomping rapturous applause. Hundreds of homegrown Drum & Bass headz filling the floor are lovin' it. The spiky b-line of *Dreadlock* spiky sends them into a frenzy. It's truly Jungle Drum & Bass land.

A VIP crowd sneak into a back room, behind a back room for a furtive smoke. If you get caught puffing here the police are involved. Each knock at the door brings tension. Inside they toke Yankee style. … A few drags then, "Pass the dutchy to the left hand side." A guy called Sacha mentions last nights' Techno party. "You like Techno?" They're all shaking their heads like I've insulted them. "No. No. Techno has no soul." These are ardent Drum & Bass fans. Out front they sing, "*Spread Love.*"

After Boomer's set we drift to a House club held in a nuclear bunker and chat more Jungle. Stars from Russia's version of *Pop Stars* invite us over to share their table and champagne. Their (former KGB) minder tops up our glasses. By 7am we're rinsed. Reach the hotel for a few hours kip before the flight. Several thousand miles from home, a Jungle Drum & Bass home is here. Just had to see it with my own eyes - feel it myself. Wake late so in true Drum & Bass style Boomer and Nastya end up driving me like mad to reach the airport in time. Flying high above the clouds we're nearing the end of this journey. I fall asleep thinking of our World of Drum & Bass.

THE ENDS

These are the last days of this journey. The writing is 98.5% and a bit done. This is one of my last nights in the studio. For months I've been saying to friends & family, "Can't come out Sorry. I'm writing (echo) … I'm in the studio." I've worked on so many projects and often forget to step back, breathe thinking, "This is wicked." Damn lucky to get this opportunity once in a lifetime but twice is humbling. Before sitting down and melding with the keyboard I pause and survey the scene. Okay Shy, this room is as bad as your studio was. Mine is covered with scribers detritus. MiniDiscs, magazines, vinyl, wristbands, flyers, CDs and papers – papers – papers cover the floor. Apart from a pathway leading out the door. It's organised chaos.

Driving home from the airport I pull a U-turn and head for Grace. Jo Groove Connection is on Bass Camp Herbal's door. The usual headz are there. Navi in smart black suit and stocking cap dances gently in the groove corner. Frost pours wine into friends' glasses. Fats sings into his mic and Groove plays his last tune. The house lights come on. Some leave for home, others head for the lock-in. I pass Rider my phone and he taps his number in: "I'll call you tomorrow."

I feel too wired to head home and drive around heading absentmindedly in search of 30 St. Mary Axe aka The Gherkin. I'm soon lost in a warren of *cul de sacs* and No Entry signs so end up walking the last few streets. The Gherkin close up is pretty awesome. Architects, like producers, never know what they'll think of next. It is visible from so many parts of London. I've seen it as I'm going out and returning home from a dance. Perhaps I like The Gherkin because it's different from all the other buildings. It's strong and has its own identity, adding something to London's skyline, standing as a metaphor for Jungle Drum & Bass.

A melange of events and proppa moments of these past months are wired into my hard drive. Dancing stage-side at Fab & Groove's 15,000 strong Glastonbury gig, any of the Innovation nights, The first time Rider dropped *Golden Girl* at Grace, 1Xtra, Jungle Fever, Andy C churning up The End, that HORRIBLE b-line London Elektricity let rip through Homelands, interviewing Bret and High Contrast – working with Navi, I'm happy my cup overflows with so many memorable moments.

As a raver and blagger it's been wicked to have had an excuse to visit all these places and meet all these characters on your behalf. Like the book is the blag. But ever since I climbed into my rusty Spitfire in '88 and headed off to Sunrise on a magical music tour, I knew that I'd want to understand what the whole thing was all about. I'm shocked to think it's a love affair that's lasted 16 years. Us forty-something brigade, grew up knowing that we'd missed the big 60s party. Then comes our own Summers of Love. I feel blessed I was drawn in, especially so to have strayed into the Jungle arena. "Watch the ride." WHAT A RIDE.

Leaving The Gherkin I'm back in the car heading through Shoreditch north to Tottenham. Tali's album is on the system. Something about *Airport Lounge* matches my mood. Remixing her words in my head her song describes my reunion with Jungle Drum & Bass. I rewind the tune all the way home:

"It's OK, I'm on my way to see your face again. Knowing there was distance between us but I still come back to you. Now and then our music needs us so I'll still come back to you. Now I must need this as I still come back to your love … Each detail of the city. Each sight and every sound … No matter where our paths will lead us I'll still come back to your love. Thinking about you and all things you might do …"